THE COMPLETE
OUTDOOR
BUILDER

UPDATED EDITION

FROM ARBORS TO WALKWAYS
150 DIY PROJECTS

COOL
SPRINGS
PRESS
Home and Garden Experts

MINNEAPOLIS, MINNESOTA

Quarto is the authority on a wide range of topics.

Quarto educates, entertains and enriches the lives of our readers—enthusiasts and lovers of hands-on living.

www.quartoknows.com

First published in 2016 by Cool Springs Press, an imprint of Quarto Publishing Group USA Inc., 400 First Avenue North, Suite 400, Minneapolis, MN 55401 USA. Telephone: (612) 344-8100
Fax: (612) 344-8692

quartoknows.com
Visit our blogs at quartoknows.com

Cool Springs Press titles are also available at discounts in bulk quantity for industrial or sales-promotional use. For details contact the Special Sales Manager at Quarto Publishing Group USA Inc., 400 First Avenue North, Suite 400, Minneapolis, MN 55401 USA.

10 9 8 7 6 5 4 3 2 1

ISBN: 978-1-59186-667-1

Library of Congress Cataloging-in-Publication Data

Names: Black & Decker Corporation (Towson, Md.)
Title: Complete outdoor builder.
Other titles: Black & Decker the complete outdoor builder
Description: Minneapolis, MN, USA : Cool Springs Press, an imprint of Quarto Publishing Group USA Inc., 2016.
Identifiers: LCCN 2015042670 | ISBN 9781591866671 (plc)
Subjects: LCSH: Garden structures--Design and construction--Amateurs' manuals. | Building, Wooden--Amateurs' manuals. | Outbuildings--Design and construction--Amateurs' manuals. | Woodwork--Amateurs' manuals. | Masonry--Amateurs' manuals. | Do-it-yourself work--Amateurs' manuals.
Classification: LCC TH4961 .C655 2016 | DDC 690/.89--dc23
LC record available at http://lccn.loc.gov/2015042670

Acquiring Editor: Mark Johanson
Project Manager: Alyssa Bluhm
Art Director: Brad Springer
Layout: Danielle Smith-Boldt

Printed in China

NOTICE TO READERS

For safety, use caution, care, and good judgment when following the procedures described in this book. The publisher and BLACK+DECKER cannot assume responsibility for any damage to property or injury to persons as a result of misuse of the information provided.

The techniques shown in this book are general techniques for various applications. In some instances, additional techniques not shown in this book may be required. Always follow manufacturers' instructions included with products, since deviating from the directions may void warranties. The projects in this book vary widely as to skill levels required: some may not be appropriate for all do-it-yourselfers, and some may require professional help.

Consult your local building department for information on building permits, codes, and other laws as they apply to your project.

CONTENTS

CONTENTS (CONT.)

Yard & Garden Structures

Treehouses & Play Structures

Outdoor Furnishings & Accessories

INTRODUCTION

In this book, the third edition of *Black & Decker The Complete Outdoor Builder*, you'll find all the classic, time-tested material from the last edition—project information that over the years helped hundreds of thousands of homeowners transform the yard and landscape into meaningful and useful space for fresh-air living. With this edition you'll also find important text and photography updates that keep classic projects relevant for today's homeowners. We also have dropped some projects that were of limited relevance to homeowners today, replacing them with many new projects to reflect new building materials and practices, as well as current homeowner interests. There were enough new projects that we even had to expand the size of the book to include them all.

The result is an encyclopedic reference ideal for the homeowner who wants a one-stop reference for all information relevant to the yard, landscape, and outdoor living. Combined with *Black & Decker The Book of Home How-To*, these two books provide a concise yet remarkably comprehensive reference for home-improvement information and instructions. Many homeowners will need nothing more than these two books, while others will find this book and its sister volume to be perfect introductions to a lifetime of satisfying home DIY practice.

Like earlier editions, *The Complete Outdoor Builder* is organized in a logical structure, from basics to accents and accessories. The first few chapters—Planning; Walkways, Steps & Patios; Decks; and Fences & Walls—deal with the landscape elements commonly known as *hardscape*. These elements include the structural bones of a landscape—the elements that closely parallel the structural elements of the house itself. These chapters deal with the framing, the walls, and the floors of your landscape. These are remarkably complete chapters, offering in-depth information on a diverse range of hardscape choices.

Later chapters then systematically treat the landscape add-ons, providing information and projects for various patio enclosures and sheds; for a variety of garden-related structures; for play and recreation projects, such as children's swing sets and play structures; and for easy-to-build outdoor furnishings and accessories to elevate to decks, patios, and landscapes to truly unique and personalized spaces.

Once again, you'll find the presentation of this background reference information and project instructions to be uniquely helpful to do-it-yourself application. The information is exhaustively complete and the photography demonstrates projects and construction steps with utter clarity. Even if (or especially if) you're a beginner, these are projects you can successfully complete if you simply practice a little diligence and patience.

Start making your outdoor dreams a reality now.

PLANNING

Homeowners no longer think of their yards as great expanses of lawn, but as outdoor living spaces. Permanent outdoor structures can add to the beauty and function of these outdoor rooms. For example, a deck can provide additional space for entertaining or relaxing, a wall can provide privacy and texture, and a walkway or path can unify areas.

But before you can begin building, you have to organize your ideas and create a plan for materials, tools, inspections, measuring, and construction. Proper planning will help you create an outdoor project that is beautiful now and will last for years to come—an important consideration, since landscaping contributes about 30 percent to your home's total value.

This opening section will provide you with all the information you need in order to plan and design the projects of your choice. We'll look at new and standard materials for outdoor projects—including wood, metal, plastic, manufactured and natural stone, and concrete—and show you how to estimate and order supplies. You will find information on basic and specialty tools and a discussion of the common types of hardware and fasteners used for outdoor projects. We'll also review the basics of building codes, including permits and inspections. And to ensure you get the results you want, we'll show you the techniques you'll need to design your own projects.

By following these planning strategies, you will save time and money and enjoy your outdoor home for years to come.

IN THIS CHAPTER:

- Building Materials
- Lumber
- Metals & Plastics
- Cast Blocks
- Natural Stone
- Concrete
- Mortar
- Estimating & Ordering Materials
- Basic Tools
- Power & Rental Tools
- Masonry Tools
- Fasteners & Hardware
- Codes & Courtesies
- Measuring
- Challenges

BUILDING MATERIALS

The building materials you choose should reflect both the function and the appearance of your outdoor project. Materials impact not only the style, but the durability, maintenance requirements, and overall cost of a project. Wood, stone, and brick are traditional favorites, but the versatility and ease of installation you get with PVC vinyl, metal, and concrete make them attractive options for certain applications.

LUMBER

Wood remains the most common building material in outdoor construction, and it is usually less expensive than stone or brick. Its versatility lends itself to just about any project, from the plain and practical to the elegant and ornate. It is ideal for decks and walkways, fences and retaining walls, pergolas and screens, outdoor furniture, and of course, outbuildings. And it is beautiful, blending with most architectural styles. It looks especially attractive in settings surrounded by trees.

Most home centers and lumberyards carry a wide selection of dimension lumber, as well as convenient preassembled fence panels, posts, pickets, rails,

balusters, floorboards, stringers, and stair railings. Inspect all lumber for flaws, sighting along each board to check for warping, twisting, or loose knots. Boards used for structural parts should have only small knots that are tight and ingrown. Inspect the end grain also. Lumber with a vertical grain will cup less as it ages. Return any boards with serious flaws.

Framing lumber—typically pine or pressure-treated pine—comes in a few different grades: Select Structural (SEL STR), Construction (CONST) or Standard (STAND), and Utility (UTIL). For most applications, Construction Grade No. 2 offers the best balance between quality and price. Utility grade is a lower-cost lumber suitable for blocking and similar uses but should not be used for structural members. Board lumber, or finish lumber, is graded by quality and appearance, with the main criteria being the number and size of knots present. "Clear" pine, for example, has no knots.

The most important consideration in choosing lumber is its suitability for outdoor use. Select a wood that is not prone to rot or insect attack. Three types are generally recommended: heart cedar, heart redwood, and pressure-treated lumber. Redwood and cedar are attractive, relatively soft woods with a natural resistance to moisture and insects—ideal qualities

Wood is the most common, and arguably the most versatile, of building materials. Carefully choose lumber that is appropriate for your project.

for outdoor applications. "Heart" or "heartwood" varieties will be identified on the grade stamp. In both redwood and cedar, heartwood has better resistance to decay than lighter-colored sapwoods. Western red cedar (WRC) or incense cedar (INC) for decks should be heartwood (HEART) with a maximum moisture content of 15 percent (MC15).

Pressure-treated pine is stronger and more durable than redwood or cedar and is more readily available and less expensive in many areas. Although this lumber has a noticeable green color due to its preservative, the wood can either be stained or left to weather to a pleasing gray.

Plywood designated as exterior-grade is made with layers of cedar or treated wood and a special glue that makes it weather-resistant. Always cover exposed plywood edges to prevent water intrusion.

Some homeowners shy away from pressure-treated lumber due to the chemicals used to treat it. Despite popular fears, the chemicals in pressure-treated pine do not easily leach into the soil, nor are they easily absorbed through the skin. In fact, it can be argued that pressure-treated lumber is actually a good environmental choice because it lasts longer in projects, thereby reducing the harvest of new trees.

When using pressure-treated lumber, however, take some common-sense precautions: avoid prolonged skin contact by wearing gloves and protective clothing, and avoid breathing the dust by wearing a particle mask.

If you live in an arid climate, such as in the Southwest, you can use untreated pine lumber because wood will not rot if its moisture content is less than 20 percent. However, it's always a good idea to use pressure-treated lumber for deck posts or any other framing members that are in contact with the ground.

Teak and white oak are hardwoods usually reserved for top-of-the-line outdoor furniture. These woods have a dense cell structure that makes them resistant to water penetration. However, because these woods are expensive, they generally aren't practical to use for large structures, such as decks or fences. They are better suited for accent pieces, such as benches or large planters.

Remember that although treated woods do resist rot, they will not last indefinitely without regular maintenance. They should have a fresh coat of stain or sealer every two years to maintain durability and appearance. Sealing cut edges of lumber—including pressure-treated wood—will prevent rotting of the end grain.

Apply a coat of sealer-preservative or staining sealer to all sides of outdoor structures. Make sure sealer is applied to all end-grain. Even pressure-treated lumber is vulnerable to moisture and rot.

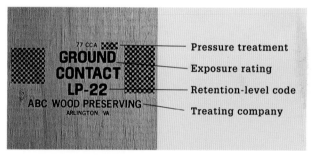

Pressure-treated lumber stamps list the type of preservative and the chemical retention level, as well as the exposure rating and the name and location of the treating company.

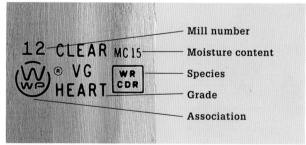

Cedar grade stamps list the mill number, moisture content, species, lumber grade, and membership association. Western red cedar (WRC) or incense cedar (INC) for decks should be heartwood (HEART) with a maximum moisture content of 15% (MC15).

11

METALS & PLASTICS

Plastic and aluminum products have become popular alternatives to traditional outdoor building materials because they are low maintenance, versatile, and easy to install. Though these materials are typically more expensive than wood and other alternatives, their durability makes them attractive options.

Plastics are now available in several colors, and they can be used in most applications where wood is appropriate. They can be found in fencing and timbers for use in decks, walkways, fences, and arbors. PVC vinyl and fiberglass-reinforced plastic (FRP) are becoming popular choices for fencing and decking materials. Many styles and sizes are available, and they are strong, versatile, and require no maintenance. Materials are often sold as kits, making installation easy. Before choosing PVC, check manufacturers' specifications on expansion and contraction variances to see if it is suitable for your project.

Composite materials blend together wood fibers and recycled plastics to create a rigid product that, unlike wood, will not rot, splinter, warp, or crack. These boards can be cut to size with a circular saw and do not require painting or staining.

Metal is often used in outdoor applications, such as in fencing and gates. Aluminum offers a sturdy, lightweight, waterproof material that is available in a variety of designs, ranging from the simple to the elaborate. Availability may be limited, so check with local building centers. Galvanized chain-link steel has long been a popular choice for fencing, because it is relatively maintenance free and can be used to create a secure outdoor wall at a reasonable price. Options such as vinyl-coated mesh and color inserts can increase privacy and boost style. Traditional wrought iron, though more expensive and less common today, is used for fencing, railings, and patio furniture to add a touch of elegance.

Copper pipe is a unique and unexpected material that is well suited to temperature swings and water exposure, making it ideal for outdoor use. This metal is inexpensive and available at nearly any home center or hardware store.

Although many of these materials may be more expensive initially, they often carry lifetime warranties, which can make them more economical than wood over time. Before choosing any alternative building material, check on restrictions with your local building department.

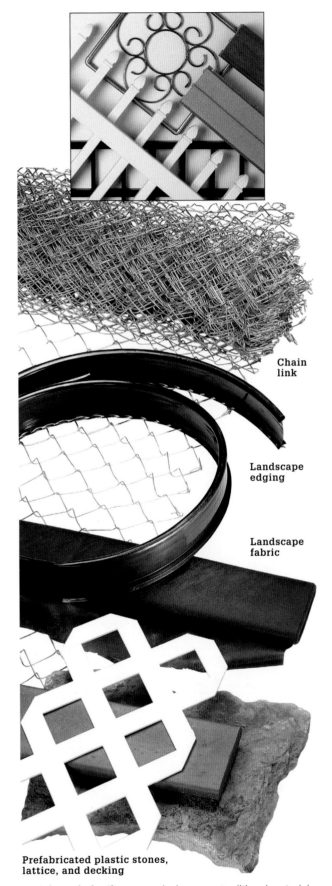

Chain link

Landscape edging

Landscape fabric

Prefabricated plastic stones, lattice, and decking

Metals and plastics are replacing more traditional materials, as they have minimal maintenance and allow environmentally conscientious consumers to use recycled products.

CAST BLOCKS

Manufactured stone is often designed to resemble natural stone, but it offers distinct advantages over the real thing. Greater uniformity makes installation easier, and it is often less expensive than natural alternatives.

Although poured concrete isn't as attractive as natural stone, new masonry techniques help it rival natural stone for visual appeal. Brick, concrete, and glass block are available in a growing variety of sizes and styles, providing the flexibility to build distinctive, reasonably priced outdoor structures. Many of these products are well-suited to do-it-yourselfers, because their weights are manageable and installation is easy.

Decorative concrete block can be used to make screen walls and is available in many colors. A decorative block wall is one of the most economical choices for a stone landscape wall.

Concrete paver slabs, available in several shapes and sizes, can be used for laying simple walkways and patios. They are available in a standard finish, a smooth aggregate finish, or can be colored and molded to resemble brick. Concrete paver slabs are relatively inexpensive and quite easy to work with. They're usually laid in a bed of sand and require no mortar. Their surface is generally finished so the smooth gravel aggregate is exposed, but they are also available in plain pavers and aggregate.

Paver bricks resemble traditional kiln-dried clay bricks, but are more durable and easier to install. Paver bricks are available in a variety of colors and geometric shapes for paving patios, walkways, and driveways. Many varieties are available in interlocking shapes that can be combined with standard bricks to create decorative patterns, such as herringbone and basket weave. Paver bricks have largely replaced clay bricks for landscape use and can be set into a bed of sand for patios and driveways, where mortar is not required.

Edging blocks are precast in different sizes for creating boundaries to planting areas, lawns, loose-fill paths, and retaining walls.

Interlocking retaining wall blocks

Molded paver slabs

Interlocking paver bricks

Exposed aggregate paver slabs

Concrete paver slabs

Brick and concrete block are available in a growing variety of sizes and styles, allowing you to build distinctive outdoor structures.

13

NATURAL STONE

Natural stone is one of the finest building materials you can use. It offers beautiful color and texture, along with unmatched durability and elegance, making it a classic building material for landscape floors, ornamental walls, retaining walls, and walkways. Because of its beauty, it is also a choice material for decorative features, such as rock gardens, ponds, fountains, and waterfalls.

These virtues come at a price, however: Natural stone is one of the more expensive building materials you can select, and it can be heavy and difficult to work with.

Natural stone includes a wide range of materials, from microscopic sands to enormous boulders and carefully cut granite, marble, limestone, slate, and sandstone. It is sold in many forms, so you'll have to choose what type, form, texture, and shade to use for your project.

Fieldstone, sometimes called river rock, is any loose stone gathered from fields, dry river beds, and hillsides. It is often used to build retaining walls, ornamental garden walls, and rock gardens, where it creates an informal, natural look. When split into smaller pieces, fieldstone can be used in projects with mortar. When cut into small pieces, or quarried stone, fieldstone is called cobblestone, a common material in walks and paths.

Ashlar, sometimes called wall stone, is quarried stone—such as granite, marble, or limestone—that has been smooth-cut into large blocks, ideal for creating clean lines with thin mortar joints. Cut stone works well for stone garden walls, but because of its expense, its use is sometimes limited to decorative wall caps.

Flagstone is large slabs of sedimentary rock with naturally flat surfaces. Limestone, sandstone, slate, and shale are the most common types of flagstone. It is usually cut into pieces up to three inches thick, for use in walks, steps, and patios. Smaller pieces—less than 16 inches square—are often called steppers.

Veneer stone is natural or manufactured stone cut or molded for use in nonload-bearing, cosmetic applications, such as facing exterior walls or freestanding concrete block walls.

Rubble is irregular pieces of quarried stone, usually with one split or finished face. It is widely used in wall construction.

Each type of stone offers a distinctive look, as well as a specific durability and workability. Often the project dictates the form of stone to use. Ask your local stone supplier to suggest a stone that meets your cost, function, and workability needs.

NOTE: You may find different terms used for various types of stone. Ask your supply yard staff to help you.

Fieldstone is stone gathered from fields, dry river beds, and hillsides. It is used in wall construction.

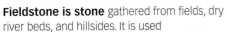

Flagstone is large slabs of quarried stone cut into pieces up to 3" thick. It is used in walks, steps, and patios.

A stone yard is a great place to get ideas and see the types of stone that are available. This stone yard includes a display area that identifies different types of stone and suggests ways they can be used.

CONCRETE

Poured concrete has long been a favorite for driveways, walkways, and patios because of its exceptional strength, but new tinting and surface finishing techniques give concrete a decorative look that makes it attractive for landscaping. It's much less expensive than natural stone, and because it's poured while in a semi-liquid state, it can be formed into curves and other shapes, such as landscape ponds or fountains. Using simple tools, you can even finish concrete to simulate brick pavers or flagstone.

Concrete is made up of a mixture of portland cement, sand, coarse gravel, and water. Premixed bags of dry concrete are available at home centers and are easy and efficient to use.

Mix concrete in a wheelbarrow for smaller projects, or rent a power mixer to blend larger amounts of cement, gravel, sand, and water quickly. Buy ready-mixed concrete for large jobs.

Timing and preparation are the most important factors in working with concrete. Concrete will harden to its final form, regardless of whether you have finished working with it. Start with smaller-scale projects until you're comfortable working with concrete. A concrete walkway is a good starter project. Recruit helpers when you're ready to take on a large project.

Premixed concrete products contain all the components of concrete. Just add water, mix, and pour.

To mix concrete ingredients in a wheelbarrow, use a ratio of 1 part portland cement (A), 2 parts sand (B), and 3 parts coarse gravel (C).

MORTAR

Masonry mortar is a mixture of portland cement, sand, and water. Ingredients, such as lime and gypsum, are added to improve workability or control "setup" time.

Every mortar mixture balances strength, workability, and other qualities. Make sure to use the mortar type that best suits your needs:

Type N is a medium-strength mortar for above-grade outdoor use in nonload-bearing (freestanding) walls, barbecues, chimneys, soft stone masonry, and tuck pointing.

Type S offers high-strength mortar for exterior use at or below grade. It is generally used in foundations, brick-and-block retaining walls, driveways, walks, and patios.

Type M is a very high strength specialty mortar for load-bearing exterior stone walls, including stone retaining walls and veneer applications.

Glass Block Mortar is a specialty white Type S mortar for glass block projects. Standard gray Type S mortar is also acceptable for glass block projects.

Refractory Mortar is a calcium aluminate mortar that does not break down with exposure to high temperatures; it is used for mortaring around firebrick in fireplaces and barbecues. Chemical-set mortar will cure even in wet conditions.

To mix mortar, always read and follow the manufacturer's specifications on the mortar mix package.

Ingredients for mixing your own mortar include portland cement, sand, and water. For high temperature, add refractory mix.

ESTIMATING & ORDERING MATERIALS

Whether pouring a small slab or building an elaborate archway, it is important to estimate the dimensions of your project as accurately as possible. This will allow you to create a complete and concise materials list and help eliminate extra shopping trips and delivery costs.

Begin compiling a materials list by reviewing your building plans. These plans should include scaled plans that will make estimating easier.

Once you have developed a materials list, add 10 percent to the estimate for each item. This will help you manage small oversights and allow for waste when cutting.

The cost of your project will depend upon which building materials you choose. But because some materials may not be readily available in your area, plan your projects and place orders accordingly. Lumber, stone, manufactured stone, and alternate materials, such as metals and plastics, can vary widely in price. It's unfortunately true that the most attractive building materials are usually the most expensive as well.

In addition to lumber, fasteners, hardware, hand tools, and power tools, many home centers also carry masonry tools and materials, such as concrete, mortar, and stucco mix, typically in premixed bags. Consider the scale of your project before buying concrete or stucco by the bag, however. For large projects, you may want to hire a ready-mix supplier to deliver fresh concrete.

If you plan on working with specialty or alternative materials, such as vinyl fencing or composite decking, many home centers will have a select range of styles and sizes onhand. Contacting manufacturers directly will lead to greater choices of products, and you will be able to place an order directly with them or be directed to a retailer near you.

Local building suppliers can be a great asset to do-it-yourselfers. The staff can offer professional advice, and yards often carry the tools and other materials necessary to complete your project. Often you can receive help in designing your project and advice on estimating the materials, applicable local building codes, and regional climate considerations.

Many centers also offer coordinating services for landscapers and contractors to work with you. You may also find class offerings in masonry construction or other techniques to help you develop the skills to complete your project.

Local brick and stone suppliers will often help you design your project and advise you about estimating materials, local building codes, and climate considerations.

How to Estimate Materials ▸

Sand, gravel, topsoil (2" layer)	surface area (sq. ft.) ÷ 100 = tons needed
Standard brick pavers for walks (2" layer)	surface area (sq. ft.) × 5 = number of pavers needed
Standard bricks for walls and pillars (4 × 8")	surface area (sq. ft.) × 7 = number of bricks needed (single brick thickness)
Poured concrete (4" layer)	surface area (sq. ft.) × .012 = cubic yards needed
Flagstone	surface area (sq. ft.) ÷ 100 = tons needed
Interlocking block (2" layer)	area of wall face (sq. ft.) × 1.5 = number of stones needed
Ashlar stone for 1-ft.-thick walls	area of wall face (sq. ft.) ÷ 15 = tons of stone needed
Rubble stone for 1-ft.-thick walls	area of wall face (sq. ft.) ÷ 35 = tons of stone needed
8 × 8 × 16" concrete block for freestanding walls	height of wall (ft.) × length of wall (ft.) × 1.125 = number of blocks needed

Amount of Concrete Needed (Cubic Feet) ▸

Number of 8"-Diameter Footings	Depth of Footings (feet)			
	1	2	3	4
2	¾	1½	2¼	3
3	1	2¼	3½	4½
4	1½	3	4½	6
5	2	3¾	5¾	7½

Dry Ingredients for Self-mix

Amount of Concrete Needed (cubic feet)	94-lb. bags of portland cement	Cubic feet of sand	Cubic feet of gravel	60-lb. bags of premixed dry concrete
1	⅙	⅓	½	2
2	⅓	⅔	1	4
3	½	1	1½	6
4	⅔	1⅓	2	8
5	1	2	3	10
10	2	4	6	20

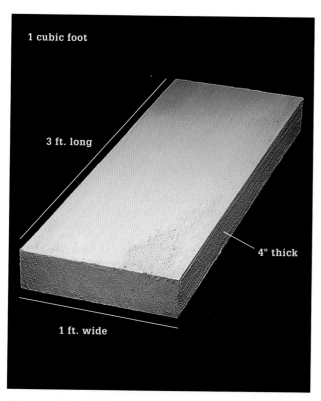

1 cubic foot

3 ft. long

4" thick

1 ft. wide

Concrete Coverage ▸

Volume	Thickness	Surface Coverage
1 cu. yd.	2"	160 sq. ft.
1 cu. yd.	3"	110 sq. ft.
1 cu. yd.	4"	80 sq. ft.
1 cu. yd.	5"	65 sq. ft.
1 cu. yd.	6"	55 sq. ft.
1 cu. yd.	8"	40 sq. ft.

Measure the width and length of the project in feet, then multiply the dimensions to get the square footage. Measure the thickness in feet (4" thick equals ⅓ ft.), then multiply the square footage times the thickness to get the cubic footage. For example, 1 ft. × 3 ft. × ⅓ ft. = 1 cu. ft. Twenty-seven cubic feet equals one cubic yard.

BASIC TOOLS

The right tool always makes the job easier. As a homeowner, you may already own many of the tools needed for the projects in this book. If you don't have the necessary tools, you can borrow them, rent them, or buy them.

If you decide to purchase new tools, invest in the highest-quality products you can afford. High-quality tools perform better and last longer than less-expensive alternatives. Metal tools should be made from high-carbon steel with smoothly finished surfaces. Hand tools should be well balanced and have tight, comfortably molded handles.

Quality tools may actually save you money over time, because you eliminate the expense of replacing worn out or broken tools every few years.

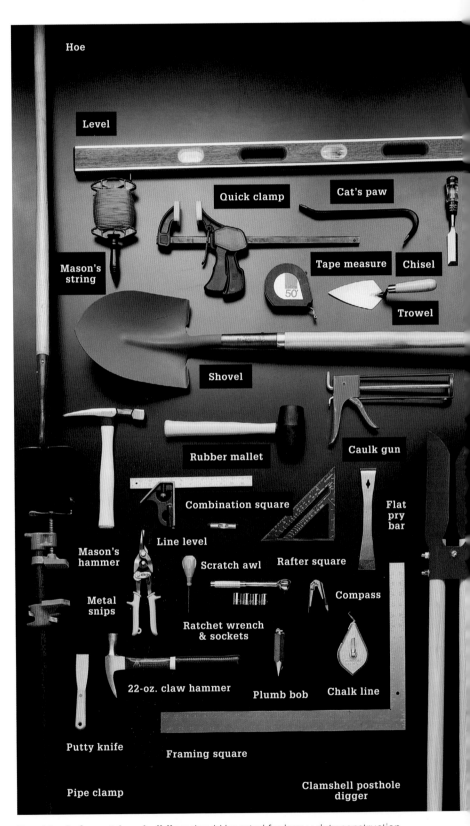

Hand tools for outdoor building should be rated for heavy-duty construction. Always purchase the highest-quality tool you can afford, there is no substitute for quality.

POWER & RENTAL TOOLS

Outdoor building projects and landscaping work often require the use of power tools and specialty tools.

Home centers will have the common power tools you will require in stock, but if your project demands a tool that you will only use once or that is expensive, consider renting. Many home centers now have rental equipment on site. Also check your local rental center outlets for tool availability.

When renting, always read the owner's manual and operating instructions to prevent damage to tools and personal injury. Some rental centers also provide training and assistance on specialty tools.

To ensure your safety, always use a ground-fault circuit-interrupter (GFCI) extension cord with power tools, and wear protective gear, such as work glasses, particle masks, and work gloves when sawing or handling pressure-treated lumber and masonry products.

Power tools you may need for outdoor building projects include: (A) Reciprocating saws (corded and cordless); (B) Circular saw or trim saw; (C) Jigsaw; (D) Cordless drill/driver.

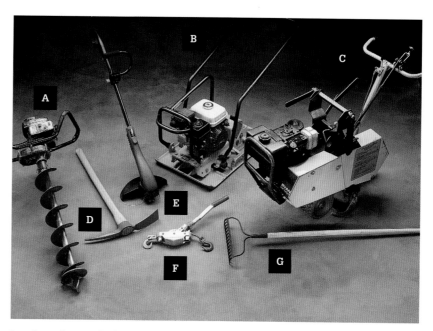

Landscaping tools for preparing sites include: power auger (A), power tamper (B), power sod cutter (C), pick (D), weed trimmer (E), come-along (F), garden rake (G).

MASONRY TOOLS

Masonry work involves two steps: preparing the site and laying the concrete. To work effectively with masonry products, you will have to buy or rent some special-purpose tools.

You may want to purchase some smaller landscaping tools, including a pick for excavating hard or rocky soil; a weed trimmer for removing brush and weeds before digging; a posthole digger for digging just one or two holes; a come-along for moving large rocks and other heavy objects without lifting; and a garden rake for moving small amounts of soil and debris.

To lay concrete you will need trowels, floats, edgers, and jointers. These are hand tools used to place, shape, and finish concrete and mortar. Chisels are used to cut and fit brick and block. You can also equip your circular saw with blades and your power drill with bits designed for use with concrete and brick.

Always make sure you have the necessary safety equipment on hand before you start a masonry project, including gloves and protective eye wear.

Mason's tools include: a darby (A) for smoothing screeded concrete; mortar hawk (B) for holding mortar; pointing trowel (C) for tuck-pointing stone mortar; wide pointing tool (D) for tuck-pointing or placing mortar on brick and block walls; jointer (E) for finishing mortar joints; brick tongs (F) for carrying multiple bricks; narrow tuck-pointer (G) for tuck-pointing or placing mortar on brick and block walls; mason's trowel (H) for applying mortar; masonry chisels (I) for splitting brick, block, and stone; bull float (J) for floating large slabs; mason's hammers (K) for chipping brick and stone; maul (L) for driving stakes; square-end trowel (M) for concrete finishing; side edger (N) and step edger (O) for finishing inside and outside corners of concrete; joint chisel (P) for removing dry mortar; control jointer (Q) for creating control joints; tile nippers (R) for trimming tile; sled jointer (S) for smoothing long joints; steel trowel (T) for finishing concrete; magnesium or wood float (U) for floating concrete; screed board (V) for screeding concrete.

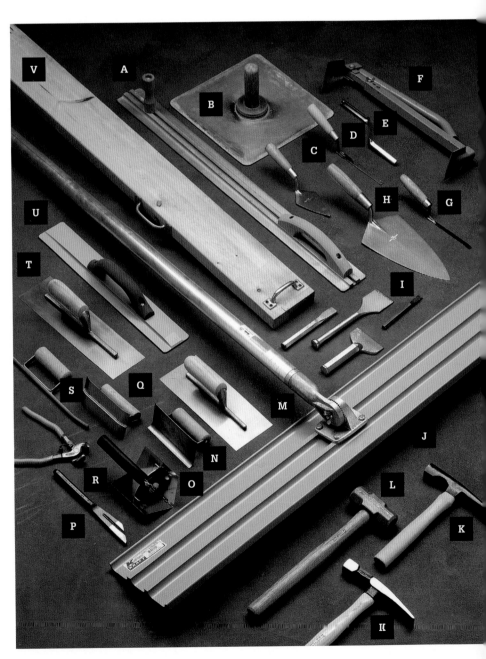

FASTENERS & HARDWARE

Because you will be building outdoor structures, the connecting hardware, fasteners, and materials you use must hold up to extreme weather conditions. The better the materials, the longer the life of the structure.

Any metal-connecting hardware and fasteners, including nails and screws, should be made from rust-resistant material, such as galvanized steel, aluminum, or stainless steel. Galvanized fasteners should be triple-dipped in zinc to resist corrosion. Although galvanized metals will not stain treated wood, they may react with natural chemicals in cedar and redwood, causing staining. Stainless steel fasteners won't cause staining in any wood, but they are expensive.

Seal screwheads set in counterbored holes with silicone caulk to prevent water damage. Also be aware that when combining dissimilar metals, you will need a plastic spacer to prevent the electrochemical reaction known as galvanic action from occurring, which causes corrosion.

A common type of hardware you'll find throughout this book is the metal anchor, used to reinforce framing connections. Most of the anchors called for in the various projects (and all of the anchors in the sheds and outbuilding projects) are commonly available at lumberyards and home centers. If you can't find what you need on the shelves, look through the manufacturer's catalog, or visit their website (see page 553). Always use the fasteners recommended by the manufacturer.

Metal connectors commonly used include: joist hanger (A), flashing (B), angled joist hanger (C), rafter tie (D), post-beam caps (E), stair cleat (F), hurricane tie (G), post anchor with washer and pedestal (H), joist tie (I), angle bracket (J).

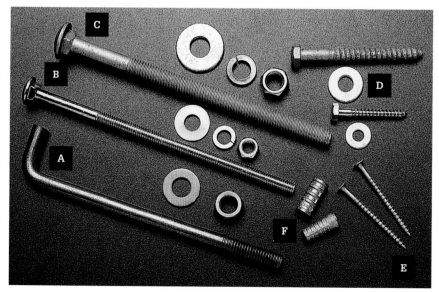

Common types of fasteners include: J-bolt with nut and washer (A), carriage bolts with washers and nuts (B, C), galvanized lag screws and washers (D), corrosion-resistant deck screws (E), masonry anchors (F).

CODES & COURTESIES

Almost anytime you build—whether indoors or out—there are local regulations you'll have to consider. Building codes, zoning ordinances, and permits are the legal issues you'll have to contend with, but you should also consider neighborhood standards and the impact your project will have on neighboring properties.

Building codes govern the materials and construction methods of your project to ensure safety, and zoning laws govern the size, location, and style of your structure to preserve aesthetic standards. Permits and inspections are required to ensure your plans meet all local building and zoning restrictions.

Requirements and restrictions vary from one municipality to another, so check the codes for your area. If your plans conflict with local codes, authorities will sometimes grant a variance, which allows you to compromise the strict requirements of the code.

Consult with your local building inspection department early in your planning process to determine if your project requires a permit and whether you must submit plans for approval. The permit process can take several weeks or months, so checking early can help you avoid unnecessary delays or changes to your plans. Then fill out the necessary forms, pay any applicable fees, and wait for your approval.

In the meantime, it's a good idea to discuss your plans with neighbors. A fence, wall, or gate on or near a property line is as much a part of your neighbors' landscapes as your own. The tall hedge you have planned for privacy, for example, may cast a dense shadow over your neighbor's sunbathing deck. The simple courtesy of apprising your neighbors of your plans can help you avoid strained relationships or even legal disputes.

You may find that discussing your plans with neighbors reaps unexpected rewards. For instance, you and your neighbor may decide to share labor and expenses by landscaping both properties at once. Or you may combine resources on a key feature that benefits both yards, such as a stone garden wall or shade tree. When several neighbors put their heads together to create an integrated landscape plan for their yards, the results benefit everyone. Individual landscapes look larger when the surrounding yards share a complementary look and style.

In addition, check with your local utility companies to pinpoint the locations of any underground electrical, plumbing, sewer, or telephone lines on your property. The locations of these features can have an obvious impact on your plans, if your project requires digging or changes to your property's grade. There is no charge to have utility companies locate these lines, and it can prevent you from making an expensive or life-threatening mistake. In many areas, the law requires that you have this done before digging any holes.

On the following pages, you'll find some common legal restrictions for typical landscape projects.

Always talk with your neighbors when planning an outdoor project. Not only will this ensure that you agree upon details such as property lines, it may also enable you to combine resources or expenses.

FENCES

- **Height:** The maximum height of a fence may be restricted by your local building code. In some communities, backyard fences are limited to 6 ft. in height, while front yard fences are limited to 3 ft. or 4 ft.—or prohibited altogether.
- **Setback:** Even if not specified by your building code, it's a good idea to position your fence 12" or so inside the official property line to avoid any possible boundary disputes. And don't assume that a neighbor's fence marks the exact boundary of your property. Before digging an elaborate planting bed up to the edge of your neighbor's fence, it's best to make sure you're not encroaching on someone else's land.
- **Gates:** Gates must be at least 3 ft. wide. If you plan to push a wheelbarrow through it, your gate width should be 4 ft.

Fences should be set back at least 1 ft. from the formal property lines.

DRIVEWAYS

- **Width:** Straight driveways should be at least 10 ft. wide; 12 ft. is better. On sharp curves, the driveway should be 14 ft. wide.
- **Thickness:** Concrete driveways should be at least 6" thick.
- **Base:** Because it must tolerate considerable weight, a concrete or brick paver driveway should have a compactable gravel base that is at least 6" thick.
- **Drainage:** A driveway should slope ¼" per foot away from a house or garage. The center of the driveway should be crowned so it is 1" higher in the center than on the sides.
- **Reinforcement:** Your local building code probably requires that all concrete driveways be reinforced with iron rebar or steel mesh for strength.

Driveways should be at least 10 ft. wide to accommodate vehicles.

SIDEWALKS & PATHS

- **Size of sidewalks:** Traditional concrete sidewalks should be 4 to 5 ft. wide to allow two people to comfortably pass one another, and 3 to 4" thick.
- **Width of garden paths:** Informal pathways may be 2 to 3 ft. wide, although steppingstone pathways can be even narrower.
- **Base:** Most codes require that a concrete or brick sidewalk be laid on a base of compactable gravel at least 4" thick. Standard concrete sidewalks may also need to be reinforced with iron rebar or steel mesh.
- **Surface & drainage:** Concrete sidewalk surfaces should be textured to provide a nonslip surface and crowned or slanted ¼" per foot to ensure that water doesn't puddle.
- **Sand-set paver walkways:** Brick pavers should be laid on a 3"-thick base of sand.

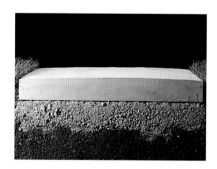

Walkways should crown in the center to provide water runoff.

STEPS

- **Proportion of riser to tread depth:** In general, steps should be proportioned so that the sum of the depth plus the riser, multiplied by two, is between 25 and 27". A 15" depth and 6" rise, for example, is a comfortable step (15 + 12 = 27), as is an 18" depth and 4" rise (18 + 8 = 26).
- **Railings:** Building codes may require railings for any stairway with more than three steps, especially for stairs that lead to an entrance to your home.

CONCRETE PATIOS

- **Base:** Concrete patios should have a subbase of compactable gravel at least 4" thick. Concrete slabs for patios should be at least 3" thick.
- **Reinforcement:** Concrete slabs should be reinforced with wire mesh or a grid of rebar.

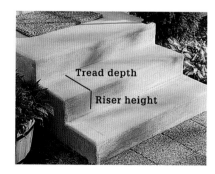

Concrete steps should use a comfortable tread depth and riser height.

Concrete patios require reinforcement with steel mesh or rebar.

Frost line

Mortared garden walls need to be supported by concrete footings.

A pool requires a protective fence to keep neighborhood children and animals from falling in.

GARDEN WALLS

- **Footings:** Mortared brick or stone garden walls more than 4 ft. in height often require concrete footings that extend below the winter frost line. Failure to follow this regulation can result in a hefty fine or a demolition order, as well as a flimsy, dangerous wall.
- **Drainage:** Dry-set stone garden walls installed without concrete footings should have a base of compactable gravel at least 6" thick to ensure the stability of the wall.

SWIMMING POOLS

- **Fences:** Nearly all building codes require a protective fence around swimming pools to keep young children and animals away from the water.
- **Location:** In some areas, building codes require that below-ground swimming pools be at least 10 ft. away from a building foundation.

SHEDS

- **Permits:** Sheds greater than 120 sq. ft. generally require a permit, but temporary buildings generally do not. Additionally, if you live in a city or a suburban association, there may be restrictions on where and how you may build a shed. If you live in a rural community, you may not need a permit if the shed will not house humans or animals.
- **Site:** Choose a location that enhances your property in all seasons. Consider setback requirements, yard grade, drainage, sun exposure, foliage, and the shed's function.
- **Size:** Choose a shed size based on what will be housed in the shed and how much room is needed to maneuver objects inside. Most sheds are built with a 3 to 4 ratio, 6-ft. wide by 8-ft. long, for example.
- **Style:** Zoning laws may dictate acceptable shed styles for your area. Try to choose a design that blends with existing home and neighborhood architecture.
- **Foundation:** The type of foundation you will need will depend on the shed's size and purpose, as well as the climate and soil conditions in your region. Cost and local building codes may also play a role in foundation type.

PORCHES

- **Permits:** Permits are required for any additions to a home. Have all gas or electrical elements added to the porch inspected before walls or floors are closed up and finished. In some areas, inspections may also be required for the footings, framing, and insulation.
- **Slope:** When building an open porch, slope floors away from the home to permit water runoff, and construct a roof overhang of 16" to enjoy the porch in the rain.
- **Cost:** To reduce costs, build a porch on a wooden deck, rather than on a concrete slab.
- **Foundation:** Always prime and paint wood support members before installation, including the ends, to prevent rot.

FIRE PITS & BARBECUES

- **Clearance:** Requirements vary by municipality, but in general, permanent open fire or barbecue pits are not permitted less than 25 ft. from your home, garage, shed, wood pile, or wooden fences.

- **Diameter:** Most cities limit the size of a pit to 3 ft. in diameter, but check your local requirements. The pit must be ringed with a noncombustible material, such as stone or driveway pavers. Some cities require a ring of sand around the pit to prevent grass fires.
- **Permits:** An inspector from the fire department will visit your site and determine whether the pit meets local safety codes. If your built-in barbecue will incorporate gas lines or electrical outlets or fixtures, additional permits and inspections will be required.
- **Burning:** Most localities do not permit burning rubbish or waste. The use of flammable or combustible liquid accelerants is generally prohibited in fire pits. Some may even restrict the size of cut wood that may be burned.
- **Safety:** Most cities require an adult present at a pit fire until all flames are extinguished. If conditions are too windy or dry, or produce excess smoke, you may be asked to extinguish all flames. A connected garden hose or other extinguisher must be near the site.

RETAINING WALLS
- **Height:** For do-it-yourself construction, retaining walls should be no more than 4 ft. high. Higher slopes should be terraced with two or more short retaining walls.
- **Batter:** A retaining wall should have a backward slant (batter) of 2 to 3" for dry-set stones; 1 to 2" for mortared stones.
- **Footings:** Retaining walls higher than 4 ft. must have concrete footings that extend down below the frost line to ensure stability.

PONDS
- **Safety:** To ensure child safety, some communities restrict landscape ponds to a depth of 12 to 18", unless surrounded by a protective fence or covered with heavy wire mesh.

DECKS
- **Structural members:** Determining the proper spacing and size for structural elements of a deck can be a complicated process, but if you follow these guidelines, you will satisfy code requirements in most areas:

BEAM SIZE & SPAN

Beam size	Maximum spacing between posts
Two 2 × 8s	8 ft.
Two 2 × 10s	10 ft.
Two 2 × 12s	12 ft.

JOIST SIZE & SPAN

Joist size	Maximum distance between beams (Joists 16" apart)
2 × 6	8 ft.
2 × 8	10 ft.
2 × 10	13 ft.

- **Decking boards:** Surface decking boards should be spaced so the gaps between boards are no more than ¼" wide.
- **Railings:** Any deck more than 24" high requires a railing. Gaps between rails or balusters should be no more than 4".
- **Post footings:** Concrete footings should be at least 8" in diameter. If a deck is attached to a permanent structure, the footings must extend below the frost line in your region.

A series of short retaining walls, rather than one tall wall, is the best way to handle a slope.

Railing balusters are required by building code to be spaced no more than 4" apart to keep small children from slipping through or being trapped between them.

Sheds larger than 100 square feet may require a permit, but temporary structures typically do not.

MEASURING

You will have to accurately measure and note the features of your yard on a rough sketch, called a yard survey. From this survey, you can draw a detailed scale drawing, called a site plan. The sketch for the yard survey can be rough, but the measurements must be exact.

If possible, enlist someone to help you take these measurements. If you haven't already done so, ask your local utility companies to mark buried utility lines.

You will also have to mark your property lines. If you don't have a plot drawing (available from the architect, developer, contractor, or possibly, the previous owner) or a deed map (available from city hall, county courthouse, title company, or mortgage bank) that specifies property lines, hire a surveyor to locate and mark them. File a copy of the survey with the county as insurance against possible boundary disputes in the future.

Measure and document the features of your yard to create a rough yard survey.

The Yard Survey ▸

Accurate yard measurements are critical for estimating quantities and cost of materials. To sketch your survey, follow these steps:

Step A: Sketch your yard and all its main features on a sheet of paper. Assign a key letter to each point. Measure all straight lines and record the measurements on a notepad.

Step B: Take triangulated measurements to locate other features, such as trees that don't lie along straight lines. Triangulation involves locating a feature by measuring its distance from any two points whose positions are known.

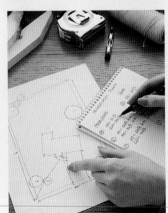

Step C: Plot irregular boundaries and curves, such as shade patterns or low-lying areas that hold moisture after a rainfall. Plot these features by taking a series of perpendicular measurements from a straight reference line, such as the edge of your house or garage.

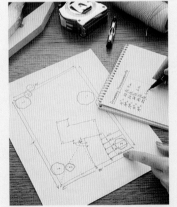

Step D: Sketch elevations to show slopes. Measure the vertical drop of a slope using different-sized stakes and string. Connect the string to the stakes so it is perfectly horizontal. Measure the distance between the string and ground at 2-ft. intervals along the string.

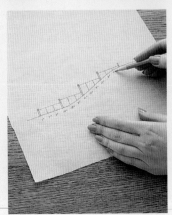

CHALLENGES

Planning an outdoor project often involves dealing with obstacles in your chosen path. You may have to go around a tree or rock outcropping, handle a hill or grade change, cross a depression, or work around buried electric, telephone, gas, cable, and water lines on your property.

You can easily cope with such challenges by removing the interference, when possible, or relocating or rerouting your structure. Contact local utility companies to locate and mark lines before you draw up plans. Law requires that these companies inspect your site on request and mark the location of buried lines.

Another option is to incorporate obstacles into your project layout. For example, on a hillside, step a fence down in level sections, or follow the contour of the slope. If a tree is in your path, try adapting your structure to incorporate the tree's current size and future growth. For example, plan a deck to flow around a large shade tree.

Rocks can be dealt with in much the same way. Incorporate boulders into wall design, or use them as focal points along a pathway.

Board, louver, basket-weave, and panel fences are good choices for stepped fences that accommodate a change in grade. More geometric in shape, they can also be more difficult to design and build.

Inset framing makes it possible to save mature trees when building a deck. Keeping trees and other landscape features intact helps preserve the value and appearance of your property.

WALKWAYS, STEPS & PATIOS

Pathways and patios transform your yard into a series of living spaces by providing a suitable surface for each room's intended purpose and activities.

By their nature, these outdoor floors must withstand heavy use and the stresses caused by seasonal weather. You will have to carefully select materials, keeping in mind the style and purpose of the area as well as the climate in your region.

There are a variety of materials available. Brick, stone, concrete, wood, and gravel can be used alone or in combinations to create attractive, durable outdoor surfaces. Look for ways to repeat materials used elsewhere in your landscape or house. For example, if you have an attractive wood fence, use the same type of wood to create a boardwalk that flows through your flower beds or garden. Or if your home has a distinctive brick façade, repeat the brick element in a matching brick paver patio or walkway.

The projects in this section illustrate the basics of paving with gravel, stone, brick, concrete, and wood. With an understanding of these techniques, you can easily complete projects as demonstrated or create variations. Many of the projects include suggestions for other materials, applications, or techniques you can apply to the basic principles.

IN THIS CHAPTER:

- Design Considerations
- Patio & Walkway Plans
- Layout & Surface Preparation
- Edging
- Loose Rock Landscape Path
- Stepping Stone Landscape Path
- Sandset Brick Walkway
- Poured Concrete Walkway
- Decorative Concrete Path
- Mortared Brick Over a Concrete Path
- Boardwalk Deck on a Slab
- Timber Garden Steps
- Flagstone Garden Steps
- Sandset Brick Patio
- Cobblestone Paver Patio
- Circular Paver Patio
- Flagstone Patio
- Creating a Permeable Subbase
- Spaced Masonry Pavers
- Concrete Slab Patio
- Mortared Paver Patio

29

DESIGN CONSIDERATIONS

In addition to the creative work of planning the look and feel of a patio space, there are several practical matters that must be addressed before you can hit the drawing board. Thinking about how you will use the patio will help you answer one of the biggest questions—how much space you'll need. The planning stage is also the time to consider environmental factors, including site drainage, sunlight, and wind, to make sure your patio will be both comfortable and usable whenever you're ready to get outside. Finally, it's a good idea (and possibly required by law) to check with your city's building department to learn about building code requirements and zoning restrictions that might affect your project plans.

USE

How you plan to spend time on your patio will influence many of your design decisions, so it's best to start the planning process by brainstorming with everyone in your household. What will be the primary uses for the space? Dining, entertaining, sunbathing, playing with the kids, enjoying the view? Once you establish the uses, see if you can accommodate all of those activities within an attractive, efficient design. For some, the solution lies simply in providing adequate space in a flexible floor plan—a quick shift in furniture, for example, can set the stage for the next activity.

In thinking about everything you hope to do on your new patio, imagine the ideal setup for each activity. For example, if you have young children, maybe you want a comfortable sitting area near an edge of the patio that's adjacent to a sandbox (or even a sandbox built into the patio; when the youngest has outgrown it, you can turn it into a planting bed). Or maybe you want some space on the patio for a baby pool or a fountain for the kids to play in.

A patio that's good for entertaining, as well as everyday uses, requires a balanced plan. Large, open areas are best for hosting parties, but can feel empty and overly exposed for a small group of diners. To accommodate both, separate expansive areas from more intimate spaces with a change in floor level or create a more personal, sheltered space by tucking a furniture set into a corner under an arbor. And don't forget to include some personal space: the perfect spot where your favorite chair is always ready for a little reading time or a quick snooze.

Visualizing Your Patio ▶

Create a quick mock-up to help you plan your patio's size, shape, and location. Mark the proposed space with rope or garden hose, and set out any furniture you'll use. See how it all looks from different points on your lot, as well as from inside the house.

If your plan is to refurbish an existing patio, think hard about what you like and dislike about the current setup. A patio that's too small can be expanded along its borders or can be connected with a walkway to a new, separate patio space designed for other uses. Often patios don't get used because they're uncomfortable or uninviting during free time. For example, if you get home from work just as the western sun is blasting the area with heat, you'll probably stay inside. The solution is a simple shade barrier that blocks those afternoon rays.

SIZE & LAYOUT

The ideal size and configuration for your patio is determined by the space needed for each activity, including plenty of room for easy access and intervening traffic. With the floor space allocated, you can begin playing around with different layouts, design elements, and shapes until the form of the space complements all of its functions. All the while, keep the big picture in mind—make sure the proportions and general design of the patio complement your house and the rest of the landscape.

HOW MUCH SPACE?

Time to think again about all the uses you have planned for the patio. If you already have the patio furniture, set it up on the proposed site and experiment with different arrangements to get a sense of how much space each furniture grouping will need. If you don't have the furniture yet, see the illustration below for suggestions on spacing. Next, decide which areas you want to be dedicated for specific activities and which can be rearranged for multiple uses. Cooking and dining areas are best as static, or *anchored*, stations, while an informal sunbathing spot defined by a couple of lounge chairs can easily be rearranged or moved as needed.

To plan traffic routes, allow a minimum of 22 inches of width for main passages between and alongside activity areas (32 inches minimum for wheelchair access). The main goal is having enough room for people to move around the patio without disrupting any activities.

TAKE A STEP BACK

As your patio plans develop, try to envision the design within its context. Does the size seem appropriate for the house and lot? How do the size and layout translate to atmosphere? While it's important to make a patio large enough for all its intended uses, there's also a risk in making it too large. With interior rooms, some people like the grandeur and openness of a sprawling great room with a cathedral ceiling, while others find the expansive space uncomfortable for personal activities like reading or quiet conversation.

Architects often design in terms of "human scale," creating spaces that are large enough to accommodate the human body in its everyday activities but small enough to provide a comfortable sense of space and enclosure. On a patio, you can establish the proper scale with clear barriers, such as fences and overheads, or with boundaries that rely more on perception—low walls, plantings, or even just a change in flooring materials.

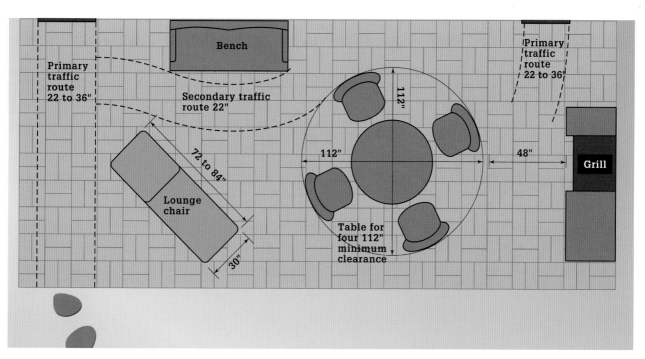

When arranging your patio, consider the placement of furniture and permanent structures as well as the space needed for primary traffic routes. These routes should have a minimum width of 22" to allow for comfortable passage throughout the patio.

ZONING LAWS, BUILDING CODES & UTILITIES

Contact local utility companies to have all utility lines marked on your property. This is necessary before digging in your yard, and it could affect your patio location. Utility companies promptly send out a representative to mark the lines.

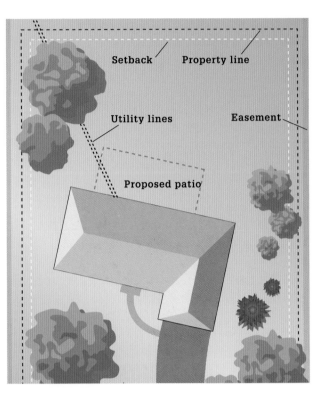

Setback   Property line

Utility lines   Easement

Proposed patio

Always check your municipality's zoning laws when planning a new patio project.

Any alterations made to your lot could fall under your municipality's zoning laws. In the case of a new patio, zoning laws might limit locations for the patio and how much ground it can cover. The latter relates to the allowable percentage of development on the lot (adding a large patio now could preclude future plans for a home addition). Also make sure the patio conforms to setback restrictions (required distance from lot lines) and easements (zones that must be accessible for utilities and other public services). Walls, fire features, or overhead structures may be subject to standards set by the local building codes, and you may need to obtain building permits.

Discuss your complete plans with an official at the local municipality's planning office for zoning laws. If you run into snags, ask about alternatives; for example, a poured concrete patio may not be allowed over an easement, but a less permanent, sandset surface may be approved.

Also, contact the local utility companies to have all utility lines marked on your property. Most states are part of the North American One Call Referral System (888-258-0808), which will contact all of the utilities in your area to have lines in your yard marked.

ACCESS

Like most recreation and relaxation areas, a patio tends to be used more often if it's easily accessible. The same is true of visual access. Full views, or even just glimpses, of the patio from several interior rooms will beckon you outdoors on nice days.

Another important consideration involves the rooms that lead to the patio. For example, if outdoor dining is one of your primary activities, locating the patio near the kitchen will prove to be an enormous convenience. Similarly, a patio used frequently for large parties should not be accessed through a bedroom or other private space. This is not only an inconvenience, guests feel uncomfortable walking through private or formal areas of a home.

ATMOSPHERE

Perhaps the most important elements of all are the everyday factors that affect the quality of life on a patio, including sunlight, noise, privacy, and views. Does the site get enough sunlight (or too much) at the times you're most likely to use it? Are noise levels acceptable—or will you need to put up a fence? Will you feel overly exposed and on display, or too shut in? Finally, what you see from the patio has a big impact on the atmosphere. If there are no good views available, add landscaping, plants, or decorations to create a pleasant view.

DEALING WITH DRAINAGE

It's not unusual that a new patio creates, or is subject to, drainage problems. One common cause is a hard paved surface that sheds water instead of absorbing it and deposits it along the lower edge of the patio. There, the water collects, creating a swampy area of grass. During heavy rains, runoff water can build up enough force to wash out flower beds bordering a patio. Drainage problems can also occur when the water has no escape, a common condition with sunken or recessed patios that are surrounded by retaining walls or ascending slopes. Additionally, adding or removing soil or plants to make room for a patio can alter natural drainage patterns, potentially resulting in an unpleasant surprise with the first good rain.

Fortunately, all of these problems can be solved with an appropriate drainage system. For patio runoff, a drainage swale or perimeter trench is usually effective. These are sloped channels or trenches that collect excess groundwater and divert it to a collection point. A trench running along the lowest edge of the patio can collect water directly from the patio surface. If the patio is at the top of a natural slope leading to a low point in the yard, a drainage swale located in the low point keeps the rest of the yard relatively dry.

Diverting excess water is only half of the battle—the water also needs a place to go. Ideally, it is collected on your property, where it filters through the soil and returns to natural aquifers. This can be achieved with a dry well or with a swale leading to a natural collection area in the landscape. Another option is to divert excess runoff to a street gutter or a storm drain, but this design must be approved by the city's planning department.

Enclosed or recessed patios may require their own drainage system, typically with some type of floor drain. The patio surface slopes toward the drain, located either in the center or along one side, where runoff water collects in a subsurface catch basin. From there, an underground drainpipe carries the water to a collection point. If you think your patio will need this type of system, consult an engineer or qualified landscape professional early in the planning process to discuss your options.

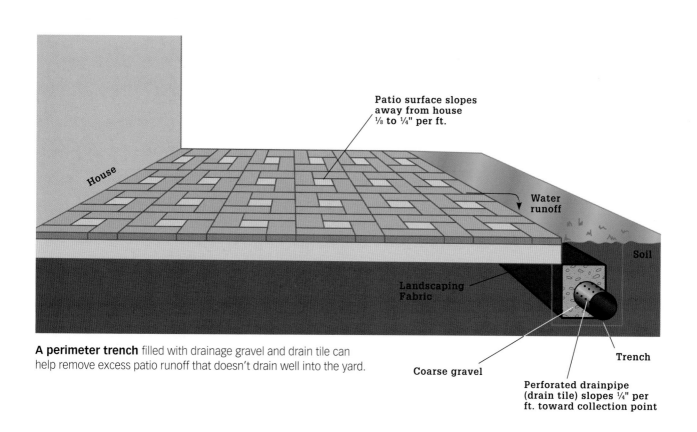

A perimeter trench filled with drainage gravel and drain tile can help remove excess patio runoff that doesn't drain well into the yard.

Patio surface slopes away from house ⅛ to ¼" per ft.

House

Water runoff

Soil

Landscaping Fabric

Coarse gravel

Trench

Perforated drainpipe (drain tile) slopes ¼" per ft. toward collection point

CLIMATE CONTROL

Careful planning can't change the weather, but it can help you make the best of prevailing conditions. By controlling or using sunlight and shade, wind, and natural air currents, you can make your patio the most comfortable place in your outdoor landscape. Consider the following:

Sunlight and shadows: The unalterable pattern of the sun is one of the few climatic systems you can count on. The tricky part is positioning your patio so it receives the right amount and intensity of sunlight at the time of day—and the season—when you'll use it most. Remember that the sun's path changes throughout the year. In summer, it rises high in the sky along the east-west axis, creating shorter shadows and more exposure overall. In winter, the sun's angle is relatively low, resulting in long shadows in the northwest, north, and northeast directions. To avoid shadows altogether, locate your patio away from the house and other structures.

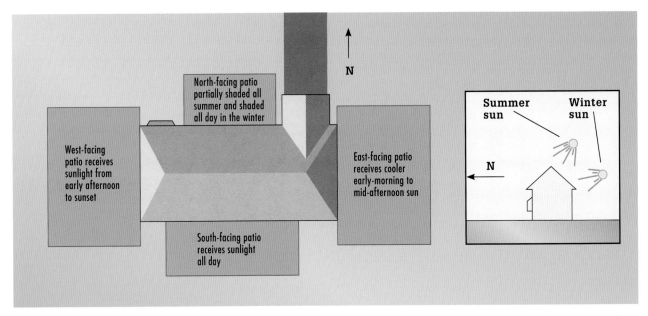

Remember to consider the amount of sunlight your patio will receive to make sure your planned project will meet your needs.

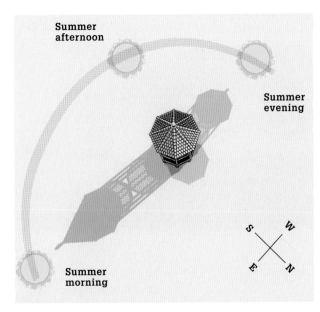

Shadows follow the east-west axis in the summer.

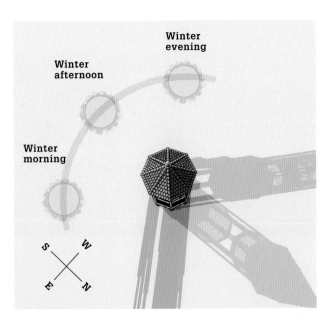

Winter shadows point to the northeast and northwest and are relatively long at midday.

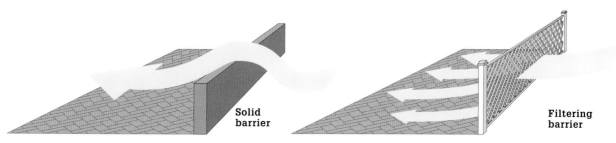

Barriers help control wind patterns around your patio. Solid barriers drive wind currents upward, creating a forcible reversal in direction. Filtering barriers allow wind to pass through, reducing its force in the process.

Wind currents can ruin your patio peace as surely as a rainstorm. Shielding yourself from wind takes careful planning and sometimes trial and error. Since you can't protect against all wind, first determine the direction of prevailing winds—the most frequent and strongest wind currents affecting your site (prevailing winds may change with the seasons)—then decide on the best location for a wind barrier. Contrary to appearances, a solid barrier often is not the most effective windbreak; these barriers force air currents to swoop over the top and then drop down on the backside, returning to full strength at a distance roughly equal to the barrier's height. A more reliable windbreak is created with a lattice or louvered fence that diffuses and weakens the wind as it passes through the barrier.

Patio materials and orientation: The surface material you choose can also affect the patio environment. Dark-colored, solid surfaces—like brick or dark stone—absorb a lot of heat during the day and may become uncomfortable to walk on in sunny areas. However, after the sun goes down, stored heat released from the paving can warm the air on the patio. Solid walls also reflect heat and can restrict cooling breezes. Because cold air sinks, low-lying patios or those positioned at the base of an incline tend to be cooler than higher areas of the landscape.

If you're building an overhead specifically for shade, experiment with alternative materials, such as bamboo screening or fabric, to filter sunlight and control wind.

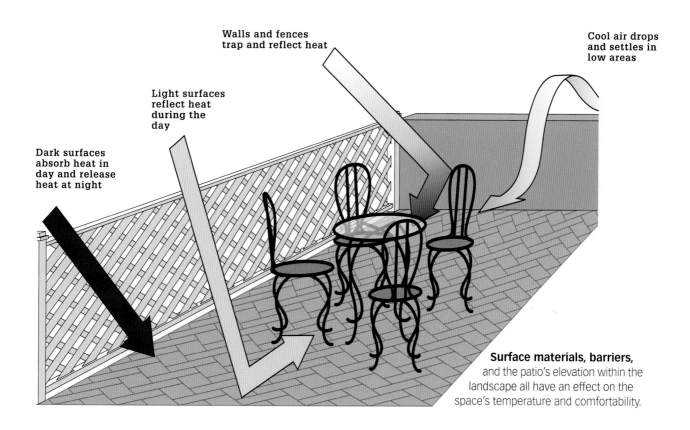

Walls and fences trap and reflect heat

Cool air drops and settles in low areas

Light surfaces reflect heat during the day

Dark surfaces absorb heat in day and release heat at night

Surface materials, barriers, and the patio's elevation within the landscape all have an effect on the space's temperature and comfortability.

PATIO & WALKWAY PLANS

This section offers a different kind of inspiration from the section on design themes. Here you'll see detailed patio and landscape plans for several different types of properties, each showing specific design solutions for making the most of the available space and existing conditions. One or more of the properties might resemble your own, but even if none of them does, don't worry; the idea is to see how various elements can be put to use and to think about how some of those solutions might work in your own plan.

The five designs, starting on the following page, are shown in *plan*, or aerial, view. This is the perspective that professionals use to do much of their design work, as it provides not only a bird's-eye view of the entire site, it's also the best way to see how the patio, walkways, and other elements relate to the house and surrounding landscape. Plan drawings of your own property can be quite helpful in designing and planning a new patio or path project (see below).

Drawing Your Own Plans ▸

Unless you need them for getting a permit or other official business, detailed drawings of your site and new projects are optional. But there are a few good reasons to map out your property and at least sketch your basic plans onto paper. Scaled drawings are good for showing relationships between elements and overall proportions within a plan, and are helpful for estimating materials and making shopping lists. If you hire out any of the work, detailed drawings will be invaluable for obtaining accurate bids and to help you keep the project on track during construction. Also, sketches are always useful for conveying or experimenting with ideas.

When making your own drawings, it's best to work from a base map, or site plan—an aerial view of the project site and as much of the surrounding area as is relevant. The site plan should include:

- The house (at least the wall adjacent to the patio), including doors, windows, and light fixtures
- Trees, significant plantings, and other landscaping features
- Gutter downspouts, outdoor faucets, and electrical outlets
- Notes about prevailing winds, lot grading (for sloping sites), and natural drainage routes
- Views (good and bad) from the patio site
- Sun and wind patterns

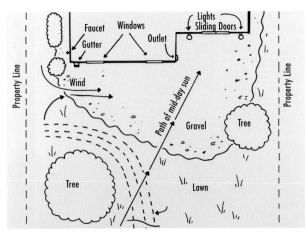

An accurately scaled site plan puts your property into perspective and helps you think like a designer. Create a plan using your own measurements or locate the plat map or original blueprints of your property (check with the local city or county planning offices or your mortgage/title company).

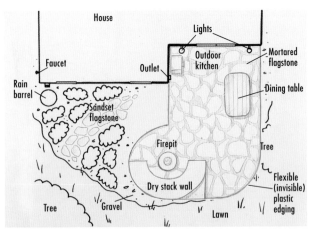

Sketch your designs onto clean copies of the site plan, or use an overlay of tracing paper for each new drawing. As you refine your plans, create more detailed, smaller-scale drawings of the patio/walkway site and immediate surroundings.

SAMPLE PATIO PLAN 1

Like most lots in established urban neighborhoods, this backyard space was short on both space and privacy. But by devoting most of the area to two patios and the rest to planting beds, this design provides ample room for entertaining, outdoor dining, and even gardening.

The main patio space is paved with cut stone for a natural yet clean look and a smooth surface that's good for nighttime parties and frequent traffic between the house and the back gate. In one corner, a flagstone coffee table and fountain define a casual "lounge" area; the fountain also helps dampen the city's noise. A vine-covered arbor (or trellis) provides shade and privacy for half of the lounge area and a portion of the smaller planting bed.

Opposite the lounge area, a cozy corner patio is the perfect stage for intimate gatherings and everyday meals. Its natural flagstone floor is two short steps up from the main patio surface. This, along with the decorative post-and-beam gate, gives the dining space a special, secluded feel. A fan-shaped arbor could be added here for shade and more privacy.

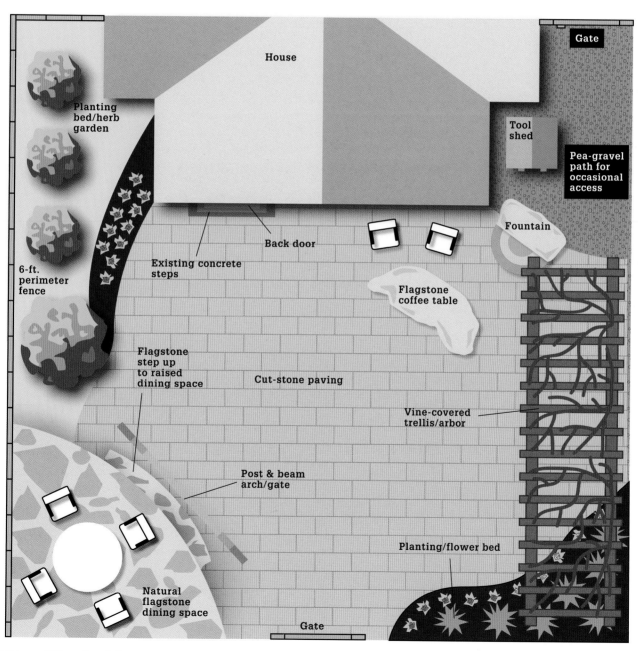

This multifunctional design adds privacy while creating multiple spaces for entertaining.

SAMPLE PATIO PLAN 2

Sloping ground can be a challenge for patio plans, but can also be an opportunity for creating dramatic features or perspectives you can't get with a flat surface. In this backyard site, the area near the middle of the house was relatively close to grade. Adding a few retaining walls allowed the patio to extend out to both sides. One retaining wall cuts into the slope along the south end of the site, providing space and a boundary for a paver walkway linking the patio to the front yard. This abuts a four-foot-tall masonry wall that carves a 90-degree space into the slope and provides a backdrop (and backsplash) for an L-shaped outdoor kitchen.

The low wall at the north end of the patio retains earth for the patio surface and helps create a lofty feel for the sitting area outside the home's master bedroom. A planter with trees provides a subtle barrier between the sitting area and the main patio space. Out on the yard's planted slope, a set of stone steps leads to gently climbing stepping stone paths laid out for either strolling through the foliage or tending to garden plants.

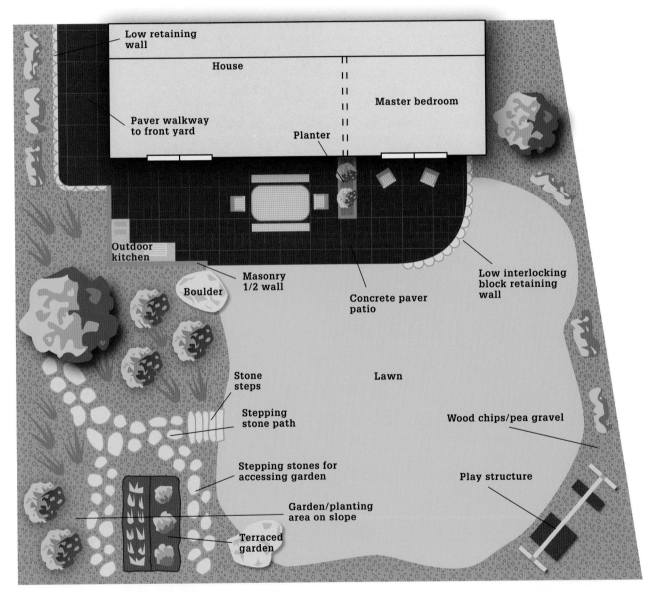

To make the most of a sloping yard, use retaining walls, steps, and paths to emphasize grand views and allow easy access to garden areas.

SAMPLE PATIO PLAN 3

This grand design, created for a large suburban or rural property, has a setting for every mood and occasion: the expansive brick patio provides an elegant venue for both formal and casual entertaining. Guests (and kids) will feel more than welcome to step out onto the lawn for backyard games or a stroll through the grounds.

In addition to its ample open space, the brick patio serves as an entryway to a screened porch—a welcome retreat for hot, wet, or buggy weather. At the other end, the patio surrounds a small sun deck designed for a few lounge chairs or perhaps a bistro set used for drinks or everyday meals.

Away from the main patio, two destinations offer getaways of distinctly different character: follow the pebbled stepping-stone path through the archway to the sun-sheltered garden view from the gazebo. Or, stroll across the lawn after dark for stargazing around the open fire on the circular gravel patio.

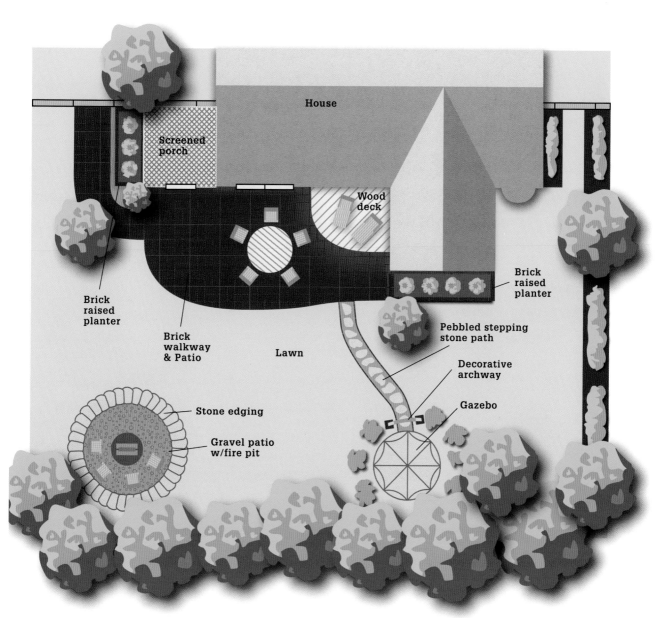

House

Screened porch

Wood deck

Brick raised planter

Brick raised planter

Brick walkway & Patio

Lawn

Pebbled stepping stone path

Decorative archway

Gazebo

Stone edging

Gravel patio w/fire pit

This design provides outdoor rooms for all purposes—gathering around a fire, dining, sunbathing, relaxing in a screened-in porch, or enjoying the view from a gazebo.

SAMPLE PATIO PLAN 4

Casual and organic in feel, this plan with sandset flagstone surfaces embodies the spirit of the ranch home, in which the patio is used as an extension of the indoor spaces. Running the full length of the home, the patio is accessible from several different rooms and is likewise visible from each.

An arbor with vine-covered trellis screen defines and shelters a dining space located just outside of the home's kitchen. And for the cook, a large planting bed adjacent to the patio provides easy access to fresh herbs, fruits, and vegetables.

An integrated sandbox keeps the kids near the house and out of the hot afternoon sun. Both the sandbox and integrated flowerbed are simply excavated areas filled with play sand over soil and landscape fabric.

In keeping with the natural look of the patio paving, flagstones are used for a well-traveled walkway between the front and back yards, while a compacted gravel path with natural stone edging creates an attractive service road leading from the shed to the back garden.

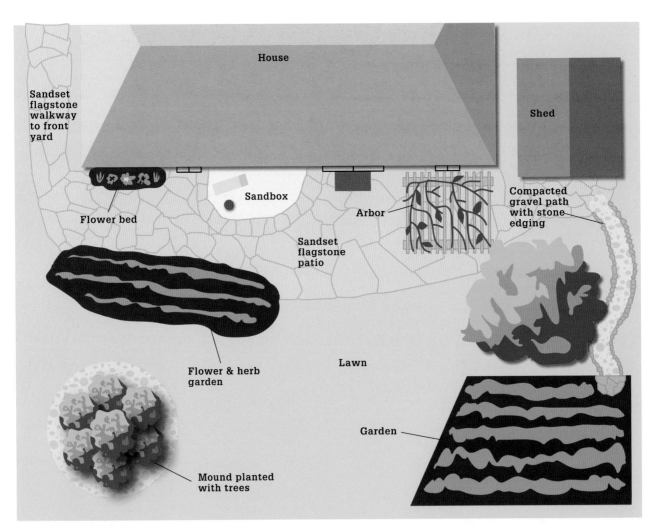

This sandset flagstone patio is accessible from multiple areas around the house, seamlessly integrating indoor and outdoor living.

SAMPLE PATIO PLAN 5

This new suburban property presented a challenge to the standard patio plan: the back of the house seemed just right for a full-sized patio, but the neighboring property was so close that the view from the patio would be dominated by the neighbor's kitchen (and *their* backyard patio). The better view was from the front of the house. Therefore, this design places the main patio space around the front door, incorporating the existing entry stoop and portico. A second, smaller patio made with circular concrete pavers serves as a landing and casual sitting area just outside the patio door leading to the back yard.

Because it faces the street, is well-integrated with the house, and is partially sheltered with overheads, the entry patio feels a lot like a traditional front porch. A low masonry wall adds definition and a sense of enclosure to the patio. However, to maintain a welcoming feel for the front entry, a large opening in the wall leaves plenty of room for the existing concrete walkway. Also, the walkway remains uninterrupted from the sidewalk to the front stoop, clearly indicating the direct route to the front door. The patio paving is level with the walkway so the entire space is useable as a patio surface when needed.

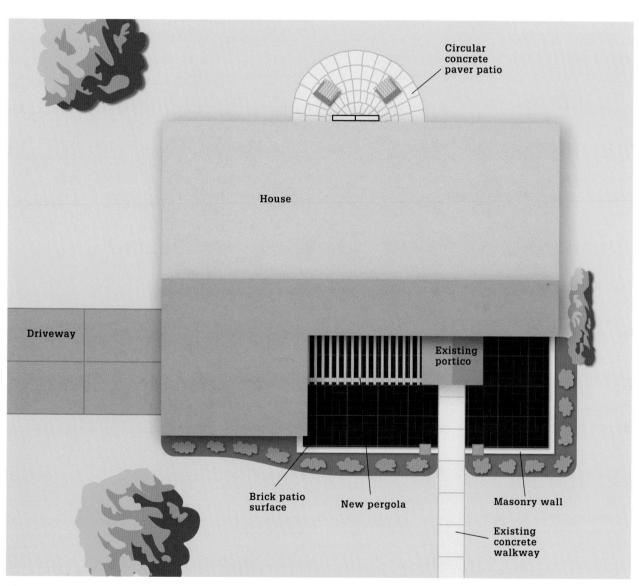

Circular concrete paver patio

House

Driveway

Existing portico

Brick patio surface

New pergola

Masonry wall

Existing concrete walkway

If the best view of your home is in the front, consider constructing a landscaped patio around your home's existing entryway, as shown in this design. A small patio in back is still a practical addition for greater privacy.

LAYOUT & SURFACE PREPARATION

The first major step of any patio project is to set up guide strings. Once that's finished, excavation begins and then a layer of gravel is added. The gravel is an essential element of patio construction: like your house's foundation, it creates a flat, stable base for building upon; and it protects the surface material by providing drainage underneath to minimize shifting and settling caused by seasonal freeze-thaw cycles.

There are a few matters to take care of before you begin the layout and surface prep work. The first is to determine the thickness of each layer of the patio construction. This includes the thicknesses of the surface material, the sand bed (if required), and the gravel subbase. For most patio types, the gravel layer should be four inches thick (after compaction). Concrete slab patios call for six inches of gravel, but this is subject to the local building code and may vary by region. The combined thicknesses of the layers minus the distance the patio surface will stand above the ground gives you the depth of the excavation.

The height of the finished patio aboveground is up to you. The standard minimum height is one inch. This ensures the patio will drain properly, but it's low enough to cut any bordering grass with a mower.

The next factor to determine is the total drop distance—the change in elevation from the high end to the low end of the patio surface. This creates the slope necessary for water runoff. Your patio should slope away from the house foundation or other adjacent structure (and preferably away from main traffic routes) at a rate of ⅛-inch per linear foot. For example, if your patio will extend 12 feet from your house, the drop distance of the patio surface will be 1½ inches. In the following project, you'll calculate the drop distance by measuring from the house (or high edge of the patio) to the batterboards at the low edge. The batterboards are set about 12 inches beyond the finished patio edges, and this additional amount makes the final drop distance more accurate than using the finished patio dimensions.

The final step before you start digging is to locate underground utility lines in the project site. Call your utility service providers or a national provider (see Resources, page 553) to have your lines marked.

Tools & Materials ▸

Drill	Lumber (2 × 2,
Circular saw	2 × 4)
Hammer	2½" coarse-thread
Level	drywall screws
Hand maul	Common nails
Mason's string	Compactable gravel
Line level	Eye and ear
Power sod cutter or	protection
lawn edger	Work gloves
Excavation tools	Rope or garden hose
Bow rake	Marking paint
Plate compactor or	Flat spade
hand tamp	U-shaped wire
Shovel	stakes (optional)
Wheelbarrow	Landscape fabric
Plumb bob	(optional)

Set up batterboards for the layout strings so you can easily remove and replace the strings without losing the slope and layout settings. A story pole—measured against temporary cross strings—makes it easy to check the depth of each layer as you work. Remember to call utility companies to have them mark utility lines in or near the project site before excavating.

HOW TO PREPARE & EXCAVATE A BUILDING SITE

Construct the batterboards from 2 × 4 lumber and 2½" screws: Cut the batterboard legs 24" long, and then taper the ends to a point. Cut the cross-pieces at 24". Align and fasten the legs perpendicular to the ends of the cross-pieces. Use a nail or screw at the top center of each crosspiece.

2 × 2 stake

Roughly mark the patio corners with 2 × 2 stakes. Cut the 2 × 2 ends to a taper (the greater the angle, the easier it will be to drive into the ground). Tap the tapered end into the ground with a hand maul or sledgehammer.

Batterboard

Drive pairs of batterboards about 2 ft. behind the stakes, holding them plumb and level. The tops of the crosspieces should be about 12" above the ground. If the patio abuts the house, drive a single 2 × 4 stake at each corner so one face of the stake is even with the planned edge of the patio.

Tie a mason's string taut between an outer batterboard nail and one of the house-side (or high edge of the patio) stakes. Attach a line level (inset) to the string and adjust the stakes as needed until the string is perfectly level.

High side

Begin setting the slope on the first layout string: stand the pole next to the batterboard and mark the height of the level mason's string. Measure between the house (or high side) stake to the batterboard, then calculate the drop distance for the string—a common slope is ¼" per linear foot.

(continued)

43

Using the story pole as a guide, drive the batterboard down until the string is even with the drop distance mark. Make sure the crosspiece remains level across the top so the string's height won't change if you move the string later.

Set up the remaining three string lines so they are even with the outer edges of the finished patio and are just touching the first string. First install the two strings parallel to the house, and use the line level to confirm they are level. The final string (parallel to the first string) will have the proper slope when it touches the intersecting strings.

Variation: Use a rope or a garden hose to lay out curved or freeform patio edges. Mark the outline onto the ground with marking paint. Once you complete the subbase, you can repeat the process to guide the installation. *Note: Curving patios still need a string layout to guide the excavation and base prep.*

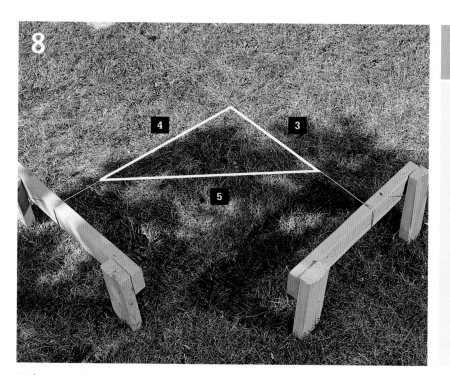

Checking for Square ▶

The traditional 3-4-5 technique can also be used for larger multiples of 3, 4, and 5. This provides greater accuracy for larger patios. For example, use 6, 8, and 10 ft.

Alternatively, you can use a long tape to measure between opposing corners of the layout. When the measurements are equal, the layout is square.

Make sure the string layout is perfectly square using the 3-4-5 squaring technique: starting at one of the string intersections, measure along one string and make a mark at 3 ft. (or a multiple of 3 ft.). Measure along the perpendicular string and mark at 4 ft. Measure between the two marks: the distance should equal 5 ft. If not, adjust the strings as needed until the measurements come out correctly. Repeat the process at the diagonally opposed corner. Mark the string positions onto the batterboard crosspieces.

Determine the finished height of the patio surface. If the patio abuts the house, the finished surface should be 1 to 3" below the typical threshold of an entry door. At the low end of the patio it's desirable to have the finished surface rise at least 1" above the surrounding ground to facilitate drainage and prevent dirt and mud from washing onto the patio.

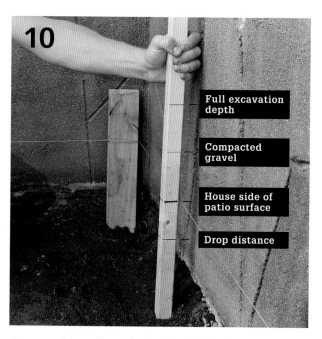

Full excavation depth

Compacted gravel

House side of patio surface

Drop distance

On your story pole, mark a top line for the distance from the string line (measured at the high edge of the patio) to the full excavation depth. A second line represents the distance from the string to the top of the compacted gravel base. Be sure to account for the thickness of the paving material and sand bed as needed.

(continued)

11

Cut the sod along the project outline using a flat-end spade or a power lawn edger. To compensate for edging, extend the excavation about 6" beyond the finished patio outline. Reserve healthy sod for covering soil backfill behind the edging.

12

Strip the sod or vegetation inside the outlined area and then excavate the construction area to a depth that allows for a 6"-thick gravel subbase, a 1" layer of sand, and the paver thickness; account for the finished height aboveground also.

13

Grade and compact the soil. First use a bow rake to achieve the proper slope, and then compact the soil with a rented plate or hand tamper. Set up temporary cross strings for reference to simplify the excavation and the gravel installation later.

14

Depth stake

Use the story pole to check the depth as you work. Drive a pair of 2 × 2 stakes outside of the original string layout, and tie on the cross string so it's just touching the layout strings. Check the depth at several points along the cross string, removing or adding soil as needed to achieve the proper depth. Once that's done, move the cross string to the next section and repeat. *Note: Thoroughly tamp any soil that's been added to a low spot to minimize future settling. For the same reason, it's best to use soil from the immediate area (instead of purchased topsoil) or fill low areas with compacted sand or gravel.*

Variation: For loose-fill patios, install a layer of high-quality landscape fabric to inhibit weed growth before adding the gravel base. Overlap rows of fabric by at least 6". If desired, pin the fabric in place with U-shaped wire stakes.

Add the first layer of compactable gravel (or start with landscape fabric; see Variation this page). Dump wheelbarrow loads of gravel into evenly distributed pods, then spread out each pod in all directions with a shovel and a bow rake. Use the rake to create a flat, smooth surface.

Thoroughly tamp each layer of gravel before adding more, as needed. If using a hand tamper, compact the gravel in 2"-thick layers; if using a plate compactor, compact every 4" of gravel. Use cross strings and the story pole to check the gravel height as you work. A straight 2 × 4 also helps for smoothing gravel prior to compacting and for checking for high and low spots.

Extend a plumb bob from the layout strings to the base to mark the exact corners and edges of the finished patio for the surface installation. Mark each point with paint or a small stake. Find and mark the corners of the patio by hanging the plumb bob from each string intersection. Proceed to the installation portion of your project.

EDGING

Edging can play many different roles in patio and walkway design. Its most practical purpose is containment—keeping the surface material in place so paving doesn't drift off into the yard. As a decorative feature, edging creates a visual border that adds a sense of order or closure to the path or patio space. This effect can be enhanced by edging with a material that contrasts with the surface material or can be made more subtle by using the same material, perhaps in a slightly different pattern. Finally, edging can serve to strengthen the patio or walkway as a hard, protective curb that stands up to years of foot traffic.

The best time to install edging depends on your application. For most sandset paving and loose material surfaces, edging is typically installed on top of the compacted gravel subbase. Edging along existing concrete slabs can be applied on top of the slab or along the sides, with the proper order determined by the finish materials.

To minimize the number of cuts required for paving, install edging after the patio surface is complete. You can also install two adjacent sides of edging to form a right angle, providing an accurate guide for starting the paver pattern, and then install the remaining two sides up against the laid pavers. A third option is to set up temporary 2 × 4 edging, which can be easily replaced with the real thing after the paving is finished.

Install professional-grade paver edging along chalk lines (chalk lines are snapped directly below the outlines you've created with the mason's strings). The paver edge should rest on the compacted gravel.

RIGID PAVER EDGING

Choose heavy-duty edging that's strong enough to contain your surface materials. If your patio or walkway has curves, buy plenty of notched, or flexible, edging for the curves. Also, buy 12-inch-long galvanized spikes: one for every 12 inches of edging plus extra for curves.

49

Invisible Edging ▸

Invisible edging is so named for its low-profile edge that stops about halfway up the side edges of pavers. The exposed portion of the edging is easily concealed under soil and sod or groundcover.

Rigid plastic edging installs easily and works well for both curved and straight walkways made from paving stones or brick pavers set in sand.

Brick pavers

Sand

Landscape fabric

Rigid plastic edging

Compactable gravel subbase

HOW TO INSTALL RIGID PAVER EDGING

Set the edging on top of a compacted gravel base covered with landscape fabric. Using your layout strings as guides, secure the edging with spikes driven every 12" (or as recommended by the manufacturer). Along curves, spike the edging at every tab, or as recommended.

Cover the outside of the edging with soil and/or sod after the paving is complete. *Tip: On two or more sides of the patio or path, you can spike the edging minimally, in case you have to make adjustments during the paving. Anchor the edging completely after the paving is done.*

BRICK PAVER EDGING

Brick edging can be laid in several different configurations (see below): on-end with its edge perpendicular to the paved surface ("soldiers"); on its long edges; or laid flat, either parallel or perpendicular to the paving. For mortared surfaces, brick can also be mortared to the edge of a concrete slab for a decorative finish (see pages 74 to 77 and 142 to 149).

(see pages 74 to 77 and 142 to 149)

Tools & Materials ▸

Flat shovel	Garden spade
Rubber mallet	Work gloves
2 × 4 (about 12" long)	Gravel
Bricks	Landscape fabric
Hand tamper	Eye protection

Brick Edging Configurations ▸

Brick "soldier" edging with ends upward

Brick set on long edges

Brick set on faces, edge-to-edge or end-to-end

HOW TO INSTALL BRICK PAVER EDGING

Excavate the edge of the patio or walkway site using a flat shovel to create a clean, vertical edge. The edge of the soil (and sod) will support the outsides of the bricks. For edging with bricks set on-end, dig a narrow trench along the perimeter of the site, setting the depth so the tops of the edging bricks will be flush with the paving surface (or just above the surface for loose materials).

Set the edging bricks into the trench after installing the gravel subbase and landscape fabric. If applicable, use your layout strings to keep the bricks in line and to check for the proper height. Backfill behind the bricks with soil and tamp well as you secure the bricks in place. Install the patio surface material. Tap the tops of the bricks with a rubber mallet and a short 2 × 4 to level them with one another (inset).

STONE EDGING

Cut stone or dressed stone makes better edging than flagstone, which often has jagged edges that create an uneven border. Semi-dressed stone, with one or more flat sides, is a good option for a more natural look.

Tools & Materials ▸

Rubber mallet
Maul
Stone chisel
Pitching chisel
Pointing chisel
Garden spade
Edging stones
Sand
Eye and ear
   protection
Work gloves
Mason's hammer

Shovel
Gravel base
Landscape fabric

Trimming Stone ▸

Trim irregular stones for a tight fit: first score a cutting line with a small stone chisel and maul, then complete the cut with a pitching chisel. Use a pointing chisel or the pick end of a mason's hammer to knock off small bumps and smooth rough edges.

HOW TO INSTALL STONE EDGING

Excavate the patio or walkway site and dig a perimeter trench to accommodate the stone edging. Add the landscape fabric and then a gravel base, as required. Place each stone into the trench and tap it with a rubber mallet to set it into the gravel. Use your layout strings to keep the edging in line and at the proper height.

Backfill behind the stones with soil and tamp with a shovel handle or a board to secure the stones in the trench. If desired, fill the spaces between stones with sand or soil to help lock them together.

CONCRETE CURB EDGING

Poured concrete edging is perfect for curves and custom shapes, especially when you want a continuous border at a consistent height. Keeping the edging low to the ground (about one inch above grade) makes it work well as a mowing strip, in addition to a patio or walkway border. Use fiber-reinforced concrete mix, and cut control joints into the edging to help control cracking.

Tools & Materials ›

Rope or garden hose
Excavation tools
Mason's string
Hand tamp
Maul
Circular saw
Drill
Concrete mixing
  tools
Margin trowel
Wood concrete
  float

Concrete edger
1 × 1 wood stakes
¼" hardboard
1" wood screws
Fiber-reinforced
  concrete
Acrylic concrete
  sealer
Eye and ear
  protection
Work gloves

Concrete edging draws a sleek, smooth line between surfaces in your yard and is especially effective for curving paths and walkways.

HOW TO INSTALL CONCRETE CURB EDGING

Lay out the contours of the edging using a rope or garden hose. For straight runs, use stakes and mason's string to mark the layout. Make the curb at least 5" wide.

Dig a trench between the layout lines 8" wide (or 3" wider than the finished curb width) at a depth that allows for a 4"-thick (minimum) curb at the desired height above grade. Compact the soil to form a flat, solid base.

Stake along the edges of the trench, using 1 × 1 × 12" wood stakes. Drive a stake every 18" along each side edge.

Build the form sides by fastening 4"-wide strips of ¼" hardboard to the insides of the stakes using 1" wood screws. Bend the strips to follow the desired contours.

Add spacers inside the form to maintain a consistent width. Cut the spacers from 1 × 1 to fit snugly inside the form. Set the spacers along the bottom edges of the form at 3-ft. intervals.

Fill the form with concrete mixed to a firm, workable consistency. Use a margin trowel to spread and consolidate the concrete.

Tool the concrete: once the bleed water disappears, smooth the surface with a wood float. Using a margin trowel, cut 1"-deep control joints across the width of the curb at 3-ft. intervals. Tool the side edges of the curb with an edger. Allow to cure. Seal the concrete, as directed, with an acrylic concrete sealer, and let it cure for 3 to 5 days before removing the form.

LANDSCAPE TIMBER EDGING

Pressure-treated landscape or cedar timbers make attractive, durable edging that's easy to install. Square-edged timbers are best for geometric pavers like brick and cut stone, while loose materials and natural flagstone look best with rounded or squared timbers. Choose the size of timber depending on how bold you want the border to look.

Tools & Materials ▸

Excavation tools
Plate compactor
  (available for rent)
Maul
Reciprocating saw
  with wood-cutting
  and metal-cutting
  blades, circular
  saw, or handsaw
Drill and ½" bit
Compacted gravel

Landscape fabric
Sand (optional)
Landscape timbers
  (pressure-treated
  or rot-resistant
  species only)
½"-diameter (#4)
  rebar
Eye and ear
  protection
Work gloves

Lumber or timber edging can be used with any patio surface material. Here, this lumber edging is not only decorative, it also holds all of the loose material in place.

HOW TO INSTALL TIMBER EDGING

During the site excavation, dig a perimeter trench for the timbers so they will install flush with the top of the patio or walkway surface (or just above the surface for loose material). Add the compacted gravel base, as required, including a 2 to 4" layer in the perimeter trench. Cut timbers to the desired length using a reciprocating saw with a long wood-cutting blade, a circular saw, or a handsaw.

Drill ½" holes through each timber, close to the ends and every 24" in between. Cut a length of ½"-diameter (#4) rebar at 24" for each hole using a reciprocating saw and metal-cutting blade. Set the timbers in the trench and make sure they lie flat. Use your layout strings as guides for leveling and setting the height of the timbers. Anchor the timbers with the rebar, driving the bar flush with the wood surface.

LUMBER EDGING

Dimension lumber makes for an inexpensive edging material and a less-massive alternative to landscape timbers; 2 × 4 or 2 × 6 lumber works well for most patios and walkways. Use only pressure-treated lumber rated for ground contact or all-heart redwood or cedar boards to prevent rot. For the stakes, use pressure-treated lumber, since they will be buried anyway and appearance is not a concern.

Tools & Materials ▸

Excavation tools
Circular saw
Compactable gravel
Drill
2× lumber for edging
2 × 4 lumber for stakes
Wood preservative

Compacted gravel
Landscape fabric
Sand
2½" galvanized deck screws
Eye and ear protection
Work gloves

Wood edging is a popular choice for simple flagstone or paver walkways and for patios with a casual look.

HOW TO INSTALL LUMBER EDGING

Excavate the patio site, and dig a perimeter trench for the boards so they will install flush with the top of the patio surface (or just above the surface for loose material). Add the gravel base, as required, including a 2 to 4" layer of gravel in the trench. Cut the edging boards to length, and seal the ends with wood preservative. Cut 2 × 4 stakes about 16" long. Set the edging boards in the trench and drive a stake close to the ends of each board and every 24" in between.

Fasten the boards to the stakes with pairs of 2½" deck screws. Where boards meet at corners and butt joints, fasten them together with screws. Use your layout strings as guides for leveling and setting the height of the edging. Backfill behind the edging to support the boards and hide the stakes.

LOOSE ROCK LANDSCAPE PATH

Loose-fill gravel pathways are perfect for stone gardens, casual yards, and other situations where a hard surface is not required. The material is inexpensive, and its fluidity accommodates curves and irregular edging. Since gravel may be made from any rock, gravel paths may be matched to larger stones in the environment, tying them in to your landscaping. The gravel you choose need not be restricted to stone, either. Industrial and agricultural byproducts, such as cinder and ashes, walnut shells, seashells, and ceramic fragments may also be used as path material.

For a more stable path, choose angular or jagged gravel over rounded materials. However, if your preference is to stroll throughout your landscape barefoot, your feet will be better served with smoother stones, such as river rock or pond pebbles. With stone, look for a crushed product in the ¼- to ¾-inch range. Angular or smooth, stones smaller than that can be tracked into the house, while larger materials are uncomfortable and potentially hazardous to walk on. If it complements your landscaping, use light-colored gravel, such as buff limestone. Visually, it is much easier to follow a light pathway at night because it reflects more moonlight.

Stable edging helps keep the pathway gravel from migrating into the surrounding mulch and soil. When integrated with landscape fabric, the edge keeps invasive perennials and trees from sending roots and shoots into the path. Do not use gravel paths near plants and trees that produce messy fruits, seeds, or other debris that will be difficult to remove from the gravel. Organic matter left on gravel paths will eventually rot into compost that will support weed growth.

A base of compactable gravel under the surface material keeps the pathway firm underfoot. For best results, embed the surface gravel material into the paver base with a plate compactor. This prevents the base from showing through if the gravel at the surface is disturbed. An underlayment of landscape fabric helps stabilize the pathway and blocks weeds, but if you don't mind pulling an occasional dandelion and are building on firm soil, it can be omitted.

Tools & Materials ▶

Mason's string	Straight 2 × 4
Hose or rope	Edging
Marking paint	Spikes
Excavation tools	Professional-grade
Garden rake	landscape fabric
Shovel	Compactable gravel
Mallet	Dressed gravel
Plate compactor	Eye and ear
Sod stripper or	protection
power sod cutter	Work gloves
Wood stakes	Circular saw
Lumber (1 × 2, 2 × 4)	Maul

CONSTRUCTION DETAILS

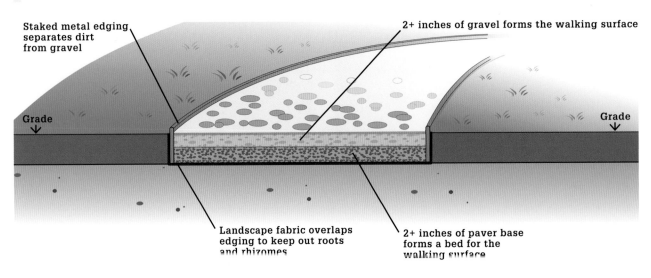

Staked metal edging separates dirt from gravel

2+ inches of gravel forms the walking surface

Grade ↓

Grade ↓

Landscape fabric overlaps edging to keep out roots and rhizomes

2+ inches of paver base forms a bed for the walking surface

Loose materials can be used as filler between solid surface materials, like flagstone, or laid as the primary ground cover, as shown here.

Make a Spacer Gauge ▸

To ensure that the edges of the pathway are exactly parallel, create a spacer bar and use it as a guide to install the edging. Start with a piece of 2 × 4 that's a bit longer than the path width. Near one end, cut a notch that will fit snugly over the edging. Trim the spacer so the distance from the notch to the other end is the planned width of the pathway.

HOW TO CREATE A GRAVEL PATHWAY

Lay out one edge of the path excavation. Use a section of hose or rope to create curves, and use stakes and string to indicate straight sections. Cut 1 × 2 spacers to set the path width and establish the second pathway edge; use another hose and/or more stakes and string to lay out the other edge. Mark both edges with marking paint.

Remove sod in the walkway area using a sod stripper or a power sod cutter (see option, at right). Excavate the soil to a depth of 4 to 6". Measure down from a 2 × 4 placed across the path bed to fine-tune the excavation. Grade the bottom of the excavation flat using a garden rake. *Note: If mulch will be used outside the path, make the excavation shallower by the depth of the mulch. Compact the soil with a plate compactor.*

Option: Use a power sod cutter to strip grass from your pathway site. Available at most rental centers and large home centers, sod cutters excavate to a very even depth. The cut sod can be replanted in other parts of your lawn.

Lay landscaping fabric from edge to edge, lapping over the undisturbed ground on either side of the path. On straight sections, you may be able to run parallel to the path with a single strip; on curved paths, it's easier to lay the fabric perpendicular to the path. Overlap all seams by 6".

Install edging over the fabric. Shim the edging with small stones, if necessary, so the top edge is ½" above grade (if the path passes through grass) or 2" above grade (if it passes through a mulched area). Secure the edging with spikes. To install the second edge, use a 2 × 4 spacer gauge that's been notched to fit over your edging (see facing page).

Stone or vertical-brick edges may be set in deeper trenches at the sides of the path. Place these on top of the fabric also. You do not have to use additional edging with paver edging, but metal (or other) edging will keep the pavers from wandering.

(continued)

Trim excess fabric, then backfill behind the edging with dirt and tamp it down carefully with the end of a 2 × 4. This secures the edging and helps it to maintain its shape.

Add a 2- to 4"-thick layer of compactable gravel over the entire pathway. Rake the gravel flat. Then, spread a thin layer of your surface material over the base gravel.

Tamp the base and surface gravel together using a plate compactor. Be careful not to disturb or damage the edging with the compactor.

Fill in the pathway with the remaining surface gravel. Drag a 2 × 4 across the tops of the edging using a sawing motion, to level the gravel flush with the edging.

Set the edging brick flush with the gravel using a mallet and 2 × 4.

Tamp the surface again using the plate compactor or a hand tamper. Compact the gravel so it is slightly below the top of the edging. This will help keep the gravel from migrating out of the path.

Rinse off the pathway with a hose to wash off dirt and dust and bring out the true colors of the materials.

STEPPING STONE LANDSCAPE PATH

A stepping stone path is both a practical and appealing way to traverse a landscape. With large stones as foot landings, you are free to use pretty much any type of fill material in between. You could even place stepping stones on individual footings over ponds and streams, making water the temporary infill that surrounds the stones. The infill does not need to follow a narrow path bed, either. Steppers can be used to cross a broad expanse of gravel, such as a Zen gravel panel or a smaller graveled opening in an alpine rock garden.

Stepping stones in a path serve two purposes: they lead the eye, and they carry the traveler. In both cases, the goal is rarely fast, direct transport, but more of a relaxing stroll that's comfortable, slow-paced, and above all, natural. Arrange the stepping stones in your walking path according to the gaits and strides of the people that are most likely to use the pathway. Keep in mind that our gaits tend to be longer on a utility path than in a rock garden.

Sometimes steppers are placed more for visual effect, with the knowledge that they will break the pacing rule with artful clusters of stones. Clustering is also an effective way to slow or congregate walkers near a fork in the path or at a good vantage point for a striking feature of the garden.

In the project featured here, landscape edging is used to contain the loose infill material (small aggregate); however a stepping stone path can also be effective without edging. For example, setting a series of steppers directly into your lawn and letting the lawn grass grow between them is a great choice as well.

Tools & Materials ▸

Mason's string
Hose or rope
Marking paint
Sod stripper
Excavation tools
Hand tamp
Wood stakes
1 × 2 lumber
Straight 2 × 4
Edging
Landscape fabric
Coarse sand

Thick steppers or
   broad river rocks
   with one flat face
¼ to ½" pond
   pebbles
2½"-dia. river rock
Eye and ear
   protection
Work gloves
Level
Rake

Choosing Steppers ▸

Select beefy stones (minimum 2½ to 3½" thick) with at least one flat side. Thinner stepping stones tend to sink into the pebble infill. Stones that are described as stepping stones usually have two flat faces. For the desired visual effect on this project, we chose steppers and 12 to 24" wide fieldstones with one broad, flat face (the rounded face is buried in the ground, naturally).

Fieldstone with a flat face

Steppers

Stepping stones blend beautifully into many types of landscaping, including rock gardens, ponds, flower or vegetable gardens, or manicured grass lawns.

HOW TO MAKE A STEPPING STONE LANDSCAPE PATH

Excavate and prepare a bed for the path as you would for the gravel pathway (see pages 58 to 61), but use coarse building sand instead of compactable gravel for the base layer. Screed the sand flat so it's 2" below the top of the edging. Do not tamp the sand. *Tip: Low-profile plastic landscape edging is a good choice because it does not compete with the pathway.*

Moisten the sand bed, then position the stepping stones in the sand, spacing them for comfortable walking and the desired appearance. As you work, place a 2 × 4 across three adjacent stones to make sure they are even with one another. Add or remove sand beneath the steppers, as needed, to stabilize and level the stones.

Pour in a layer of larger infill stones (2"-dia. river rock is seen here). Smooth the stones with a garden rake. The infill should be below the tops of the stepping stones. Reserve about ⅓ of the larger diameter rocks.

Add the smaller infill stones that will migrate down and fill in around the larger infill rocks. To help settle the rocks, you can tamp lightly with a hand tamper, but don't get too aggressive—the larger rocks might fracture easily.

Scatter the remaining large infill stones across the infill area so they float on top of the other stones. Eventually, they will sink down lower in the pathway and you will need to lift and replace them selectively to maintain the original appearance.

VARIATIONS

Move from a formal space to a less orderly area of your landscape by creating a pathway that begins with closely spaced steppers on the formal end and gradually transforms into a mostly-gravel path on the casual end, with only occasional clusters of steppers.

Combine concrete stepping pavers with crushed rock or other small stones for a path with a cleaner, more contemporary look. Follow the same basic techniques used on these two pages, setting the pavers first, then filling in between with the desired infill material(s).

SANDSET BRICK WALKWAY

Sandset brick is a good choice of material for a walkway for the same reasons that make it a great patio surface—it's easy to work with, it lends itself equally well to traditional paving patterns and creative custom designs, and it can be installed at a leisurely pace because there's no mortar or wet concrete involved. The timeless look of natural clay brick is especially well-suited to walkways, where the rhythmic patterns of geometric lines create a unique sense of movement that draws your eye down the path toward its destination.

In this walkway project, all of the interior (*field*) bricks are arranged in the installation area and then the curving side edges of the walk are marked onto the set bricks to ensure perfect cutting lines. After the edge bricks are cut and reset, border bricks are installed followed by rigid paver edging to keep everything in place. This is the most efficient method for installing a curving path. Straight walkways can follow the standard process of installing the edging and border bricks (on one or both sides of the path, as applicable) before laying the field brick, as is done in the brick patio project.

With standard brick, you'll need to set the gaps with spacers cut from ⅛-inch hardboard, as shown in this project.

Tools & Materials ▸

Tape measure
¾" braided rope
Marking paint
Excavation tools
Plate compactor
Mason's string
Stakes
Hand tamp
2- or 4-ft. level
Drill bits
Rubber mallet
Straightedge
Trowel
Masonry saw
Push broom
1 × 2 or 2 × 2 lumber
Compactable gravel
Straight 2 × 4
Duct tape

Coarse sand
Landscape fabric
Landscape staples
Brick paver units
Plastic patio edging
⅛" hardboard
Paver joint sand
Eye and ear protection
Work gloves
12" galvanized spikes
Maul

A curving brick walkway can be as much a design statement as a course for easy travel. Curves require more time than straight designs, due to the extra cutting involved, but the results can be all the more stunning.

HOW TO INSTALL A SANDSET BRICK WALKWAY

Lay out the walkway curved edges using ¾" braided rope (or use mason's strings for straight sections; shown as variation). Cut 1 × 2 or 2 × 2 spacers to the desired path width and then place them in-between the ropes for consistent spacing. Mark the outlines along the inside edges of the ropes onto the ground with marking paint.

Excavate the area 6" outside of the marked lines along both sides of the path. Remove soil to allow for a 4"-thick subbase of gravel, a 1" layer of sand, and the thickness of the brick pavers (minus the height of the finished paving above the ground). The finished paving typically rests about 1" aboveground for ease of lawn maintenance. Thoroughly tamp the area with a plate compactor.

Spread out an even layer of compactable gravel— enough for a 4"-thick layer after compaction. Grade the gravel to follow a downward slope of ¼" per foot (most long walkways slope from side to side, while shorter paths or walkway sections can be sloped along their length). Use a homemade slope gauge to screed the gravel smooth and to check the slope as you work (see step 5, page 43). Tamp the subbase thoroughly with the plate compactor, making sure the surface is flat and smooth and properly sloped.

(continued)

Cover the gravel base with professional-grade landscape fabric, overlapping the strips by at least 6". If desired, tack the fabric in place with landscape staples.

Spread a 1"-layer of coarse sand over the landscape fabric. Screed the sand with a board so it is smooth, even, and flat.

Tamp the screeded sand with a hand tamper or a plate compactor. Check the slope of the surface as you go.

Spacer

Begin the paving at one end of the walkway, following the desired pattern. Use ⅛"-thick hardboard spacers in-between the bricks to set the sand-joint gaps. *Tip: It's best to start the paving against a straightedge or square corner. If your walkway does not connect to a patio or stoop, set a temporary 2 × 4 with stakes at the end of the walkway to create a straight starting line.*

Option: If your walkway includes long straight sections between curves, set up guidelines with stakes and mason's strings to keep the ends of the courses straight as you pave.

Set the next few courses of brick, running them long over the side edges. With the first few courses in place, tap the bricks with a rubber mallet to bed them into the sand.

Lay out the curved edges of the finished walkway using ¾" braided rope . Adjust the ropes as needed so that the cut bricks will be roughly symmetrical on both edges of the walkway. Also measure between the ropes to make sure the finished width will be accurate according to your layout. Trace along the ropes with a pencil to mark the cutting lines onto the bricks.

(continued)

Variation: Cut field bricks after installing the edging. Mark each brick for cutting by hlding it in position and drawing the cut line across the top face.

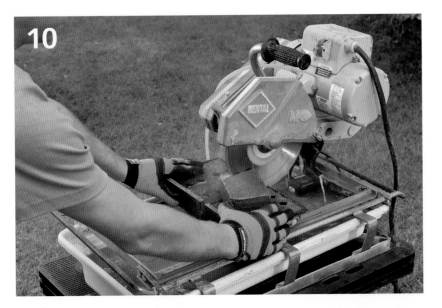

Cut the bricks with a rented masonry saw (wet saw), following the instructions from the tool supplier. Make straight cuts with a single, full-depth cut. Curved cuts require multiple straight cuts made tangentially to the cutting line. After cutting a brick, reset it before cutting the next brick.

Align the border bricks (if applicable) snug against the edges of the field paving. Use a straightedge or level to make sure the border units are flush with the tops of the field bricks. Set the border bricks with a rubber mallet. Dampen the exposed edges of the sand bed, and then use a trowel to slice away the edge so it's flush with the paving.

Install rigid paver edging (bendable) (see page 49) or other edge material tight against the outside of the walkway.

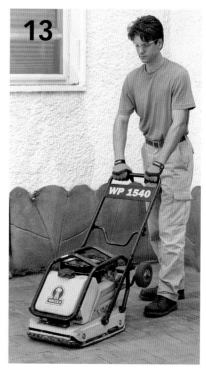

Fill and tamp the sand joints one or more times until the joints are completely filled. Sweep up any loose sand.

Soak the surface with water and let it dry. Cover the edging sides with soil and sod or other material, as desired.

POURED CONCRETE WALKWAY

If you've always wanted to try your hand at creating with concrete, an outdoor walkway is a great project to start with. The basic elements and construction steps of a walkway are similar to those of a poured concrete patio or other landscape slab, but the smaller scale of a walkway makes it a much more manageable project for first-timers. Placing the wet concrete goes faster, and you can easily reach the center of the surface for finishing from either side of the walkway.

Like a patio slab, a poured concrete walkway also makes a good foundation for mortared surface materials, like pavers, stone, and tile. If that's your goal, be sure to account for the thickness of the surface material when planning and laying out the walkway height. A coarse broomed or scratched finish on the concrete will help create a strong bond with the mortar bed of the surface material.

The walkway in this project is a 4-inch-thick by 26-inch-wide concrete slab with a broom finish for slip resistance. It consists of two straight, 12-ft.-long runs connected by a 90 degree elbow. After curing, the walkway can be left bare for a classic, low-maintenance surface, or it can be colored with a permanent acid stain. When planning your walkway project, consult your city's building department for recommendations and construction requirements.

Tools & Materials ▸

Drill, bits
Circular saw
Mason's string
Line level
Excavation tools
2- or 4-ft. level
Plate compactor
Heavy-duty wire
    cutters or bolt
    cutters
Concrete mixing
    tools
Shovel
Hammer
Magnesium float
Edger tool
Groover tool
Magnesium trowel
Push broom
Lumber (2 × 2,
    2 × 4)
Drywall screws
    (2½", 3½")

⁷⁄₁₆" hardboard siding
Compactable gravel
6 × 6" 10/10 welded
    wire mesh (wwm)
Tie wire
2" bolsters
Isolation board
    and construction
    adhesive
Release agent
4,000 psi concrete
    (or as required by
    local code)
Clear polyethylene
    sheeting
Eye and ear
    protection
Work gloves
4" deck screws
#3 rebar (optional)
Wood stakes
Tape measure

Poured concrete walkways can be designed with straight lines, curves, or any angles you desire. The flat, hardwearing surface is ideal for frequently traveled paths and will stand up to heavy equipment and decades of snow shoveling.

SLOPING A WALKWAY

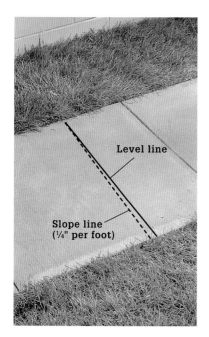

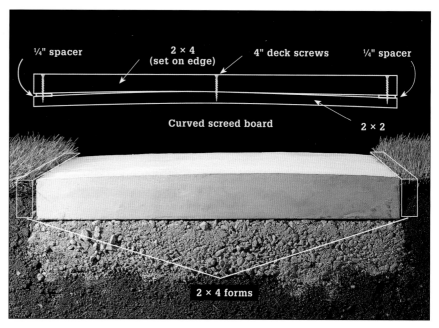

Straight slope: Set the concrete form lower on one side of the walkway so the finished surface is flat and slopes downward at a rate of ¼" per foot. Always slope the surface away from the house foundation or, when not near the house, toward the area best suited to accept water runoff.

Crowned slope: When a walkway does not run near the house foundation, you have the option of crowning the surface so it slopes down to both sides. To make the crown, construct a curved screed board by cutting a 2 × 2 and a 2 × 4 long enough to rest on both sides of the concrete form. Sandwich the boards together with a ¼"-thick spacer at each end, then fasten the assembly with 4" deck screws driven at the center and the ends. Use the board to screed the concrete (see step 8, page 76).

REINFORCING A WALKWAY

As an alternative to the wire mesh reinforcement used in the following project, you can reinforce a walkway slab with metal rebar (check with the local building code requirements). For a 3-ft.-wide walkway, lay two sections of #3 rebar spaced evenly inside the concrete form. Bend the rebar as needed to follow curves or angles. Overlap pieces by 12" and tie them together with tie wire. Use wire bolsters to suspend the bar in the middle of the slab's thickness.

HOW TO INSTALL A POURED CONCRETE WALKWAY

Lay out the precise edges of the finished walkway using stakes (or batterboards) and mason's string (see pages 43 to 47 for additional help with setting up and using layout strings). Where possible, set stakes 12" or so outside of the walkway edges so they're out of the way. Make sure any 90° corners are square using the 3-4-5 measuring technique. Level the strings, then lower the strings on one side of the layout to create a downward slope of ¼" per foot (if the walkway will be crowned instead of sloped to one side, keep all strings level with one another. Cut away the sod or other plantings 6" beyond the layout lines on all sides of the site.

Excavate the site for a 4- to 6"-thick gravel subbase, plus any subgrade (below ground level) portion of the slab, as desired. Measure the depth with a story pole (see page 45) against the high-side layout strings, making sure to use a slope gauge to grade the slope ¼" per foot away from foundations. Tamp the soil thoroughly with a plate compactor.

Cover the site with a 4- to 6"-layer of gravel and screed the surface flat, checking with a slope gauge to set the proper grade. Compact the gravel so the top surface is 4" below the finished walkway height. Reset the layout strings at the precise height of the finished walkway.

Build the concrete form with straight 2 × 4 lumber so the inside faces of the form are aligned with the strings. Drive 2 × 4 stakes for reinforcement behind butt joints. Align the form with the layout strings, and then drive stakes at each corner and every 2 to 3 ft. in between. Fasten the form to the stakes so the top inside corner of the form boards are just touching the layout strings. The tops of the stakes should be just below the tops of the form.

Add curved strips made from ¼- to ⅜"-thick plywood hardboard or lauan to create curved corners, if desired. Secure curved strips by screwing them to wood stakes. Recheck the gravel bed inside the concrete form, making sure it is smooth and properly sloped.

Lay reinforcing wire mesh over the gravel base, keeping the edges 1 to 2" from the insides of the form. Overlap the mesh strips by 6" (one square) and tie them together with tie wire. Prop up the mesh on 2" bolsters placed every few feet and tied to the mesh with wire. Install isolation board where the walkway adjoins other slabs or structures. When you're ready for the concrete pour, coat the insides of the form with a release agent or vegetable oil.

Drop the concrete in pods, starting at the far end of the walkway. Distribute it around the form by placing it (don't throw it) with a shovel. As you fill, stab into the concrete with the shovel, and tap a hammer against the back sides of the form to eliminate air pockets. Continue until the form is evenly filled, slightly above the tops of the form.

(continued)

Immediately screed the surface with a straight 2 × 4: two people pull the board backward in a side-to-side sawing motion with the board resting on top of the form. As you work, shovel in extra concrete to fill low spots or remove concrete from high spots, and re-screed. The goal is to create a flat surface that's level with the top of the form.

Float the concrete surface with a magnesium float, working back and forth in broad arching strokes. Tip up the leading edge of the tool slightly to prevent gouging the surface. Stop floating once the surface is relatively smooth and has a wet sheen. Be careful not to over-float, indicated by water pooling on the surface. Allow the bleed water to disappear and the concrete to harden sufficiently (see page 144).

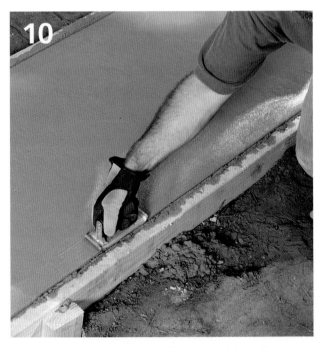

Use an edger to shape the side edges of the walkway along the wood form. Carefully run the edger back and forth along the form to create a smooth, rounded corner, lifting the leading edge of the tool slightly to prevent gouging.

Mark the locations of the control joints onto the top edges of the form boards, spacing the joints at intervals 1½ times the width of the walkway.

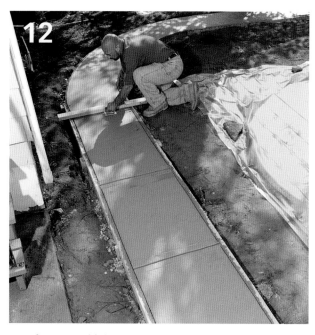

Cut the control joints with a 1" groover guided by a straight 2 × 4 held (or fastened) across the form at the marked locations. Make several light passes back and forth until the groove reaches full depth, lifting the leading edge of the tool to prevent gouging. Remove the guide board once each joint is complete. If desired, smooth out the marks made by the groover using a magnesium trowel.

Create a nonslip surface with a broom finish: starting at the far side edge of the walkway, steadily drag a broom backward over the surface in a straight line using a single pulling motion. Repeat in single, parallel passes (with minimal or no overlap), and rinse off the broom bristles after each pass. The stiffer and coarser the broom, the rougher the texture will be.

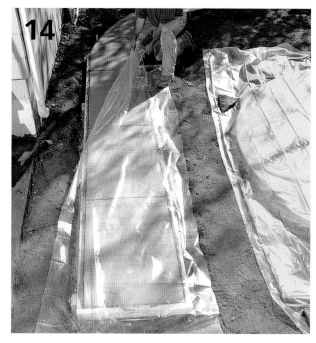

Cure the concrete by misting the walkway with water, then covering it with clear polyethylene sheeting. Smooth out any air pockets (which can cause discoloration), and weight down the sheeting along the edges. Mist the surface and reapply the plastic daily for 1 to 2 weeks.

DECORATIVE CONCRETE PATH

A well-made walkway or garden path not only stands up to years of hard use, it enhances the natural landscape and complements a home's exterior features. While traditional walkway materials like brick and stone have always been prized for both appearance and durability, most varieties are quite pricey and often difficult to install. As an easy and inexpensive alternative, you can build a new concrete path using manufactured forms. The result is a beautiful pathway that combines the custom look of brick or natural stone with all the durability and economy of poured concrete.

Building a path is a great do-it-yourself project. Once you've laid out the path, you mix the concrete, set and fill the form, then lift off the form to reveal the finished design. After a little troweling to smooth the surfaces, you're ready to create the next section—using the same form. Simply repeat the process until the path is complete. Each form creates a section that's approximately two square feet using one 80-lb. bag of premixed concrete. This project shows you all the basic steps for making any length of pathway, plus special techniques for making curves, adding a custom finish, or coloring the concrete to suit your personal design.

Tools & Materials ▸

Excavation and site preparation tools	Liquid concrete colorant
Concrete mold	Clear polyethylene sheeting
Wheelbarrow or mixing box	Polymer-modified jointing sand or mortar mix
Shovel	
Margin trowel or concrete finishing trowel	Compactable gravel (optional)
Fiber-reinforced concrete mix	Level
	Broom or stiff brush
Work gloves	Eye and ear protection

Concrete path molds are available in a range of styles and decorative patterns. Coloring the wet concrete is a great way to add a realistic look to the path design.

Basketweave Brick

Country Stone Pattern

Running Bond Brick

European Block Brick

HOW TO CREATE A STRAIGHT OR 90° DECORATIVE CONCRETE PATH

Prepare the project site by leveling the ground, removing sod or soil as needed. For a more durable base, excavate the area and add 2 to 4" of compactable gravel. Grade and compact the gravel layer so it is level and flat. See pages 42 to 47 for detailed steps on layout and site preparation.

Mix a batch of concrete for the first section, following the product directions (see page 80 to add color, as we have done here). Place the form at the start of your path and level it, if desired. Shovel the wet concrete into the form to fill each cavity. Consolidate and smooth the surface of the form using a concrete margin trowel.

Promptly remove the form, and then trowel the edges of the section to create the desired finish (it may help to wet the trowel in water). For a nonslip surface, broom the section or brush it with a stiff brush. Place the form against the finished section and repeat steps 2 and 3 to complete the next section.

After removing each form, remember to trowel the edges of the section to create the desired finish. Repeat until the path is finished. If desired, rotate the form 90° with each section to vary the pattern. Cure the path by covering it with polyethylene sheeting for 5 to 7 days, lifting the plastic and misting the concrete with water each day.

(continued)

5

Fill walkway joints with sand or mortar mix to mimic the look of hand-laid stone or brick. Sweep the sand or dry mortar into the section contours and spaces between sections. For mortar, mist the joints with water so they harden in place.

Custom Surfacing Tip ▸

Create custom surface finishes by pressing small stones or pea gravel into the wet concrete or by brushing on a layer of sand. Apply finish materials after the concrete has reached its initial set (thumb print hard) but is still damp—approximately one hour after placing.

Coloring Your Concrete ▸

Adding colorant to the concrete mix is the easiest method and produces consistent results:

1. Combine liquid concrete colorant with water and mix into each bag-quantity of dry concrete mix, following the manufacturer's instructions. Blend thoroughly for consistent coloring, then add clean water to the mix, as needed, to achieve the proper consistency for pouring the concrete.

2. After placing and finishing the path sections, cure the concrete carefully to produce the best color quality. If curing conditions will be less than ideal, apply concrete sealer to ensure slow, even curing and good coloring.

Coloring gives molded concrete a more natural-looking finish and is great for blending your path or walkway into your landscape design.

HOW TO CREATE A CURVED DECORATIVE CONCRETE PATH

After removing the form from a freshly poured section (see page 79, steps 1 through 3), reposition the form in the direction of the curve and press down to slice off the inside corner of the section (photo left). Trowel the cut edge (and the rest of the section) to finish. Pour the next section following the curve (photo right). Cut off as many sections as needed to complete the curve. Cure the path by covering it with plastic sheeting for 5 to 7 days, lifting the plastic and misting the concrete with water each day.

Sprinkle the area around the joint or joints between pavers with polymer-modified jointing sand after the concrete has cured sufficiently so that the sand does not adhere. Sweep the product into the gap to clean the paver surfaces while filling the gap.

Mist the jointing sand with clean water, taking care not to wash the sand out of the joint. Once the water dries, the polymers in the mixture will have hardened the sand to look like a mortar joint. Refresh as needed.

MORTARED BRICK OVER A CONCRETE PATH

If you're looking to make over an aging concrete walkway, you can't beat the looks and performance of mortared brick paving. The flat, finished surface is ideal for both heavy foot traffic and garden equipment and is nearly as maintenance-free as plain concrete, while the formal elegance of brick is a dramatic upgrade over a timeworn, gray slab. If your plans include new paving over an old concrete patio, a walkway is also the perfect opportunity to develop your skills before tackling the larger patio surface—the materials and techniques are the same for both applications.

Start your walkway project with a careful examination of the concrete path: as the structural foundation of your new surface, the concrete must be stable and relatively flat. Large cracks and uneven surfaces indicate movement of the concrete structure, often due to problems with the gravel base and/or inadequate drainage under the slab. Since these ailments won't go away with the new paving, you can either decide to replace the old concrete with a newly poured walkway or consider a mortarless surface, such as sandset brick. With that in mind, minor surface problems, such as fine cracks and cosmetic flaws, will not likely affect new mortared paving.

When shopping for pavers, consider the added height of the new surface, the paving pattern you desire, and the material of the pavers themselves. Natural clay brick pavers are available in standard (approximately 2⅜ inches) and thinner (approximately 1½ inches) thicknesses. Concrete pavers are installed using the same techniques, and they come in a range of sizes, thicknesses, and shapes. In any case, be sure to choose straight-sided pavers, as irregular or interlocking shapes make for unnecessarily tricky mortar work. Consult with knowledgeable staff at your masonry supplier to learn about paver materials and mortar suitable for your project and the local climate.

Tools & Materials ▸

Shovel	Brick or concrete
Mortar mixing tools	pavers
Mason's trowel	½" plywood
V-shaped mortar tool	Straight 2 × 4
(jointing tool)	or 2 × 6
Rubber mallet	Clear polyethylene
4-ft. level	sheeting
Mortar bag	Eye and ear
Type S mortar (or other	protection
recommended type)	Various work gloves
Coarse rag	

The natural, warm color of brick is a dramatic yet DIY-friendly upgrade for a tired looking gray slab.

HOW TO INSTALL MORTARED BRICK OVER A CONCRETE PATH

Dig a trench around the concrete path, slightly wider than the thickness of one paver. Dig the trench so it is about 3½" below the concrete surface (for standard-sized pavers).

Sweep the old concrete, then hose off the surface and sides with water to clear away dirt and debris. Soak the pavers with water before mortaring; dry pavers absorb moisture, weakening the mortar strength. Mix a small batch of mortar according to manufacturer's directions. For convenience, place the mortar on a scrap of plywood.

½"

Install edging bricks by applying a ½"-layer of mortar to the side of the concrete slab and to one side of each brick. Set bricks into the trench, against the concrete. Brick edging should be ½" higher than the thickness of the brick pavers.

Finish the joints on the edging bricks with a V-shaped mortar tool, then mix and apply a ½"-thick bed of mortar to one end of the sidewalk using a trowel. Mortar hardens very quickly, so work in sections no larger than 4 sq. ft.

(continued)

Make a screed board for smoothing the mortar by notching the ends of a straight 2 × 4 or 2 × 6 to fit between the edging bricks. The depth of the notches should equal the thickness of the pavers. Drag the screed across the mortar bed until the mortar is smooth.

Lay the paving bricks one at a time into the mortar, maintaining a ½" gap between pavers. (A piece of scrap plywood works well as a spacing guide.) Set the pavers by tapping them lightly with a rubber mallet.

As each section of pavers is completed, check with a straightedge or level to make sure the tops of the pavers are even. If a paver is too high, press it down or tap it with the rubber mallet; if too low, lift it out and butter its back face with mortar and reset it.

When all the pavers are installed, use a mortar bag to fill the joints between the pavers with fresh mortar. Work in 4-sq.-ft. sections, and avoid getting mortar on the tops of the pavers.

9 Use a V-shaped mortar tool to finish the joints as you complete each 4 sq.-ft. section. For best results, finish the longer joints first, then the shorter joints. Use a trowel to remove excess mortar.

10 Let the mortar dry for a few hours, then scrub the pavers with a coarse rag and water. Cover the walkway with polyethylene sheeting and let the mortar cure for at least 24 hours. Remove sheeting, but do not walk on the pavers for at least three days.

Variation: As an alternative to paving over an entire walkway (if the old concrete still looks good), add a decorative touch with a border of mortared pavers along the edges. The same treatment is great for dressing up the exposed edges of a concrete patio, stoop, or steps. To install edging along a walkway, follow the basic techniques shown in steps 1 to 4 on page 83, but set the pavers flush with the walkway surface. Position the pavers horizontally or vertically, depending on the height of the walkway and the desired effect. After the pavers are set and tooled, follow step 10 above to complete the job.

BOARDWALK DECK ON A SLAB

There's no need to let a cracked, aging concrete patio ruin the look and enjoyment of your backyard. You can build a very simple deck platform right over the failing slab with very little effort or expense. Make no mistake though, the result will be a beautiful new outdoor platform that improves the look of the home and the yard.

This is an independent deck; the structure is not attached to the house, but is instead laid atop the slab and allowed to move with any shifting in the concrete. It's constructed on a simple frame base laid level with sleepers over the concrete itself. This means that the deck will be very close to the ground and subject to a great deal of moisture. Only certain types of decking will tolerate those conditions. We've used pressure-treated pine deckboards.

The design of the deck is a plain rectangle and can easily be constructed over a weekend. We've spruced up the look a bit by laying the decking in a standard

"Boardwalk" pattern. More complex patterns would make the deck surface look even more impressive— just remember to do yourself a favor and work the patterns out on graph paper before cutting any decking. Proper planning will inevitably save a lot of waste.

Turn a boring or failing concrete slab into an attractive walkout or entertainment space with a short utility or "Boardwalk" deck installed on top of it.

Supplies

Galvanized metal corner brackets (16)
2" and 3" galvanized deck screws
2" composite shims
Circular saw
Miter saw
Power drill and bits
Treated lumber (2 × 4 and 2 × 2)

Caulk gun and glue
Level
8" plastic shims
Chalk line
Stain
Work gloves
Eye and ear protection

Cutting List

Key	Qty	Size	Part	Material
A	3	1½ x 3½ x 128"	Frame side	PT pine
B	2	1½ x 1½ x 128"	Nailer	PT pine
C	2	1½ x 3½ x 76"	Frame end	PT pine
D	60	1½ x 3½ x (cut to fit)	Decking	PT pine

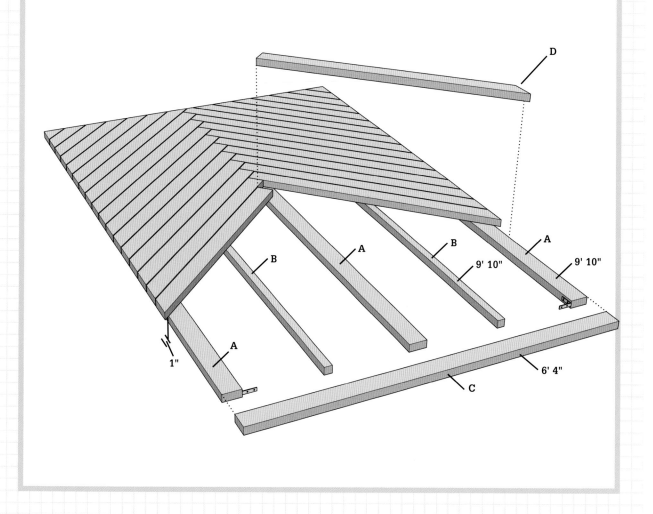

HOW TO BUILD A BOARDWALK DECK

Build and assemble the frame offsite by cutting and measuring 10-ft. 2 × 4s to length and securing them together with galvanized metal corner brackets.

Install the nailer joists by measuring and cutting parallel boards to the length of the frame. Use 2" deck screws and galvanized metal corner brackets to secure the nailer joists to the frame.

Clear away any dust and debris from the concrete slab. Set the frame atop the slab and use 8" plastic shims to level it. Glue shims in place and cut off excess so shims are flush with the frame.

Use a level as you work with the shims to ensure an even plane on which to build the deck.

Remove the frame from the slab before installing the decking. Stagger the 2 × 4s in a crosshatch pattern in opposing 45° angles from the center nailing joist. Attach the boardwalk pattern to the frame using 3" deck screws. Boards should abut one another the length of the joist and allow for at least 1" of overhang from the frame.

Mark 1" overhang on all sides of the frame using a chalk line, and cut off excess decking using a circular saw equipped with a carbide blade.

Use a helper to install the decking atop the concrete slab, checking for level and using shims to adjust as necessary.

Clear away dust and debris and stain the decking as desired.

CONSTRUCTION DETAILS: TIMBER STEP FRAMES

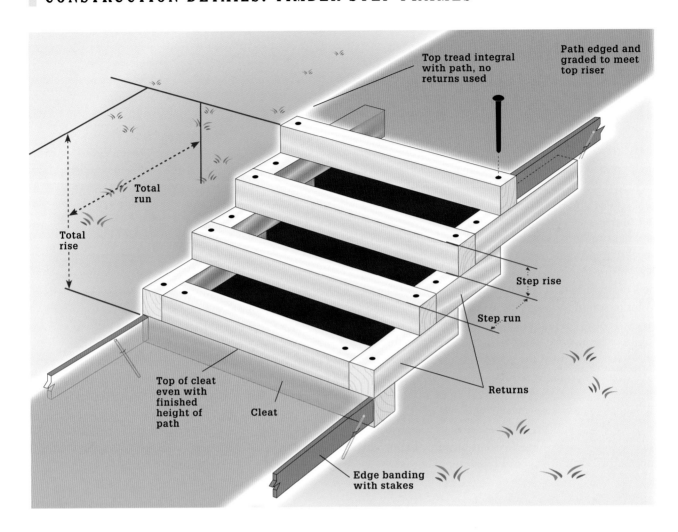

Top tread integral with path, no returns used

Path edged and graded to meet top riser

Total run

Total rise

Step rise

Step run

Top of cleat even with finished height of path

Cleat

Returns

Edge banding with stakes

Cutting Timbers ▸

Large landscape timbers (6 × 6" and bigger) can be cut accurately and squarely with a circular saw, even though the saw's cutting capacity isn't big enough to do the job completely. First, draw cutting lines on all four sides of the timber using a speed square as guide. Next, cut along the line on all four sides with the saw set for maximum blade depth. Finally, use a hand saw to finish the cut. For most DIYers, this will yield a straighter cut than saws that can make the cut in one pass, such as a reciprocating saw.

Cut and position the returns and the first riser. Using a 2 × 4 as a level extender, check to see if the backs of the returns are level with each other and adjust by adding or removing gravel in the trenches. Drill four ⅜"-dia. holes and fasten the first riser and the two returns to the cleat with spikes.

Excavate and add tamped gravel for the second set of returns. Cut and position the second riser across the ends of the first returns, leaving the correct unit run between the riser faces. Note that only the first riser doesn't span the full width of the steps. Cut and position the returns, check for level, then pre-drill and spike the second riser and returns to the returns below.

Build the remaining steps in the same fashion. As you work, it may be necessary to alter the slope with additional excavating or backfilling (few natural hills follow a uniform slope). Add or remove soil as needed along the sides of the steps so that the returns are exposed roughly equally on both sides. Also, each tread should always be higher than the neighboring ground.

Install the final riser. Typically, the last timber does not have returns because its tread surface is integral with the path or surrounding ground. The top of this timber should be slightly higher than the ground. As an alternative, you can use returns to contain pathway material at the top of the steps.

(continued)

Lay and tamp a base of compactable gravel in each step tread area. Use a 2 × 4 as a tamper. For proper compaction, tamp the gravel in 2" or thinner layers before adding more. Leave about 2" of space in each tread for the surface material.

Fill up the tread areas with gravel or other appropriate material. Irregular crushed gravel offers maximum surface stability, while smooth stones, like the river rock seen here, blend into the environment more naturally and feel better underfoot than crushed gravel and stone.

Create or improve pathways at the top and bottom of the steps. For a nice effect, build a loose-fill walkway using the same type of gravel that you used for the steps. Install a railing, if desired or if required by the local building code.

HOW TO BUILD TIMBER & CONCRETE GARDEN STEPS

Mark the sides of the step site with stakes and string. The stakes should be positioned at the front edge of the bottom step and the back edge of the top step.

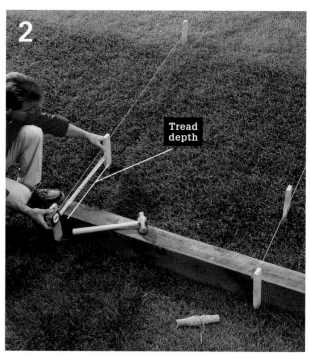

Add the width of the timber (5") to the tread depth, then measure back this distance for the stakes and drive additional stakes to mark the back edge of the first step. Connect these stakes with string to mark the digging area for the first step.

Tools & Materials ▸

Supplies for Timber & Concrete Steps:	
Mason's string	Stiff brush
Tape measure	Hand tamp
Excavation tools	Carpenters' square
Saw	Wood stakes
Level	5 × 6 landscape timbers
Drill and 1" space bit with bit extension	1" pipe
	12" galvanized spikes
Maul	Plastic sheeting
Rake	Compactable gravel
Wheelbarrow	2 × 4 lumber
Trowel	Premixed concrete
Hoe	Seed gravel (½")
Wood float	Burlap
Concrete edging tool	Muriatic acid
	Work gloves
	Eye and ear protection

Excavate for the first step, creating a flat bed with a very slight forward slope, no more than ⅛" from back to front. The front of the excavation should be no more than 2" deep. Tamp the soil firmly.

(continued)

Arrange the timbers to form the step frame and endnail them together with 12" spikes.

Set the timber frame in position. Use a carpenter's square to make sure the frame is square, and adjust as necessary. Drill two 1" guide holes in the front timber and the back timber, 1 ft. from the ends, using a spade bit and bit extension.

Anchor the steps to the ground by driving a 2½-ft. length of ¾" pipe through each guide hole until the pipe is flush with the timber. When pipes are driven, make sure the frame is level from side to side and has the proper forward pitch. Excavate for the next step, making sure the bottom of the excavation is even with the top edge of the installed timbers.

Drive pipes here

Build another step frame and position it in the excavation so the front timber is directly over the rear timber on the first frame. Nail the steps together with three 12" spikes, then drill guide holes and drive two pipes through only the back timber to anchor the second frame.

Continue digging and installing the remaining frames until the steps reach full height. The back of the last step should be at ground level.

Staple plastic over the timbers to protect them from wet concrete. Cut away the plastic so it does not overhang into the frame opening.

Pour a 2" layer of compactable gravel subbase into each frame, and use a 2 × 4 to smooth it out.

Mix concrete in a wheelbarrow, adding just enough water so the concrete holds its shape when sliced with a trowel.

Shovel concrete into the bottom frame, flush with the top of the timbers. Work the concrete lightly with a garden rake to help remove air bubbles, but do not overwork the concrete.

(continued)

Screed the concrete by dragging a 2 × 4 across the top of the frame. If necessary, add concrete to low areas and screed again until the surface is smooth and free of low spots.

While the concrete is still wet, scatter mixed gravel on the surface. Sand-and-gravel suppliers and garden centers sell colorful gravel designed for seeding. For best results, select a mixture with stones no larger than ½" in diameter.

Press the seeded gravel into the surface of the concrete using a concrete float, until the tops of the stone are flush with the surface of the concrete. Remove any concrete that spills over the edges of the frame using a trowel.

Pour concrete into the remaining steps, screeding and seeding each step before moving on to the next. For a neater appearance, use an edging tool (inset) to smooth the cracks between the timbers and the concrete as each step is finished.

When the sheen disappears from the poured concrete (4 to 6 hours after pouring), use a float to smooth out any high or low spots in each step. Be careful not to force seeded gravel too far into the concrete. Let the concrete dry overnight.

After concrete has dried overnight, apply a fine mist of water to the surface, then scrub it with a stiff brush to expose the seeded gravel.

Variation: To create a nonslip surface on smooth concrete without seeding, draw a stiff-bristled brush or broom once across the concrete while it is still wet.

Remove the plastic from the timbers, and cover the concrete with burlap. Allow the concrete to cure for several days, spraying it occasionally with water to ensure even curing. *Note: Concrete residue can be cleaned from timbers using a solution of 5% muriatic acid and water.*

Stone steps blend natural elegance and beauty for a stunning landscape feature in any yard. Depending on how stylized the design is and the type of stone (natural shaped or cut square), the steps can enhance either a formal or casual outdoor living area.

FLAGSTONE GARDEN STEPS

Flagstone steps are perfect structures for managing natural slopes. Our design consists of broad flagstone treads and blocky ashlar risers, commonly sold as wall stone. The risers are prepared with compactable gravel beds on which the flagstone treads rest. For the project featured here, we purchased both the flagstone and the wall stone in their natural split state (as opposed to sawn). It may seem like overkill, but you should plan on purchasing 40 percent more flagstone, by square foot coverage, than your plans say you need. The process of fitting the stones together involves a lot of cutting and waste.

The average height of your risers is defined by the height of the wall stone available to you. These rough stones are separated and sold in a range of thicknesses (such as 3 to 4 inches), but hand-picking the stones helps bring them into a tighter range. The more uniform the thicknesses of your blocks, the less shimming and adjusting you'll have to do. (Remember, all of the steps must be the same size, to prevent a tripping hazard.) You will also need to stock up on slivers of rocks to use as shims to bring your risers and returns to a consistent height; breaking and cutting your stone generally produces plenty of these.

Flagstone steps work best when you create the broadest possible treads: think of them as a series of terraced patios. The goal, once you have the stock in hand, is to create a tread surface with as few stones as possible. This generally means you'll be doing quite a bit of cutting to get the irregular shapes to fit together. For a more formal look, cut the flagstones along straight lines so they fit together with small, regular gaps.

Tools & Materials ▸

Tape measure
Mason's string
Marking paint
Line level
Torpedo level
4-ft. level
Excavation tools
Maul
Hand tamp
Wood stakes
Lumber (2 × 4, 4× 4)
Straight 2 × 4
Landscape fabric
Compactable gravel
Coarse sand

Wall stone
Flagstone
Stone chisels
Stone and block adhesive
Rubber mallet
Eye and ear protection
Work gloves
Small brush
Spade
Granite or polymeric sand

CONSTRUCTION DETAILS

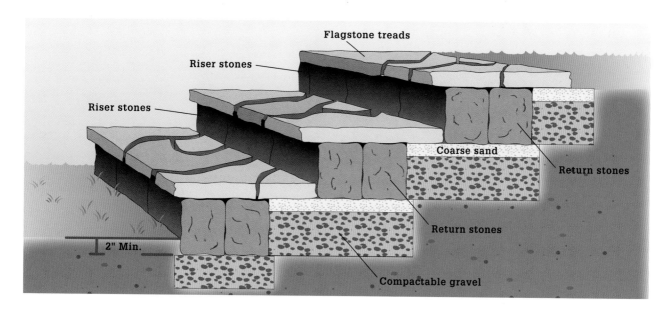

Flagstone treads

Riser stones

Riser stones

Coarse sand

Return stones

Return stones

2" Min.

Compactable gravel

Step Variations ▶

Pave the slope. Sometimes the best solution for garden steps is simply to lay some broad, flat rocks down on a pathway more or less as you find it. Make some effort to ensure that the surface of each rock is relatively flat and safe to walk on. Do not use this approach on steep slopes (greater than 2 in 12) or in heavily traveled areas.

These terraces are made from large flagstone steppers supported by stacked riser stones. They function as steps in managing the slope, but they look and feel more like a split-level patio. For a natural look and the best visual effect, terrace-type steps should mimic the topography of your yard.

Cut stone blocks that are roughly uniform in size are laid in a step formation to create a stately passageway up this small hill. A hand-formed mortar cap adorns the sides of the outdoor stairway for a more finished appearance.

Stacked slabs cannot be beat for pure simplicity, longevity, and ease of maintenance. The initial cost is high, and stacking stones that weigh several hundred pounds (or more) does require professionals with heavy equipment. But once these lovely garden steps are in place they'll stay put for generations with hardly any attention beyond a simple hosing off.

HOW TO BUILD FLAGSTONE GARDEN STEPS

Measure the height and length of the slope to calculate the rise and run dimensions for each step (see page 23 for help with designing and laying out steps). Plot the footprint of your steps on the ground using marking paint. Purchase wall stones for your risers and returns in a height equal to the rise of your steps. Also buy flagstone (with approx. 40% overage) for the step treads.

Begin the excavation: for the area under the first riser and return stones, dig a trench to accommodate a 4"-layer of gravel, plus the thickness of an average flagstone tread. For the area under the back edge of the first step's tread and the riser and return stones of the second step, dig to accommodate a 4"-layer of gravel, plus a 1"-layer of sand. Compact the soil with a 2 × 4 or 4 × 4.

Add a layer of compactable gravel to within 1" of the planned height and tamp. Add a top layer of compactable gravel and level it side to side and back to front. This top layer should be a flagstone's thickness below grade. This will keep the rise of the first step the same as the following steps. Leave the second layer of gravel uncompacted for easy adjustment of the riser and return stones.

Set the riser stones and one or two return stones onto the gravel base. Level the riser stones side to side by adding or removing gravel as needed. Level the risers front to back with a torpedo level. Allow for a slight up-slope for the returns (the steps should slope slightly downward from back to front so the treads will drain). Seat the stones firmly in the gravel with a hand maul, protecting the stone with a wood block.

(continued)

Line the excavated area for the first tread with landscape fabric, draping it to cover the insides of the risers and returns. Add layers of compactable gravel and tamp down to within 1" of the tops of the risers and returns. Fill the remainder of the bed with sand and level it side to side with a 2 × 4. Slope it slightly from back to front. This layer of sand should be a little above the first risers and returns so that the tread stones will compact down to sit on the wall stones.

Set the second group of risers and returns: first, measure the step/run distance back from the face of your first risers and set up a level mason's string across the sand bed. Position the second-step risers and returns as you did for the first step, except these don't need to be dug in on the bottom because the bottom tread will reduce the risers' effective height.

Fold the fabric over the tops of the risers and trim off the excess. Set the flagstone treads of the first step like a puzzle, leaving a consistent distance between stones. Use large, heavy stones with relatively straight edges at the front of the step, overhanging the risers by about 2".

Fill in with smaller stones near the back. Cut and dress stones where necessary using stone chisels and a maul or mason's hammer. Finding a good arrangement takes some trial and error. Strive for fairly regular gaps, and avoid using small stones as they are easily displaced. Ideally, all stones should be at least as large as a dinner plate.

Adjust the stones so the treads form a flat surface. Use a level as a guide, and add wet sand under thinner stones or remove sand from beneath thicker stones until all the flags come close to touching the level and are stable.

Shim between treads and risers with thin shards of stone. (Do not use sand to shim here). Glue the shards in place with block and stone adhesive. Check each step to make sure there is no path for sand to wash out from beneath the treads. You can settle smaller stones in sand with a mallet, but cushion your blows with a piece of wood.

Complete the second step in the same manner as the first. The bottoms of the risers should be at the same height as the bottoms of the tread on the step below. Continue building steps to the top of the slope. *Note: The top step often will not require returns.*

Fill the joints between stones with sand by sweeping the sand across the treads. Use coarse, dark sand such as granite sand, or choose polymeric sand, which resists washout better than regular builder's sand. Inspect the steps regularly for the first few weeks and make adjustments to the heights of stones as needed.

SANDSET BRICK PATIO

Traditional clay brick pavers set in sand make for one of the simplest yet most rewarding patio projects. The installation process is straightforward and, because there's no mortar involved, you can complete the work at your own pace. The overall installation time depends on the patio's design.

Square-edged patios require fewer cuts and thus less time than curved designs. But if you want something out of the ordinary, sandset brick is a good material to work with—the small units are perfect for making curves and custom features; even if you have a lot of cuts, you can make them quickly and accurately with a rented masonry saw.

To pave with any of the classic patterns, such as running bond or herringbone, you'll start at one corner of your patio border or edging. To ensure accurate layout, check that the sides of the edging form a 90-degree angle at the starting corner. If you're not using edging or any kind of formal border, set up mason's strings to guide the brick placement.

If you go with clay brick without spacing lugs, use spacers cut from a sheet of ⅛-inch-thick hardboard to help set accurate sand-joint gaps as you lay the units.

Tools & Materials ▶

Tape measure
Circular saw
Drill
Excavation tools
Mason's string
Stakes
Line level
Plate compactor (available for rent)
Hand tamp
4-ft. level
Rubber mallet
Push broom
Brick paver units
Lumber (2 × 2, 2 × 4)
2½" drywall screws
Compactable gravel
Work gloves

Professional-grade landscape fabric
U-shaped wire stakes (optional)
Rigid paver edging
1"-dia. pipe
Coarse sand
Straight 2 × 4
⅛" hardboard
Plywood scrap
Paver joint sand
Rake
Trowel
Masonry saw
Eye and ear protection
Maul
Galvanized spikes (for edging)

Brick pavers set in sand create a classic patio surface that's more casual than mortared pavers. The inherent flexibility of the sandset finish allows for easy repair and maintenance or changes in the design over time. It also creates good drainage.

HOW TO INSTALL A SANDSET BRICK PATIO

Set up batterboards and layout strings in a square or rectangle that's about 1 ft. larger than the excavation area (see pages 42 to 47 for detailed steps on layout and site preparation). Measure to make sure the string layout is square, and set the strings to follow a ⅛" per foot downward slope in the desired direction using a line level for guidance. Mark the excavation corners with stakes. The edges of the excavation should extend about 6" beyond the finished patio footprint.

Remove all sod and vegetation inside the area, reserving healthy sod for patching in around the finished patio.

Excavate the area to a depth that allows for a 6"-thick gravel subbase, a 1" layer of sand, and the paver thickness; account for the desired height of the finished surface above the surrounding ground. Use cross strings and a story pole to check the depth as you work.

Add an even 3"-layer of compactable gravel over the entire site, and then tamp with a plate compactor. Repeat with another 3" layer. The completed 6" gravel base prior to compacting must be smooth and flat, and it must follow the slope of the layout strings.

Install a layer of high-quality landscape fabric. Overlap rows of fabric by at least 6". If desired, pin the fabric in place with U-shaped wire stakes.

(continued)

Install rigid paver edging along two adjacent sides of the patio area, creating a perfect 90° corner. *Option: If you've laid out the pavers and taken precise measurements, you can install edging along three or four sides of the patio, as desired.* Trim the fabric along the back of the edging. Lay down lengths of 1"-dia. pipe in parallel lines about 3 to 6 ft. apart.

Add a 1"-thick layer of coarse sand. Smooth it out with a rake so it just covers the pipes. Dampen the sand with water, then pack it down lightly with a hand tamp.

Screed the sand perfectly flat using a straight, long 2 × 4: rest the board on top of the pipes, and pull it backward with a side-to-side sawing motion. Fill in low spots with sand as you work. Dampen, tamp, and screed the sand again until the surface is smooth and flat and firmly packed. Remove the pipe(s) in the area where you will begin the paving.

Fill the depression left by the pipe with sand, and then smooth it out with a short board or a trowel. Tamp the area with the hand tamp, and smooth again as needed so the filled-in area is perfectly flat. *Note: Repeat this step as needed during the paving process.*

10

Begin setting the border bricks, starting at the right-angle corner of the patio edging, using ⅛" hardboard spacers if necessary. Complete the border row that will be parallel to the first course of field brick, and continue several feet up the perpendicular side edge. For gentle curves, use full bricks set with slightly angled (wedge-shaped) sand joints; tighter curves require cut bricks for a good fit.

11

Field units

Border units

Set the first course of field brick. These bricks should be centered over the sand joints of the completed border row. Use a mason's string tied between two bricks to align the leading edges of the first-course bricks. After setting several bricks, tap them with a rubber mallet to bed them into the sand layer. Complete the first field course, and then add some border units along the edge.

12

Snug a piece of edging against the installed brick and anchor it in place. *Note: Install the remaining edging as the paving progresses.* Continue setting the brick using the mason's string and spacers for consistent spacing and alignment.

Cutting Pavers & Bricks ▸

If your design requires cuts, use a masonry saw (tub saw). These water-lubricated cutting tools are available for rent at most building centers and stone yards.

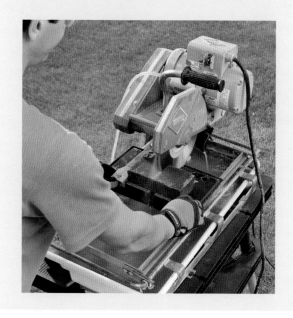

(continued)

13

Check each 4-ft. section for level to make sure the bricks are even across the top. Remove low or high bricks and add or remove sand beneath to bring them flush with the surrounding bricks. Work atop a plywood platform to prevent displacing the bricks. Complete the paving.

Variation: If your patio design includes curves or rounded corners, mark bricks for cutting curves by holding each brick in position and marking the desired cutting line onto the top face, then make the cuts with a masonry saw.

14

Spread sand over the surface, then sweep the sand to fill the joints. Sweep the surface clean, and then tamp the surface with the plate compactor to settle the sand in the joints and lock the bricks in place.

15

Fill and tamp the sand joints one or more times until the joints are completely filled after compaction. Sweep up any loose sand.

16

Soak the surface with water and let it dry. If necessary, fill and tamp again, then hose off the surface and let it dry.

90° herringbone patterns require bricks that are twice as long as they are wide. Start the pattern with two bricks set in the corner of your edging (edging must form a precise 90° angle). Add half-bricks next to the ends of the first two bricks. Complete the next row, zigzagging full bricks following the first row. Repeat the zigzag pattern for the remaining field bricks, adding half-bricks at the ends of rows as needed.

45° herringbone patterns require bricks that are twice as long as they are wide. Starting from a precise 90° corner, set the first row with two right-angle half-bricks. Complete the second row with two right-angle half-bricks flanking a full brick. Begin each remaining field row zig-zagging full bricks and finishing with right-angle half-bricks or trimmed bricks beveled at 45°.

Basketweave patterns require bricks that are twice as long as they are wide. To avoid cuts (on square or rectangular patios), you can install edging on only one side and use it as a baseline for the paving. Install the remaining three sides of edging after all bricks are laid. Snap a chalk line down the center of the sand bed, making sure it is perpendicular (90°) to the baseline edging. Working from the centerline out for each section, lay bricks in a pyramid shape, setting 12 bricks total in the first row, 8 in the second row, and 4 in the third row. Complete the paving by adding to each row incrementally to maintain the pyramid shape. This ensures that every row stems from the centerline to keep the layout straight.

Pinwheels allow you to avoid cuts (on square or rectangular patios) by installing edging on only two adjacent sides, starting from a precise 90° corner. Install the remaining edging after the paving is complete. Set each square pattern using four full bricks, as shown here, then fill the center cavity with a half-brick. For added accent, the centerpiece can be a unique color, but it must be the same thickness as the full bricks. Do not use a thinner brick for the center and compensate for the difference with additional sand; the brick will eventually sink and create an uneven surface.

These convenient interlocking pavers are made with DIYers in mind. They are easy to install and often come with fully plotted patterns for simple design preparation and installation.

COBBLESTONE PAVER PATIO

Concrete pavers have advanced by leaps and bounds from the monochromatic, cookie-cutter bricks and slabs associated with first-generation versions. The latest products feature subtle color blends that lend themselves well to organic, irregular patterns. A tumbling process during manufacturing can further "age" the pavers so they look more like natural cobblestones. The technological advances in the casting and finishing processes have become so sophisticated that a well-selected concrete paver patio could look as suitable in a traditional European square as in a suburban backyard.

When choosing pavers for a patio, pick a style and blend of shapes and sizes that complements your landscape. Use the materials used on your house's exterior and other stone or masonry in your yard to inform your decisions on colors and shade. Be aware that some paver styles require set purchase amounts, and it's not always possible to return partially used pallets of material, so order carefully.

In this project, we lay a cobblestone patio that uses three sizes of pavers. Such pavers may be purchased by a fraction of a pallet, or band, minimizing leftovers. We've also included a row of edge pavers to create a pleasing border around the patio. When shopping for your own patio materials, bring a drawing of your patio plans with exact measurements to your stone yard or landscape supplier. Based on your chosen pattern, the sales staff will be able to tell you how much stone in each size you'll need to purchase.

The patio in this project was created using the following sizes and proportions of cobblestone concrete pavers:

Field pavers—70 percent 6 × 9-inch cobble rectangles, 30 percent 6 × 6-inch cobble squares

Border pavers—3 × 6-inch cobble rectangles

Tools & Materials ▸

Excavation tools	Masonry saw
Wheelbarrow	Push broom
4-ft. level	Concrete pavers
Hand maul	Compactable gravel
Wood stakes	Coarse sand
Chalk line	Plastic edging and
Mason's string	spikes
Line level	Joint sand
Square-nose spade	Eye and ear
1"-dia. metal pipes	protection
2 × 4 lumber	Work gloves
Scrap plywood	Tape measure
Plate compactor	Shovel

Cobblestones ▸

Today, the word *cobblestone* more often refers to cast concrete masonry units that mimic the look of natural cobblestones. Although they are tumbled to give them a slightly aged appearance, cast concrete cobbles are more uniform in shape, size, and color. This is an advantage when it comes to installation, but purists object to the appearance.

Cobblestone Paver Patio—Construction Details

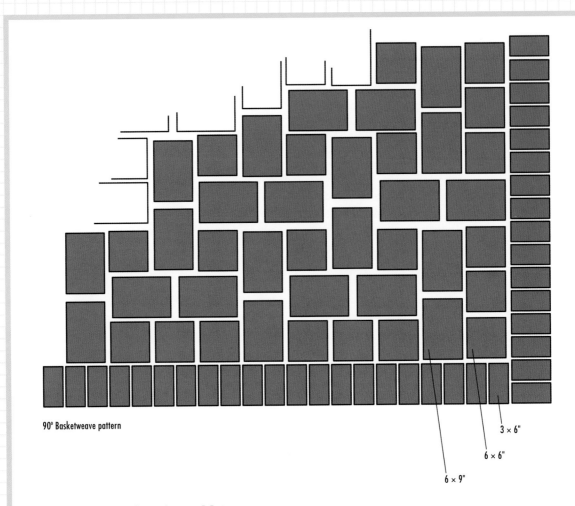

90° Basketweave pattern

3 × 6"

6 × 6"

6 × 9"

Cross-section of patio and base

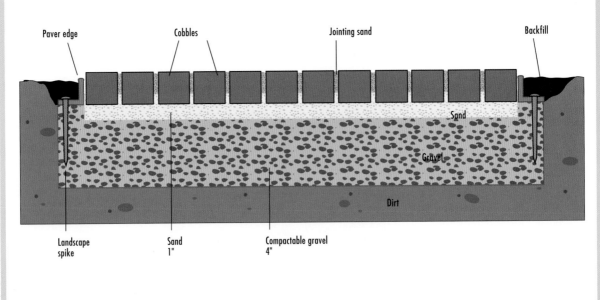

Paver edge

Cobbles

Jointing sand

Backfill

Sand

Gravel

Dirt

Landscape spike

Sand 1"

Compactable gravel 4"

HOW TO BUILD A COBBLESTONE PAVER PATIO

Mark the corners of the finished patio with stakes, and remove any sod or other plantings in the area. Set up grade stakes and mason's strings to guide the excavation and establish a downward slope of ⅛" per foot away from the house foundation.

Variation: Use batterboards and mason's strings to establish the layout of the project area. See pages 42 to 47 for detailed instructions.

Excavate the site to a depth that accommodates a 4" gravel subbase, a 1" layer of sand, and the thickness of the pavers (minus the desired height above the ground). Extend the excavation 6" beyond the patio footprint. Use the layout strings or grade stakes to check the depth and slope as you work. Tamp the soil with a plate compactor.

Add compactable gravel for a 4"-thick layer after compaction. Screed the gravel flat with a straight 2 × 4 and use a level or the layout strings to make sure the surface is properly sloped. Compact the gravel thoroughly with a plate compactor.

(continued)

4

Set up a new string layout to guide the edging installation using stakes and mason's string. The strings should represent the inside edges of the edging material. To make sure the layout has square corners, measure diagonally between the corners: the layout is square when the measurements are equal.

5

Rigid paver edge   Paver edge spikes

Install rigid paver edging along one side edge of the patio: snap a chalk line directly under the layout string along the edge, and then remove that string. Set the edging to the line and secure it with paver edge spikes, driving in the spikes only partially (in case you have to make adjustments later).

Screed (2 × 4)

Drive pipes here

Screed guides (1" pipe)

Lay lengths of 1"-dia. metal pipe in the project area to serve as screed guides. Fill the patio area with coarse building sand to the tops of the pipes. Screed the sand smooth and flat using a long, straight 2 × 4, pulling the board back and forth with a sawing motion. Remove the pipes, fill the voids with sand, and smooth the surface flat. *Tip: Dampen the sand before screeding.*

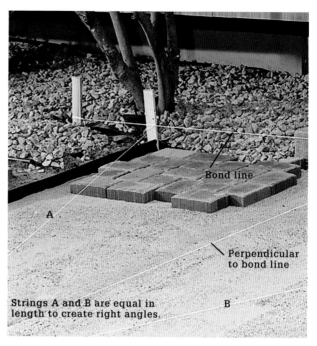

Set the pavers in the chosen pattern, starting at the 90° corner formed by the patio edging and an adjacent layout string (called the bond line). Lay border pavers along one or both edges before setting the field pavers. For now, simply lay the pavers in place; later, you will bed them into the sand with the plate vibrator.

Option: Use additional layout strings to help guide the paver pattern. Set up a string that is perpendicular to the bond line, using it to align courses every few feet. Tie equidistant strings between the corners and the end of the perpendicular string to assure a right angle with the bond line.

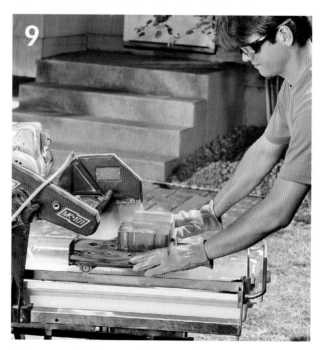

Install the remaining pieces of edging as you near the opposite side and end of the patio, leaving enough room for the final course of field pavers (plus border units, if applicable). Cut away the edges of the sand bed so the edging rests on the gravel base only. *Tip: If you don't need to cut pavers along the edges, you can install the edging after all of the pavers are laid.*

Cut pavers to fit as needed to complete the paving using a rented masonry saw (also see Making Curves on page 118). It's preferable to cut pavers a little too small than to have very tight fits; the joint sand will fill small gaps. With the paving complete, drive the edging stakes into the rigid edging to lock the pavers in place.

(continued)

Sweep joint sand over the pavers using a push broom. Continue adding sand and sweeping until the joints between pavers are nearly filled to the top surface.

Tamp the patio surface with the plate compactor. Move the compactor in circular motions, working from the outside in and overlapping rings as you go. Repeat Steps 10 and 11 until the joints are completely filled after compaction. *Note: Some paver manufacturers recommend sweeping excess sand from the pavers before compacting.*

Making Curves ▸

At rounded corners and curves, install border pavers (A) in a fan pattern with even gaps between the pavers. Gentle curves may accommodate full-sized border pavers, but for sharper turns you usually need to cut tapers into the paver edges so you don't end up with wide gaps at the outside. When using border pavers in a curved layout, the field pavers will need to be trimmed to fit the odd spaces created where the field and borders intersect (B).

Choosing Pavers & Patterns ▸

The number of purchasing options available when you shop for pavers makes it possible to create just about any patio layout pattern you can imagine. There is nothing stopping you from going wild and creating a layout that's truly one-of-a-kind. Most landscape centers will also work with you to create a layout for your patio that employs tested design ideas and uses pavers in a very efficient manner and with as little cutting as possible.

Another option for DIY designers is to visit the website of the paver manufacturer (you should be able to get the information from your paver dealer). Many of these have applications where you can choose a basic style you like (such as the patterns shown here) and enter the size of your planned patio. You'll receive a printout of what the pattern should look like, along with a shopping list for the materials you'll need, all the way down to sand and spikes for your paver edging.

A traditional brick running-bond pattern can be created using rectangular pavers.

This basketweave pattern is made with squares and large rectangles. A border of small rectangles completes the design.

Cobblestone paving with squares and large and small rectangles create this circular pattern.

CIRCULAR PAVER PATIO

Tools & Materials ▶

Concrete pavers are available in a range of sizes and shapes, making it easy to create distinctive patterns without a lot of cuts. This circular patio is made with a complete set of shaped concrete pavers. To create a perfect circle, all you have to do is set the pavers following the manufacturer's installation diagram, and no cuts are needed (although some sets have center pieces that must be cut before installation).

Circular paver sets are commonly sold in fixed starter sizes, and you can add units as needed to enlarge the circle. You may have to purchase additional pavers as complete sets or in full-pallet quantities and use only what you need. Circular pavers are ideal for building freestanding patios because their shape makes for a nice decorative feature.

Circular saw
Hammer
Drill
Excavation tools
Mason's string
Line level
Plate compactor
Trowel
Flathead screwdriver
Shovel
Push broom
Circular paver units
16d nails
Duct tape
Lumber (2 × 2, 2 × 4)

Marking paint
2½" drywall screws
Compactable gravel
Landscape fabric
1 or 1½" pipe
Straight 2 × 4
Washed concrete
  sand
Scrap plywood
Plastic patio edging
Paver joint sand
Eye and ear
  protection
Work gloves
Tape measure

A circular patio is visually dynamic and its shape makes it uniquely suited to intimate outdoor dining and entertaining spaces. When shopping for pavers, ask about color and texture options. Some suppliers may allow you to mix and match finishes for a personalized look.

As a design feature, a circle naturally draws the eye toward its center. This makes a circular patio the perfect setting for a round patio table and chairs or for highlighting a central decorative feature, such as a fountain or statuary. A circle is also the best configuration for creating an intimate seating area surrounding a fire pit. In addition to patio spaces, small circles can be used as landing areas along a curving paver walkway, while an open ring of circular pavers can be used as a border around a planting bed.

The patio in this project follows a standard sandset installation. Mortaring a patio like this would be far more difficult than sandsetting, due to the irregularity of the paver joints. For the sandset process, it's easiest to lay the pavers first, and then install flexible plastic edging around the perimeter to lock the units in place. If your patio plan calls for numerous cuts, rent a masonry saw, or *tub saw*, for making the cuts. Otherwise, you can make a few cuts with a circular saw fitted with a masonry blade. Before you get started, it will help to review the detailed information on laying out the project site and preparing the gravel base (see pages 42 to 47).

Circular Paver Materials ▶

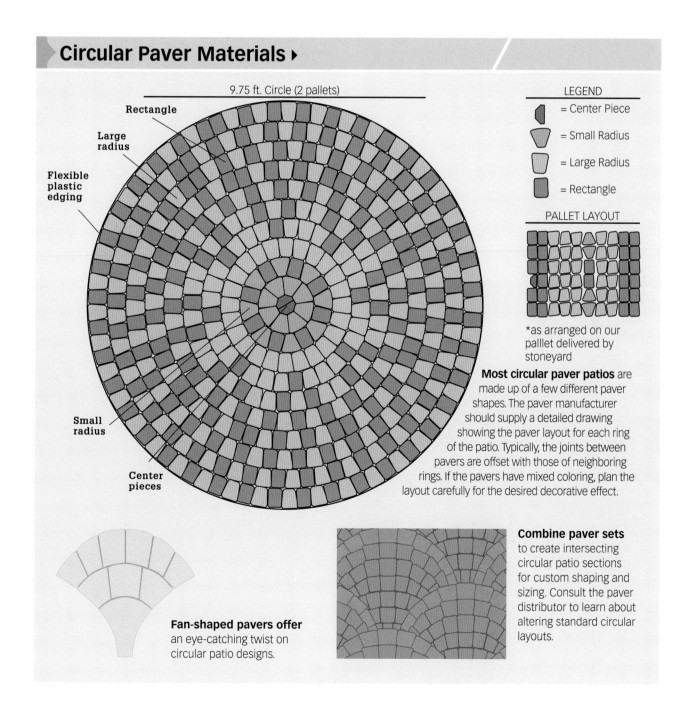

9.75 ft. Circle (2 pallets)

Rectangle

Large radius

Flexible plastic edging

Small radius

Center pieces

LEGEND

▬ = Center Piece

▬ = Small Radius

▬ = Large Radius

▬ = Rectangle

PALLET LAYOUT

*as arranged on our palllet delivered by stoneyard

Most circular paver patios are made up of a few different paver shapes. The paver manufacturer should supply a detailed drawing showing the paver layout for each ring of the patio. Typically, the joints between pavers are offset with those of neighboring rings. If the pavers have mixed coloring, plan the layout carefully for the desired decorative effect.

Fan-shaped pavers offer an eye-catching twist on circular patio designs.

Combine paver sets to create intersecting circular patio sections for custom shaping and sizing. Consult the paver distributor to learn about altering standard circular layouts.

HOW TO INSTALL A CIRCULAR PAVER PATIO

WALKWAYS, STEPS & PATIOS

Create a center pivot for defining the patio layout. Drive a stake at the exact center of the desired location for the finished patio. Cut a straight 2 × 2 about 12" longer than the radius of the patio. Drill a large pilot hole at one end of the board, and fasten the board to the center of the stake with a single nail. *Note: For large patio areas, use a string tied to a center nail instead of a board (inset).*

Mark the ground for excavation. Measuring out from the nail, mark the board at a distance equal to the radius, plus 6". Tape a can of marking paint to the board so the spray nozzle is centered on the mark (inset). Spray a continuous line onto the ground while pivoting the board to create a complete circle. Set up batterboards and leveled layout strings in a square that's about 1 ft. larger than the excavated area. Remove all sod and other vegetation inside the marked circle.

Measure diagonally between opposing corners and adjust the strings as needed until the measurements are equal (the layout is square). Slope two of the parallel layout strings at ¼" per foot using the distance between the batterboards to calculate the drop distance generally dropping away from your house.

Excavate the site to the depth recommended by the paver manufacturer. Make sure the soil is smooth, well compacted, and properly sloped to ⅛" per foot.

Prepare the subbase with a 4" layer of gravel. Thoroughly compact the gravel with a plate compactor.

Check the depth with cross strings and a story pole as you work (shown). The completed base must be smooth and flat and follow the slope setting.

Install landscape fabric over the gravel subbase. Overlap the edges of fabric strips by 6". Trim the fabric as needed, leaving the ends a little long for now. *Note: This helps keep the sand base in place longer.*

Set two lengths of 1"-dia. pipe on top of the landscape fabric so that one piece spans the full diameter of the gravel base and the other spans across the base about ¼ of the way in from the side of the circle. Align the pipes parallel to each other. Fill half of the patio site with sand even with the tops of the pipes.

Use a straight 2 × 4 to screed the sand level with the pipes. Move the short pipe to the opposite side of the site to complete the other half of the sand layer. Remove the pipes and then fill all depressions with sand. *Tip: Moisten sand prior to screeding.*

(continued)

Position the center paver, then measure out to the edge of the site in several places to confirm that it is centered. *Tip: Work on top of a piece of plywood to avoid disturbing the sand bed.*

Set the first ring of pavers around the center paver. Check their positions carefully, and make sure the spacing lugs are oriented correctly. If the pavers don't have lugs, gap them according to the manufacturer's specifications. *Note: Do not hammer or tamp the pavers into the sand bed unless the manufacturer directs otherwise.*

Set the remaining pavers, completing each ring according to your layout diagram. Be sure to offset the paver joints between rows. The pavers may be labeled, requiring them to be installed in a specific order as you work around the circle. After a sizable area is laid, work from your plywood platform set atop the pavers.

Install rigid paver edging along the patio's perimeter. Set the edging on top of the gravel subbase but not the sand bed. *Tip: Dampening the sand bed along the patio edge makes it easy to cut the sand away cleanly with a trowel before setting the edging.*

14

Inspect the paving to make sure all joints are aligned properly and all gaps are consistent. Make minor adjustments to pavers as needed using a flathead screwdriver as a pry bar. Be careful not to mar the paver edges as you pry.

15

Shovel joint sand over the entire patio surface, then use a push broom to sweep the sand over the pavers to fill the joints. Repeat as needed until the joints are completely filled, then sweep off excess sand.

16

Set the pavers into the sand bed using a plate compactor. Make a first pass along the perimeter of the patio, then compact the interior with parallel back-and-forth passes, overlapping the preceding pass slightly as you go. *Note: Avoid excessive tamping to prevent damage to the paver surfaces.* Add another application of sand. Tamp the surface, but make the interior passes perpendicular to those of the first tamping runs.

17

Refill the joints with sand a final time and sweep the surface clean. Spray thoroughly with water to settle the joint sand.

Sandset flagstone patios blend nicely with natural landscapes. Although flagstone evokes a natural feel, the patio can appear rustic or formal. This patio has clean, well-tamped joints and straight, groomed edges along the perimeter that lends to a formal feel. Plantings in the joints or a rough, natural perimeter would give the same patio a more relaxed, rustic feel.

FLAGSTONE PATIO

Flagstones make a great, long-lasting patio surface with a naturally rough texture and a perfectly imperfect look and finish. Randomly shaped stones are especially suited to patios with curved borders, but they can also be cut to form straight lines. Your patio will appear more at home in your landscape if the flagstones you choose are of the same stone species as other stones in the area. For example, if your gravel paths and walls are made from a local buff limestone, look for the same material in limestone flags.

Flagstones usually come in large slabs, sold as flagstone, or in smaller pieces (typically 16 inches or smaller), sold as *steppers*. You can make a patio out of either. Larger stones will make a solid patio with a more even surface, but the bigger ones can require three strong people to position, and large stones are hard to cut and fit tightly. If your soil drains well and is stable, flagstones can be laid on nothing more than a layer of sand. However, if you have unstable clay soil that becomes soft when wet, start with a four-inch-thick foundation of compactable gravel (see pages 42 to 47) under your sand.

There are a few different options for filling the spaces between flagstones. One popular treatment is to plant them with low-growing perennials suited to crevice culture. For best results, use sand-based soil between flagstones when planting. Also, stick to very small plants that can withstand foot traffic. If you prefer not to have a planted patio, simply fill the joints with sand or fine gravel—just be sure to add landscape fabric under your sand base to discourage weed growth.

Tools & Materials ▸

Mason's string	Stiff-bristle brush
Line level	Circular saw with
Rope or hose	masonry blade
Excavation tools	Plugs or seeds for
Spud bar	groundcover
Broom	Eye and ear
Stakes	protection
Marking paint	Work gloves
1" (outside	¾" plywood
diameter) pipe	3½" deck screws
Coarse sand	Pointing chisel
Straight 2 × 4	Pitching chisel
Flagstone	Stone chisel
Spray bottle	Hand maul
Stone edging	Dust mask
Sand-based soil or	Chalk or a crayon
joint sand	Square-nose spade
Lumber (2 × 2,	Crushed stone
2 × 4)	Ashlar
Drill	Mortar
Mason's trowel	Capstones

Adding a Stone Wall ▸

A dry stone wall is a simple, beautiful addition to a flagstone patio. A wall functions as extra seating, a place to set plants, or extra countertop or tabletop space. It also provides visual definition to your outdoor space.

Construction Details

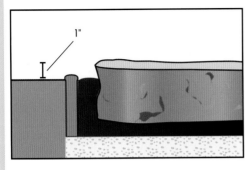

1"

Lay flagstones so their tops are approximately ½ to 1" above the surrounding ground. Because natural stones are not uniform in thickness, you will need to adjust sand or dirt beneath each flagstone, as needed.

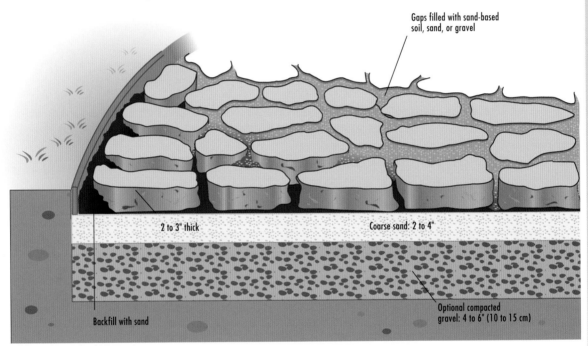

Gaps filled with sand-based soil, sand, or gravel

2 to 3" thick

Coarse sand: 2 to 4"

Backfill with sand

Optional compacted gravel: 4 to 6" (10 to 15 cm)

A typical sandset patio has a layer of coarse sand for embedding the flagstones. A subbase of compactable gravel is an option for improved stability and drainage. The joints between stones can be filled with sand, gravel, or soil and plants. Edging material is optional.

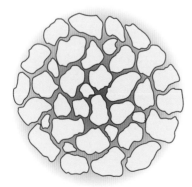

Irregular flagstones look natural and are easy to work with in round layouts.

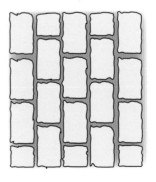

Flagstones that are cut into rectangular shapes can be laid in square or rectangular patterns with uniform gaps.

HOW TO BUILD A SANDSET FLAGSTONE PATIO

Outline the patio base using string and stakes for straight lines and/or a rope or hose for curves. The base should extend at least 2 to 4" beyond the edges of the flagstones, except where the patio will butt up to a wall. Transfer the outline to the ground with marking paint. Remove any sod and vegetation within the base area.

Set up layout strings to guide the excavation using stakes or batterboards (see pages 42 to 47 for detailed steps on layout and site preparation). Excavate the base to a depth of 2" plus the stone thickness plus ½ to 1". Slope the ground away from the house foundation at a rate of ¼" per foot.

Lay sections of 1" pipe across the project area to serve as screed gauges. These allow you to strike off sand at a consistent depth when you drag a screed board over them. *Note: Since large flagstones can be held in place adequately by the surrounding soil, edging for the patio is optional; it often looks best to allow neighboring groundcover to grow up to the edges of the stones. If you do plan to use edging, install it now.*

Fill the site with coarse sand slightly above the screed gauges. With a helper, drag a straight 2 × 4 across the screed gauges to level off the sand. Use a screed board that's long enough so that you can avoid stepping in the sand. Work the screed in a back-and-forth sawing motion. Remove the pipes once each section is finished, fill in the voids, and smooth the surface flat.

(continued)

Arrange your flagstones into groups according to size and shape. As a general rule, start paving with the broadest stones and fill in around them with increasingly smaller pieces, but appearance and sight lines are also important: if there is one nice stone with a flat surface and good color, feature it in the center of the patio. Or, if some of the patio will be visible from the house, choose nicer stones for these areas.

Begin by laying large, thick stones around the perimeter of the patio. Leave a consistent gap of about 1" between stones by matching pieces like a puzzle and cutting and dressing stones as needed. The outer edge of the patio should form smooth curves (or straight lines) without jutting pieces or abrupt irregularities. Level stones as needed by prying up with a spud bar and adding or removing sand underneath.

Fill in around the larger stones with smaller pieces cut to fit the spaces, as needed, working from the outside in. After setting a band of stones a few courses wide, lay a 2 × 4 across the stones to make sure they're level with one another. Add or remove sand below to adjust their height, and dampen the sand occasionally to make it easier to work with.

Fill the joints between stones with sand-based, weed-seed-free soil. Sweep the soil across the patio surface to fill the cracks, and then water the soil so it settles. Repeat as needed until the soil reaches the desired level. Plant plugs or seeds for groundcover to grow up between the stones, if desired.

Variation: To finish the patio with sand instead of soil and plants, spread sand over the patio and sweep across the stones with a push broom to fill the joints. Pack the sand with your fingers or a piece of wood. Spray the entire area with water to help compact the sand. Let the patio dry. Repeat filling and spraying until the joints are full and the stones are securely locked in place.

Choosing Soil & Plants for Your Patio ▸

Sand-based soil (also called "patio planting" soil) is the best material to use for planting between flagstones. This mixture of soil and sand sweeps easily into joints, and it resists tight compaction to promote healthy plant growth, as well as surface drainage. Regular soil can become too compacted for effective planting and drainage and soil from your yard will undoubtedly contain weeds. Sand-based soil is available in bulk or by the bag and is often custom-mixed at most large garden centers.

As for the best plants to use, listed below are a few species that tend to do well in a patio application. Ask a local supplier what works best for your climate.

- Alyssum
- Rock cress
- Thrift
- Miniature dianthus
- Candytuft
- Lobelia
- Forget-me-not

- Saxifrage
- Sedum
- Thymus
- Scotch moss
- Irish moss
- Woolly thyme
- Mock strawberry

Patio "planting soil" (for planting between stones) is available in bulk or bags at most garden centers. It is good for filling cracks because the sand base makes it dry and smooth enough to sweep into cracks, yet the black compost will support plant growth. Because it is bagged, you can be assured it doesn't come with weeds.

CREATING A PERMEABLE SUBBASE

Most patios made with rock or masonry units should have a stable subbase of compacted rock or gravel, usually beneath a layer of coarse sand into which the surfacing materials are set. Typically, these subbase layers are 6 to 8 inches thick, depending on your soil conditions—loose, loamy, or sandy soil needs a thicker subbase. A standard subbase made from compactable gravel (called Class II or Class V in most areas) hardens to form a solid mass when it is compacted. Water runoff will not penetrate such a subbase. But as patio builders have begun to place a higher value on water retention and minimizing runoff, they have developed permeable subbases that accomplish the same result by stabilizing the patio, but allow water runoff to seep through into the subsoil below instead of running off and into the wastewater collection system.

They key to a permeable subbase is called open-grade drainage rock in most areas. Where Class II and Class V are sifted with fine pulverized material (usually limestone) that hardens, ungraded drainage rock is just the rock. Most landscape materials stores carry it in two sizes: ¾-inch aggregate and 1½-inch aggregate. The prevailing wisdom suggests laying a layer of the larger rock first, compacting it, and then topping it off with a compacted layer of the smaller drainage rock before you put down your sand bed (if you are using one). Once you've created a permeable subbase, it will look very much like a traditional subbase and you build upon it using the same techniques. However, note that a permeable subbase is of little value if you top it with an impermeable or minimally permeable surfacing, such as interlocking pavers. Use either material that allows water to drain through it (such as pervious pavers), or install impermeable materials with large enough gaps between the individual members that the water will run off the pavers or stones and drain down through the gaps.

A permeable subbase looks a little like a typical compacted gravel subbase, but because the open-grade drainage rock is devoid of fines it does not form a solid layer and thus it allows water to run through, not off.

Tools & Materials ▸

Stakes and mason's line
Tape measure
Maul
Shovels or other excavation tools
Wheelbarrow
Hand tamper
Landscape rake
Plate compactor
Level
Ear and eye protection
Sturdy shoes/boots
Work gloves
Large (1½" diameter) open-grade drainage rock
Smaller (¾" diameter) open-grade rock
Landscape fabric or geogrid textile (optional)
Edging
Coarse sand or pulverized granite (optional)

Coarse setting sand

¾"-dia. open-grade drainage rock

1½"-dia. open-grade drainage rock

The thickness of your permeable subbase depends on the soil conditions. For stable soil with good drainage, a 4 to 6" subbase is adequate. If you have loamy or sandy soil, go as thick as 10", with a layer of larger-diameter drainage rock. Adding an underlayment of geogrid textile will help stabilize the subbase in such cases. An underlayment is not helpful in stable soil with good drainage.

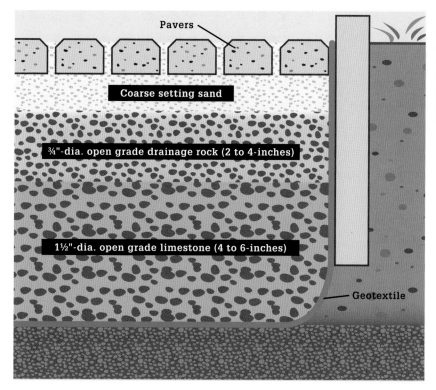

Pavers

Coarse setting sand

¾"-dia. open grade drainage rock (2 to 4-inches)

1½"-dia. open grade limestone (4 to 6-inches)

Geotextile

The components of a permeable subbase, from bottom to top, include a 4 to 6" layer of 1½" diameter open-grade drainage rock (limestone is shown here); above that, a 2 to 4" layer of open-grade rock; a top layer of coarse sand or pulverized granite for use as a setting bed for flagstone or masonry units.

HOW TO INSTALL A PERMEABLE SUBBASE

Minimum slope: ½" per 10 ft. away from house

Line level

Story pole

Drive corner posts with a maul and outline the patio area. Run mason's lines between the corner posts. Ideally, the patio should slope away from an adjoining house at a rate of around ½" for every 10 ft. Set a level line along the edges of the patio perpendicular to the house. Adjust the line downward to create the ¼" per 1-ft. slope.

Begin excavating the site. A typical permeable subbase is 8" below grade when you allow for the thickness of the setting layer and the pavers or other surfacing. Use your layout strings to establish your digging depth. Measure the distance from the mason's line to the ground and add the depth of your excavation—8" in the project seen here. Make a story pole with markings that match the distance from the planned bottom of the excavation to the mason's line. Keep the lines in place as you dig (this does create an obstacle but it is the best way to assure that you don't overdig).

Excavate the patio site using the story pole as a depth guide. Be sure to call (in the US, simply dial "811") and have any utility lines flagged before you begin digging. Be careful not to dig too deeply, as the best base for your subbase is undisturbed earth. Once the excavation is complete, remove the strings and prepare for the installation of the subbase.

Create a Wheelbarrow Path ▸

Create a temporary pathway from the subbase rock to the site using wood planks, old pavers, or any other surface you can create. This will minimize damage to your yard and make the heavy wheelbarrows safer to operate.

A permeable base is made with open-grade rock, which is simply landscape rock that has no fines or binders, as typical subbase (often called Class V or Class II) does. The bottom layer should be rock that is not smooth and has diameters of 1½" to 2" inches. Spread a 2- to 4"-deep layer of rock over the excavation area. OPTION: Install a layer of landscape fabric over the site to inhibit weeds. Landscape fabric can be installed under the subbase or on top of the subbase, but must be under the setting base layer.

Spread the rock out into an even layer. Use a garden rake or landscape rake to spread it. The subbase should extend past the planned edges of the project area by at least 10" on all open sides.

Tamp the rock to compact it. You can use a hand tamper, but for best results use a rented plate compactor. This is a very important part of creating a solid patio base, so be sure to be diligent with your efforts. Compact the rock as you go: do not compact more than 2" of material at one time. Wear foam ear plugs or other ear protection.

Add additional layers of large rock until the base layer is at least 4" thick. Then, switch to a smaller open-grade rock for the next layer. Here, ¾"-dia. buff limestone is being used. Add, spread, and compact the smaller-grade rock until the leveled surface follows the grade of the patio and the surface of the rock layer is 2", plus the thickness of your surfacing material, below grade at the top of the worksite. This completes your permeable subbase. Add a sand setting layer and pavers according to the demands of your project.

SPACED MASONRY PAVERS

A bit of space between each paver and its neighbor is all it takes to turn a mostly impervious surface like masonry pavers into something that replenishes groundwater and spares storm drains. You have several options for building these earth-friendly gaps into your project:

- **Spaced conventional pavers.** Boost the earth friendliness of standard concrete pavers or bricks by installing them with several inches of a gap between them. Filling the voids with river rock or creeping plants permits water to drain easily.

- **Mounting grids.** Plastic mounting not only locks in pavers a consistent space from each other, they help keep the installation smooth and level.

- **Pavers with pre-formed spacers.** Some pavers come with small nubs that separate them just enough to allow for drainage. They install as quickly and easily as conventional pavers.

For this project, you'll also need to prepare a deep substrate of coarse, angular gravel to handle the water (see Creating a Permeable Subbase, pages 132 to 135). Your soil type will dictate its depth. At the extreme, you may have to excavate 10 to 12 inches to make room for 8 inches of ¾- to 1½-inch open-graded stone, followed by at least 2 inches of coarse sand or screenings as a setting bed.

The project that follows uses widely spaced 16-inch by 16-inch pavers. One advantage of large pavers is that they look best if laid out so only whole pieces are used. No cutting! Once the substrate and edging is in place, use spacers and a taut line to install the pavers.

The 16 x 16" wet-cast concrete pavers would shed rainwater and runoff if they were butted against one another in the traditional manner. By leaving a 3" gap filled with pulverized granite, you create a route for water to soak into the permeable subbase and subsoil.

Tools & Materials ›

Safety glasses, gloves, ear protection	Rigid paver edging, galvanized spikes
Tape measure	Scrap plywood and 2× for making spacers
Circular saw	
Hammer	¾ to 1½" open-grade stone for base
Drill driver, bits	
Excavation tools	Coarse sand or screenings for setting bed
Stakes	
Mason's string	
Line level	Pea gravel, river rock, crushed granite, or sand to fill gaps
Plate compactor	
Rubber mallet	
Rake	Topsoil (if adding plants)
Trowel	
Lengths of 1" metal conduit	Plants

Using Spacers ▶

One of the least expensive ways to make an earth-friendly patio is to install conventional pavers with extra space between them for drainage. Any amount of spacing helps, whether a mere ¼-inch gap filled with coarse sand or 3 inches or more for stone or plantings. The consistent geometry of conventional pavers makes it relatively easy to achieve straight courses. However, once you introduce a gap you'll need to contrive spacers to help keep the gap consistent and the pavers neatly lined up. Guides can range from a few strips of ¼-inch hardboard to 2× and plywood combinations made to suit your arrangement.

Simple strips of ¼" hardboard or plywood work fine as gap guides. Adding a scrap of 1 × 2 makes them easier to use. Make several so they are always handy. This relatively small gap works well with smaller cast concrete pavers similar in size to brick pavers.

For a 1½" gap, use a 2 × 2 as a spacer. Adding a scrap of ½" plywood to ride on the paver tops makes the spacer easier to handle and helps you level adjacent pavers. This spacing is good with medium-sized pavers, such as these 8 × 16 concrete pavers.

To install a grid of square pavers, make a cross spacer about 16" by 16". Two 2 × 2s gives you a roughly 3-inch gap without having to rip a 2 × 4. Add the cross made of ¼- to ¾" plywood to match to the thickness of the pavers and hold the 2 × 2s together. For ease of use, attach a 1 × 2 handle. This is the spacer used for the featured project to follow, which uses large 16 × 16" pavers.

HOW TO INSTALL A SPACED-PAVER PATIO

Prepare a permeable subbase that extends at least 10" past the planned borders of the patio where possible. Install rigid paver edging around the border of the patio area to contain the coarse sand or crushed granite setting base material.

Embed 1"-dia. pieces of conduit into the sand at 4- to 6-ft. intervals, making sure the conduit pieces are flush with one another and follow any slope you want to build into the patio (a ½" in 10-ft. slope away from the house is a good minimum). Scrape a piece of straight 2 × 4 along strips of adjoining conduit to level the paver setting medium. Slowly move the 2 × 4 back and forth in a sawing motion. Avoid walking on the setting bed once it is smooth. Remove the conduit and backfill the depressions.

Lay a setting bed that is at least 2" thick on top of the subbase. Level the setting bed. Do not use a power plate compactor on this bed, as it will make adjusting the pavers very difficult. It is okay to use a hand tamper to level things out and lightly compact the material.

Starting at a corner, set four tiles, using a cross spacer (see previous page) to position the pavers. *Note: When using spacers to lay out a patio next to a house, always start at the house and work outward. In cases (such as the example seen here) where you are working in a closed corner, choose that corner to start. That way, if the corner is slightly out of square, which is common, you can make it up at the open sides of the patio where it is less noticeable.*

(continued)

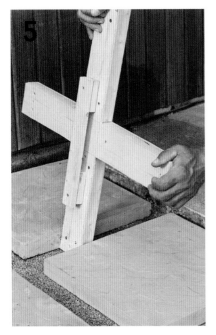

Continue to set pavers onto the setting bed, fanning outward from the corner where you started. Rely on the spacer to position the pavers, and go back to recheck the gaps as you work. For best results, make many spacers and leave them in place as you work.

Once you've set several pavers, also check to make sure you are staying level. Lay a straight 2 × 4 across the tops and look for gaps between the straightedge and the pavers.

Add or remove bedding base from beneath the pavers as needed to bring them to level. Use some restraint here, as it is very easy to throw off your layout by adding too much bedding.

Use a rubber mallet and a scrap of 2 × 4 to adjust out-of-kilter pavers. Again, use restraint here and be mindful of the lines formed by the grid pattern. Even slight deviations will show up very clearly.

Place all the pavers, then add filler between the pavers. Here, the same crushed (also called composted) granite that was used for the setting base is used to fill in the gaps. Keep a supply of the material around, as it is likely you'll need to refresh it from time to time as the level gets lower.

Option: Fill the spaces between the pavers with topsoil or potting soil so you can add attractive groundcover plants that don't mind being underfoot. Some may even add a pleasant fragrance as you walk across them. For areas with full sun, consider Creeping Thyme or Elfin Thyme. In partial sun, Goldmoss Sedum, Chamomile, Dichondra, and Irish Moss work well. In shady areas, go with Corsican Sandwort or Sweet Woodruff. Or, simply plant grass.

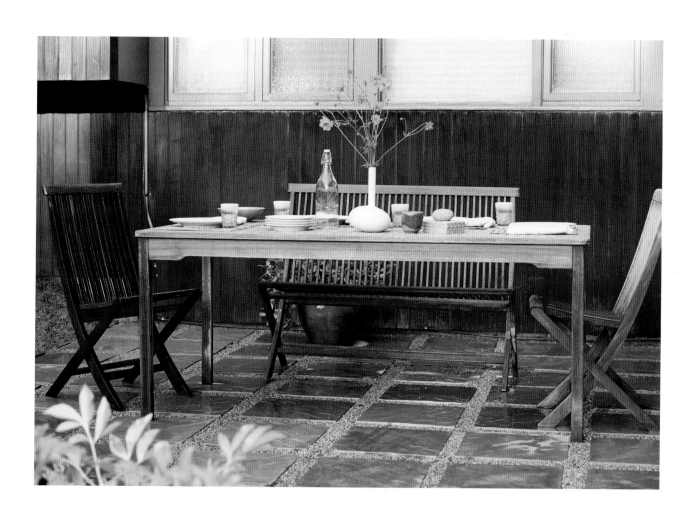

The moldable nature of poured concrete makes it ideal for creating patios with curves and custom shapes in addition to perfect squares and rectangles. If your patio plans call for a neighboring concrete walkway, see pages 72 to 77.

CONCRETE SLAB PATIO

Few outdoor surfaces are as heavy duty as a properly poured concrete slab. As a patio material, poured concrete is tough to beat. The surface is flat, smooth, easy to clean, and about as close to maintenance-free as you can get. A concrete slab is also the best foundation for permanent finishes like mortared brick, tile, and stone. And if you like the simplicity and durability of a bare concrete patio but flat gray doesn't suit your design scheme, you can always apply an acid stain, dry pigment colors, or concrete paint (rated for exterior use) for custom coloring effects without compromising the surface's performance.

If you've never worked with poured concrete before, you'll find that most of the work lies in preparing the site and building the forms for containing and shaping the wet concrete. Once the concrete is mixed or delivered to your site, time is of the essence, and the best way to ensure quality results is to be prepared with strong forms, the right tools, and an understanding of each step of the process. And it never hurts to have help: you'll need at least two hardworking assistants for the placing and finishing stages.

This patio project follows the steps for building a small (100 square feet or so) slab that can be poured and finished all at once. The patio featured here is a circular, freestanding structure slightly more than 10 feet in diameter. If you are building a patio of any shape that abuts your house, always isolate it from the house with an isolation board and slope the surface so water drains away from the foundation. A smaller slab is much more manageable for amateurs. Larger slabs often require that you place and tool the wet concrete in workable sections, and these steps must continue simultaneously until the entire slab is filled and leveled before the concrete begins to set. Therefore, it's a good idea to seek guidance and/or assistance from a concrete professional if your plans call for a large patio.

Because they are permanent structures, concrete patios are often governed by local building codes, and you might need a permit for your project—especially if the patio abuts a permanent structure. Before you get started, contact your city's building department to learn about permit requirements and general construction specifications in your area, including:

- Zoning restrictions
- Depth of gravel subbase
- Concrete composition
- Slab thickness and slope
- Internal reinforcement (wire mesh, rebar, etc.)
- Control joints
- Moisture barrier under slab (not a common requirement)

Concrete Coverage ▸

Volume	Slab Thickness	Surface Area
1 cubic yard	2"	160 square feet
1 cubic yard	3"	110 square feet
1 cubic yard	4"	80 square feet
1 cubic yard	5"	65 square feet
1 cubic yard	6"	55 square feet
1 cubic yard	8"	40 square feet

Tools & Materials ▸

Drill
Circular saw
Hand maul or
    sledgehammer
Mason's string
Stakes
Marking paint
Line level
Excavation tools
Bow rake
Level
Plate compactor or
    hand tamper

Eye protection
Plumb bob
Chalk line
Hammer
Hardboard lap siding
Bolt cutters
Concrete mixing tools
Shovel or masonry hoe
Wheelbarrow
Bull float
Edger
1" groover
Magnesium trowel

Push broom
Lumber (1 × 2,
    2 × 4)
Compactable
    gravel
Screws
6 × 6" 10/10 welded
    wire mesh
Tie wire
2" wire bolsters
Work gloves
Square-nose spade
Safety protection

Isolation board
    and construction
    adhesive
Concrete form release
    agent
4,000 psi concrete (or
    as required by local
    code)
Clear polyethylene
    sheeting
Lawn edger (available
    for rent)

CONSTRUCTION DETAILS

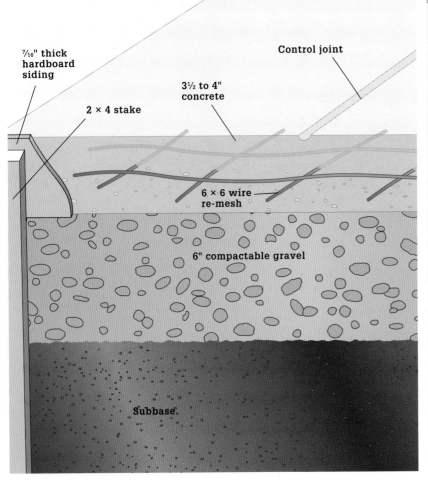

Well-constructed forms and properly prepared foundational elements will ensure your slab is structurally sound.

Labels in diagram:
7/16" thick hardboard siding
2 × 4 stake
3½ to 4" concrete
Control joint
6 × 6 wire re-mesh
6" compactable gravel
Subbase

When is Concrete Ready to Finish? ▸

Floating wet concrete causes the heavy materials in the mix to sink below the surface, leaving a layer of water—know as bleed water—on the surface. To achieve an attractive and durable finish, let the bleed water disappear before proceeding with the final finishing steps (edging, control joints, and finish troweling). How long this takes depends on the air temperature, humidity, and sun exposure; you just have to watch and wait.

Once the bleed water dries, test the concrete for hardness by stepping on it: if your foot sinks in no more than ¼", the concrete is ready for finishing. Be extra diligent with any areas exposed to the sun or wind, as they can dry much faster than other spots. *Note: Air-entrained concrete (commonly used for cold-weather pours) doesn't show bleed water, so you have to rely on the step test to know when it's time to start finishing.*

HOW TO BUILD A ROUND CONCRETE PATIO

Establish layout lines for the site excavation using batterboards, mason's string, and inverted marking paint. Set the lines so they reach at least 12" beyond the work area on all sides. Plan for the gravel base to extend 12" beyond the slab. Use two pairs of perpendicular batterboards with strings to establish the centerpoint of a round patio (where the strings intersect). To create a rough outline for the patio excavation, drive a stake at the centerpoint and then attach a string to the top of the stake. Tape the other end of the string to a can of inverted marking paint so the distance from the stake to the can equals the radius of the circle, including the gravel base; mark the outline.

Cut the sod on the perimeter of the excavation area to define where to dig. For better access, first remove the batterboards (or at least the strings). A lawn edger works well for cutting the outline into the sod (be sure to wear safety equipment).

Story pole

Excavate the site for a 6- to 8"-thick compactable gravel subbase plus any sub-grade (below ground level) portion of the slab. If building next to your house, grade the soil so it slopes away from the house at ⅛" per foot. Measure down from the leveled cross strings with a story pole to gauge the depth as you work. Compact the soil after grading using a plate compactor or a hand tamper.

(continued)

Patio Next to a House ▸

If your patio will butt up to a house or another permanent structure, you should use the house or structure as your starting point for setting slope and establishing a patio layout. Snap a chalk line onto the house foundation at the precise elevation of the top of the finished slab. This should be 1 to 3" below any patio door threshold. You can use this line for reference during the site prep, the concrete pour, and finishing.

1 to 3"

Fill the excavation area with a 4"-thick layer of compactable gravel. Use an upside-down bow or garden rake to move the rock around. Rake the rock until it is level and follows the grade of the soil base.

Use a plate compactor to tamp the first 4" of graded compactable gravel. Add another 2 to 4" layer of gravel until the top surface will compact to the finished level. Use cross strings and the story pole to make sure the subbase is uniform and follows the ⅛" per ft. slope. Tamp until the gravel is compacted and at the correct height relative to your lines.

Set level lines for the form height. Replace batterboards and retie the mason's lines so they are level. If you are making a circular patio, as seen here, add intermediate stakes between the batterboards and the tie lines to divide the circle into at least eight segments. Drop a plumb bob from the point where the lines intersect, and drive a stake at this centerpoint. Use this stake to create a string guide and redraw the patio outline (inset).

Drive stakes for anchoring the forms around the perimeter of the patio, just outside the outline. Drive the stakes deep enough that they will be beneath the tops of the forms. Use a hand maul or sledgehammer to drive the stakes. To prevent them from splitting, use a scrap 2 × 4 as a hammer block to absorb the blows. Drive a stake at each point where a string intersects the patio outline.

Install forms. Here, 7⁄16"-thick pieces of hardboard lap siding have been rip-cut into 3½" strips to make bendable forms. Cut each strip long enough to span three stakes as it follows the patio outline. Screw the strip to the middle stake first, making sure the top is the correct distance down from the layout string. Bend the form to follow the outline and attach it to the other stakes.

Drive stakes behind the forms anywhere where the strips require additional bending or anchoring to follow the round outline. Attach the forms to the stakes. *Note: If you are installing straight 2 × 4 forms, drive screws through the outsides of the stake and into the form boards to make them easier to remove later.*

(continued)

Lay wire mesh over the gravel base, keeping the edges 1 to 2" from the insides of the form. Overlap the mesh strips by 6" and tie them together with tie wire. Prop up the mesh on 2" wire bolsters placed every few feet and tied to the mesh with wire. If required, install isolation board along the house foundation.

Place 4,000 psi concrete in the form, starting at the side farthest from the concrete source. Before pouring, construct access ramps so wheelbarrows can roll over the forms without damaging them, and coat the insides of the form with a release agent or vegetable oil to prevent the forms from sticking. Distribute the concrete with a shovel or masonry hoe. As you fill, hammer against the outsides of the forms to eliminate air pockets.

Screed the surface with a long, straight 2 × 4: have two people pull the board backward in a side-to-side sawing motion, with the board resting on top of the form. As you work, shovel in extra concrete to fill the low spots or remove concrete from high spots, and re-screed. The goal is to create a flat surface that's level with the top of the form.

Float the concrete surface with a bull float: without applying pressure, push and pull the float in straight, parallel passes, overlapping each pass slightly with the next. Slightly tip up the leading edge of the float to prevent gouging the surface. Stop floating once the surface is relatively smooth and has a wet sheen. Be careful not to over-float, indicated by water pooling on the surface. Allow the bleed water to disappear.

Use an edger to shape all edges of the slab that contact the wood form. Carefully run the edger back and forth along the form to create a smooth, rounded corner. Slightly lift the leading edge of the tool as needed to prevent gouging.

Cut a control joint (if required) using a 1" groover guided by a straight 2 × 4. In most cases, you'll need to erect a temporary bridge to allow access for cutting in the center of the patio. Take great care here. Be sure to cut grooves while concrete is still workable. Make several light passes back and forth until the groove reaches full depth, lifting the leading edge of the tool to prevent gouging.

Flatten ridges and create a smooth surface with a magnesium trowel. This will create a smooth surface that takes a finish well once the concrete has dried. Another finishing option is simply to skip the additional floating. Then, before the concrete dries completely, brush lightly with a push broom to create a nonslip "broomed" surface.

Cure the concrete by misting the slab with water, then covering it with a single piece of polyethylene sheeting. Smooth out any air pockets (which can cause discoloration), and weight the sheeting along the edges. Mist the slab and reapply the plastic daily for 1 to 2 weeks.

MORTARED PAVER PATIO

Setting brick or concrete pavers into mortar is one of the most beautiful—and permanent—ways to dress up an old concrete slab patio. The paving style used most often for mortared pavers is the standard running bond pattern, that is also the easiest pattern to install.

Mortared pavers are appropriate for old concrete slabs that are flat, structurally sound, and relatively free of cracks. Minor surface flaws are generally acceptable, however existing slabs with significant cracks or any evidence of shifting or other structural problems will most likely pass on those same flaws to the paver finish. When in doubt, have your slab assessed by a qualified mason or concrete contractor to learn about your options.

Pavers for mortaring include natural clay brick units in both standard thickness (2⅜ inch) and thinner versions (1½ inch) and concrete pavers in various shapes and sizes. Any type you choose should be square-edged, to simplify the application and finishing of the mortar joints. When shopping for pavers, discuss your project with an expert masonry supplier. Areas that experience harsh winters call for the hardiest pavers available, graded SW or SX for severe weather. Also make sure the mortar you use is compatible with the pavers to minimize the risk of cracking and other problems.

Tools & Materials ▸

Stiff brush or broom	⅜ or ½" plywood
Rented masonry saw	Spray bottle
Mason's trowel	Isolation board
Mortar mixing tools	Mortar
4-ft. level	Burlap
Rubber mallet	Plastic sheeting
Mortar bag	Notched board
Jointing tool	Mason's string
Pointing trowel	Straight 2 × 4
Concrete cleaner or	Eye and ear
pressure washer	protection
Brick or concrete	Push broom
pavers	Work gloves

Nothing dresses up an old concrete patio like mortared pavers. The mortaring process takes more time and effort than many finishing techniques, but the look is timeless; and the surface is extremely durable.

HOW TO INSTALL A MORTARED PAVER PATIO

Prepare the patio surface for mortar by thoroughly cleaning the concrete with a commercial concrete cleaner and/or a pressure washer. Make sure the surface is completely free of dirt, grease, oil, and waxy residue.

Mist the concrete with water to prevent premature drying of the mortar bed, and then mix a batch of mortar as directed by the manufacturer. *Tip: Install isolation board along the foundation wall if the paving abuts the house; this prevents the mortar from bonding with the foundation.*

Dry-lay the border pavers along the edge of the patio slab. Gap the pavers to simulate the mortar joints using spacers cut from plywood equal to the joint thickness (⅜ or ½" is typical). Adjust the pavers as needed to create a pleasing layout with the fewest cuts possible. Mark the paver locations on the slab and then set pavers aside.

Begin laying the border pavers by spreading a ½"-thick layer of mortar for three or four pavers along one edge of the patio using a mason's trowel. Lay the first few pavers, buttering the leading edge of each with enough mortar to create the desired joint thickness. Press or tap each paver in place to slightly compress the mortar bed. If necessary, cut bricks with a rented masonry saw.

(continued)

Remove excess mortar from the tops and sides of the pavers. Use a level to make sure the pavers are even across the tops, and check the mortar joints for uniform thickness. Tool the joints with a jointer as you go. Repeat the process to lay the remaining border pavers. Allow mortar to dry.

Option: To conceal the edges of a raised slab, build wood forms similar to concrete forms. Set a gap between the forms and slab equal to the paver thickness plus ½".

Dry lay the field pavers without buttering them. Use the plywood spacers to set the gaps for mortar joints. Cut end pavers as needed with a rented masonry saw. *Tip: Keep the courses straight by setting the pavers along a string line referenced from the border pavers. Remove dry-laid pavers.*

Spacer

Notched screed

Spread and then screed mortar for the field pavers. Trowel on a ½"-thick layer of mortar inside the border, covering only about 3 or 4 sq. ft. to allow for working time before the mortar sets. Screed the mortar to a uniform ½" thickness using a notched board set atop the border pavers (set the interior end on a lumber spacer, as needed).

As you work, check the heights of the pavers with a level or a straight 2 × 4 to make sure all units are level with one another. If a paver is too high, press it down or tap it with a rubber mallet; if too low, lift it out and butter its back face with mortar and reset it. Repeat steps 6 through 8 to complete the paver installation, and then let the mortar bed dry.

Fill the paver joints with fresh mortar using a mortar bag to keep the paver faces clean. Within each working section, fill the long joints between courses first, and then do the short joints between the paver ends. Overfill the joints slightly.

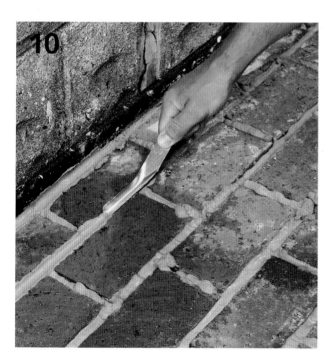

Tool the joints with a jointing tool—again, complete the long joints first and then fill the next section. As the mortar begins to set (turns from glossy wet to flat gray) in each tooled section, scrape off excess mortar with a pointing trowel, being careful not to smear mortar onto the pavers.

Let the mortar joints dry for a few hours, and then scrub the pavers with a wet burlap rag to remove excess mortar and any other residue. Cover the surface with plastic for 48 hours. Remove the plastic, and let the surface cure undisturbed for one week before using the patio.

DECKS

A deck is the perfect way to create a comfortable and practical outdoor living space, whether for cookouts with family and friends or time alone with a cup of coffee and the Sunday paper.

A great deck design makes the best possible use of available outdoor space while meshing gracefully with the beauty and functionality of your home. Decks provide options for almost every space configuration—from wraparound decks that take advantage of small yards by using the space surrounding the house, to detached decks located anywhere in the yard.

This section begins with important information on working with your local building officials and codes to prepare you for obtaining a building permit before you begin construction.

Next, you will find basic deck building techniques showing you how to lay out and install the deck you have designed on paper. Step-by-step instructions explain how to build each component of a basic deck: ledgers, footings, posts, beams, joists, decking, stairs, and railings. The specific tools and materials required for each of these techniques are listed. Also, information regarding the recent trends in alternative decking materials, such as plastic/wood composites and PVC vinyl, are discussed, complete with full how-to steps.

Everything is here to help you design, plan, and build a cost-effective deck that will provide years of enjoyment. All you have left to do now is choose from one of the seven popular designs included here and begin planning your new deck.

IN THIS CHAPTER:

- Deck Building Codes
- Building a Deck: A Step-by-Step Overview
- Installing a Ledger
- Locating Post Footings
- Digging & Pouring Footings
- Installing Posts
- Installing Beams
- Hanging Joists
- Laying Decking
- Building Stairs
- Deck Railing Basics
- Floating Octagon Island Deck
- Deck Benches
- Deck Skirting

DECK BUILDING CODES

Even modest decks are required to meet building codes, and for good reason. An improperly constructed deck can be a safety hazard, eyesore, and can even devalue your home. That's why any deck project should begin with some research into local codes.

Although codes will vary from place to place, most are based on the International Residential Code, which was last updated in 2015. Talk to your local building department; most will supply a list of relevant deck-building codes for your area and will answer questions you might have about compliance on your particular project. If you're using a contractor to build your deck, make sure he is up to date on the latest codes. For more information on deck codes and good building practices, go online and download a free PDF copy of "Prescriptive Residential Deck Construction Guide" published by the American Wood Council (see Resources, page 553).

The following pages show examples of code-compliant building details. This is by no means comprehensive. Use this section as a way to familiarize yourself with the most important code requirements you should know when designing and building your deck.

Post-footing diameter and depth are essential for proper deck support. The requirements differ from locality to locality based on frost level (the footing should be poured below frost level). Be aware that requirements for minimum footing diameter have become more stringent in recent years; footings that support important structural members, such as beams, often need to be 12 in. or 16 in. or even wider in diameter. The 8-in.dia. concrete tube forms you see at the building center are best reserved for fence posts.

Ledger flashing (usually metal or reinforced plastic) must be positioned according to code—wrapping over the top of the ledger and under the building paper and siding—to prevent water from infiltrating between the ledger and the wall.

Beam overhangs or "cantilever" are strictly regulated by code and vary depending on the type of wood and thickness of the beam. Generally, the cantilever should not exceed 1" in length for every 4" of joist span. If you want to design a cantilever in your deck greater than one-quarter of the span of the beam, you will probably need to use steel beams.

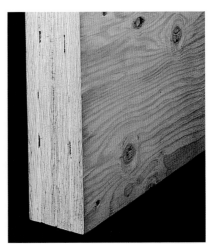

Engineered beams, such as a laminated wood product or steel girder, should be used on decks with very long joist spans, where standard dimension lumber is not adequate for the load. Engineered beams for decks must be rated for exterior use.

Railings are required by local codes for decks more than 30" above the ground and must usually be at least 36" in height. Bottom rails must be positioned with no more than 4" of open space below them. Balusters, whether vertical or horizontal, can be spaced no more than 4" apart.

Stairs must be at least 36" wide, although 48" is preferable. Vertical step risers should be a maximum of 7¾" high—if left open, the opening must not be greater than 4". Treads should be a minimum of 10" deep. Variation among risers, or among treads, should not exceed ⅜". Railing tops should be 34" to 38" above tread nosings, and a grippable handrail is required for stairs of more than four treads. You should also install a landing pad at the base of the stairs of at least 3 ft. × 3 ft.

Beams or joists must either sit on top of posts in an approved saddle, or be notched into a post that is at least 6 × 6". Either 4 × 4" or 4 × 6" lumber can be used for posts 8 ft. high or less (measured to the underside of the beam). Longer posts must be 6 × 6". Joists cannot be attached to posts with through-bolts, even when mortises have been cut into the posts.

Beam assemblies. Laminated deck beams (two or more pieces of dimensional lumber are attached face-to-face) must be fastened together with staggered rows of 10d galvanized nails or 3" deck screws, spaced 16" on center. Beams of three members must be secured from both sides. Exterior construction adhesive is also recommended for the lamination.

Deck footing sizes vary and are calculated based on both the load of the deck and the makeup of the soil. Local codes usually specify a formula for calculating post-footing sizes, but bigger is better. Posts can be connected to footings with a post base hardware or sunk into the cement of the footings (generally, a post base is preferred because it eliminates ground contact that can cause the post to rot).

Ledger and rim joists. The house siding must be removed prior to fastening a ledger to a rim joist. Use either ⅜" or ½" diameter by 4" long galvanized lag screws (check with your local building department) or through-bolts with washers and nuts. The fasteners must be staggered in two rows, spaced appropriately: 2" from ends and top, 5½" between fasteners on 2 × 8 ledger; 6½" on 2 × 10; and 7½" on 2 × 12.

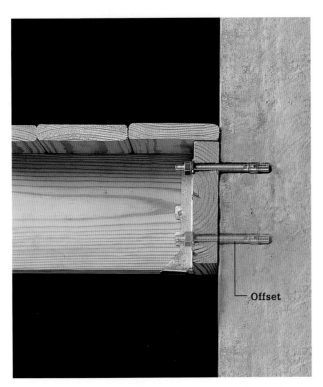

Offset

Ledgers and concrete walls. Ledgers fastened to solid concrete must be attached with bolts and washers driven into approved expansion, epoxy, or adhesive anchors.

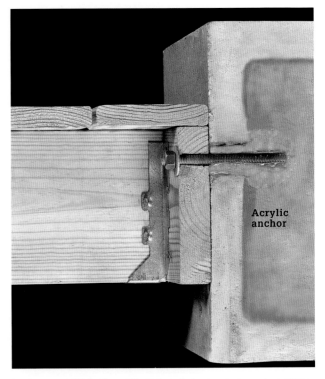

Acrylic anchor

Ledgers and block walls. When fastening ledgers to hollow concrete block walls, secure the attachment bolts to the wall with approved epoxy anchors (also called acrylic anchors).

Railing posts. Code no longer allows for railing posts to be notched where they attach to the deck rim. Posts should be fastened to deck rim joists with pairs of through-bolts and washers and nuts, or attached to the decking with appropriate post base hardware.

Stair lighting. Deck stairs must be illuminated at night from a light located at the top of the landing. The light can be switch-controlled from inside the house, motion-controlled, or used in conjunction with a timer switch.

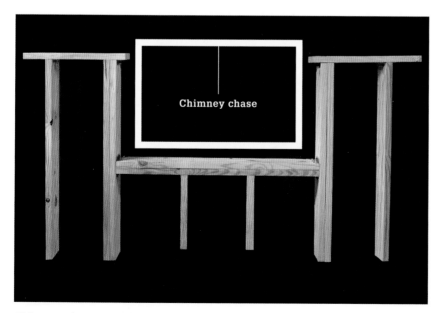

Chimney chase

Chimney chases and bays. When framing a deck around a chimney or bay window, a suitable double header must be added where the ledger is spliced to accommodate the obstruction. The type of header shown here can span a maximum of 6 ft.

Joist

Rim joist

Rim joist connections. Attach rim joists to the end of each joist with a minimum of three #10 × 3" exterior wood screws. Secure the decking to both the rim joist and the perpendicular joist using the same deck screws.

You may toenail joists to a beam only if the deck is attached to the house. Best practice is to secure joists to the beam using a hurricane clip.

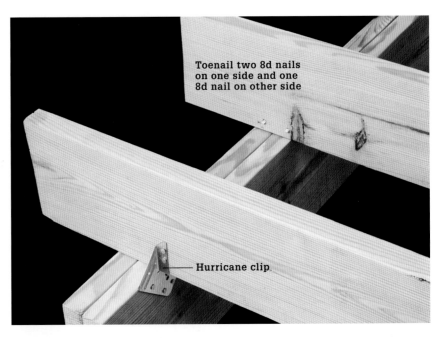

Toenail two 8d nails on one side and one 8d nail on other side

Hurricane clip

Install staggered fasteners on the ledger board using spacing specified in the table below.

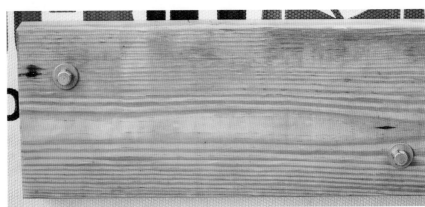

Location of Lag Screws and Bolts in Band Joists and Deck Ledger Boards ▸

	TOP EDGE	BOTTOM EDGE	ENDS	ROW SPACING
LEDGER	≥ 2"	≥ ¾"	≥ 2" & ≤ 5"	≥ 1⅝" & ≤ 5"
DIMENSION LUMBER BAND JOIST	≥ ¾"	≥ 2"	≥ 2" & ≤ 5"	≥ 1⅝" & ≤ 5"

Deck Ledger Attachment Using Screws or Bolts ▸

JOIST SPAN	≤ 6 FT.	> 6 FT. & ≤ 8 FT.	> 8 FT. & ≤ 10 FT.	> 10 FT. & ≤ 12 FT.	> 12 FT. & ≤ 14 FT.	> 14 FT. & ≤ 16 FT.	> 14 FT. & ≤ 18 FT.
				CONNECTOR SPACING O.C.			
½" lag screw with ≤ ½" sheathing	30"	23"	18"	15"	13"	11"	10"
½" lag bolt with ≤ ½" sheathing	36"	36"	34"	29"	24"	21"	19"
½" lag bolt with ≤ 1" sheathing or ≤ ½" sheathing and ≤ ½" stacked washers	36"	36"	29"	24"	21"	18"	16"

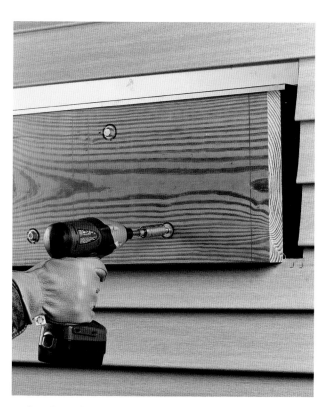

Ledger boards should be pressure-treated lumber that's at least 2 × 8 in size. The ledger board should be the same width as the joists that will be supported by it.

Use the correct size galvanized steel or stainless steel joist hanger. Attach the joist hanger using the fastener specified by the hanger manufacturer. Install a fastener in every round and oblong hole.

One way to attach a beam to a 6 × 6 post is to notch the post and secure the beam using ½" diameter galvanized steel machine bolts and washers. Or, you can mount beams on top of posts with galvanized post cap hardware.

Joists may not be attached to posts with through bolts, even when mortises are cut into the posts to house the joists.

BUILDING A DECK: A STEP-BY-STEP OVERVIEW

BUILDING DECKS: A STEP-BY-STEP OVERVIEW

Deck-building is a project you'll tackle in stages, no matter what deck design you choose. The photos on these next four pages provide an overview of the primary stages involved in a typical deck project. The chapters that follow will explore each of these stages in depth.

In this overview, an old, worn deck is replaced with a slightly larger new deck with approximately 180 square foot of outdoor living space (not including the steps). As decks go, it's average in size and the structural techniques are standard. The deck is supported by a ledger board attached to the rim joist of the home, and three main posts set atop large concrete footings. A second set of smaller posts supports the stairs. The 2 × 2 railing balusters are custom-cut on site and topped with a 2 × 6 cap. The structural elements are all made with pressure-treated pine; the decking and the more visible lumber is also pressure-treated pine, but it is pre-colored to a cedar tone so it does not require a finish coating.

An average size deck built with standard construction practices is still a major undertaking. Be sure to plan well and arrange for plenty of help at key points, such as when digging and pouring the footings and installing the central beam. In most areas any deck attached to the home requires a building permit issued by your municipality, and there likely will be several on-site inspections required. For this deck, inspection of the footing holes was needed to confirm that they are sufficiently wide and that they extended past the frostline (here, a minimum of 42 inches deep). An additional inspection was done once the undercarriage was completed (before the decking was installed), and a final inspection also was required.

Before

Install a ledger to anchor the deck to the house and to serve as reference for laying out footings (pages 166 to 171). Use batterboards and mason's strings to pinpoint the right locations for the footings, and check to make sure the layout is square by measuring the diagonals: if diagonal measurements are the same, the layout is square.

Pour concrete post footings (pages 172 to 183), and install metal post anchors (pages 183 to 188). Set and brace the posts, attach them to the post anchors, and mark the posts for cutting at the point where the beam will be attached (page 189). (continued)

Fasten the beam to the main posts with post caps (pages 190 to 195). Install the outside joists and the header joist, using galvanized nails. Measure between the outer rim joists and then cut and install a front rim joist parallel to the ledger.

Install the internal joists using metal joist hangers at the ledger (pages 196 to 201). Attach the other ends using hangers or nails according to your approved plan.

5

Lay decking boards, and trim them to length after installation (pages 202 to 204). If desired for appearance, clad the structural members with fascia boards (page 204).

6

Build the deck stairs (pages 206 to 209). If three or more stairs are built a grippable handrail is required.

7

Install a railing around the deck and stairway (pages 210 to 219). A railing adds a decorative touch and is required on any deck that is more than 30" above the ground.

INSTALLING A LEDGER

DECKS

The first step in building an attached deck is to fasten the ledger to the house. The ledger anchors the deck and establishes a reference point for building the deck square and level. The ledger also supports one end of all the deck joists, so it must be attached securely to the framing members of the house.

If your deck's ledger is made from pressure-treated lumber, make sure to use hot-dipped, galvanized lag screws and washers to attach it to the house. Ordinary zinc-coated hardware will corrode and eventually fail if placed in contact with ACQ pressure-treating chemicals. For additional strength on large decks—and where the framing structure will permit it—use through-bolts instead of lag screws, tightening down with a washer and nut on the opposite side. Install the ledger so that the surface of the decking boards will be 1 inch below the indoor floor level. This height difference prevents rainwater or melted snow from seeping into the house. Deck fasteners and flashing must be installed precisely according to code. Make sure you know what local codes require and follow them to the letter when installing the ledger.

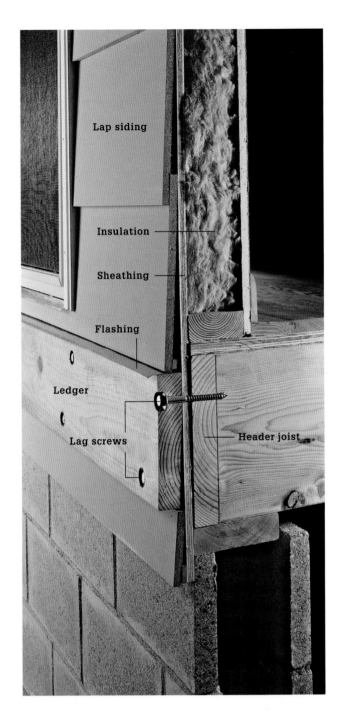

A deck ledger (shown in cross section) is usually made of pressure-treated lumber. Lap siding is cut away to expose sheathing and to provide a flat surface for attaching the ledger. Galvanized flashing tucked under siding prevents moisture damage to wood. Countersunk ½ × 4" lag screws hold ledger to header joist inside house. If there is access to the space behind the header joist, such as in an unfinished basement, attach the ledger with carriage bolts, washers, and nuts.

Tools & Materials ▸

For all surfaces:
Pressure-treated lumber
2 × 4s for braces
Drill and bits
Galvanized (triple zinc plated)
    lag screws and 1⅜" washers
Silicone caulk
Pencil
Pry bar

Z-flashing
    (galvanized steel or plastic)
Level
Circular saw
Caulk gun
8d galvanized common nails
Hammer
Ratchet wrench or impact driver
Building paper or moisture barrier

Work gloves
Eye and ear protection
Optional:
Wood chisel
Metal snips
Awl
Rubber mallet
Masonry anchors for ½" lag
    screws (for masonry walls)

HOW TO CUT OUT SIDING FOR A LEDGER BOARD

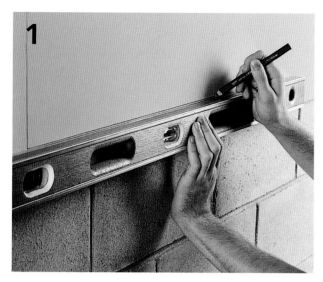

1

Draw an outline showing where the deck will fit against the house, using a level as a guide. Include the thickness of the outside joists and any decorative facing boards that will be installed.

2

Cut out the siding along the outline, using a circular saw. Set the blade depth to the same thickness as the siding, so that the blade does not cut into the sheathing.

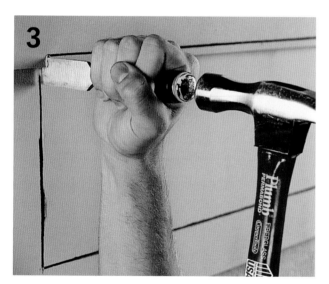

3

Use a chisel to cut the siding at the ends of the cutout or anywhere the circular saw cannot reach. Hold the chisel with the bevel side facing into the cutout area. Use a claw hammer to pry off the siding and a pry bar as necessary to pop stubborn nails holding siding over the cutout area.

4

Measure and cut the ledger from pressure-treated lumber. Remember that the ledger will be shorter than the overall length of the cutout.

Sizing Your Ledger Opening ▸

A wood ledger board should be made from 2× stock that is pressure treated or naturally rot resistant. Pressure-treated pine is by far the most common material. The ledger should be at least a 2" × 8" width, but it cannot be narrower than the joists that hang from it. Best practice is to use lumber of the same dimension as the joists. When sizing the ledger length, be sure to allow for the metal joist hanger flanges at the end- add at least an inch or two per end for nailing the hangers.

(continued)

Should the lag screws used to attach your ledger board be counterbored? More often than not, deck builders will drill guide holes and counterbore them so the head of each lag screw and its washer is recessed below the exposed surface of the board. Many building inspectors will point out, however, that in most cases a counterbore is unnecessary and its function is purely cosmetic. In fact, by reducing the thickness of the board at the point of attachment you are actually weakening the holding power. A 2 × 8 with a ½ inch deep counterbore will have only 1 inch of wood at the point of attachment. Other than appearance, the only real advantage to counterboring the lag screws is that it allows you to mount joist hangers with the flanges over the screw heads if that is where they fall in your layout.

Self-tapping ledger screws do not require pilot holes or washers and have low-profile heads so they do not interfere with joist hanger installation.

These days, many professional deck builders skirt the issue entirely by using self-tapping ledger screws, which are now allowed by most codes. Typically smaller in diameter and featuring star-drive screw heads, these fasteners can be driven directly into the ledger and rim joist with no pilot holes. They are also made from reinforced metal that has much greater shear strength than the steel used in inexpensive forged lag screws. The low-profile screw heads do not interfere significantly with hanger installation. If you wish to use these screws, check with your building inspector first to make sure they are allowed by your codes and to confirm which size screw they recommend.

HOW TO ATTACH A LEDGER TO A RIM JOIST

Remove the old ledger board if you are replacing a deck. Also inspect and remove any deteriorated wood in and around the ledge installation area. If you are installing a deck where none was previously, create a cutout in the siding (see previous page).

Install a backing of building paper or self-adhesive moisture barrier in the ledger opening, making sure the material is securely tucked behind the siding and it extends past the gap where the rim joist meets the foundation wall. Tuck Z-flashing (galvanized steel or plastic) behind the siding to create coverage for the top of the ledger. Overlap vertical joints in the flashing by at least 4". Friction fit the flashing only—do not penetrate it with fasteners.

DECKS

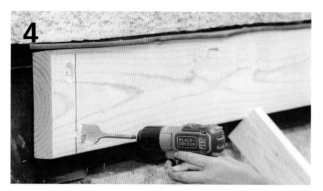

Position the ledger board in the opening, propping it from below with 2 × 4 braces to hold it in place. Tack the ledger in place with 8d galvanized nails.

Attach the ledger board with lag screws. Many codes allow ⅜" dia. lags, but many also require ½" dia. fasteners—check with your local building inspector. The lags should be installed in pairs with the fasteners offset by at least 1" so they are not aligned. Spacing should be no closer than 16" apart. If you are counterboring for the lags (See Sidebar, previous page) drill the counterbore first (top photo) and then the guide hole (bottom).

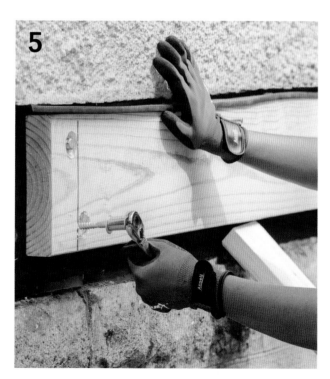

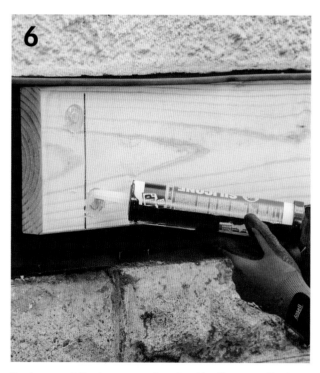

Attach the ledger to the wall with ⅜ or ½ × 4" lag screws and washers, using a ratchet wrench and socket or an impact driver.

Seal around the lag screw heads with silicone caulk. Also seal the crack between the wall and the sides and bottom of the ledger. Apply a full bead of the silicone caulk between the top of the Z-flashing and the top of the cutout in the siding.

HOW TO ATTACH A LEDGER TO A MASONRY FOUNDATION WALL

Measure and cut the ledger. The ledger should be slightly shorter than the overall length of the outline. Mark and drill ½"-deep counterbores (1⅜" dia.) for the lag screws you'll use to attach the ledger, according to your plan. Drill the counterbore first and then drill the smaller guide holes for the lag screw shanks.

Draw an outline of the deck on the wall, using a level as a guide. Center the ledger in the outline, and brace in position. Mark the pilot-hole locations on the wall, using an awl or nail. Remove the ledger.

Drill anchor holes 3" deep into the wall, using a masonry bit large enough for the anchors.

Drive lead masonry anchors for ½" lag screws into the holes, using a rubber mallet.

Attach the ledger to the wall with ½ × 4" lag screws and washers, using a ratchet wrench or impact driver. Tighten screws firmly, but do not overtighten.

Seal the cracks between the wall and ledger with silicone caulk. Also seal the lag screw heads.

HOW TO ATTACH A LEDGER TO STUCCO

Draw the outline of the deck ledger on the wall, using a level as a guide. The ledger should be located so you'll be attaching it securely to the rim joist of your house. Measure and cut the ledger, and drill pilot holes at lag screw locations. Brace the ledger against the wall, and transfer the hole locations onto the stucco, using a nail or awl.

Remove the ledger. Drill guide holes through the stucco layer of the wall, using a ½" masonry bit.

Extend each pilot hole through the sheathing and into the rim joist, using a ⅜" bit. Reposition the ledger and brace it in place.

Attach the ledger to the wall with lag screws and washers, using a ratchet wrench and socket or an impact driver. Seal the lag screw heads and the cracks between the wall and ledger with silicone caulk.

LOCATING POST FOOTINGS

Establish the exact locations of all concrete footings by stretching mason's strings across the site. Use the ledger board as a starting point. These perpendicular layout strings will be used to locate holes for concrete footings and to position metal post anchors on the finished footings. Anchor the layout strings with temporary 2 × 4 supports, called "batterboards". You may want to leave the batterboards in place until after the footings are dug. That way, you can use the strings to accurately locate the J-bolts in the concrete.

Tools & Materials ▸

Tape measure	Plumb bob
Felt-tipped pen	2 × 4s
Circular saw	10d nails
Drill	2½" drywall screws
Screwgun	Mason's strings
Framing square	Masking tape
Masonry hammer	Wire flags or stakes
Claw hammer	Work gloves
Batterboards	Eye and ear protection
Line level	

Mason's strings

Batterboards

Plumb bob

Mason's strings stretched between the ledger and the batterboards are used to position footings for deck posts. Use a plumb bob and wire flags or stakes to mark the ground at the exact centerpoints of footings. Always double check your measurements at this point because any variations can have critical consequences for the rest of the construction."

HOW TO LOCATE POST FOOTINGS

1

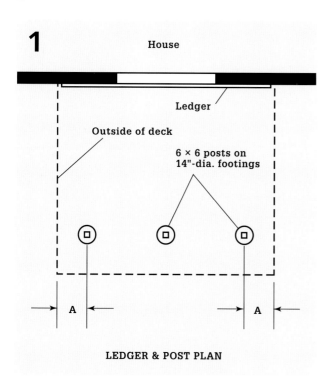

LEDGER & POST PLAN

Use your design plan to find distance (A). Measure from the side of the deck to the center of each outside post. Use your elevation drawings to find the height of each deck post.

2

Cut 2 × 4 stakes for batterboards, each about 8" to 12" longer than post height. Trim one end of each stake to a point, using a circular saw. Cut 2 × 4 crosspieces, each about 2 ft. long.

3

Assemble the batterboards by attaching crosspieces to the stakes with 2½" wallboard screws. Crosspieces should be about 2" below the tops of the stakes.

4

Transfer measurement A (step 1) to the ledger, and mark reference points at each end of the ledger. String lines will be stretched from these points on the ledger. When measuring, remember to allow for outside joists and facing that will be butted to the ends of the ledger. (continued)

Drive a batterboard 6" into the ground, about 2 ft. past the post location. The crosspiece of the batterboard should be parallel to the ledger.

Drive a 10d nail into the bottom of the ledger at the reference point (step 4). Tie a mason's string to the nail.

Extend the mason's string so that it is taut and perpendicular to the ledger. Use a framing square as a guide. Secure the string temporarily by wrapping it several times around the batterboard.

Check the mason's string for square using the "3-4-5 method." First, measure along the ledger 3 ft. from the mason's string and mark a point, using a felt-tipped pen.

Measure the mason's string 4 ft. from the edge of the ledger, and mark with masking tape.

Measure the distance between the marks. If the string is perpendicular to the ledger, the distance will be exactly 5 ft. If necessary, move the string left or right on the batterboard until the distance between the marks is 5 ft.

Drive a 10d nail into the top of the batterboard at the string location. Leave about 2" of nail exposed. Tie the string to the nail.

(continued)

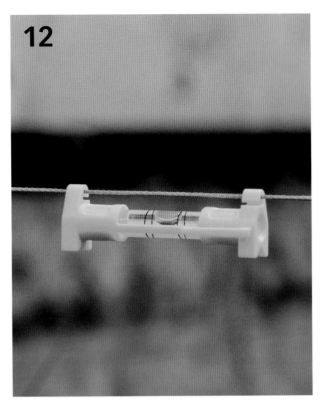

12

Hang a line level on the mason's string. Raise or lower the string until it is level. Locate the other outside post footing, repeating steps 5 to 12.

13

Measure along the mason's strings from the ledger to find the centerpoint of the posts. Mark the centerpoints on the strings, using masking tape.

14

Drive additional batterboards into the ground, about 2 ft. outside of the mason's strings and lined up with the post centerpoint marks (step 13).

15

Align a third cross string with the centerpoint marks on the first strings. Drive 10d nails in the new batterboards, and tie off the cross strings on the nails. The cross string should be close to, but not touching, the first strings.

16

Check the strings for square by measuring distances A-B and C-D. Measure the diagonals A-D and B-C from the edge of the ledger to the opposite corners. If the strings are square, measurement A-B will be the same as C-D, and diagonal A-D will be the same as B-C. If necessary, adjust the strings on the batterboards until they are square.

17

Measure along the cross string and mark the centerpoints of any posts that will be installed between the outside posts.

18

Use a plumb bob to mark the post centerpoints on the ground, directly under the marks on the mason's strings. Drive a stake into the ground at each point. Remove the mason's strings before digging the footings.

DIGGING & POURING FOOTINGS

Concrete footings provide solid support for deck posts. Check your local codes to determine the size and depth of footings required for your area. For all but the smallest decks and some stairways, today's codes usually specify that post footings be at least 12 inches in diameter, and often as big as 16 inches. In cold climates, footings must be deeper than the soil frost line, which can be as deep as 48 inches in the continental US. To help protect posts from water damage, footings are generally poured so that they are at least 2 inches above ground level. You can create footings by pouring concrete directly into a hole with a form on top to create the aboveground portion, or turn to the more common solution of a tube-shaped form that allows you to pour the post you need quickly and easily.

Before digging, consult local utilities for the locations of any underground electrical, telephone, or water lines that might interfere with footings. Many municipalities require that post footing holes.

Tools & Materials ›

Power auger and/or
   posthole digger
Tape measure
Shovel
Reciprocating saw
   or handsaw
Torpedo level
Masonry hoe
Trowel
Long rod (for tamping)
Plumb bob
Utility knife

Concrete tube forms
Concrete (dry bagged
   mix or readymix)
J-bolts
Wheelbarrow
Concrete mixer
   (optional)
Scrap 2 × 4s
Gloves
Dust mask
Eye and ear protection

Post-hole diggers are relatively inexpensive and extremely useful. Digging a large deck footing hole will take a long time, but you can work at your own pace. You can also make the hole any size you wish (power augers are limited to three or four standard bit sizes).

Power Augers ▸

A power auger can be a terrific timesaver, but using one is still a very labor-intensive job—especially if the soil in your project site is full of rocks or roots. With the exception of very loose soil, using a two-person auger generally requires that you raise the tool up and down in the hole as you dig, which takes a good deal or teamwork and some brute strength. Even lifting the auger out of a 4'-deep hole is strenuous enough that good back support is highly recommended, as is hearing protection. One-person power augers are available for rent, but if your hole is 12 inches or wider in diameter, you'll need a two-person tool because you generally can't get bits bigger than 8 inches for one-person augers.

Estimating Concrete for Tube Forms ▸

FOOTING DEPTH	NUMBER OF 60-LB. BAGS FOR EACH SIZE (DIAMETER OF TUBE)				FOOTING DEPTH	NUMBER OF 80-LB. BAGS FOR EACH SIZE (DIAMETER OF TUBE)			
	6"	8"	10"	12"		6"	8"	10"	12"
1 ft.	1	1	2	2	1 ft.	1	1	1	2
2 ft.	1	2	3	4	2 ft.	1	2	2	3
3 ft.	2	3	4	6	3 ft.	2	3	3	4
4 ft.	2	4	5	7	4 ft.	2	3	4	6

HOW TO DIG & PREPARE HOLES FOR FOOTINGS

Dig holes for post footings with a clamshell digger or power auger, centering the holes on the layout stakes. For holes deeper than 35", use a power auger.

Measure hole depth. Local building codes specify depth of footings. Cut away tree roots, if necessary, using a pruning saw.

Pour 2" to 3" of loose gravel in the bottom of each footing hole. Gravel will provide drainage under concrete footings.

Add 2" to hole depth so that footings will be above ground level. Cut concrete tube forms to length, using a reciprocating saw or handsaw. Make sure the cuts are straight.

Insert the tubes into footing holes, leaving 2" of the tube above ground level. Check the tops of the tubes for level and adjust as necessary. Pack soil around the tubes to hold them in place.

HOW TO MIX CONCRETE BY HAND

Empty one or two bags of dry concrete mix into a wheelbarrow or a mortar box. *Note: concrete is sold in both 60- and 80-pound bags so be sure to use the correct bag size when calculating how much you'll need. Blend the dry mix with a masonry hoe to break up any hard clumps.*

Form a hollow in the center of the dry mix, and slowly pour a small amount of water into the hollow. Blend it in using the masonry hoe. Be sure to wear protective gloves and a dust mask.

Add more water gradually, mixing thoroughly until the concrete is firm enough to hold its shape when sliced with a trowel.

HOW TO MIX CONCRETE WITH A CONCRETE MIXER

Eye protection

Particle mask or half-mask respirator

Empty premixed concrete bags into a mortar box or wheelbarrow. Form a hollow in the mound of dry mix, and then pour water into the hollow. Start with ¾ of the estimated water amount per 80-lb. bag.

Work the material with a hoe, continuing to add water until a pancake batter consistency is achieved. Clear out any dry pockets from the corners. Do not overwork the mix. Also, keep track of how much water you use in the first batch so you will have a reliable guideline for subsequent batches.

HOW TO POUR CONCRETE FOOTINGS IN A TUBE FORM

Dig postholes and insert a concrete tube form of the correct size (page 179). The tube form should be stabilized and level, with the top at least 2" above grade. An easy way to stabilize it is simply to drive a single drywall screw through the inside surface of the form and into scrap 2 × 4 braces. You can also backfill around the form with dirt, but it's better to do this after the concrete footing is dry so you can properly tamp the backfill dirt without worrying about damaging the tube form or knocking it out of level. Pour concrete slowly into the tube form, guiding concrete from the wheelbarrow with a shovel. Fill about half of the form, using a long rod to tamp the concrete, filling any air gaps in the footing. Then fill the form to the top, crowning it slightly.

Use a 2 × 4 scrap as a screed to strike off excess concrete and create a relatively smooth surface. The concrete still should crown slightly in the form—this allows it to shed water once it is cured.

Insert a J-bolt at an angle into the wet concrete at the center of the footing. *Note: If you are pouring multiple footings (normally the case) double-check the location and alignment of the J-bolts compared to your layout lines. Adjust the J-bolts if necessary by re-setting them.*

4

Lower the J-bolt slowly into the concrete, wiggling it slightly to eliminate any air gaps and let the concrete fill back in around the bolt shank. *Tip: Wrap a little duct tape around the threaded end of the bolt to protect the part that will be exposed from the wet concrete.*

5

Set the J-bolt so ¾" to 1" is exposed above the concrete.

6

Suspend a plumb bob from your layout lines (re-tie them if you had to remove them to excavate the holes) and confirm that the J-bolts are still in proper location and alignment.

7

Use a torpedo level to make sure the J-bolt is plumb. If necessary, adjust the bolt and repack the concrete. Let the concrete cure, then cut away the exposed portion of tube with a utility knife if its appearance bothers you. Backfill around the footing with dirt, tamping it into the hole with the end of a 2 × 4 as you fill.

INSTALLING POSTS

Posts support the deck beams and transfer the weight of the deck, as well as everything on it, to the concrete footings. They create the above-ground foundation of your deck. Your building inspector will verify that the posts you plan to use are sized correctly to suit your deck design.

Choose post lumber carefully so the posts will be able to carry these substantial loads for the life of your deck. Pressure-treated lumber is your best defense against rot or insect damage. Select posts that are straight and free of deep cracks, large knots, or other natural defects that could compromise their strength. Try not to cut off the factory-treated ends when trimming the posts to length; they contain more of the treatment chemicals and generally last longer than cut ends. Face the factory ends down against the post hardware where water is more likely to accumulate.

Use galvanized metal post anchors to attach the posts to concrete footings. If posts are set directly on concrete, the ends won't dry properly. You'll also have a harder time making the necessary mechanical connection to the footings. Post anchors have drainage holes and pedestals that raise the ends of the wood above the footings and improve drainage. Make sure the posts are installed plumb for maximum strength.

Tools & Materials ▶

Pencil	6d galvanized
Framing square	common nails
Ratchet wrench	10d galvanized joist
and sockets	hanger nails
(or impact driver)	2" drywall screws
Tape measure	Lumber for posts
Power miter saw	Long, straight
or circular saw	2 × 4, 1 × 4s
Hammer	Pointed 2 × 2 stakes
Drill/driver	Safety equipment
Level	Work gloves
Speed square	Eye and ear protection
Metal post anchors	
J-bolts	
Nuts and washers	
for J-bolts	

HOW TO ATTACH POST ANCHORS

Mark the top of each footing as a reference line for installing post anchors. Lay a long, straight 2 × 4 flat across two or three concrete footings, parallel to the ledger, with one edge tight against the J-bolts.

Draw a reference line across each concrete footing, using the edge of a 2 × 4 as a guide. Remove the 2 × 4.

Place a metal post anchor on each concrete footing, and center it over the J-bolt. (continued)

185

Hand-thread a nut into each J-bolt, and use a framing square to make sure the post anchor is positioned square to the reference line drawn on the footing.

Tighten each nut securely with a ratchet wrench or impact driver.

HOW TO SET POSTS

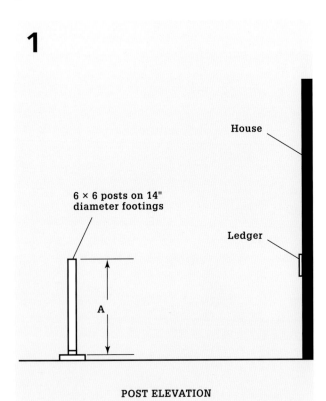

1

6 × 6 posts on 14"
diameter footings

House

Ledger

A

POST ELEVATION

Use the elevation drawing from your design plan to find the length of each post (A). Add 6" to the length for a cutting margin.

Cut posts with a circular saw or power miter saw. Make sure factory-treated ends of posts are square. If necessary, square them by trimming with a power miter saw or circular saw.

Place the post in the anchor and tack it into place with a single 6d galvanized common nail. Do not drive the nail all the way in.

Brace the post with a 1 × 4. Place the 1 × 4 flat across the post so that it crosses the post at a 45º angle about halfway up.

Attach the brace to the post temporarily with a single 2" drywall screw.

Drive a pointed 2 × 2 stake into the ground next to the end of the brace. (continued)

Use a level to make sure the post is plumb. Adjust the post, if necessary.

Attach the brace to the stake with two 2" drywall screws.

Plumb and brace the post on the side perpendicular to the first brace.

Attach the post to the post anchor with 10d galvanized joist hanger nails. (You can also mark the post and then remove it and cut it on the ground, then nail it in place.)

11

Position a straight board with one end on the ledger and the other end across the face of the post. Level the board. Draw a line on the post along the bottom of the board. This line indicates the top of the joists.

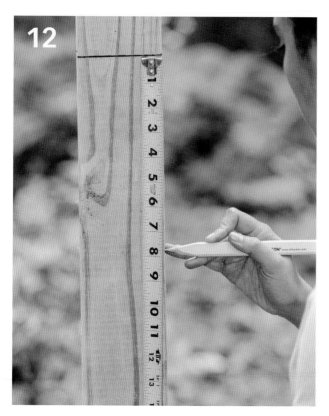

12

From the line shown in step 11, measure down and mark the posts a distance equal to the width of the joists.

13

Use a square to draw a line completely around the post. This line indicates the top of the beam. From this line, repeat steps 11 and 12 to determine the bottom of the beam.

INSTALLING BEAMS

Deck beams attach to the posts to help support the weight of the joists and decking. Installation methods depend on the deck design and local codes, so check with a building inspector to determine what is acceptable in your area.

In a saddle beam deck, the beam is attached directly on top of the posts. Metal fasteners, called post-saddles, are used to align and strengthen the beam-to-post connection. The advantage is that the post bears the weight of the deck.

A notched-post deck requires 6 × 6 posts notched at the post top to accommodate the full size of the beam. The deck's weight is transferred to the posts, as in a post-and-beam deck.

In years past, a third style of beam construction, called sandwiching, was also generally acceptable for deck construction. It consisted of two beams that straddled both sides of the post, connected by long through bolts. Because this method has less strength than the saddle or notched styles, it is no longer acceptable under most building codes.

▶ Tools & Materials ▸

Tape measure
Pencil
Circular saw
Paint brush
Speed square or
   combination
   square
Drill/driver and bits
Ratchet wrench
   and sockets
   or impact driver
Caulk gun
Reciprocating saw
   or handsaw
Pressure-treated
   lumber
Clear sealer-
   preservative
2½" galvanized
   deck screws

10d joist hanger
   nails or 8d
   galvanized nails
Exterior-grade
   construction
   adhesive
Hammer
Wood preservative
Carriage bolts with
   washers and nuts
Silicone caulk
2-part post saddle
   or 1-piece saddle
   hardware
Clamps
Work gloves
Eye and ear
   protection

Deck beams, resting in a notch on the tops of the posts and secured with through bolts and nuts, guarantee strong connections that will bear the weight of your deck.

Fabricating Beams ▸

Support beams for decks usually are fabricated on site by laminating two or three lengthy pieces of dimensional lumber together. The lumber, 2 × 8 or larger, should be exterior-rated. Pressure-treated pine is a good choice. Some deckbuilders cut strips of ½-inch-thick exterior plywood to the same dimension as the beam members and sandwich the plywood between the boards. This increases the dimensional stability of the beam, making it less likely to warp or twist. It also increases the bearing strength and has the added advantage of increasing the total thickness of the beam so it fits neatly into a post saddle designed for 4× lumber (3½-inches actual thickness). However, plywood is not a required element in deck beams and may be left out if only for visual reasons.

To make a laminated beam, select two straight boards of the same dimension, taking particular care to avoid lumber that is twisted or crowned. Lay the boards face to face to see which alignment comes closest to flush on all sides. Apply exterior-grade construction adhesive to one board and lay the mating board onto it. Drive a pair of 10d nails near the end of the assembly to pin the boards together. Then, clamp the beam members together every two to three feet, forcing the boards into alignment as you go, if necessary. Drive 10d nails in a regular, staggered pattern every 12 to 16 inches or so. Flip the beam over and repeat the nailing pattern from the other side. For added strength, cross-nail the beams at about a 30-degree angle periodically. If the beam stock is longer than the required beam length, wait until the beam is assembled before you trim it to length. Finally, apply wood preservative to any cut end before you install the beam.

Tip ▸

Beams may be installed to support the deck joists from below, or you may choose to attach joist hangers to the sides of the beams and hang the joists so the tops are flush with the beam, as seen here.

HOW TO MAKE A POST/BEAM CONNECTION USING A TWO-PIECE SADDLE

Measure along the beam to mark the post locations, making sure the ends of the boards of a doubled beam are flush. Mark both the near and far edges of each post onto the beam.

Use a speed square or combination square to transfer the post marks onto the top and then the opposite face of the beam, allowing you to make sure the post and post hardware align with both faces.

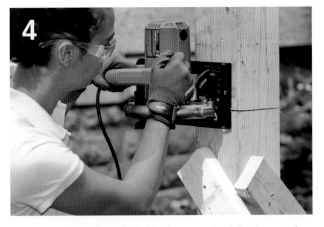

Cut the post to final height after securing it in place. Make two passes with a circular saw and finish with a reciprocating saw or handsaw. Take your time and try and get the cut as smooth and flat as possible.

Fabricate the beam by face-nailing two (or three, depending on your plan) pieces of identically sized dimensional lumber. See previous page.

5

Set both halves of the two-part post saddle on top of the cut post, spread as far apart as they can go. With a helper, lower the beam into position on the post and then slide the two halves of the saddle flush against the side of the beam.

6

Trace along the outside edge of each saddle half to mark their position onto the top of the post. Remove the two-part saddle and the beam.

7

Replace the saddle parts onto the post, aligned with the reference marks you drew. Nail each saddle half to the post by driving joist hanger nails or 8d galvanized nails through the holes in the nailing flanges. Attach saddles on each post on which the beam will bear.

8

Replace the beam in position and secure it to the posts by driving nails through the top nailing flanges of the saddle and into the beam.

DECKS

HOW TO MAKE A POST/BEAM CONNECTION USING A ONE-PIECE SADDLE

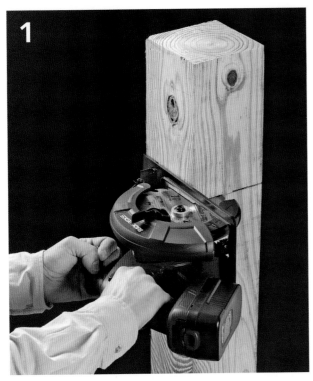

1

Cut the post to final height after securing it in place. Make two passes with a circular saw and finish with a reciprocating saw.

2

Attach the saddle hardware to the top of the post using joist hanger screws, 10d galvanized common nails, or joist hanger nails. You must drive a fastener at every predrilled hole in the saddle hardware.

3

Set the beam into the saddle, making sure the sides of the saddle align with the layout marks on the beam.

4

Secure the beam into the saddle by driving galvanized common nails or joist hanger screws through the predrilled holes in the top half of the saddle.

DECKS

HOW TO INSTALL A BEAM FOR A NOTCHED-POST DECK

Remove 6 × 6 posts from post anchors and cut to finished height. Measure and mark a notch at the top of each post, sized to fit the thickness and width of the beam. Trace the lines on all sides using a framing square.

Use a circular saw to rough-cut the notches, then switch to a reciprocating saw or hand saw to finish. Reattach posts to the post anchors, with the notch-side facing away from the deck.

With someone's help, lift the beam (crown side up) into the notches. Align the beam and clamp it to the post. Counterbore two ½"-deep holes, using a 1⅜" spade bit, then drill ½" pilot holes through the beam and post, using a ½" auger bit.

Insert carriage bolts in to each pilot hole. Add a washer and nut to the counterbore-side of each, and tighten using a ratchet. Seal both ends with silicone caulk. Apply self-sealing membrane to top surfaces of beam and posts if necessary.

HANGING JOISTS

Joists provide support for the decking boards. They are attached to the ledger and header joist with galvanized metal joist hangers and are nailed or strapped to the top of the beam.

For strength and durability, use pressure-treated lumber for all joists. The exposed outside joists and header joist can be faced with composite or cedar boards for a more attractive appearance.

Tools & Materials ▸

Tape measure
Pencil
Hammer
Combination square
Circular saw or power miter saw
Paintbrush
Drill

Twist bits (⅛", ¼")
Pressure-treated lumber
Joist-hanger hardware
10d joist hanger nails
Scrap board spacer
10d and 16d galvanized
    common nails

Clear sealer-preservative
Joist angle brackets
Metal corner brackets
Galvanized metal or stainless
    steel joist hangers
Work gloves
Eye and ear protection

Metal joist hangers attached to rim joists or ledgers are practically foolproof for hanging intermediate deck joists. Look for hanger hardware that is triple-dipped galvanized metal or stainless steel.

HOW TO HANG JOISTS

1

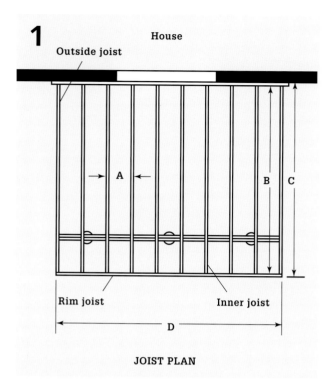

Use your deck plan to find the spacing (A) between joists, and the length of inner joists (B), outside joists (C), and rim joist (D). Measure and mark lumber for outside joists, using a combination square as a guide. Cut joists with a miter or circular saw. Seal cut ends with clear sealer-preservative.

2

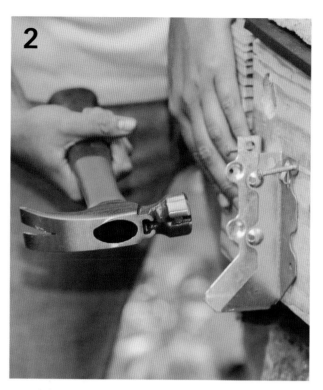

Attach joist hanger hardware near each end of the ledger board, according to your layout. Previous building codes allowed you to face nail the joists into the ends of the ledger, but this is no longer accepted practice. Attach only enough fasteners to hold the hanger in position while you square up the joist layout.

3

Attach the outside joists to the top of the beam by toenailing them with 10d galvanized common nails.

4

Trim off the ends of structural lumber to get a clean straight edge. (continued)

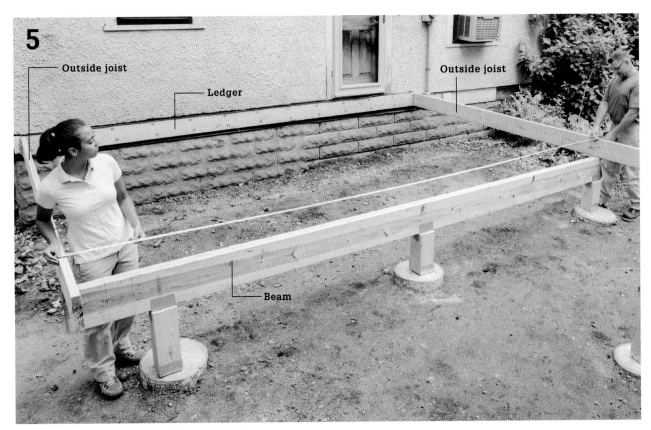

5

Outside joist

Ledger

Outside joist

Beam

Measure and cut the rim joist. Seal cut ends with clear sealer-preservative. Drill ⅛" pilot holes at each end of the rim joist. Attach the rim joist to ends of outside joists with 16d galvanized common nails. For extra reinforcement, add metal corner brackets to the inside corner joints.

6

Finish nailing the end joist hangers, making sure you have a joist hanger nail in every punched hole in the hanger.

7

Measure along the ledger from the edge of the outside joist, and mark where the joists will be attached to the ledger.

8

Draw the outline of each joist on the ledger, using a square as a guide.

9

Measure along the beam from the outside joist, and mark where joists will cross the beam. Draw the outlines across the top of both beam boards.

10

Measure along the header joist from the outside joist, and mark where joists will be attached to the header joist. Draw the outlines on the inside of the header, using a square as a guide. Install the joist hangers on the rim joist.

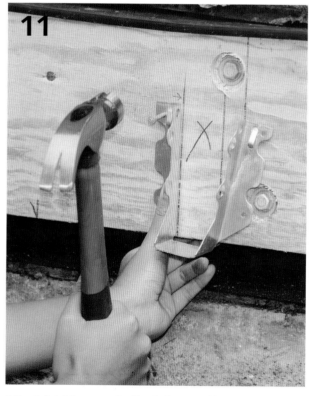

11

Attach joist hangers to the ledger. Position each hanger so that one of the flanges is against the joist outline. Nail one flange to framing members with 10d galvanized joist hanger nails.

(continued)

12

Cut a scrap board to use as a spacer. Hold the spacer inside each joist hanger, then close the hanger around the spacer.

13

Nail the remaining side flange to the framing member with 10d joist hanger nails. Remove the spacer.

14

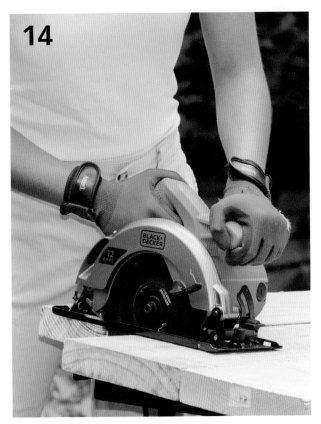

Measure and mark lumber for joists, using a combination square as a guide. Cut joists with a circular saw or power miter saw.

15

Seal cut ends with clear sealer-preservative. Place the joists in the hangers with crowned edge up.

16

Attach the ledger joist hangers to the joists with joist hanger nails. Drive nails into both sides of each joist.

17

Align the joists with the outlines drawn on the top of the beam. Anchor the joists to the beam by toenailing from both sides with 10d galvanized nails.

Alternate Method ▸

Fasten joists to beams using H-fit joist ties for strength and durability.

Option: End nail the joists to reinforce the connections by driving 10d galvanized nails through the rim joist and into the inner joists. If you will not be cladding the rim joists and it will be visible, use 10d galvanized finish nails.

LAYING DECKING

Buy decking boards that are long enough to span the width of the deck, if possible. If you have to use more than one, butt the boards end-to-end over a joist. Stagger butted joints so that they do not overlap row to row.

Install decking so that there is a gap approximately ⅛ inch between boards to provide drainage. You can use a nail as a spacer between rows. Some wood boards naturally "cup" as they age. Lay the boards with the bark side facing down, so that any cupping occurs on the bottom side, and to prevent the board from holding water on the top.

The common installation method for wood decking is shown here. We've limited the discussion to face-screwing boards to joists, but you can nail the boards down as well. However, nailing is rarely used on modern decking because it requires as much work, and nails inevitably pop down the road. Screws are just more efficient. If you do decide to nail boards down, use 10d galvanized common nails, angling the nails toward each other to improve holding power. Composite and plastic deck boards are never nailed down. For a much sleeker appearance, you can choose from the large

Tools & Materials ▸

Tape measure
Circular saw
Screwgun
Hammer
Drill
⅛" twist bit
Pry bar
Chalk line
Jigsaw or handsaw
Decking boards

2½" corrosion-resistant deck screws
Galvanized common nails (8d, 10d)
Redwood or cedar facing boards
Decking spacer tool
Work gloves
Eye and ear protection

number of "invisible" fasteners on the market. The technology for these has come a long way and, whether you're using wood, composite, or another type of deck boards, hidden fasteners are an easy and quick option to screwing the boards down. In any case, always follow the installation instructions and methods recommended by the manufacturer of the product you select.

HOW TO LAY DECKING

Position the first row of decking flush against the house. The first decking board should be perfectly straight, and should be precut to proper length. Attach the first decking board by driving a pair of 2½" corrosion-resistant deck screws into each joist.

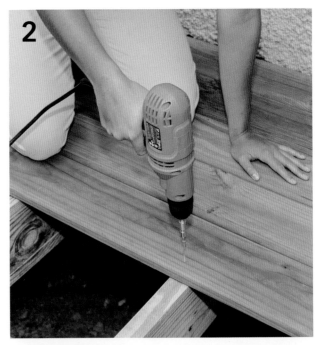

Position remaining decking boards so that ends overhang outside joists. Space boards about ⅛" apart. Attach boards to each joist with a pair of 2½" deck screws driven into each joist.

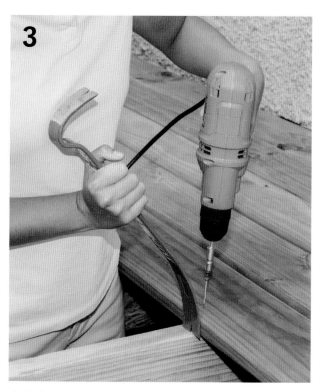

If the boards are bowed, use a pry bar to maneuver them into position while fastening.

Drill ⅛" pilot holes in the ends of boards before attaching them to the outside joists. Pilot holes prevent screws from splitting decking boards at ends.

After every few rows of decking are installed, measure from the edge of the decking board to the edge of header joist. If the measurements show that the last board will not fit flush against the edge of the deck, adjust board spacing.

Adjust board spacing by changing the gaps between boards by a small amount over three or four rows of boards. Very small spacing changes will not be obvious to the eye. *Tip: Although 10d common nails can be used as spacers to keep gaps even, a decking spacer tool (inset) is easier to manage.*

(continued)

Use a chalk line to mark the edge of the decking flush with the outside of deck. Cut off decking, using a circular saw. Set the saw blade ⅛" deeper than the thickness of the decking so that the saw will not cut the side of the deck. At areas where the circular saw cannot reach, finish the cutoff with a jigsaw or handsaw.

8

For a more attractive appearance, clad the exposed structural members of the deck with fascia boards. Miter cut the corners, and attach the boards with deck screws or 8d galvanized nails. Generally, it is preferable to have the decking overlap the top edges of the fascia so you are not creating a gap where debris can collect. If you are using non-wood decking, many decking manufacturers offer non-wood fascia and trim that match the color, style and texture of the decking.

COMPOSITE AND PVC DECKING

Lay composite decking as you would wood decking (pages 202 to 203). Position with the factory crown up so water will run off, and space rows ⅛" to ¼" apart for drainage.

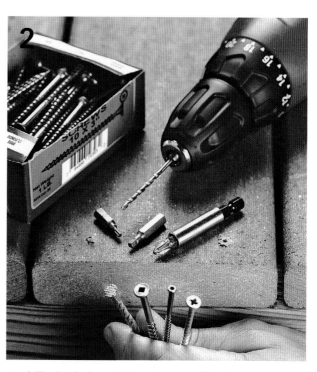

Predrill pilot holes at ¾ the diameter of the fasteners, but do not countersink. Composite materials allow fasteners to set themselves. Use the fastener recommended by the manufacturer.

Cut away for clarity

Alternate Method: Attach composite decking with self-tapping composite screws. These specially designed screws require no pilot holes. If the decking "mushrooms" over the screw head, use a hammer to tap the decking back in place.

Lay remaining decking. For boards 16-ft. or shorter, leave a gap at deck ends and any butt joints, ¹⁄₁₆" for every 20°F difference between the temperature at the time of installation and the expected high temperature for the year.

BUILDING STAIRS

How you build stairs and railings for your deck is perhaps the most tightly regulated portion of the building code related to decks. Whenever you are in doubt about measurements for deck stairs—or wondering if you even need to install stairs in the first place—consult the local building codes or local building inspector. Basically, designing deck stairs involves four calculations:

The number of stairs depends on the vertical drop of the deck—the distance from the deck surface to the nearest ground level.

Rise is the vertical space between treads. The proper rise prevents stumbling on the stairs. Most codes call for a maximum rise of 7¾ inches; a lower rise generally makes it easier to ascend or descend the stairs. The thickness of one tread is added to the space between steps to determine actual rise.

Run is the depth of the treads, and is usually a minimum of 10 inches, although the deeper the tread, the more comfortable the stairs will be. Stair step thickness is also dictated by code and is usually a minimum of 1 inch, although most builders use 2× lumber for stair steps. A convenient way to build step treads is by using two 2 × 6s.

Span is calculated by multiplying the run by the number of treads. The span helps you locate the end of the stairway so that you can properly position the posts.

Specifications for other elements such as the stringers and the method of attachment used to connect stairs to decking are also usually mandated in local codes. For instance, stringers normally have to be at least 1½ inches thick.

Although there are different ways to construct stairs, the same basic code requirements apply to any staircase used with a deck.

Tools & Materials ▸

Tape measure	Drill	Metal post anchors	3" deck screws
Pencil	⅛" twist bit	2 × 12 lumber	or through-bolts
Framing square	1⅜" spade bit	2 × 6 lumber	10d common nails
Level	Ratchet wrench	Metal cleats	16d galvanized common nails
Plumb bob	Caulk gun	¼" × 1¼" lag screws	Silicone caulk
Clamshell posthole digger	Sand	Joist angle brackets	Long, straight 2 × 4
Wheelbarrow	Portland cement	10d joist hanger nails	Pointed stakes
Hoe	Skewable joist hangers	½ × 4" lag screws	Masking tape
Circular saw	Gravel	and 1⅜" washers	Work gloves
Hammer	J-bolts	Metal tread cleats	Eye and ear protection

HOW TO MAKE STAIR STRINGERS

1

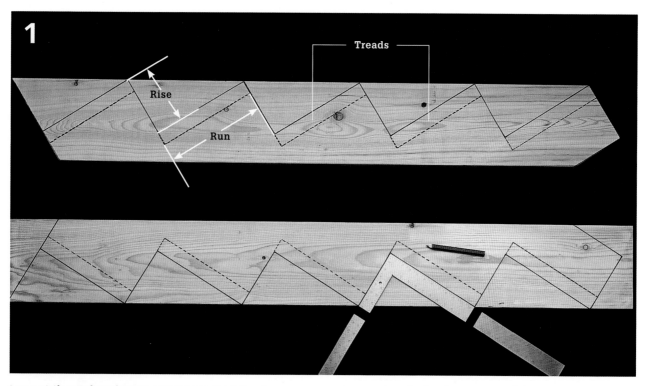

Treads

Rise

Run

Lay out the stair stringers. Use tape to mark the rise measurement on one leg of a framing square, and the run measurement on the other leg. Beginning at one end of the stringer, position the square with tape marks flush to edge of the board, and outline the rise and run for each step. Then draw in the tread outline against the bottom of each run line. Use a circular saw to trim the ends of the stringers as shown. (When cutting the stringers for stairs without metal cleats, just cut on the solid lines.)

2

Attach metal tread cleats flush with the bottom of each tread outline, using ¼" × 1¼" lag screws. Drill ⅛" pilot holes to prevent the screws from splitting the wood.

3

Attach angle brackets to the upper ends of the stringers, using 10d joist hanger nails. Brackets should be flush with the cut ends of the stringers.

HOW TO BUILD BASIC DECK STAIRS

Use the stairway elevation drawings to confirm your design, including the locations of the stair stringers and posts. Use a pencil and framing square to outline where stair stringers will be attached to the side of the deck.

Locate the post footings according to your plan. Lay a straight 2 × 4 on the deck so that it is level and square to the side of the deck. Measure out along the 2 × 4 and use a plumb bob or level to mark the ground at footing centerpoints.

Dig holes and pour the footings for posts. Attach metal post anchors to the footings and install the posts. Check with your building department to find out if 6 × 6 posts are now required. See pages 172 to 183 for more information on locating and pouring footings.

Attach the stair stringers to the deck joist that supports them, using skewable joist hangers designed for use with stair stringers. Here, a prefabricated four-step stringer cut from pressure-treated pine is shown.

5

Attach the bottoms of the stringer to the stair railing posts using several 3" deck screws or through-bolts.

6

Attach a 2 × 4 brace to the bottom ends of the stringers to help prevent racking. You'll need to trim 1½" from the bottom end of any intermediate stringers so the ends of the brace will butt against the inside faces of the outer stringers. Measure from the outside edges of the outer stringers to find the required tread length. Add an inch of overhang to each end if you wish.

7

Begin positioning the treads on the stringers, starting at the top. Two 5/4 × 6" decking boards or two 2 × 6 boards are just the right width to create a stair tread. The top of the tread on the top step should be flush with the decking.

8

Attach the stair treads with 3" deck screws. Especially when working on the outer stringers where the screws are near the ends of the board you should drill pilot holes for the screws.

9

Finish installing the treads, using a spacer such as a 10d common nail to maintain and check the gaps between tread boards. If your staircase has more than three steps you're required to install a railing with a graspable handrail.

DECK RAILING BASICS

Railings must be sturdy and firmly attached to the framing members of the deck. Never attach railing posts to the surface decking. Check local building codes for guidelines regarding railing construction. Most codes require that railings be at least 36 inches above decking. Vertical balusters should be spaced no more than 4 inches apart. In some areas, a grippable handrail may be required for any stairway over four treads. Check with your local building inspector for the building codes in your area.

Tools & Materials ▸

Tape measure
Pencil
Power miter saw
Drill
Twist bits (⅛", ⅜")
1⅜" spade bit
Combination square
Awl
Ratchet wrench
    or impact driver
Caulk gun
Reciprocating saw
Circular saw
Jigsaw with
    wood-cutting blade
Miter saw
Level

Clear sealer-preservative
Railing lumber (4 × 4s,
    2 × 6s, 2 × 4s,
    2 × 2s)
⅜ × 4½" lag screws
    and 1⅜" washers
Silicone caulk
2½" corrosion-resistant
    deck screws
10d galvanized
    common nails
Work gloves
Eye and ear protection

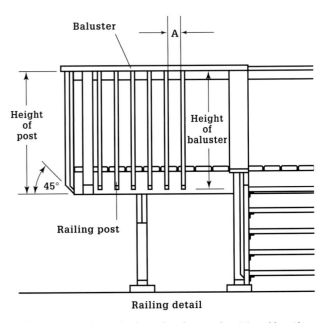

Railing detail

Refer to your deck design plan for spacing (A) and length of railing posts and balusters. Balusters should be placed so that there is no more than a 4" gap between adjacent balusters. Posts should be spaced no more than 6 ft. apart.

Railings are mandatory safety features for any deck that's more than 30" above grade. There are numerous code issues and stipulations that will dictate how you build your deck railings. Consult with your local building inspector for any code clarification you may need.

TYPES OF RAILINGS

Vertical balusters are a traditional look, well suited to a range of home and deck styles, and the most common type of railing construction used on decks. The balusters can be made of wood, metal, or composite to vary the look.

Horizontal railings are often used on low, ranch-style homes. Horizontal railings are made of vertical posts, two or more wide horizontal rails, and a railing cap. There should be no more than 4" between the horizontal railings.

Lattice panels add a decorative touch to a deck. They also provide extra privacy and are the easiest railing filler to install.

Railing Codes ▸

Railings are required by building codes on any deck that is 30" above existing grade, although they are handy even on lower decks. The style of railing is, however, not mandated by code. You can choose from among the many railing styles to match the architectural style of your home, or—as is more commonly done—pick a railing style that complements the deck itself. Wood railings can be fabricated in many different styles; composite railings are usually matched in both color and detailing to the deck color and style. Synthetic railings can even be formed into complex curving shapes as necessary. Codes may require that you add easily gripped handrails on stairs with more than four risers. Always check with your local building department to ensure compliance with local codes.

Preshaped products let you easily build decorative deck railings. Railing products include shaped handrails, balusters, and posts.

HOW TO INSTALL A WOOD DECK RAILING

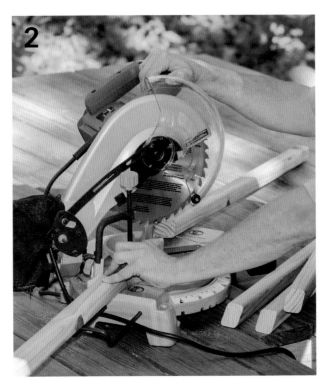

Measure and cut 4 × 4 posts, using a power miter saw or circular saw. Cut the tops of the posts square, and cut the bottoms at a 45º angle. Seal cut ends of lumber with clear sealer-preservative.

Measure and cut the balusters for the main deck railing, using a power miter saw or circular saw. Cut the tops of the balusters square, and cut the bottoms at a 45º angle. Seal cut ends of lumber with clear sealer-preservative.

Drill two ⅜" pilot holes spaced 2" apart through the bottom end of each post. Counterbore each pilot hole to ½" depth, using a 1⅜" spade bit.

Drill two ⅛" pilot holes spaced 4" apart near the bottom end of each baluster. Drill two ⅛" pilot holes at the top of each baluster, spaced 1½" apart.

Measure and mark the position of posts around the outside of the deck, using a combination square as a guide. Plan to install a post on the outside edge of each stair stringer.

Position each post with the beveled end flush with the bottom of the deck. Plumb the post with a level. Insert a screwdriver or the ⅜" drill bit into the pilot holes and mark the side of the deck.

Remove the post and drill ⅜" holes into the side of the deck.

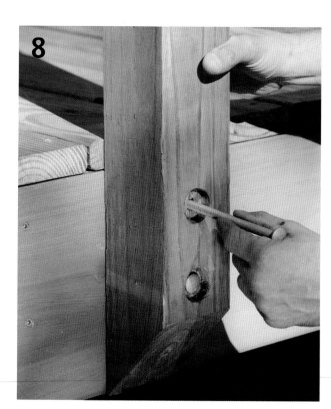

Attach railing posts to the side of the deck with ⅜ × 4½" lag screws and washers, using a ratchet wrench or impact driver. Seal the screw heads with silicone caulk.

Measure and cut 2 × 4 side rails. Position the rails with their edges flush to the tops of the posts, and attach them to the posts with 2½" corrosion-resistant deck screws.   (continued)

10

Join 2 × 4s for long rails by cutting the ends at 45° angles. Drill ⅛" pilot holes to prevent nails from splitting the end grain, and attach the rails with 10d galvanized nails. (Screws may split mitered ends.)

11

Attach the ends of rails to the stairway posts, flush with the edges of the posts, as shown. Drill ⅛" pilot holes, and attach the rails with 2½" deck screws.

12

At a stairway, measure from the surface of the decking to the top of the upper stairway post (A).

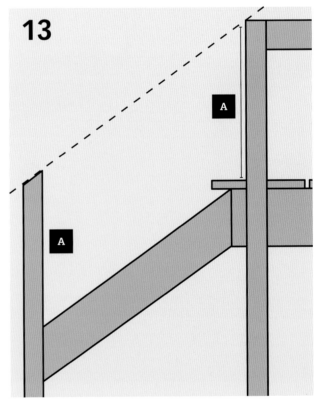

13

Transfer measurement A to the lower stairway post, measuring from the edge of the stair stringer.

14

Rail parallel

Position a 2 × 4 rail against the inside of the stairway posts. Align the rail with the top rear corner of the top post and with the pencil mark on the lower post. Have a helper attach the rail temporarily with 2½" deck screws.

15

Stair rail

Deck rail

Mark the outline of the post and the deck rail on the back side of the stairway rail.

16

Mark the outline of the stairway rail on the lower stairway post.

17

Mark a plumb cutoff line at the bottom end of the stairway rail. Remove the rail. (continued)

18

Extend the pencil lines across both sides of the stairway post, using a combination square as a guide and straightedge.

19

Cut off the lower stairway post along the diagonal cutoff line, using a reciprocating saw or circular saw.

20

Use a circular saw to cut the stairway rail along the marked outlines.

21

Position the stairway rail flush against the top edge of the posts. Drill ⅛" pilot holes, then attach the rail to the posts with 2½" deck screws.

22

Use a spacer block to ensure equal spacing between not to exceed 4 balusters. Beginning next to a plumb railing post, position each baluster tight against the spacer block, with the top of the baluster flush to the top of rail. Attach each baluster with 2½" deck screws.

23

For the stairway, position the baluster against the stringer and rail, and adjust for plumb. Draw a diagonal cutoff line on top of the baluster, using the top of the stair rail ensuring that the space does not exceed 4" as a guide. Cut the baluster on the marked line, using a power miter saw. Seal the ends with clear sealer-preservative.

24

Beginning next to the upper stairway post, position each baluster tight against the spacer block, with the top flush to the top of the stair rail. Predrill and attach the baluster with 2½" deck screws.

25

Position the 2 × 6 cap so that the edge is flush with the rail's inside edge. Drill ⅛" pilot holes and attach the cap to the rail with 2½" deck screws every 12". Drive screws into each post and into every third baluster. For long caps, bevel the ends at 45°. Drill ¹⁄₁₆" pilot holes and nail to the post with 10d nails. (continued)

26

At the corners, miter the ends of the railing cap at 45º. Drill ⅛" pilot holes, and attach the cap to the post with 2½" deck screws.

27

At the top of the stairs, cut the cap so that it is flush with the stairway rail. Drill ⅛" pilot holes and attach the cap with 2½" deck screws.

28

Measure and cut the cap for the stairway rail. Mark the outline of the post on the side of the cap, and bevel cut the ends of the cap. Position the cap over the stairway rail and balusters so that the edge of the cap is flush with the inside edge of the rail.

29

Drill ⅛" pilot holes and attach the cap to the rail with 2½" deck screws driven every 12". Also drive screws through the cap into the stair post and into every third baluster.

WOOD RAILING STYLE VARIATIONS

Vertical baluster railings are a popular style because they complement most house styles. To improve the strength and appearance of the railing, the advanced variation shown here uses a "false mortise" design. The 2 × 2 balusters are mounted on 2 × 2 horizontal rails that slide into mortises notched into the posts.

Horizontal railing best visually complements ranch-style or modern houses with predominantly horizontal lines. For improved strength and a more attractive appearance, the style shown here features 1 × 4 rails set on edge into dadoes cut in the faces of the posts. A cap rail running over all posts and top rails helps unify and strengthen the railing.

Wall-style railing is framed with short 2 × 4 stud walls attached flush with the edges of the deck. The stud walls and rim joists are then covered with siding materials, usually chosen to match the siding on the house. A wall-style railing creates a more private space and visually draws the deck into the home, providing a unified appearance.

Stairway railings are required for any stairway with more than three steps. They are usually designed to match the style used on the deck railing.

FLOATING OCTAGON ISLAND DECK

Sometimes all you need is a simple, easy-to-build platform to complete an otherwise perfect backyard. The project shown here is an "island deck," detached from the house and requiring no ledger attachment.

That means it has the simplest of foundations; a set of pre-cast concrete pier blocks that are simply set in place, making them far easier to work with than poured footings. The piers are cast to a standardized shape and size: 10 inches square and 10 inches high, with slots in the top to accommodate joists and posts. Because the pier blocks are not secured in the ground, the deck "floats." This allows for movement in response to settling and the freeze-thaw cycle of the soil. Floating pier decks meet most local codes—but check yours just to be sure.

This deck is also low enough to the ground that it won't require a handrail (unless, in your particular case, the yard slopes severely off to one side).

Cutaway View

Tools & Materials

Preformed concrete pier blocks (25)
3" galvanized deck screws
Circular saw
Miter saw
Power drill and bits

Stain or sealer
Level
Chalk line
Work gloves
Eye and ear protection

Cutting List

Key	Qty	Size	Part	Material
A	8	1½ x 5½ x 49¾"	Joist	PT pine
B	25	3½ x 3½ x (cut to fit)	Post	PT pine
C	6	1½ x 5½ x 13½"	Spreader	PT pine
D	22	1½ x 5½ x (cut to fit)	Decking	PT pine

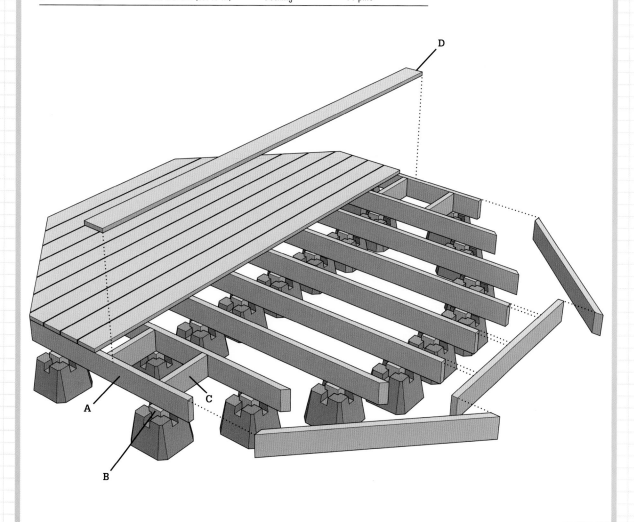

Overall size: 10 × 10 ft.

Framing Plan

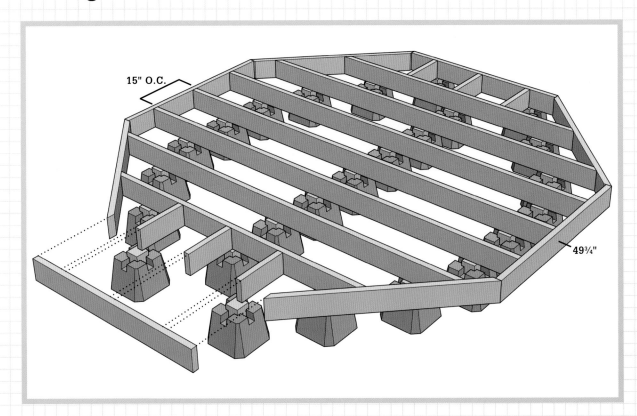

15" O.C.

49¾"

Decking Detail

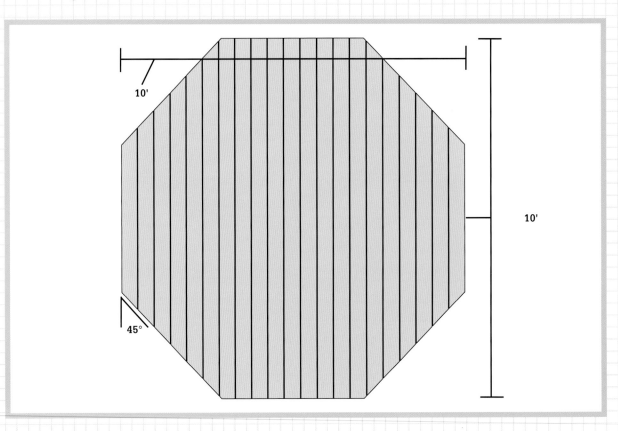

10'

10'

45°

HOW TO BUILD A FLOATING OCTAGON DECK

POSITION THE PIERS

Clear any large rocks or debris from the area over which the deck will be positioned. Measure and mark the locations for the pier blocks. Set out the pier blocks for the center of the deck; you'll start by building the center "box" rectangle off of which all the other joists will be leveled.

Position three rows of three blocks each. The rows for this deck were placed 46½ inches OC row to row, with 1½ inches OC between the pier blocks in each row. Check that each pier block is level, adding or removing dirt underneath to level it as necessary.

BUILD THE CENTER BOX

Set a 10-foot-long 2 × 6 joist on edge in the slots of the three pier blocks along one end of each row. Hold a carpenter's level along the top of the joist as a helper raises or lowers the lowest end of the joist.

Position the piers accurately to ensure a stable deck. They need to be the proper distance from each other and level side to side.

Leveling a joist is a job that calls for a helper. You'll need to focus on the precise measurements for the posts, if any.

Once the posts are cut, it's important to check the joists for level in place. Only screw the joists down when the preliminary "box" for the frame is complete.

(continued)

The first two opposite band joists complete the box.

With the helper holding the joist level, measure any gaps between the bottom of the joist and the pier block sockets.

Cut 4 × 4 posts to match the gap measurements, and place the posts in the pier block sockets. Set the 2 × 6 joist on top of the posts, if any, and check for level again. Adjust as necessary.

Repeat the process with a joist set in the sockets of the outside blocks on the other end of each row. Position the joist as before, and check level with the aid of a helper. Once you've established level along the length of the second joist, make sure the joists are level side to side.

Now cut 2 × 6 band joists for the ends of the floor joists. The band joists will be 49¾ inches long. Measure and mark the band joist so that it will extend equal lengths from both sides of where it is screwed to the floor joists.

Check diagonal measurements of the foundation center box. This must be square because the rest of the deck is built off the box. If the diagonal measurements are off at all, adjust the "box" until they match.

Complete the center of the deck frame by screwing the center joist into place, attaching it to the band joists on either end.

DECKS

Use 3-inch deck screws to screw the band joists to each end of the floor joists to create the center box of the deck floor frame.

Ensure this box is square by measuring diagonally both ways. If the frame is square, the diagonal measurements should be exactly the same.

Position the center joist in this box, cutting 4 × 4 posts as necessary to keep the joist level along its length and in relation to the two outside joists. Screw the band joist into the end of the center floor joist, completing the frame center box. Screw the joists to their 4 × 4 posts in toenail fashion.

COMPLETE THE FRAME

Measure and set the remaining pier blocks in place on both sides of the center frame box. There should be a row of three piers and a row of two piers on each side of the center box, as shown in the Framing Plan (page 222).

Cut and position the outer floor joists in the octagon, leveling them in place as before.

Install the blocking to support the side piers. Once level, screw the outside joist to the 4 × 4 posts (if any) with the joist positioned so that the overhang on both sides is equal.

(continued)

9

Drive 3" screws through the mitered ends to secure the band joists to one another. Use three screws per connection. Complete the outside frame by screwing diagonal band joists onto the mitered ends of the middle floor joists, and to the band joists.

10

Install the decking boards, allowing for overhang that will be trimmed at the end of construction.

Cut the shorter outside floor joists to length. Set them in place in the outside piers, and measure and level as before. Cut 4 × 4s as necessary, and set the outside joists in position. Miter the two outside joist ends 22½°. Screw all joists to the posts in toenail fashion.

Complete the outside frame by cutting the remaining six band joists. Miter the ends of the four diagonal band joists 22½° before installing them. Drill pilot holes and screw the band joists to the spacer blocks using 3-inch deck screws. Install the remaining joists. At each end, the band joists will extend beyond the outside row of pier blocks so no blocks will be visibly exposed at the edge of the deck.

INSTALL THE DECKING

Begin laying the decking at one edge of the octagon, so that the decking lays perpendicular to the floor joists. Place the first deck board into position with its edge aligned with the edge of the band joist. Screw down each decking board using two 3-inch deck screws per joist.

Continue laying the decking, allowing the boards to overhang the edges of the band joists. Maintain a ⅛-inch gap between boards.

When all the decking boards have been screwed down, snap a chalk line along the edges over which the deck boards hang; use a circular saw equipped with a carbide blade to cut the deck board ends so that the decking is flush with the band joists.

Stain, paint, or finish the deck as you prefer, including the rim joists. Add other built-on structures to suit your needs.

Lay the rest of the decking boards by screwing them down to the joists, maintaining a ⅛" spacing between boards.

Use a circular saw equipped with a carbide blade to make quick work of trimming the ends of the deck boards, leaving a clean edge.

DECK BENCHES

A well-designed deck bench can often serve double duty. Installed along the perimeter of a low-lying deck, a long bench adds visual interest to what is often a fairly uninteresting uniform shape. Benches with built-in backs can stand in for railings on higher decks, ensuring the safety, as well as comfort, of everyone.

You can build fully enclosed deck benches to create useful additional storage—a handy way to hide sporting goods and cookout gear when they are not in use. Benches are also the perfect partner to planters, visually linking one or more independent mini-gardens.

Of course, the most important role any deck bench fulfills is that of accessible, durable, and comfortable seating on the deck. If you can measure accurately and operate a miter saw precisely, you can complete this bench in a weekend. It's a good idea to drive screws up through the underside of the deck into the legs so that the screws are completely invisible.

Tools & Materials ▸

Tape measure	2 × 4 lumber	Pressure-treated 2 × 4s	Long, thin spike or awl
Circular saw	2 × 6 lumber	3" galvanized deck screws	Wood glue
Miter saw	3 prefab braces and hardware	2½" decking screws	Finish
Power drill	1" spade bit	5 × ⅜" lag screws	Work gloves
4 × 4 lumber	Depth gauge	⅜" lag bolts and washers	Eye and ear protection
1 × 4 lumber	⅜" drill bit	Bar clamps	

Improve the look and comfort of a deck with a built-in bench. Building one is fairly easy, whether you're retrofitting an existing deck or adding one as part of a brand-new platform.

HOW TO BUILD A DECK-MOUNTED BENCH

Cut six 15"-long legs from 4 × 4s. Cut 3 bases from the same material as the legs. Each base should be 4" long.

Place a leg on the worktable with a scrap piece underneath. Mark and drill a 1" hole, ½" deep, 1½" up from the bottom of the leg on the outside face (use a depth gauge on a spade bit). Change to a ⅜" bit to complete the pilot hole, drilling a hole in the center of the larger hole, and through the other side of the leg.

Drill identical base holes on all the other legs. Place a base in position against the inside edges of two legs, aligned with the bottom of the legs. Stick a long thin spike, awl, or other marking device through the hole to mark the location of the pilot holes on each end of the base.

Remove the base and drill ¼" pilot holes into the ends at the marks. Repeat with all the bases and mark each base for the legs it goes with.

(continued)

Measure and cut the leg top plates. These can be pressure-treated 2 × 4s because they won't be visible once the bench is assembled. Cut three plates 16½" long. Make marks on the long edges of the plates 2¾" from each end.

Complete the leg assemblies by aligning the edge marks on each top plate with the outside edges of the legs, and drilling two pilot holes through the top of the plate into each leg. Attach the plates to the legs with 3" screws.

Cut three 2 × 6s, each exactly 6 ft. long, for the seat. Lay them side by side, clamped together with the ends aligned. Mark the leg positions across the boards. The end leg units should be 2" from each end. The center leg unit should be centered along the span. *Note: Make attaching the legs to the decking easier and more secure by determining leg position along the deck before attaching them to the seat. Center each leg board on top of a decking board so that you can screw into the center of the board to secure the legs.*

Set the leg assemblies in place, upside down on the 2 × 6s, using the marks for reference. Screw through the bottom of the top plates into the seat boards. Use two 2½" decking screws per 2 × 6, for each leg unit.

9

Cut two 2 × 4 side frame pieces 6'3" long, and two end pieces 19½" long. Miter each edge 45° and dry fit the frame around the outside of the bench seat.

10

Assemble the frame by attaching the end pieces to the ends of the 2 × 6s, and the side pieces to the pressure-treated top plates. Use 3" deck screws to secure the frame pieces in place. Drill pilot holes through the miters and screw the frame pieces to each other.

11

Position the bench on the deck. Mark the leg base locations. Remove the bench and drill pilot holes for each base, down through the base and deck board. Use a spade bit to countersink the holes. Drive ⅜" lag screws down through the bases into the deck boards. Put the bench into position and secure it to the bases using ⅜" lag bolts and washers.

12

For a more finished look, cut plugs from the same wood as the legs, and glue them into place to cover the lag bolt heads in the sides of the legs. Sand as necessary, and finish the bench with whatever finish you prefer.

VARIATION: HOW TO BUILD AN EDGE-MOUNTED BENCH

This project is an edge-mounted bench built by using prefab braces (See Resources, page 553) that make constructing the bench much easier. It has a canted back that allows a person to lean back and relax, and is mounted right to the band joist. We've built this as a double bench, with mitered boards on one side so that the benches look like a continuous unit.

Tools & Materials ▸

Miter saw
Tape measure
2 × 6 Lumber
2 × 4 Lumber
1" screws

2½" deck screws
Power drill & bits
Prefab deck braces and hardware
Work gloves
Eye and ear protection

Attach the first bracket centered along the band joist 6" from where the bench will end. Screw it to the decking and band joist using the 1½" screws and washers provided, screwing through the holes in the bracket.

Attach the second bracket on the band joist, no more than 24" away from the first bracket. Screw two brackets to the adjacent band joist in exactly the same pattern.

Measure and mark six 2 × 6s for the seats and top caps of the benches. The boards should be same width on the inside edge as the band joist, mitered out to the wider back edge 22½°, so that the members of each bench butt flush against each other.

Cut four 2 × 4 back supports 41" long. Miter the top ends 12°. Position each back support in a bracket, mark the 2 × 4 through the holes in the brackets, and drill for the mounting bolts. Attach the back supports with the 2½" bolts supplied, using washers on both sides.

DECKS

Position the top cap on top of the back supports, leaving a ¾" overhang in the back. Drill pilot holes and screw the top caps to the back supports with 2½" deck screws, with the mitered edges meeting on the inside corner between the two bench segments. Screw the seat boards into position the same way, driving the supplied 1" screws up through the bottom of the leg brackets, into the 2 × 6 seat boards.

Measure and miter twelve 2 × 4 back and leg boards in the same way as you did the seat and top cap boards, but with the boards on edge. Butt the top back board up underneath the top cap, so that the mitered end is positioned on the inside corner between the two bench segments. Screw it into the back supports using 2½" deck screws. Attach the two remaining back boards in the same way, leaving a 2" gap between the boards.

Position the seat skirt on the front of the bench seat in the same way you positioned the seat boards. Mark and drill pilot holes, and screw the skirt to the front 2 × 6 using 2½" deck screws. Screw the first leg board into position using 1" screws driven through the holes in the bracket, and screw 2 × 4 blocks as spacers.

Attach the back, seat, and leg boards on the adjacent bench section in the same way, making sure that the mitered edges leave a 1" gap between the two bench sections. *Inset: Install added support behind the back boards where the adjacent benches meet using scrap blocking and deck screws.*

DECK SKIRTING

Elevated decks are often the best solution for a sloped yard or a multi-story house. A deck on high can also take advantage of spectacular views. But the aesthetic drawback to many elevated decks is the view from other parts of the yard. The supporting structure can seem naked and unattractive.

The solution is to install deck skirting. Skirting is essentially a framed screen attached to support posts. Skirting effectively creates a visual base on an elevated deck and adds a more finished look to the entire structure. It looks attractive on just about any deck.

There are many different types of skirting. The project here uses lattice skirting, perhaps the most common and easiest to install. But you can opt for solid walls of boards run vertically or horizontally, depending on the look you're after and how much time and money you're willing to spend. However, keep in mind that lattice allows for air circulation underneath the deck. If you install solid skirting, you may need to add vents to prevent rot or other moisture related conditions under the deck. Codes also require that you allow access to egress windows, electrical panels, and other utilities under the deck, which may involve adding a gate or other structure to the skirting.

Regardless of the design, the basic idea behind building skirting is to create a supporting framework that runs between posts, with the skirting surface attached to the framework. Obviously, this provides the opportunity to add a lot of style to an elevated deck. The lattice skirting shown here is fairly easy on the eyes. If you choose to use boards instead, you can arrange them in intriguing patterns, just as you would design a showcase fence for your property. You can use wood skirting of the same species as the decking, or vary the material to create a more captivating look. You can even build in a storage space underneath the deck—a perfect location for lawnmowers, leaf blowers, and other yard equipment.

Tools & Materials ▸

Measuring tape	¾" exterior grade lattice panel
Speed square	1 × 4 pressure-treated lumber
Circular saw	2" galvanized finish nails
Miter saw	Angle and T braces
Power drill & bits	¾" galvanized screws
3" deck screws	Paint or other finish
Work gloves	Eye and ear protection

HOW TO INSTALL DECK SKIRTING

Determine the length of the skirting sections by measuring the space between posts. Measure on center and mark the posts. At corners, measure from the outer edge of the corner post to the center of the next post in line. Determine the height of the skirting by measuring from the top of a post to grade leaving at least 1" between the skirt bottom and ground.

Snap a chalk line 1" above the bottom of the post, and use a speed square to find the angle of the slope. Cut the top and side frame sections for the skirting from 1 × 4 pressure-treated lumber. You can also use cedar or other rot- and insect-resistant material.

Cut the ends of the frame pieces to fit. Assemble the 1 × 4 frame using galvanized angle brackets.

Cut the ¾" lattice to dimensions of the frame, using a circular saw or jigsaw. Align the lattice on the back of the 1 × 4 frame, and screw the lattice to the frame about every 10" using ¾" galvanized screws.

Install each finished lattice skirting section as soon as it is assembled. Align the edges of the frame with the marks you've made on the posts and drill pilot holes through the front of the frame and lattice into the post. Screw the section to the post with 3" galvanized deck screws, using a screw at the top, bottom, and middle of the frame.

Optional: If the length between posts is greater than 8 ft., add stiles in the frame to support extra lattice panels. Cut 1 × 4 stiles to length so that they fit between the top and bottom rails. Screw it in place by using a 4" or larger T brace on the back of the frame. Then nail the lattice in place.

Once the skirting is in place, finish it to match the deck or your house. If you have access to spray equipment, you'll find that lattice can be painted much faster with it than with a brush or roller.

FENCES & WALLS

Crawling across a rolling field or guarding a suburban home, a fence or wall defines space and creates a backdrop for the enclosed landscape. Its materials, style, shape, and colors set a tone that may even tell you something about what you'll find on the other side.

Traditional picket fences conjure up images of cottage gardens and children playing. Post and rail fences often surround rustic landscapes or pastures; long expanses of a white board fence can make you believe there might be horses over the next hill. Privacy fences, such as board and stringer, or security fences, such as chain link, produce images of swimming pools sparkling in the sun.

Landscape walls can serve many purposes: They can define property boundaries, separate living areas within the yard, and screen off unpleasant views or utility spaces. Durable masonry walls, such as glass block, concrete block, stone, or stone veneer, can introduce new textures and patterns into your landscape, while living walls, like the framed trellis wall, can provide beautiful backdrops for your favorite vines or lush border gardens.

Using simple building techniques, the projects in this section offer a wide variety of choices for practical, visually appealing fences and walls. Properly constructed, the fences or walls you build should last decades with little maintenance.

IN THIS CHAPTER:

- Fence & Wall Materials
- Wood Panel Fences
- Picket Fence
- Post & Board Fences
- Split Rail Fence
- Virginia Rail Fence
- Wood Composite Fence
- Vinyl Panel Fence
- Ornamental Metal Fence
- Chain Link Fence & Gate
- Bamboo Fence
- Invisible Dog Fence
- Patio Wall
- Outdoor Kitchen Walls & Countertop
- Dry Stone Wall
- Interlocking Block Retaining Wall
- Timber Retaining Wall

FENCE & WALL MATERIALS

As with most building projects, choosing the right materials for your fence or wall is really a question of priorities. In other words, what do you value most in the finished product: Appearance? Durability? Ease of maintenance? Security? Cost? Ultimately, your decision will involve a combination of priorities (and most likely some compromises). And often the function and style of a fence or wall narrows the choices for you. For example, if you're building a fence for privacy, you can automatically rule out metal fencing. Here's an overview of the most popular fence and wall materials.

WOOD

Wood is still the most commonly used material for fences and is really the only one that allows for custom designs and details. Durability, cost, and appearance have everything to do with the type and quality of wood you choose. For a painted fence and for structural members (posts and stringers) that aren't highly visible on unpainted fences, the best and cheapest option is pressure-treated (PT) lumber. Unfinished, it doesn't look as good as other wood types, but it's strong and highly rot-resistant, and you can't see it once it's painted. Choose PT lumber

rated for "ground contact" for all posts and any pieces that will be within 6 inches of the ground. Kiln-dried lumber (often labeled KDAT, for "kiln-dried after treatment") is less likely to warp or split than surfaced-dry (S-Dry) lumber.

If you want to stain and seal your fence or leave it unfinished to let it weather naturally, your two standard options are cedar and redwood. Both are naturally rot-resistant, depending on the grade of the lumber. Heartwood (or "all-heart") lumber, which comes from the dense center of the tree, is the most resistant to rot and, in the case of redwood, insects. Sapwood comes from the softer outer portion of the tree and is no more resistant to decay than other softwoods, like pine. Most cedar and redwood lumber you'll find is a mixture of heartwood and softwood, therefore offering varying degrees of limited decay resistance. Discuss your project with knowledgeable staff at a good lumberyard; they can suggest appropriate grades for your project and budget (and the local climate). *Note: When structural strength is important, many fence builders recommend using only PT lumber for all fence posts, due to its superior strength and decay resistance over most cedar and redwood lumber.*

For a small, highly visible and decorative fence, you might consider splurging on a sustainably harvested tropical hardwood, such as ipé, ironwood, meranti, or cambera. Choose these products carefully: the wood should be suitably rot-resistant for your application and local climate, and it should come from a supplier certified for sustainable forestry.

ORNAMENTAL METAL

Sold in preassembled panels and precut posts made of steel, aluminum, or iron, ornamental metal fencing has a distinctive, formal look reminiscent of traditional wrought iron fences. Most products come prefinished with tough, weather-resistant coatings, making metal fencing one of the lowest-maintenance types you can buy. Steel and aluminum versions are lighter in weight and less expensive than iron fencing and are readily available through home centers and fencing suppliers. Iron fencing made for easy installation is available through specialty manufacturers and distributors.

Always use galvanized or stainless steel hardware and fasteners when building fences.

CHAIN LINK

Chain link is the ultimate utility fence—durable, secure, and virtually maintenance-free. Made of rust-resistant galvanized steel, chain link fencing comes in ready-to-assemble parts and is easily worked into custom lengths and configurations. Installing chain link is a little more involved than with other types of pre-fab fencing, but the technique is pretty straightforward once you get the hang of it.

WOOD COMPOSITE

Because it's made with wood fibers and plastic, wood composite fencing may be considered an alternative to both wood and vinyl fencing. And it's an environmentally friendly choice to boot. Composite fencing can be made almost entirely from recycled plastic and recycled or reclaimed wood materials (not counting metal brackets and rail stiffeners). Like vinyl, it won't rot and never needs painting. Like wood, it has a solid feel and a non-glare finish. Composite fencing come in ready-to-assemble kits and installs much like many vinyl fence products.

VINYL

Vinyl fencing is popular for its long life, minimal maintenance requirements (essentially none), and the fact that it comes in many styles based on traditional wood fence designs. As such, vinyl is generally considered an alternative to painted wood fencing. Installation of the various post-and-panel fence systems is relatively simple, provided you follow the manufacturers' instructions carefully.

BAMBOO

Bamboo occupies its own category because it's not wood—it's grass—and because it has such a unique decorative quality that can turn any fence into a conversation piece. Most bamboo fences are made with preassembled panels (consisting of size-matched canes tied together with wire) set into a wood framework. You can also find materials for building an all-bamboo fence, or you can cover an existing fence with preassembled panels. Bamboo can be tooled and finished with ordinary tools and materials and is an environmentally friendly material.

FENCE & GATE HARDWARE

All metal hardware and fasteners used for building fences must be corrosion-resistant. This includes hinges, latches, and brackets, as well as screws, nails, and other fasteners. For fastener materials,

Stone, brick, and block are timeless, sturdy fence-building materials that stand the test of time.

choose hot-dipped galvanized or stainless steel (not aluminum) when working with pressure-treated wood; with cedar and redwood lumber, galvanized, stainless steel, and aluminum fasteners offer corrosion resistance, but only stainless steel is guaranteed not to discolor the wood.

STONE

Natural stone is a timeless building material for walls, offering unmatched beauty and durability. Cut stone (called ashlar) is the best choice for most wall applications. Its relatively flat surfaces make it easy to stack for a strong, uniform structure. Other types of stone for building include fieldstone (naturally shaped, irregular stones gathered from fields) and rubble (lower-quality irregular stone pieces used primarily for infill in stone walls).

BRICK & CONCRETE BLOCK

Clay brick and concrete block are equally well suited to outdoor wall projects. By itself, brick is clearly the more decorative choice, while walls made of block are quicker to build (whether mortared or mortarless) and make a great foundation for decorative finishes like stucco or veneer stone.

LANDSCAPE BLOCK

Landscape blocks are manufactured concrete units that come in several different forms. All types are uniformly shaped and sized, making them exceptionally easy to work with. In addition to the familiar blocks made specifically for retaining walls, you can now buy building-type landscape blocks designed for do-it-yourself walls, columns, steps, and planters.

WOOD PANEL FENCES

Prefabricated fence panels take much of the work out of putting up a fence, and (surprisingly) using them is often less expensive than building a board and stringer fence from scratch. They are best suited for relatively flat yards, but may be stepped down on slopes that aren't too steep.

Fence panels come in many styles, ranging from privacy to picket. Most tend to be built lighter than fences you'd make from scratch, with thinner wood for the stringers and siding. When shopping for panels, compare quality and heft of lumber and fasteners as well as cost.

Purchase panels, gate hardware, and gate (if you're not building one) before setting and trimming your posts. Determine also if panels can be trimmed or reproduced from scratch for short sections.

The most exacting task when building a panel fence involves insetting the panels between the posts. This requires that preset posts be precisely spaced and perfectly plumb. In our inset panel sequence (pages 243 to 245), we set one post at a time as the fence was built, so the attached panel position can determine the spacing, not the preset posts.

An alternative installation to setting panels between posts is to attach them to the post faces (pages 246 to 247). Face-mounted panels are more forgiving of preset posts, since the attachment point of stringers doesn't need to be dead center on the posts.

Wood fence panels usually are constructed in either six- or eight-foot lengths. Cedar and pressure-treated pine are the most common wood types used in making fence panels, although you may also find redwood in some areas. Generally, the cedar panels cost one-and-a-half to two times as much for similar styles in PT lumber.

When selecting wood fence panels, inspect every board in each panel carefully (and be sure to check both sides of the panel). These products are fairly susceptible to damage during shipping.

Building with wood fence panels is a great time-saver and allows you to create a more elaborate fence than you may be able to build from scratch.

Tools & Materials ▸

Pressure-treated cedar or redwood 4 × 4 posts
Prefabricated fence panels
Corrosion-resistant fence brackets or panel hangers
Post caps
Corrosion-resistant deck screws (1", 3½")

Prefabricated gate & hardware
Wood blocks
Colored plastic
Tape measure
Plumb bob
Masking tape
Stakes and mason's string
Gravel

Clamshell digger or power auger
Hand tamp
Level
2 × 4 lumber
Circular saw, hand saw, or reciprocating saw
Concrete
Drill
Line level

Clamps
Scrap lumber
Shovel
Hammer
Speed square
Eye and ear protection
Work gloves
Permanent marker
Hinges (3)

PANEL BOARD PATTERN VARIATIONS

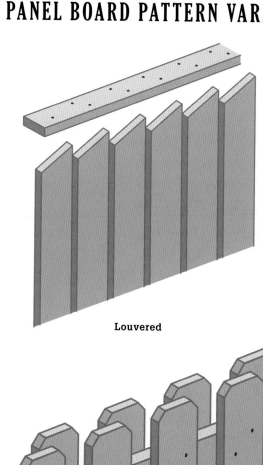

Louvered

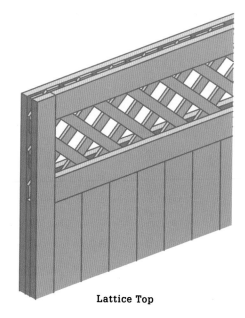

Lattice Top

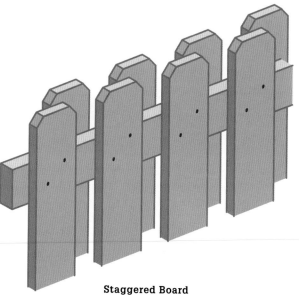

Staggered Board

Stockade

INSTALLING FENCE PANELS

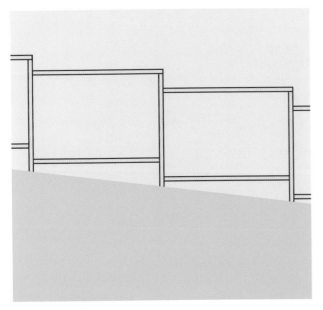

On a sloped lot, install the panels in a step pattern, trying to keep a consistent vertical drop between panels. It is difficult to cut most preassembled panels, so try to plan the layout so only full-width panels are used.

Metal fence panel hangers make quick work of hanging panels and offer a slight amount of wiggle room if the panel is up to ½" narrower than the space between posts.

With some panel styles, the best tactic is to flatten the lower tab after attaching it to the post and then bend it up or down against the panel frame once the panel is in place.

Setting all of the posts in concrete at one time and then installing the panels after the concrete sets has advantages as well as disadvantages. On the plus side, this approach lets you pour all of the concrete at the same time and provides good access so you can make absolutely certain the posts are level and plumb. On the downside, if the post spacing is off even a little bit, you'll need to trim the panel (which can be tricky) or attach a shim to the post or the panel frame (also tricky). Most panel manufacturers recommend installing the posts as you go.

FENCES & WALLS

HOW TO BUILD A WOOD PANEL FENCE

Lay out the fenceline, and mark the posthole locations with colored plastic (inset). Space the holes to fit the fence panels, adding the actual post width (3½" for 4 × 4 posts) plus ¼" for brackets to the panel length. *Tip: For stepped fences, measure the spacing along a level line, not along the slope.*

Dig the first posthole for a corner or end post using a clamshell digger or power auger. Add 6" of gravel to the hole, and tamp it flat. Set, plumb, and brace the first post with cross bracing.

Dig the second posthole using a 2 × 4 spacer to set the distance between posts (cut the spacer to the same length as the stringers on the preassembled fence panels).

Fill the first posthole with concrete or with tamped soil and gravel. Tamp the concrete with a 2 × 4 as you fill the hole. Let the concrete set.

(continued)

5

Install the stringer brackets onto the first post using corrosion-resistant screws or nails. Shorter fences may have two brackets, while taller fences typically have three. *Note: The bottom of the fence siding boards should be at least 2" above the ground when the panel is installed.*

6

Set the first panel into the brackets. Shim underneath the free end of the panel with scrap lumber so that the stringers are level and the panel is properly aligned with the fenceline. Fasten the panel to the brackets with screws or nails.

7

Mark the second post for brackets. Set the post in its hole and hold it against the fence panel. Mark the positions of the panel stringers for installing the brackets. Remove the post and install the stringer brackets, as before.

8

Reset the second post, slipping the ends of the panel stringers into the brackets. Brace the post so it is plumb, making sure the panel remains level and is aligned with the fenceline. Fasten the brackets to the panel with screws or nails.

Anchor the second post in concrete. After the concrete sets, continue building the fence, following steps 5 to 8. *Option: You can wait to fill the remaining postholes with concrete until all of the panels are in place.*

Attach the post caps after trimming the posts to their finished height (use a level mason's line to mark all of the posts at the same height). Install the gate, if applicable; see below.

Installing a Prefab Gate ▸

To install a prefabricated gate, attach three evenly spaced hinges to the gate frame using corrosion-resistant screws (left). Follow the hardware manufacturer's directions, making sure the hinge pins are straight and parallel with the edge of the gate. Position the gate between the gate posts so the hinge pins rest against one post. Shim the gate to the desired height using wood blocks set on the ground (right). Make sure there is an even gap (reveal) between the gate and the latch post, and then fasten the hinges to the hinge post with screws (inset).

HOW TO BUILD A FACE-MOUNTED PANEL FENCE

Set the posts for your project (see page 243). Since spacing is less critical for face-mounted panels than for inset panels, you can install all of the posts before adding the panels, if desired. Lay out the posts according to the panel size, leaving about ¼" for wiggle room. *Note: Spaces before end, corner, and gate posts must be smaller by half the post width, so that the end of the fence panel covers the entire post face.* Set the posts in concrete.

Trim the posts to height. For level or nearly level fences, mark the desired post height on the end posts, allowing for a 2" min. space between the bottom edge of the panels and the ground. Stretch a mason's string between the end/corner posts, and mark the infill posts at the string level. Cut the posts with circular saw, reciprocating saw, or handsaw.

Position the first panel. To mark the height for all of the panels, run a mason's string between the end/corner posts to represent the top of the top panel stringers. Use a line level to make sure the line is level. Also make sure the panel will be at least 2" above the ground when installed. Set the first panel onto blocks so the top stringer is touching the mason's string.

4

Fasten the first panel. Holding the panel in position, drill pilot holes and fasten each stringer to the post with 3½" deck screws. Use two screws at each stringer end. At end, corner, and gate posts, the stringers should run all the way across the post faces.

Install the remaining panels. Repeat steps 3 and 4 to install the rest of the panels. *Tip: If any posts are off layout, resulting in a stringer joint falling too close to the edge of a post, add a 24"-long brace under the butted stringer ends; the brace should have the same thickness as the stringer stock.* Add post caps and other details, as desired.

Variation: Face-mounted privacy fence panels may be fastened to post faces through the panels' vertical frame members. To use this technique, make sure the panel edges are perfectly plumb before fastening, and butt the panels tightly together (or as directed by the manufacturer).

PICKET FENCE

The quintessential symbol of American hominess, the classic picket fence remains a perennial favorite for more than its charm and good looks. It's also a deceptively effective boundary, creating a clear line of separation while appearing to be nothing more than a familiar decoration. This unique characteristic of a welcoming barrier makes the picket fence a good choice for enclosing an area in front of the house. It's also a popular option for separating a vegetable or flower garden from the surrounding landscape.

Building a custom picket fence from scratch is a great do-it-yourself project. The small scale and simple structure of the basic fence design make it easy to add your own creative details and personal touches. In this project, you'll see how to cut custom pickets and build a fence using standard lumber (plus an easy upgrade of adding decorative post caps). As an alternative, you can build your fence using prefab fence panels for the picket infill (see pages 246 to 247). You can also buy precut pickets at home centers, lumberyards, and online retailers to save on the work of cutting your own.

Traditionally, a picket fence is about three to four feet tall (if taller than four feet, a picket fence starts to look like a barricade) with 1 × 3 or 1 × 4 pickets. Fence posts can be spaced anywhere up to eight feet apart if you're using standard lightweight pickets. Depending on your preference, the posts can be visible design elements or they can hide behind a continuous line of pickets. Spacing between the pickets is a question of function and taste: go with whatever spacing looks best and fulfills your functional needs.

Tools & Materials ▸

Tools and materials for setting posts	Hammer
Mason's string	Galvanized or stainless steel finish nails
Line level	Spacer
Circular saw	Speed square
Jigsaw	Eye and ear protection
Drill	Clamps
Power miter saw	Paint brush
Sander	Tape measure
2-ft. level	16d galvanized common nails
Lumber (4 × 4, 2 × 4, 1 × 4)	Wood sealant or primer
Deck screws (3½, 2")	Work gloves
Finishing materials	Pencil
Post caps (optional)	Finish materials

A low picket fence adds curb appeal and a cozy sense of enclosure to a front yard or entry area without blocking views to or from the house.

PICKET FENCE STYLES

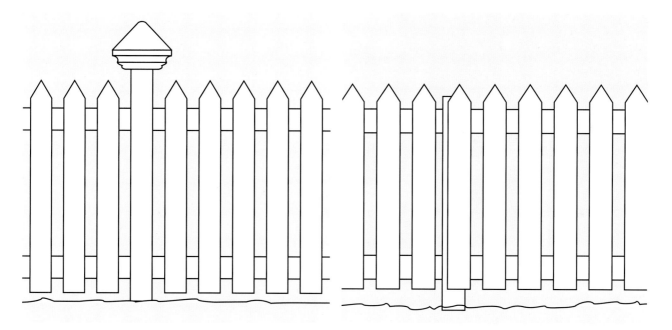

Highlighting the posts (left) gives the fence a sectional look, and the rhythm of the pickets is punctuated by the slower cadence of the posts. To create this effect, mount the stringers on edge, so the pickets are flush with—or recessed from—the front faces of the posts. Hiding the posts (right) creates an unbroken line of pickets and a somewhat less structural look overall. This effect calls for stringers installed flush with—or over the front of—the post faces.

HOW TO BUILD A PICKET FENCE

Install and trim the posts according to your plan (see pages 243 and 246). In this project, the pickets stand at 36" above grade, and the posts are 38" (without the post caps). Set the posts in concrete, and space them as desired—but no more than 96" on center.

Mark the stringer positions onto the posts. Measure down from each post top and make marks at 8 and 28½" (or as desired for your design). These marks represent the top edges of the two stringer boards for each fence section.

(continued)

3

Install the stringers. Measure between each pair of posts, and cut the 2 × 4 stringers to fit. Drill angled pilot holes, and fasten the stringers to the posts with 3½" deck screws or 16d galvanized common nails; drive one fastener in the bottom and top edges of each stringer end.

Calculating Picket Spacing ▸

Determine the picket quantity and spacing. Cut a few pickets (steps 5 to 7) and experiment with different spacing to find the desired (approximate) gap between pickets. Calculate the precise gap dimension and number of pickets needed for each section using the formula shown in the example here.

Total space between posts: 92.5"
Unit size (picket width + approx. gap size):
    3.5" + 1.75" = 5.25"
Number of pickets (post space ÷ unit size):
    92.5" ÷ 5.25" = 17. 62 (round down for slightly
    larger gaps; round up for slightly smaller gaps)
Total picket area (# of pickets × picket width):
    17 × 3.5" = 59.5"
Remaining space for gaps (post space -
    total picket area): 92.5" - 59.5" = 33"
Individual gap size (total gap space ÷
    (# of pickets + 1)): 33" ÷ 18 = 1.83"

4

Cut the pickets to length using a power miter saw. To save time, set up a stop block with the distance from the block to blade equal to the picket length. *Tip: If you're painting the fence, you can save money by cutting the pickets from 12-ft.-long boards of pressure-treated lumber. In this project, the pickets are 32" long; each board yields 4 pickets.*

5

Shape the picket ends as desired. For straight-cut designs, use a miter saw with a stop block on the right side of the blade (the first pass cuts through the picket and the block). If the shape is symmetrical, such as this 90° point, cut off one corner, and then flip the board over and make the second cut—no measuring or adjusting is needed.

Variation: To cut pickets with decorative custom shapes, create a cardboard or hardboard template with the desired shape. Trace the shape onto each picket and make the cuts. Use a jigsaw for curved cuts. Gang several cut pieces together for final shaping with a sander.

Prime or seal all surfaces of the posts, stringers, and pickets; and then add at least one coat of finish (paint, stain, or sealer), as desired. This will help protect even the unexposed surfaces from rot.

Set up a string line to guide the picket installation. Clamp a mason's string to two posts at the desired height for the tops of the pickets. *Note: To help prevent rot and to facilitate grass trimming, plan to install the pickets at least 2" above the ground.*

Install the pickets. Using a cleat spacer cut to the width of the picket gap, set each picket in place and drill even pairs of pilot holes into each stringer. Fasten the pickets with 2" deck screws. Check the first picket (and every few thereafter) for plumb with a level before piloting.

Add the post caps. Wood post caps (with or without metal cladding) offer an easy way to dress up plain posts while protecting the end grain from water. Install caps with galvanized or stainless steel finish nails, or as directed by the manufacturer. Apply the final finish coat or touch-ups to the entire fence.

POST & BOARD FENCES

Post and board fences include an endless variety of simple designs in which widely spaced square or round posts support several horizontal boards. This type of fence has been around since the early 1700s, when it began to be praised for its efficient use of lumber and land and its refined appearance. The post and board is still a great design today. Even in a contemporary suburban setting, a classic, white three- or four-board fence evokes the stately elegance of a horse farm or the welcoming, down-home feel of a farmhouse fence bordering a country lane.

Another desirable quality of post and board fencing is its ease in conforming to slopes and rolling ground. In fact, it often looks best when the fence rises and dips with ground contours. Of course, you can also build the fence so it's level across the top by trimming the posts along a level line. Traditional agricultural versions of post and board fences typically include three to five boards spaced evenly apart or as needed to contain livestock. If you like the look of widely spaced boards but need a more complete barrier for pets, cover the back side of the fence with galvanized wire fencing, which is relatively unnoticeable behind the bold lines of the fence boards. You can also use the basic post

and board structure to create any number of custom designs. The fence styles shown in the following pages are just a sampling of what you can build using the basic construction technique for post and board fences.

Tools & Materials ›

Tools and materials for setting posts	Primer and paint or stain
Mason's string	3" stainless steel screws
Line level	Combination square
Circular saw	Eye and ear protection
Speed square	Lumber (1 × 6, 1 × 4,
Clamps	2 × 6, 1 × 3)
Circular saw	Deck screws
Drill	(2", 2½", 3½")
4 × 4 posts	8d galvanized nails
Finishing materials	Scrap 2 × 4
Bar clamps	Work gloves
Chisel	Pencil
Post levels	

A low post and board fence, like traditional picket fencing, is both decorative and functional, creating a modest enclosure without blocking views. The same basic fence made taller and with tighter board spacing becomes an attractive privacy screen or security fence.

HOW TO BUILD A CLASSIC POST & BOARD FENCE

Set the posts in concrete, following the desired spacing. Laying out the posts at 96" on center allows for efficient use of lumber. For smaller boards, such as 1 × 4s and smaller, set posts closer together for better rigidity.

Trim and shape the posts with a circular saw. For a contoured fence, measure up from the ground and mark the post height according to your plan (post height shown here is 36"). For a level fence, mark the post heights with a level string. If desired, cut a 45° chamfer on the post tops using a speed square as an edge guide to ensure straight cuts. Prime and paint (or stain and seal) the posts.

Mark the board locations by measuring down from the top of each post and making a mark representing the top edge of each board. The traditional three-board design employs even spacing between boards. Use a speed square to draw a line across the front faces of the posts at each height mark. Mark the post centers on alternate posts using a combination square or speed square and pencil. For strength, it's best to stagger the boards so that butted end joints occur at every other post (this requires 16-ft. boards for posts set 8 ft. apart). The centerlines represent the location of each butted joint.

(continued)

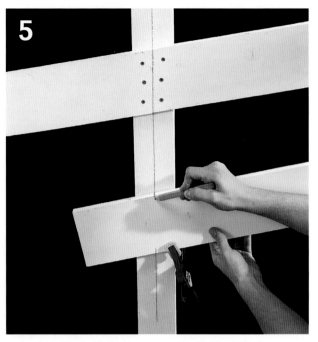

Install 1 × 6 boards. Measure and mark each board for length, and then cut it to size. Clamp the board to the posts, following the height and center marks. Drill pilot holes and fasten each board end with three 2½" deck screws or 8d galvanized box nails. Use three fasteners where long boards pass over posts as well.

Mark for mitered butt joints at changes in elevation. To mark the miters on contoured fences, draw long centerlines onto the posts. Position an uncut board over the posts at the proper height, and then mark where the top and bottom edges meet the centerline. Connect the marks to create the cutting line, and make the cut. *Note: The mating board must have the same angle for a symmetrical joint.*

Variation: This charming fence style with crossed middle boards calls for a simple alteration of the classic three-board fence. To build this version, complete the installation of the posts and top and bottom boards, following the same techniques used for the classic fence. *Tip: If desired, space the posts closer together for steeper cross angles.* Then, mark long centerlines on the posts, and use them to mark the angled end cuts for the middle boards. When installed, the middle boards lap over each other, creating a slight bow in the center that adds interest to the overall look.

HOW TO BUILD A NOTCHED POST & BOARD FENCE

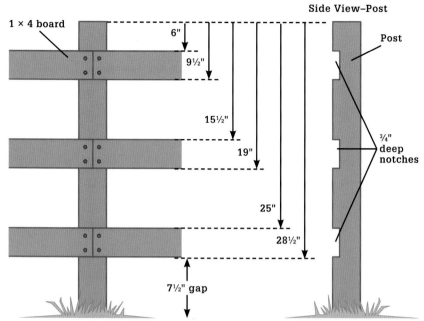

1 × 4 board

6"

9½"

15½"

19"

25"

28½"

7½" gap

Side View–Post

Post

¾"
deep
notches

The notched-post fence presents a slight variation on the standard face-mounted fence design. Here, each run of boards is let into a notch in the posts so the boards install flush with the post faces. This design offers a cleaner look and adds strength overall to the fence. In this example, the boards are 1 × 4s so the posts are set 6 ft. on center; 1 × 6 or 2 × 6 boards would allow for wider spacing (8 ft.). *Note: Because the notches must be precisely aligned between posts, the posts are set and braced before the concrete is added. Alternatively, you can complete the post installation and then mark the notches with a string and cut each one with the posts in place.*

Cut and mark the posts. Cut the 4 × 4 posts to length at 66". Clamp the posts together with their ends aligned, and mark the notches at 6, 9½, 15½, 19, 25, and 28½" down from the top ends.

Create the notches. Make a series of parallel cuts between the notch marks using a circular saw with the blade depth set at ¾". Clean out the waste and smooth the bases of the notches with a chisel.

Install the posts and boards. Set the posts in their holes and brace them in place using a level string to align the notches. Secure the posts with concrete. Prefinish all fence parts. Install the 1 × 4 boards with 2" deck screws (driven through pilot holes) so their ends meet at the middle of each post.

HOW TO BUILD A CAPPED POST & BOARD FENCE

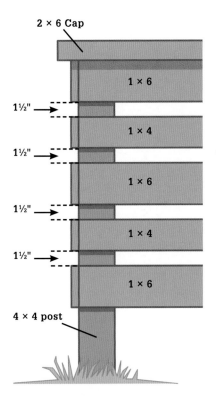

2 × 6 Cap

1 × 6

1½"

1 × 4

1½"

1½"

1 × 6

1½"

1 × 4

1½"

1 × 6

4 × 4 post

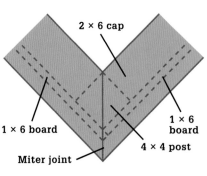

2 × 6 cap

1 × 6 board

Miter joint

1 × 6 board

4 × 4 post

Top View–Detail

A cap rail adds a finished look to a low post and board fence. This fence design includes a 2 × 6 cap rail and an infill made of alternating 1 × 4 and 1 × 6 boards for a decorative pattern and a somewhat more enclosed feel than you get with a basic three-board fence. The cap pieces are mitered over the corner posts. Where cap boards are joined together over long runs of fence, they should meet at a scarf joint—made with opposing 30 or 45° bevels cut into the end of each board. All scarf and miter joints should occur over the center of a post.

FENCES & WALLS

Install and mark the posts. Set the 4 × 4 posts in concrete with 72" on-center spacing (see page 243). Trim the post tops so they are level with one another and approximately 36" above grade. Prefinish all fence parts. Use a square and pencil to mark a vertical centerline on each post where the board ends will butt together.

Install the boards. For each infill bay, cut two 1 × 4s and three 1 × 6s to length. Working from the top of the posts down, fasten the boards with 2½" deck screws driven through pilot holes. Use a 1½"-thick spacer (such as a 2 × 4 laid flat) to ensure even spacing between boards.

Add the cap rail. Cut the cap boards so they will install flush with the inside faces and corners of the posts; this creates a 1¼" overhang beyond the boards on the front side of the fence. Fasten the cap pieces to the posts with 3½" deck screws driven through pilot holes.

HOW TO BUILD A MODERN POST & BOARD PRIVACY FENCE

This beautiful, modern-style post and board fence is made with pressure-treated 4 × 4 posts and clear cedar 1 × 3, 1 × 4, and 1 × 6 boards. To ensure quality and color consistency, it's a good idea to hand-pick the lumber, and choose S4S (surfaced on four sides) for a smooth, sleek look. Alternative materials include clear redwood, ipé, and other rot-resistant species. A high-quality, UV-resistant finish is critical to preserve the wood's natural coloring for as long as possible.

Install the posts, spacing them 60" on-center (see page 243) or as desired. Mark the tops of the posts with a level line, and trim them at 72" above grade. *Note: This fence design is best suited to level ground.* Cut the fence boards to length. If desired, you can rip down wider stock for custom board widths (but you'll have to sand off any saw marks for a finished look).

Fasten the boards to the post faces using 2½" deck screws or 8d galvanized box nails driven through pilot holes. Work from the top down, and use ⅞"-thick wood spacers to ensure accurate spacing.

Add the battens to cover the board ends and hide the posts. Use 1 × 4 boards for the infill posts and 1 × 6s for the corner posts. Rip ¾" from the edge of one corner batten so the assembly is the same width on both sides. Fasten the battens to the posts with 3" stainless steel screws (other screw materials can discolor the wood).

SPLIT RAIL FENCE

The split rail, or post and rail, fence is essentially a rustic version of the post and board fence style (pages 252 to 257) and is similarly a good choice for a decorative accent, for delineating areas, or for marking boundaries without creating a solid visual barrier. Typically made from split cedar logs, the fence materials have naturally random shaping and dimensions, with imperfect details and character marks that give the wood an appealing hand-hewn look. Natural weathering of the untreated wood only enhances the fence's rustic beauty.

The construction of a split rail fence couldn't be simpler. The posts have holes or notches (called mortises) cut into one or two facets. The fence rails have trimmed ends (called tenons) that fit into the mortises. No fasteners are needed. Posts come in three types to accommodate any basic configuration: common posts have through mortises, end posts have half-depth mortises on one facet, and corner posts have half-depth mortises on two adjacent facets. The two standard fence styles are two-rail, which stand about three feet tall, and three-rail, which stand about four feet tall. Rails are commonly available in 8- and 10-feet lengths.

In keeping with the rustic simplicity of the fence design, split rail fences are typically installed by setting the posts with tamped soil and gravel instead of concrete footings (frost heave is generally not a concern with this fence, since the joints allow for plenty of movement). This comes with a few advantages: the postholes are relatively small, you save the expense of concrete, and it's much easier to replace a post if necessary. Plan to bury about a third of the total post length (or 24 inches minimum). This means a three-foot-tall fence should have 60-inch-long posts. If you can't find long posts at your local home center, try a lumberyard or fencing supplier.

Tools & Materials ▶

Mason's string
Shovel
Clamshell digger
   or power auger
Digging bar
   (with tamping
   head) or 2 × 4
Level
Reciprocating saw
   or handsaw
Tape measure
Stakes
Soil
Nails

Precut split rail fence
   posts and rails
Compactable gravel
   (bank gravel
   or pea gravel)
Plastic tags
Lumber and screws for
   cross bracing
Wheelbarrow
Line level
Shovel
Eye and ear protection
Work gloves

A split rail fence looks great as a garden backdrop or a friendly boundary line. The rough-hewn texture and traditional wood joints are reminiscent of homesteaders' fences built from lumber cut and dressed right on the property.

HOW TO BUILD A SPLIT RAIL FENCE

Determine the post spacing by dry-assembling a fence section and measuring the distance between the post centers. Be sure the posts are square to the rails before measuring.

Set up a string line using mason's string and stakes to establish the fence's path, including any corners and return sections. Mark each post location along the path using a nail and plastic tag.

Dig the postholes so they are twice as wide as the posts and at a depth equal to ⅓ the total post length plus 6". Because split posts vary in size, you might want to lay out the posts beforehand and dig each hole according to the post size.

Add 6" of drainage gravel to each posthole. Tamp the gravel thoroughly with a digging bar or a 2 × 4 so the layer is flat and level.

(continued)

5

Set and measure the first post. Drop the post in its hole, and then hold it plumb while you measure from the ground to the desired height. If necessary, add or remove gravel and re-tamp to adjust the post height.

6

Brace the post with cross bracing so it is plumb. Add 2" of gravel around the bottom of the post. Tamp the gravel with a digging bar or 2 × 4, being careful not to disturb the post.

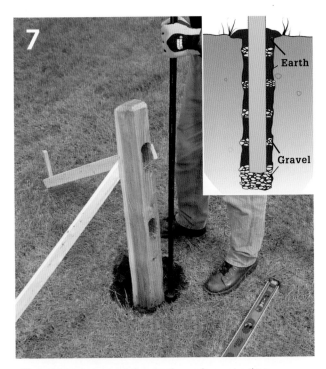

7

Earth

Gravel

Fill and tamp around the post, one layer at a time. Alternate between 4" of soil and 2" of gravel (inset), tamping each layer all the way around the post before adding the next layer. Check the post for plumb as you work. Overfill the top of the hole with soil and tamp it into a hard mound to help shed water.

8

Assemble the first section of fence by setting the next post in its hole and checking its height. Fit the rails into the post mortises, and then brace the second post in place. *Note: Set all the posts at the same height above grade for a contoured fence. For a level fence, see Variation, right.*

Variation: For a fence that remains level across the top, set up a level mason's line strung between two installed fence posts or between temporary supports. Set all of the posts so their tops are just touching the line.

Secure the second post by filling and tamping with alternate layers of gravel and soil, as with the first post. Repeat steps 5 through 9 to complete the fence. *Tip: Set up a mason's string to help keep the posts in a straight line as you set them.*

Custom Details ▸

Custom-cut your rails to build shorter fence sections. Cut the rails to length using a reciprocating saw and long wood blade or a handsaw (be sure to factor in the tenon when determining the overall length). To cut the tenon, make a cardboard template that matches the post mortises. Use the template to mark the tenon shape onto the rail end, and then cut the tenon to fit.

Gates for split rail fences are available from fencing suppliers in standard and custom-order sizes. Standard sizes include 4 ft. for a walk-through entrance gate and 8 or 10 ft. for a drive-through gate. For large gates, set the side posts in concrete footings extending below the frost line.

4

Dig the first pair of postholes using a clamshell digger. Make the holes about three times the width of one post and 18 to 24" deep. Because of the fence's inherent flexibility, the posts don't need to extend below the frost line.

5

6

Place two posts in each hole, leaving enough room for a rail to pass in between them. Hold the posts plumb, and backfill the holes with soil, compacting it moderately to allow for some movement of the posts, if necessary.

Thread a rail through the post pairs, propping it up near the ends with rocks or landscape blocks. Cinch the top ends of the posts together with clothesline or rope to keep them parallel. The rail should extend past the posts an equal distance at both ends.

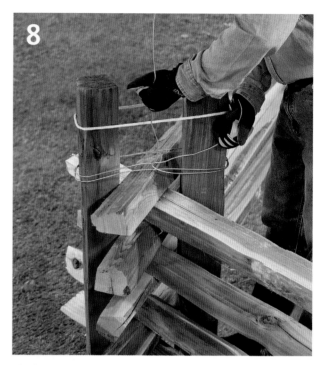

Continue building the fence in the same fashion.
Remember to alternate the rail placement to keep the rails roughly level. You can use chunks of scrap wood from the rail or post material as spacers to help level uneven rails, if desired.

Bind the post pairs with wire once the fence sections are complete. Wrap 9-gauge galvanized wire a couple of times around the post, directly above the top-most rail. Twist the wire ends together a couple of times, leaving longish tails after the twist.

Tighten the wire with a screwdriver. Twist the wire tails around the shaft of a large screwdriver a few times, and then rotate the screwdriver in a circle (as if you're applying a tourniquet) until the wire is tight and begins to bite into the posts. Trim the wire tails and twist them under or drive them into the wood for safety.

Drive the posts in further, if necessary, to stiffen up the post and rail junctures. Protect the tops of the post with a wood block. You can also tamp around the posts with a digging bar to stabilize them. If necessary, trim the post tops of each pair so they are even.

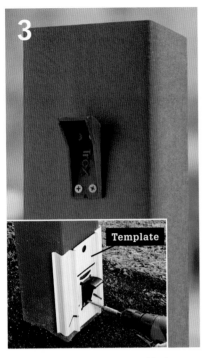

Install the post brackets with the provided screws, using the manufacturer's template (inset) to center the brackets on the post faces. Install the bottom bracket onto each post first, measure up from the bracket and mark the position of the top bracket, and then install the top bracket.

Assemble each bottom stringer by sliding the composite cladding pieces over the sides of the aluminum stringer channel. For short fence sections, see step 5.

Cut a stringer as needed for short sections of fence. Cut the aluminum channel with a hacksaw. Trim the composite cladding pieces to match the channel with a circular saw and carbide-tipped wood blade.

Set the stringer onto the bottom post brackets. Check the stringer with a level. If necessary, remove the stringer and adjust the bracket heights (you may have to adjust top brackets as well to maintain the proper spacing).

Fasten the stringer ends to the post brackets using the provided screws.

Trim the upper outside corner of the first picket so it will clear the top post bracket using a circular saw and carbide-tipped wood blade.

FENCES & WALLS

Install the first picket by slipping its bottom end into the stringer channel. Align the picket to the top post bracket, and fasten the picket to the post with three evenly spaced screws.

Assemble the fence panel by fitting the pickets together along their interlocking side edges and sliding their bottom ends into the stringer channel.

Fit the last picket into place after trimming its top corner to clear the post bracket, as you did with the first panel. Fasten the picket to the post with three screws, as in step 9.

Set the top rail over the ends of the pickets until the rail meets the top post brackets.

Secure the top rail to each top post bracket, using the provided screws, driving the screws through the top of the rail and into the bracket.

Add the post caps, securing them to the posts with galvanized finish nails or an approved adhesive. *Tip: Some fence manufacturers offer more than one cap style (inset).*

FENCES & WALLS

VINYL PANEL FENCE

The best features of vinyl fencing are its resilience and durability. Vinyl fencing is made with a form of tough, weather-resistant, UV-protected PVC (polyvinyl chloride), a plastic compound that's found in numerous household products, from plumbing pipe to shower curtains. A vinyl fence never needs to be painted and should be guaranteed for decades not to rot, warp, or discolor. So if you like the styling of traditional wood fences, but minimal maintenance is a primary consideration, vinyl might just be your best option. Another good option is wood composite fencing (see pages 266 to 269), which comes in fewer styles than vinyl but is environmentally friendly and can replicate the look of wood fencing.

Installing most vinyl fencing is similar to building a wood panel fence. With both materials, it's safest to set the posts as you go, using the infill panels to help you position the posts. Accurate post placement is critical with vinyl, because many types of panels cannot be trimmed if the posts are too close together. Squeezing the panel in can lead to buckling when the vinyl expands on hot days, while setting the posts too far apart results in unsightly gaps.

Given the limited workability of most vinyl panels, this fencing tends to work best on level or gently sloping ground. Keep in mind that installation of vinyl fences varies widely by manufacturer and fence style.

Tools & Materials ▶

Mason's string	Vinyl fence materials
Shovel	(with hardware,
Clamshell digger	fasteners, and
or power auger	decorative accessories)
Circular saw	Pea gravel
Drill	Concrete
Tape measure	Pressure-treated 4 × 4
Hand maul	(for gate, if applicable)
Line level	PVC cement or screws
Post level	(optional)
Clamps or duct tape	Work gloves
Concrete tools	Post caps
Stakes	Eye and ear protection
2 × 4 lumber	

Vinyl fencing is now available in a wide range of traditional designs, including picket, post and board, open rail, and solid panel. Color options are generally limited to various shades of white, tan, and gray.

HOW TO INSTALL A VINYL PANEL FENCE

Lay out the first run of fence with stakes and mason's string. Position the string so it represents the outside or inside faces of the posts (you'll use layout strings to align the posts throughout the installation). Mark the center of the first post hole by measuring in from the string half the post width.

Dig the first posthole, following the manufacturer's requirements for diameter and depth (improper hole dimensions can void the warranty). Add 4 to 6" (or as directed) of pea gravel to the bottom of the hole and tamp it down so it is flat and level using a 2 × 4 or 4 × 4.

Attach the fence panel brackets to the first post using the provided screws. Dry-fit a fence panel into the brackets, then measure from the top of the post to the bottom edge of the panel. Add 2" (or as directed) to represent the distance between the fence and the ground; the total dimension is the posts' height above the ground.

Set up a post-top string to guide the post installation. Using the post height dimension, tie a mason's string between temporary 2 × 4 supports so the string is centered over the post locations. Use a line level to make sure the string is level. Measure from the string to the ground in several places to make sure the height is suitable along the entire fence run.

(continued)

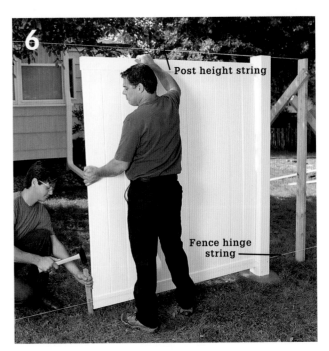

Set the first post. Drop the post in its hole and align it with the fenceline string and height string. Install cross bracing to hold the post perfectly plumb. *Tip: Secure bracing boards to the post with spring-type clamps or duct tape.* Fill the posthole with concrete and let it set completely.

Determine the second post's location by fitting a fence panel into the brackets on the first post. Mark the ground at the free edge of the panel. Measure out from the mark half the post width to find the center of the post hole (accounting for any additional room needed for the panel brackets.)

Complete the fence section. Dig the hole for the second post, add gravel, and tamp as before. Attach the panel brackets to the second post, set the post in place and check its height against the string line. Assemble the fence section with the provided screws (inset). Confirm that the fence panel is level. Brace the second post in place (as shown) and anchor it with concrete. Repeat the same layout and construction steps to build the remaining fence sections.

Cutting Panels ▸

Cut panels for short runs on solid-panel fencing (if straight along the top) per manufacturer's recommendations.

Add the post caps. Depending on the product, caps may be installed with PVC cement or screws, or they may be fitted without fasteners. Add any additional decorative accessories, such as screw caps, to complete the installation.

INSTALLING A VINYL FENCE GATE

Hang the gate using the provided hardware. Fasten the hinges to the gate panel with screws. Position the gate in line with the infill fence panels, and screw the hinges to the hinge post. Install the latch hardware onto the gate and latch post. Close the gate, position the gate stops against the gate rails, and fasten the stops to the latch post with screws.

Post Infills ▸

Reinforce the hinge post with a pressure-treated 4 × 4 inserted inside the post. Set the post in concrete following the same steps used for fence sections. Check carefully to make sure the post is plumb, as this will ensure the gate swings properly. Install the latch post according to the manufacturer's specified dimension for the gate opening.

ORNAMENTAL METAL FENCE

Ornamental metal fencing is so called to distinguish it from the other common metal fence material, chain link, which makes a useful fence, but is far from ornamental. Ornamental metal fences arguably offer the best combination of strength, durability, and visibility of any standard fence type. In general, most ornamental metal fences are modern iterations of traditional iron, or "wrought iron," fencing and offer a similarly elegant, formal look (if perhaps not the same heft and handcrafted character).

Today, most ornamental metal fencing is made with galvanized steel or aluminum. Both are finished with durable powder coatings for weather resistance, and most fence systems are based on modular components designed for easy DIY installation. Comparing the two materials, appearances are virtually identical, while aluminum is lighter in weight. It also tends to carry a longer warranty than steel products, probably because aluminum is a naturally rust-proof material. The other type of ornamental fence is iron, which is available in a variety of forms, including bolt-together modular systems.

Thanks to its exceptional security and visibility, ornamental metal fencing is a very popular choice for upscale yards. That's why most manufacturers offer gates (with welded construction for strength) and code-compliant locking hardware as standard options. Some fence lines include special infill panels and gates with closer picket spacing than standard panels. If you're installing your fence as a pool surround, check the local codes for requirements.

Tools & Materials ›

Mason's string	Lumber and screws
Tape measure	for cross bracing
Shovel	Wheelbarrow
Clamshell digger	Masking tape
or power auger	Marking paint
Clamps or duct tape	Level
Drill	Hacksaw
Concrete tools	Drainage gravel
Post level	Eye and ear
Stakes	protection
2 × 4 or 4 × 4 lumber	Work gloves
Modular fence materials	1 × 3 or 1 × 4 lumber
Concrete	Permanent marker

Ornamental steel, aluminum, and iron fences come in prefabricated panels up to 6 ft. in height and 8 ft. in length, with matching posts and optional decorative details. The most common color option is black (the better to mimic the look of wrought iron), but some products come in white, bronze, and other colors.

HOW TO INSTALL AN ORNAMENTAL METAL FENCE

Lay out the fenceline with stakes and mason's string. Start at the corners, driving stakes a few feet beyond the actual corner so that the strings intersect at 90° (as applicable). Mark the approximate post locations onto the strings using tape or a marker.

Mark the first post location with ground-marking spray paint. Assemble the panel onto the first post and align it in the corner with the mason's strings.

Dig the first posthole, following the manufacturer's specifications for depth and diameter. Shovel drainage gravel into the hole, and tamp it with a 2 x 4 or 4 x 4. Set the post in the hole and measure its height above the ground. If necessary, add or remove gravel until the post top is at the recommended height.

First post

Post level

Plumb and anchor the first post. Position the post perfectly plumb using a post level. Brace the post with cross bracing. Use clamps to secure the bracing to the post. Fill the hole with concrete and let it set.

Drill pilot holes for the brackets into the second post and first panel. Align the fence assembly with the first post and mark for the second post hole. Prepare the post hole as you did in step 3.

(continued)

6

Fill the second posthole with concrete and let it set. Here, we have a temporary brace to hold the post plumb and at the desired height. The first panel, complete with posts on either sides, is now set. Remaining posts along this fenceline can be set by positioning posts with spacers to save time (see tip on this page).

7

Align the second panel on the other side of the corner post. Follow instructions in steps 2 through 5 to set the post and install the panel. Repeat the same process to install the remaining fence sections. You can save time by positioning the posts with spacers (see tip on this page).

Variation: For brick pillar corners, columns, or the side of a house, install manufacturer-provided wall brackets. If wall brackets do not come with the standard installation package of your metal fence, contact the manufacturer.

Spacing Posts ▸

Spacers help you locate the posts without having to measure or install each panel for every post. The panels are then added after the post concrete has set. Create each spacer with two 1 × 3 or 1 × 4 boards. Cut board(s) to fit flush from outside edge to outside edge of the first and second post (once they are set in concrete). Clamp the board in between an anchored post and the next post to be installed. It is best to position spacer boards near the top and bottom of the posts. With the boards in place, the linear spacing should be accurate, but always check the new post with a level to make sure it is plumb before setting it in concrete. Use a level mason's string to keep the post brackets at the same elevation.

HOW TO CUT METAL

Measure and mark panels for cuts. Hold the panel up to the final post in the run and mark the cutting line. Often, designs will not accommodate full panels around the entire fence perimeter.

Cut panels to the appropriate length using a hacksaw, as needed.

Old (and Old-fashioned) Iron Fencing ▶

Traditional iron fencing—commonly called "wrought iron"—has been adorning and securing homes and other buildings for many centuries and is still the gold standard of ornamental metal fencing. The oldest forms of wrought iron fences were made with individually hand-forged pieces, while cast-iron fences were assembled from interchangeable pieces of molded iron. Wrought iron, the material, is a pure form of iron that contains very little carbon. Most modern iron fences are made of a form of steel, not wrought iron.

While new iron fencing can still be made by the hand of a blacksmith, it's also commonly available in preassembled panels and modular posts, much like the steel and aluminum fencing sold at home centers. Some iron fencing must be welded together on-site (by professional installers), while some is assembled with bolts, making it suitable for DIY installation. Many styles of prefab iron fencing can be surprisingly affordable.

If you have your heart set on the timeless look and feel of iron, search online for local fabricators and dealers of real iron fencing. You can also hunt through local architectural salvage shops, where you can find antique iron fence panels, posts, finials, and other adornments. Their condition may not be perfect, but the patina of weathering and marks of use only add to the character of old iron fencing.

Whether it was made yesterday or in the 1800s, iron fencing offers enduring beauty and unmatched durability, making it worth the splurge on a small fence or a front entry gate.

CHAIN LINK FENCE & GATE

If you're looking for a strong, durable, and economical way to keep pets and children in—or out—of your yard, a chain link fence may be the perfect solution. Chain link fences require minimal maintenance and provide excellent security. Erecting a chain link fence is relatively easy, especially on level property. Leave contoured fence lines to the pros. For a chain link fence with real architectural beauty, consider a California-style chain link with wood posts and rails (see pages 283 to 284).

A 48-inch-tall chain link fence—the most common choice for residential use—is what we've demonstrated here. The posts, fittings, and chain link mesh, which are made from galvanized metal, can be purchased at home centers and fencing retailers. The end, corner, and gate posts, called terminal posts, bear the stress of the entire fence line. They're larger in diameter than line posts and require larger concrete footings. A footing three times the post diameter is sufficient for terminal posts. A properly installed stringer takes considerable stress off the end posts by holding the post tops apart.

When the framework is in place, the mesh must be tightened against it. This is done a section at a time with a winch tool called a come-along. As you tighten the come-along, the tension is distributed evenly across the entire length of the mesh, stretching it taut against the framework. One note of caution: it's surprisingly easy to topple the posts if you over-tighten the come-along. To avoid this problem, tighten just until the links of the mesh are difficult to squeeze together by hand.

Instructions for installing a chain link gate are given on page 282. If you're building a new fence, it's a good idea to test-fit the gate to make sure the gate posts are set properly before you complete the fence assembly.

Tools & Materials ›

Supplies for setting posts
Mason's string
Ratchet wrench
Pliers
Hacksaw or pipe cutter
Chain link fence materials and hardware
Duct tape
Tie wire
Circular saw, reciprocating saw, or handsaw
Drill
Come-along with spread bar and wire grip
Hog ring pliers
4 × 4 posts
2 × 4 lumber

3" deck screws or 16d galvanized common nails
Post finials or caps
Tension wire
Large galvanized fence staples
Hog rings
Lumber for cross bracing
Level
Permanent marker
Speed square
Clamps
Eye and ear protection
Hammer
Tape measure
Pencil
Work gloves
Privacy fabric tape
Vinyl privacy slats

Chain link fencing is a strong, durable, and inexpensive way to create a barrier, increase your property's security, or keep pets safely inside.

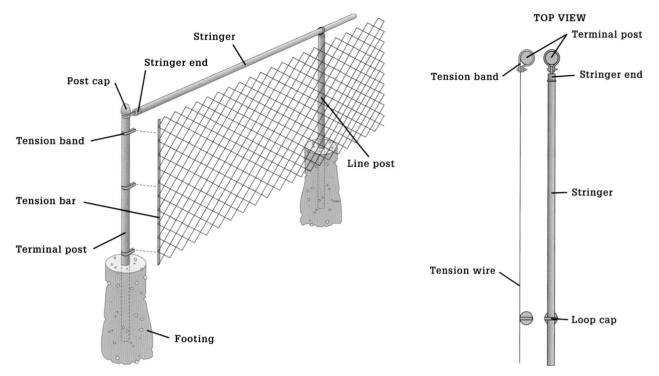

TOP VIEW

Fittings are designed to accommodate slight alignment and height differences between terminal posts and line posts. Tension bands, which hold the mesh to the terminal posts, have one flat side to keep the mesh flush along the outside of the fence line. The stringer ends hold the top stringer in place and keep it aligned. Loop caps on the line posts position the top stringer to brace the mesh.

HOW TO INSTALL A CHAIN LINK FENCE

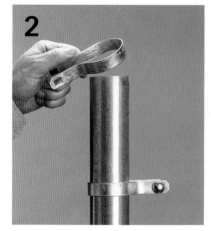

Install the posts. Lay out the fenceline, spacing the posts at 96" on-center (see page 243 for laying out and setting posts). Dig holes for terminal posts 8" in diameter with flared bottoms; dig holes for line posts at 6". Make all postholes 30" deep or below the frost line, whichever is deeper. Set the terminal posts in concrete so they extend 50" above grade. Run a mason's string between terminal posts at 46" above grade. Set the line posts in concrete so their tops are even with the string. If desired, stop the concrete 3" below ground level and backfill with soil and grass to conceal the concrete. *Tip: When plumbing and bracing posts, use duct tape to secure cross bracing to the posts.*

Position the tension bands and stringer ends on the gate and end terminal posts, using a ratchet wrench to tighten the bands with the included bolt and nut. Each post gets three tension bands: 8" from the top, 24" from the top, and 8" above the ground (plus a fourth band at the bottom of the post if you will use a tension wire). Make sure the flat side of each band faces the outside of the fence and points into the fence bay. Also add a stringer end to each post, 3" down from the top.

(continued)

3

Add bands and ends to the corner posts. Each corner post gets six tension bands, two at each location: 8" and 24" from the top and 8" from the bottom (plus two more at the bottom for a tension wire, if applicable). Also install two stringer ends, 3" from the top of the post. Orient the angled side up on the lower stringer end and the angled side down on the upper stringer end.

4

Top each terminal post with a post cap and each line post with a loop cap. Make sure the loop cap openings are perpendicular to the fenceline, with the offset side facing the outside of the fenceline.

5

Begin installing the stringer, starting at a terminal post. Feed the non-tapered end of a stringer section through the loop cap on the nearest line post, then into the stringer end on the terminal post. Make sure it's snug in the stringer end cup. Continue feeding stringer sections through loop caps, and join stringer sections together by fitting the non-tapered ends over the tapered ends. If necessary, use a sleeve to join two non-tapered ends.

6

Measure and cut the last stringer section to fit to complete the stringer installation. Measure from where the taper begins on the preceding section to the end of the stringer end cup. Cut the stringer to length with a hacksaw or pipe cutter. Install the stringer.

Secure the chain link mesh to a terminal post, using a tension bar threaded through the end row of the mesh. Anchor the bar to the tension bands so the mesh extends about 1" above the stringer. The nuts on the tension bands should face inside the fence. If applicable, install a tension wire as directed by the manufacturer. Unroll the mesh to the next terminal post, pulling it taut as you go.

Stretch the mesh toward the terminal post using the come-along. Thread a spread bar through the mesh about 48" from the end, and attach the come-along between the bar and terminal post. Pull the mesh until it's difficult to squeeze the links together by hand. Insert a tension bar through the mesh and secure the bar to the tension bands. Remove excess mesh by unwinding a strand. Tie the mesh to the stringer and line posts every 12" using tie wire. See page 282 to install a gate.

Weaving Chain Link Mesh Together ▸

If a section of chain link mesh comes up short between the terminal posts, you can add another piece by weaving two sections together.

With the first section laid out along the fenceline, estimate how much more mesh is needed to reach the next terminal post. Overestimate 6" or so, so you don't come up short again.

Detach the amount of mesh needed from the new roll by bending back the knuckle ends of one zig-zag strand in the mesh. Make sure the knuckles of the same strand are undone at the top and bottom of the fence. Spin the strand counter-clockwise to wind it out of the links, separating the mesh into two.

Place this new section of chain link at the short end of the mesh so the zig-zag patterns of the links line up with one another.

Weave the new section of chain link into the other section by reversing the unwinding process. Hook the end of the strand into the first link of the first section. Spin the strand clockwise until it winds into the first link of the second section, and so on. When the strand has connected the two sections, bend both ends back into a knuckle. Attach the chain link mesh to the fence framework.

HOW TO INSTALL A CHAIN LINK GATE

Set fence posts in concrete spaced far enough apart to allow for the width of the gate plus required clearance for the latch. Position the female hinges on the gate frame, as far apart as possible. Secure with nuts and bolts (orient nuts toward the inside of the fence).

Set the gate on the ground in the gate opening, next to the gatepost. Mark the positions of the female hinges onto the gate post. Remove the gate and measure up 2" from each hinge mark on the gatepost. Make new reference marks for the male hinges.

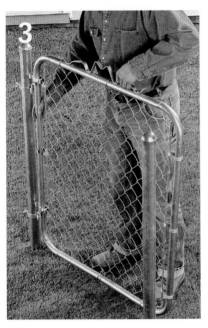

Secure the bottom male hinge to the gatepost with nuts and bolts. Slide the gate onto the bottom hinge. Then, lock the gate in with the downward-facing top hinge.

Test the swing of the gate and adjust the hinge locations and orientations, if needed, until the gate operates smoothly and the opposite side of the gate frame is parallel to the other fence post. Tighten the hinge nuts securely.

Attach the gate latch to the free side of the gate frame, near the top of the frame. Test to make sure the latch and gate function correctly. If you need to relocate a post because the opening is too large or too small, choose the latch post, not the gate post.

HOW TO BUILD A CALIFORNIA-STYLE CHAIN LINK FENCE

Install the posts. Set the 4 × 4 fence posts in concrete, spacing them at 6 to 8 ft. on center. The posts should stand at least 4" taller than the finished height of the chain link mesh. See page 243 for help with laying out your fenceline and installing the posts.

Trim the posts so they are 4" higher than the installed height of the chain link mesh. Mark the post height on all four sides of each post, and make the cuts with a circular saw, reciprocating saw, or handsaw.

Add 2 × 4 top stringers between each pair of posts. Mark reference lines 4" down from the tops of the posts. Cut each stringer to fit snugly between the posts. Fasten the stringers with their top faces on the lines using 3" deck screws or 16d galvanized common nails driven through angled pilot holes.

Wrap tension wire around a terminal post, about 1" above the ground. Staple the wire with a galvanized fence staple, and then double back the tail of the wire and staple it to the post.

(continued)

Staple the tension wire to the line posts after gently tightening the wire (using a come-along with a wire grip) and securing the loose end of the wire to the opposing terminal post. Option: You can install 2 × 4 bottom stringers in place of a tension wire.

Add finials or decorative caps to the post tops for a finished look and to help protect the end grain of the wood.

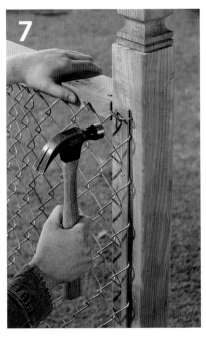

Secure the fence mesh to the first terminal post using a tension bar threaded through the end row of the mesh. Fasten the bar to the posts with a fence staple every 8". Make sure the bar is plumb and the top of the mesh overlaps the top stringer (and bottom stringer, if applicable).

Unroll the mesh toward the other terminal post, and then stretch the mesh gently with a come-along (see step 8, page 281). Secure the end of the mesh to the post with a tension bar and staples, as before. Remove any excess mesh by unwinding a strand (see page 281).

Attach the bottom edge of the mesh to the tension wire every 2 ft., using hog rings tightened with hog ring pliers. Staple the mesh to the stringers every 2 ft. and to the line posts every 12".

Privacy fabric tape cuts the wind and provides partial privacy. It's purchased in rolls with a limited number of color options. It is relatively inexpensive, but threading it through the chain link mesh is time consuming.

Vinyl privacy slats create vertical lines and are easier to install than tape. They're available in a limited number of colors at most building centers. Some varieties of strips also have a grass-like texture.

BAMBOO FENCE

Bamboo is one of nature's best building materials. It's lightweight, naturally rot-resistant, and so strong that it's used for scaffolding in many parts of the world. It's also a highly sustainable resource, since many species can be harvested every three to five years without destroying the plants. Yet, perhaps the best feature of bamboo is its appearance—whether it's lined up in orderly rows or hand-tied into decorative patterns, bamboo fencing has an exotic, organic quality that adds a breath of life to any setting.

Bamboo is a grass, but it shares many properties with wood. It can be cut, drilled, and sanded with the same tools, and it takes many of the same finishes, including stains and exterior sealers. And, just like wood, bamboo is prone to splitting, though it retains much of its strength even when subject to large splits and cracks. In general, larger-diameter poles (which can be upwards of 5 inches) are more likely to split than smaller (such as ¾-inch-dia.) canes.

Bamboo fencing is commonly available in eight-foot-long panels made from similarly sized canes held together with internal or external wires. The panels, which are rolled up for easy transport, can be used as infill within a new wood framework, or they can attach directly to an existing wood or metal fence. Both of these popular applications are shown here. Another option is to build an all-bamboo fence using large bamboo poles for the posts and stringers and roll-up panels for the infill.

Tools & Materials ▶

Tools and materials for laying out and setting posts	Pliers
Circular saw or reciprocating saw	Deck screws (3", 2½", 2")
Drill	Bamboo fence panels with ¾"-dia. (or as desired) canes
Countersink-piloting bit	Level
Wire cutters	Tape measure
Lumber (4 × 4, 2 × 4, 1 × 4, 2 × 6)	Eye and ear protection
	Galvanized steel wire
	Work gloves

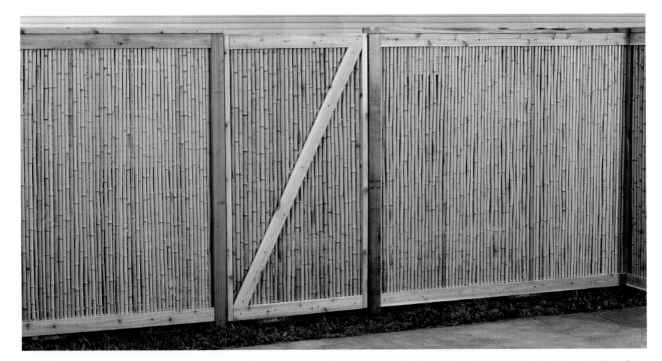

Quality bamboo for fencing isn't hard to find, but you can't pick it up at your local lumberyard. The best place to start shopping is the internet (see Resources, page 553). Look for well-established suppliers who are committed to sustainable practices. Most suppliers can ship product directly to your home.

HOW TO BUILD A WOOD-FRAME BAMBOO FENCE

Install and trim the 4 × 4 posts according to the size of your bamboo panels, setting the posts in concrete (see page 243). For the 6 × 8-ft. panels in this project, the posts are spaced 100" on-center and are trimmed at 75" tall (refer to the manufacturer's recommendations).

Install the top 2 × 4 stringers. Cut each stringer to fit snugly between the posts. Position the stringer on edge so it is flush with the tops of the posts and with the back or front faces of the posts. Fasten the stringer with 3" deck screws driven through angled pilot holes. Use one screw on each edge and one on the inside face of the stringer, at both ends.

Mark the location of each bottom stringer. The span between the top of the top stringer and bottom of the bottom stringer should equal the bamboo panel height plus about 1". Cut and install the bottom stringers in the same fashion as the top stringers. Here, the bottom stringer will be installed 2" above the ground for rot prevention. Unroll the bamboo panels.

Flatten the bamboo panels over the inside faces of the stringers. Make sure the panels fit the frames on all sides. Using a countersink-piloting bit (inset), drill a slightly countersunk pilot hole through a bamboo cane and into the stringer at a top corner of the panel. Fasten the corner with a 2" deck screw, being careful not to overtighten and split the bamboo.

(continued)

5 Screws   2 × 4

Fasten the rest of the panel with screws spaced 12" apart. Stagger the screws top and bottom, and drive them in an alternating pattern, working from one side to the other. Repeat steps 4 and 5 to install the remaining bamboo panels.

Reducing Panel Length ▸

To shorten the length of a bamboo panel, cut the wiring holding the canes together at least two canes beyond the desired length using wire cutters. Remove the extra canes, and then wrap the loose ends of wire around the last cane in the panel.

6

Cover the top and bottom ends of the panels with 1 × 4 battens. These finish off the panels and give the fence a similar look on both sides. Cut the battens so the ends are flush against the inside faces of the posts and fasten them to the panels and stringers with 2½" deck screws driven through pilot holes.

7

Add the top cap. Center the 2 × 6 top cap boards over the posts so they overhang about 1" on either side. Fasten the caps to the posts and stringers with 3" deck screws. Use miter joints for corners, and use scarf joints (cut with opposing 30° or 45° bevels) to join cap boards over long runs.

HOW TO COVER AN OLD FENCE WITH BAMBOO

Unroll and position a bamboo panel over one or both sides of the existing fence. Check the panel with a level and adjust as needed. For rot prevention, hold the panel 1 to 2" above the ground. *Tip: A 2 × 4 laid flat on the ground makes it easy to prop up and level the panel.*

Fasten the panel with deck screws driven through the bamboo canes (and fence siding boards, if applicable) and into the fence stringers. Drill countersunk pilot holes for the screws, being careful not to overtighten and crack the bamboo. Space the screws 12" apart, and stagger them top and bottom (see page 288).

Install the remaining bamboo panels, butting the edges together between panels for a seamless appearance. If the fence posts project above the stringer boards, you can cut the bamboo panels flush with the posts. To trim the panels, follow the technique shown in the Tip on page 288.

Variation: To dress up a chain link fence with bamboo fencing, simply unroll the panels over the fence and secure them every 12" or so with short lengths of galvanized steel wire. Tie the wire around the canes or the panel wiring and over the chain link mesh.

INVISIBLE DOG FENCE

The invisible, or underground, pet fence can be the perfect option for those who love dogs but not necessarily dog fences. The pet fence is invisible because the actual boundary is nothing more than a thin electrical wire buried an inch or so underground. It can also be laid into hard walkway and driveway surfaces and can be installed above ground, on fences and other fixed structures. This makes it easy to create a continuous barrier to enclose any or all of your property as well as specific areas inside the boundary, such as a garden or swimming pool. Invisible fences can also be used for cats, provided they meet the weight minimum for safe use.

Here's how the pet fence works: the boundary wire receives a constant electrical signal from a small, plug-in transmitter located in the house or other protected space. Your pet is fitted with a special collar that picks up the signal in the wire and responds accordingly: if your pet approaches the boundary area, the collar beeps and vibrates to give him warning that the boundary is near. If he continues beyond the warning zone, he is given an electrical shock by the collar contacts—a clear message to back away from the boundary.

Invisible pet fences effectively contain dogs of all types and are suitable for small and large properties—up to 10 acres, in some cases. However, it's important to make sure this type of system is right for your needs and your pet. While most dogs quickly learn to respect the system, it's always possible for a dog to breach the boundary (a high-spirited pooch may be especially prone to doing so). And keep in mind that this fence will not prevent other dogs from entering your yard. After installing the fence, it's critical that you take the time to train your dog properly so that he knows where the boundary lines are and understands the correction system. The fence manufacturer should provide detailed training instructions.

Tools & Materials ›

Tape measure (100-ft.)	Screws
Drill	Stapler and staples
Straightened coat hanger	(for wood fence
Flat spade	installation only)
Paint stir-stick	Electrical tape
Circular saw and	Zip ties (for
masonry blade	metal fence
Concrete or	installation only)
asphalt caulk or	Wire stripper
patching material	Wire nuts
Shop vacuum	Silicone caulk
Pet fence kit	Caulk gun
Eye and ear potection	Work gloves

A properly trained pet will stay within the invisible boundary, as long as the animal wears the collar that is part of the invisible fence system.

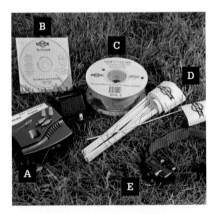

Invisible pet fence systems are available in complete kits and can be installed in a day. The basic components for installation (photo above) include from left to right: a transmitter and power cord (A), installation manual or disc (B), boundary wire (C), boundary flags (D), and receiver collar (E).

BOUNDARY LAYOUT OPTIONS

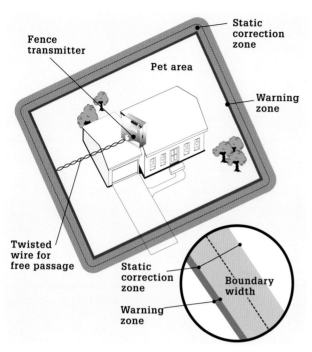

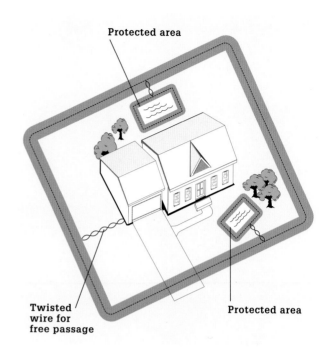

A perimeter layout uses a single run of wire encircling the house and grounds. A single section of twisted wire runs from the boundary to the transmitter. *Note: Twisting the boundary wire around itself cancels the signal, creating a "free passage" area for your pet.*

Protecting areas within a perimeter boundary is achieved by looping the wire around the area and returning to the boundary. Twisting the wire between the boundary and protected inner area allow for free passage around the protected area.

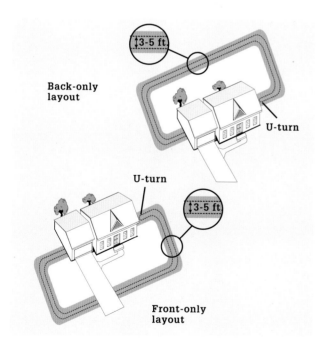

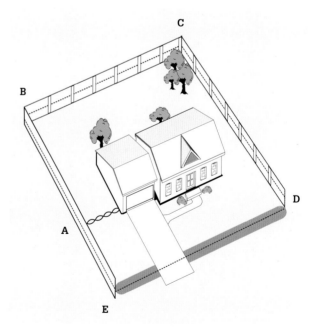

A front or back-only layout requires a doubled loop of wire to complete the boundary circuit. Starting at the transmitter, the wire encircles the containment area and then doubles back, maintaining a 3- to 5-ft. space (or as directed) between runs to prevent canceling the signal.

Incorporating a fence into the boundary can help deter your dog from jumping over or digging under the fence. The wire can be fastened directly to the fence and/or can be buried in front of the fence. Burial allows you to protect gate openings. Run wires from the transmitter to A, A to B, B to C, C to D, D to E, E to A, and then twist wire from A to transmitter.

HOW TO INSTALL AN INVISIBLE DOG FENCE

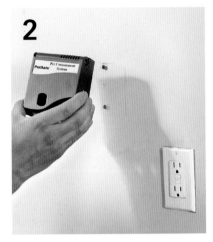

Plan the layout of the boundary wire. With a helper, use a 100-ft. tape measure to determine the total distance of the wire run. Factor in extra length for twisted (free passage) sections and for making adjustments. Order additional wiring, if necessary. *Tip: Use the boundary flags that come with the kit to temporarily mark the corners and other points of the wire route.*

Mount the transmitter on the inside of an exterior wall, near a standard 120-volt receptacle. The location can be in the house, garage, basement, or crawlspace and must be convenient, protected from the elements, not subject to freezing temperatures, and must be at least 3 ft. (or as recommended) from appliances or other large metal objects. Mount the transmitter with appropriate screws.

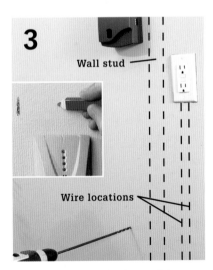

Wall stud

Wire locations

Drill a hole through the wall for routing the boundary wire. The hole can be just large enough to fit the wire (which will likely be twisted at this point; see step 5). Alternatively, you can route the wire through a window, door, or crawlspace/basement-wall vent, provided the wire will be safe from damage. Identify stud and wire locations before you drill but shut off electrical power to be safe.

Begin running the wire along the planned route. Be sure to leave extra wire for twisting at the termination point of the boundary (transmitter location), if applicable. Turn corners with the wire gradually, not at sharp angles.

5

Twist the wire onto itself to cancel the signal for free passage areas, as desired. With a helper holding the wire at the end of a loop (start of twisted section), circle the spool around the wire to create 10 to 12 twists per linear foot (or as recommended). Be sure not to exceed the maximum length of twisted wire.

6

Splice together multiple boundary wires (required only when the boundary distance exceeds the length of wire provided with kit). Strip ½" of insulation from the ends of both wires using a wire stripper. Hold the ends together and join them with a wire nut, twisting the nut on tightly. Tug on the wires to make sure they're held by the nut.

7

Seal inside and around the wire nut with silicone caulk to create a waterproof connection and prevent corrosion. When the caulk has dried completely, reinforce the connection with electrical tape. *Tip: Make note of each splice location, as these are the most common points of boundary wire failure.*

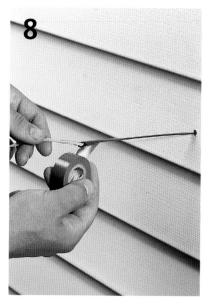

8

Fish the ends of the boundary wire through the house wall (termination of the boundary run) using a straightened coat hanger. Wrap the wire ends around the fish tape bend and secure them with electrical tape. Once through the wall, twist the wires to provide free passage from the house to the boundary line, as appropriate for your layout.

(continued)

9

Connect the wire ends to the transmitter after stripping ½" of insulation from each end. Secure the wires to the appropriate terminals on the transmitter. Plug in the transmitter and set the boundary controls for testing the system, as directed.

10

Test the system using the receiver collar and testing tool. Adjust the collar settings as directed. Walk toward the boundary wire while holding the collar at the pet's neck height. Note when the warning and correction signals are activated, indicated by the testing tool. Test the system in multiple locations. Make adjustments to the settings and/ or boundary wire as needed.

11

Excavate grass or soil, making a continuous cut 1 to 3" deep. Drive a spade into the ground, then rock the handle back and forth to widen the cut slightly, creating a straight or gently curving slot.

12

Lay the boundary wire into the slot, using a paint stir-stick to seat it into the bottom of the slot. Be careful not to kink or damage the wire. Carefully close the slot by stepping along its length with one foot on either side of the slot.

13

Cut slots into concrete or asphalt driveways and walks using a circular saw with a masonry blade. Vacuum the slot clean, and then lay the boundary wire into the slot. Seal over the slot with high-quality concrete or asphalt caulk or patching compound.

Option: Use existing control joints to pass the boundary wire over concrete drives and walks. Control joints are the shallow grooves formed in the concrete to help control cracking. Clean and vacuum the joint, then lay in the wire. Cover the joint with concrete caulk.

FENCES & WALLS

14

Fasten the boundary wire to fences, as directed by the manufacturer. Use staples for wood fences and plastic zip ties for metal fences (or simply weave the wire through chain link mesh). To protect gate openings, bury the wire in the ground in front of the opening.

15

Position the boundary flags using the collar to find the inside edge of the warning zone. Move toward the boundary until the collar beeps (warning signal) and place a flag at that location. Place a flag every 10 ft. (or as directed) over the entire boundary area. Fit the collar to your pet as directed to begin the training. After training period, remove flags (follow manufacturer instructions).

PATIO WALL

Perhaps due to the huge popularity of interlocking concrete wall block, which made building retaining walls a great do-it-yourself project, you can now find concrete landscape blocks made for a range of applications, including patio walls, freestanding columns, raised planters, and even outdoor kitchens. The blocks shown in this project require no mortar and are stacked up just like retaining wall units. Yet unlike retaining wall blocks, these "freestanding" units have at least two faceted faces, so the wall looks good on both sides. And they have flat bottoms, allowing them to be stacked straight up without a batter (the backward lean required for most retaining walls).

Solid concrete blocks for freestanding walls come in a range of styles and colors. Products that come in multiple sizes produce walls with a highly textured look that mimics natural stone, while walls made with uniform blocks have an appearance closer to weathered brick. Many block products can be used for both curved and straight walls, and most are compatible with cap units that give the wall an architecturally appropriate finish, as well as a great surface for sitting.

The wall in this project forms a uniform curve to follow the shape of a circular patio. It's built over a base of compacted gravel, but you could build the same wall right on top of a concrete patio slab. Keep in mind that freestanding walls like this are typically subject to height limits, which might range from 20 to 36 inches or higher. Walls with straight sections or gentle curves may need a supporting feature, such as a column or 90-degree turn or jog, to stabilize the wall.

Tools & Materials ▸

Mason's string	Wood stakes
Landscape marking paint	Straight board
	Compactable gravel
Excavation tools	Concrete wall block and cap units
Line level	
Plate compactor or hand tamp	Concrete adhesive
	Tape measure
Rake	Eye and ear protection
4-ft. level	Circular saw with masonry blade (optional)
Caulk gun	
Brickset or pitching chisel	Heavy rope or garden hose
	Wheelbarrow
Hand maul	Work gloves
Stone chisel	

Landscape block for freestanding walls is versatile and an easy material with which to build. You can use it to create low walls of almost any shape, plus columns, steps, and other features. Quality block manufacturers offer a variety of styles and textures, along with compatible specialty and accessory pieces for a well-integrated look.

LAYING OUT FREESTANDING BLOCK WALLS

Draw the rough outline of the wall onto the ground with a can of marking paint. First measure the wall blocks and/or align a few blocks in place as guides. To mark end columns, first measure the blocks and then use the marking paint to outline the footprint of the column (inset).

Freeform curving walls: Use heavy rope or a garden hose to lay out the wall's shape. Follow the rope with marking paint to transfer the outline to the ground. To mark the other side of the wall and the edges of the excavation, reposition the rope or hose the appropriate distance away from the first mark and trace with paint.

Straight walls: Mark the outlines of the wall and/or excavation with stakes and mason's string. Position one string, then measure from it to position any remaining strings as needed. *Tip: Leave the stakes marking one of the wall faces in the ground; you'll use them later to align the wall block.*

HOW TO BUILD A FREESTANDING PATIO WALL

Remove the sod and other plantings inside the excavation area. For a gravel base, the excavation should extend 6" beyond the wall on all sides. If you are building adjacent to a sandset patio with pavers, take care not to disturb the rigid paver edging. Alternatively, fully excavate the ground around patio to compensate for wall addition and install new edging around perimeter. Follow your manufacturer's instructions.

Set up level lines to guide the excavation using stakes and mason's string. For curved walls, you may need more than one string. Level the string with a line level (make sure multiple strings are level with one another). Measure from the string to ground level (grade), and then add 12" (or as directed by the block manufacturer)—this is the total depth required for the excavation.

Use a story pole to measure the depth as you complete the excavation. To make a story pole, mark the finished depth of the excavation onto a straight board, and use it to measure against the string; this is easier than pulling out your tape measure for each measurement.

Tamp the soil in the trench with a rented plate compactor or a hand tamp. The bottom of the trench should be flat and level, with the soil thoroughly compacted. Take care not to disturb or damage adjacent structures.

Spread compactable gravel over the trench in an even 2- to 3"-thick layer. Tamp the gravel thoroughly. Add the remaining gravel and tamp to create a 6"-thick layer after compaction.

Check the gravel base with a level (or a level taped to a straight board) to make sure the surface is uniform and perfectly level. Add gravel to any low spots and tamp again.

Set the first course. If you're using more than one thickness of block, select only the thicker units for the first course. Lay out the blocks in the desired pattern along the layout line, butting the ends together for complete contact. If necessary, cut blocks to create the desired curve (see step 10). Place a 4-ft. level across the blocks to make sure they are level and flat across the tops.

Set the second course. Begin the course at the more visible end of the wall. Set the blocks in the desired pattern, making sure to overlap the block joints in the first course to create a bond pattern. Alternate different sizes of block regularly, and check the entire course with a level. If necessary, cut a block for the end of the wall.

(continued)

9

End each course with a piece no narrower than 6". If necessary, position a full unit at the end of the wall, then measure back and cut the second-to-last unit to fit the space. Glue small end pieces in place with concrete adhesive.

10

Cut blocks using a brickset or pitching chisel and a maul. First score along the cutting line all the way around the block, and then chisel at the line until the block splits. You can also cut a deep score line (on thick block) or cut completely through (on thin block) using a circular saw with a masonry blade.

Cut Facets ▶

Round over the cut edges of blocks to match the original texture. Using a stone chisel and mason's hammer or maul, carefully chip along the edges to achieve the desired look.

11

Complete the remaining courses, following the desired pattern. Be sure to maintain a bond with the course below by overlapping the joints in the lower course. For the top two courses, glue each block in place with concrete adhesive.

12

Install the cap blocks. Trapezoidal cap block may fit your wall's curve well enough without cuts (for gentle curves, try alternating the cap positions). If cuts are necessary, dry-fit the pieces along the wall, and plan to cut every other block on both side edges for an even fit. Set all caps with concrete adhesive. Backfill along the wall to bury most or all of the first course.

HOW TO ADD DECORATIVE COLUMNS TO A WALL

Set the first course of each column after completing the first wall course (middle-of-wall columns are set along with each wall course). Use four full blocks for the first course, butting the column blocks against the end wall block. Check the column blocks for level. *Note: Prepare the ground as seen on pages 298 to 299.*

Glue the second course and all subsequent courses in place with concrete adhesive or according to the manufacturer's specifications.

Cap the column with special cap units, or create your own caps with squares of flagstone. Glue cap pieces in place with concrete adhesive or mortar in between them, following the manufacturer's instructions. *Tip: The hollow space in the column's center is ideal for running wiring for adding a light fixture on top of a cap.*

OUTDOOR KITCHEN WALLS & COUNTERTOP

Loaded with convenient work surfaces and a dedicated grill space, the outdoor kitchen has changed backyard grilling forever. This roomy kitchen can be the perfect addition to any patio or garden retreat. It's made entirely of concrete blocks and not only looks great, it's also incredibly easy to build.

The design of this kitchen comes from a manufacturer (see Resources, page 553) that supplies all of the necessary masonry materials on two pallets. As shown, the project's footprint is about 98 × 109 inches and includes a 58-inch-wide space for setting in a grill. Square columns can provide work surfaces on either side of the grill, so you'll want to keep them conveniently close, but if you need a little more or a little less room for your grill, you can simply adjust the number of blocks that go into the front wall section enclosing the grill alcove.

Opposite the grill station is a 32-inch-tall countertop capped with large square pavers, or patio stones, for a finished look. This countertop has a lower surface for food prep and a higher surface for serving or dining. A low side wall connects the countertop with the grill area and adds just the right amount of enclosure to complete the kitchen space.

Tools & Materials ▸

Masonry outdoor
   kitchen kit (concrete
   wall block, concrete
   patio stones)
Chalk line
Framing square
Straight board
Level
Caulk gun
Exterior-grade
   concrete adhesive
Tape measure
Eye and ear protection
Work gloves

This all-masonry outdoor kitchen comes ready to assemble on any solid patio surface, or you can build it over a prepared gravel base anywhere in your landscape (check with the manufacturer for base requirements). For a custom design, similar materials are available to purchase separately and the installation would be more or less the same as shown here. Discuss the project with the manufacturer for specifics. If you decide to build just a part of this kitchen (the bar, for example), review the setup and site prep steps at the beginning of this project.

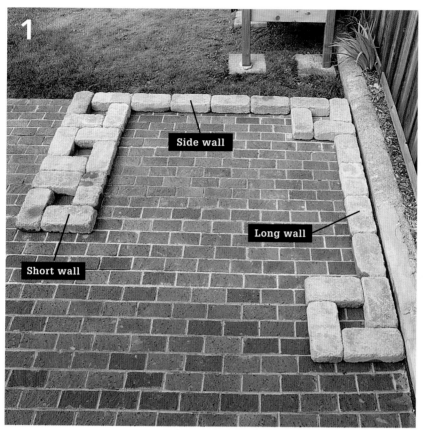

Dry-lay the project on the installation surface. This overview of the first course of blocks shows how the kitchen is constructed with five columns and two wall sections. Laying out the first course carefully and making sure the wall sections are square ensures the rest of the project will go smoothly.

Create squared reference lines for the kitchen walls after you remove the dry-laid blocks. Snap a chalk line representing the outside face of the front wall. Mark the point where the side wall will meet the front wall. Place a framing square at the mark and trace a perpendicular line along the leg of the square. Snap a chalk line along the pencil line to represent the side wall, or use the edge of a patio as this boundary (as shown). To confirm that the lines are square, mark the front-wall line 36" from the corner and the side-wall line 48" from the corner. The distance between the marks should be 60". If not, re-snap one of the chalk lines until the measurements work out.

(continued)

Begin laying the first course of block. Starting in the 90° corner of the chalk lines, set four blocks at right angles to begin the corner column. Make sure all blocks are placed together tightly. Set the long wall with blocks laid end to end, followed by another column.

Finish laying the first course, including two more columns, starting at the side wall. Use a straight board as a guide to make sure the columns form a straight line. To check for square, measure between the long wall and the short wall at both ends; the measurements should be equal. Adjust the short-wall columns as needed.

Set the second course. Add the second course of blocks to each of the columns, rotating the pattern 90° to the first course. Set the blocks for the long and side walls, leaving about a 2" gap in between the corner column and the first block. Set the remaining wall blocks with the same gap so the blocks overlap the joints in the first course.

Set the third course. Lay the third-course blocks using the same pattern as in the first course. For appearance and stability, make sure the faces of the blocks are flush with one another and that the walls and columns are plumb. Use a level to align the blocks and check for plumb.

Install the remaining courses. The higher courses of wall block are glued in place. Set the courses in alternating patterns, as before, gluing each block in place with concrete adhesive.

Build the short wall overhang. Starting at one end of the short wall, glue wall blocks along the tops of the columns with concrete adhesive. Position blocks perpendicular to the length of the short wall, overhanging the columns by 3".

Complete the short wall top. Create the counter surface for the short wall by gluing patio stones to the tops of the columns and overhanging blocks. Position the stones for the lower surface against the ends of the overhanging blocks. Position the upper-surface stones so they extend beyond the overhanging blocks slightly on the outside ends and a little more so on the inside ends.

Cap the corner columns. Finish the two corner columns with wall blocks running parallel to the side wall. Glue the cap pieces in place on the columns using concrete adhesive. Make sure the blocks are fitted tightly together.

DRY STONE WALL

You can construct a low stone wall without mortar, using a centuries-old method known as "dry laying." With this technique, the wall is actually formed by two separate stacks that lean together slightly. Each stone overlaps a joint in the previous course. This technique avoids long vertical joints, resulting in a wall that is attractive and strong. The position and weight of the two stacks support each other, forming a single, sturdy wall.

While dry walls are simple to construct, they do require a fair amount of patience. The stones must be carefully selected and sorted by size and shape. They must also be correctly positioned in the wall so that weight is distributed evenly. Long, flat stones work best. A quarry or aggregate supply center will have a variety of sizes, shapes, and colors to choose from. For this project you'll need to purchase a number of stones in these four sizes:

- Shaping: half the width of the wall
- Tie: the same width as the wall
- Filler: small shims that fit into cracks
- Cap: large, flat stones, wider than the wall

Because the wall relies on itself for support, a concrete footing is unnecessary, but the wall must be at least half as wide as it is tall. This means some stones may need to be shaped or split to maintain the spacing and structure of the wall.

Tools & Materials ▸

Circular saw with masonry blade	Rough-textured rag
Hand sledge	Compactable gravel
Mason's chisel	Excavation tools
4-ft. level	Mason's string
Mason's trowel	Wood stakes
Stones of various shapes and sizes	Tape measure
Cap stones	Eye and ear protection
Type M mortar	Work gloves

A dry stone wall is one of the oldest and strongest styles of garden wall out there. The wall's two stacks of stones rely on one another for support.

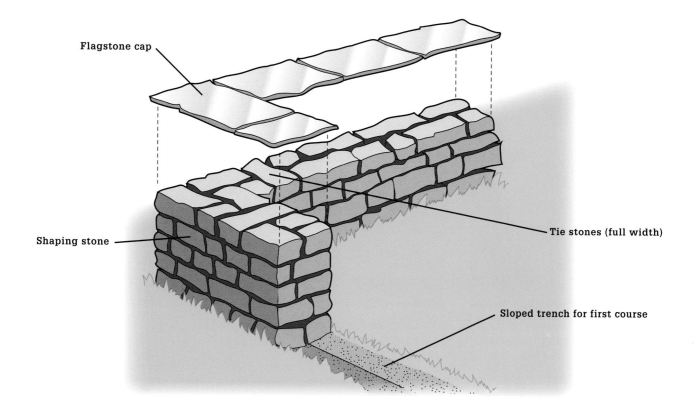

Flagstone cap

Shaping stone

Tie stones (full width)

Sloped trench for first course

HOW TO BUILD A DRY STONE WALL

Lay out the wall site with stakes and mason's string. Dig a 24"-wide trench that is 6" deep at the edges and 8" deep in the center, creating a slight V shape by evenly sloping the sides toward the center. Compact any loose soil. Add a 2"-layer of gravel, but do not compact it.

Shaping stones (½ wall width)

Lay two rows of shaping stones along the bottom of the trench. Position them flush with the edges of the trench and sloping toward the center, staggering joints. Use stones similar in height. If stones have uneven surfaces, position them with the uneven sides facing down.

Form a corner by laying the last stone of the outer row so it covers the end of the stone in the outer row of the adjacent wall course. Lay the inner row in the same manner.

(continued)

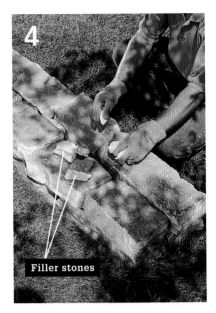

Tie stone

Lay the second course and fill any significant gaps between the shaping stones with rubble and filler stones.

Filler stones

Lay the stones for the second course corner so they cover the joints of the first course corner. Form corners using the same steps as for forming the first course corner. Use stones that have long, square sides. Place tie stones across the width of each wall just before the corner. Build the wall ends in this same way. Use stones of varying lengths so that each joint is covered by the stone above it. Wedge filler stones into any large gaps.

Lay the third course. Work from the corner to the end of the wall. If necessary, shape or split the final stones of the course to size with a masonry saw or hand sledge and chisel. Place tie stones approximately every 36". Lay shaping stones between the tie stones. Make sure to stagger the joints; stones of varying lengths will help offset them. Continue to place filler stones into any cracks on the surface or sides of the wall. Continue laying courses, maintaining a consistent height along the wall and adding tie stones to every third course. Check for level as you go.

When the wall is about 36" high, check for level. Trowel mortar onto the center of the wall, in at least 6" from the edges. Center the capstones and set them as close together as possible. Carefully fill the cracks between the capstones with mortar. Let any excess mortar dry until crumbly, then brush it off. After two or three days, scrub off any residue using water and a rough-textured rag.

Slopes & Curves ▸

If slope is an issue along your wall site, you can easily build a stepped wall to accommodate it. The key is to keep the stones level so they won't shift or slide with the grade, and to keep the first course below ground level. This means digging a stepped trench.

Lay out the wall site with stakes and mason's string. Dig a trench 4 to 6" deep along the entire site, including the slope. Mark the slope with stakes at the bottom where it starts, and at the top where it ends.

Begin the first course along the straight-line section of the trench, leading up to the start of the slope. At the reference stake, dig into the slope so a pair of shaping stones will sit level with the rest of the wall.

To create the first step, excavate a new trench into the slope, so that the bottom is level with the top of the previous course. Dig into the slope the length of one-and-a-half stones. This will allow one pair of stones to be completely below the ground level, and one pair to span the joint where the new trench and the stones in the course below meet.

Continue creating steps, to the top of the slope. Make sure each step of the trench section remains level with the course beneath. Then fill the courses, laying stones in the same manner as for a straight-line wall. Build to a maximum height of 36", and finish by stepping the top to match the grade change, or create a level top with the wall running in to the slope.

If you'd like a curved wall or wall segment, lay out each curve, as demonstrated on page 297. Then dig the trench as for a straight wall, sloping the sides into a slight V toward the center. Lay the stones as for a straight wall, but use shorter stones; long, horizontal stones do not work as well for a tight curve. Lay the stones so they are tight together, offsetting the joints along the entire stretch. Be careful to keep the stone faces vertical to sustain the curve all the way up the height of the wall.

If the wall goes up- or downhill, step the trench, the courses, and the top of the wall to keep the stones level.

To build a curved wall, lay out the curve using a string staked to a center point as a compass. Then, dig the trench and set stones using the same techniques as for a straight wall.

HOW TO BUILD A RETAINING WALL USING INTERLOCKING BLOCK

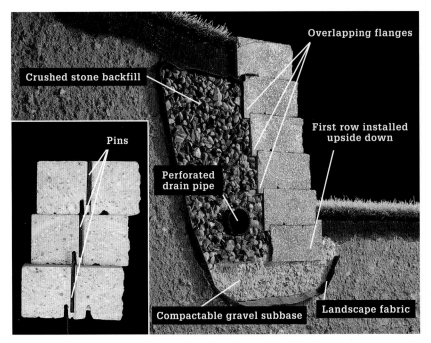

Crushed stone backfill

Overlapping flanges

Pins

Perforated drain pipe

First row installed upside down

Compactable gravel subbase

Landscape fabric

Interlocking wall blocks do not need mortar. Some types are held together with a system of overlapping flanges that automatically set the backward pitch (batter) as the blocks are stacked, as shown in this project. Other types of blocks use fiberglass pins (inset).

Excavate the hillside, if necessary. Allow 12" of space for crushed stone backfill between the back of the wall and the hillside. Use stakes to mark the front edge of the wall. Connect the stakes with mason's string, and use a line level to check for level.

Dig out the bottom of the excavation below ground level, so it is 6" lower than the height of the block. For example, if you use 6"-thick block, dig down 12". Measure down from the string in multiple spots to make sure the bottom base is level.

Line the excavation with strips of landscape fabric cut 3 ft. longer than the planned height of the wall. Make sure all seams overlap by at least 6".

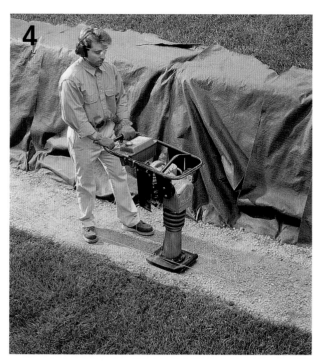

Spread a 6" layer of compactable gravel over the bottom of the excavation as a subbase and pack it thoroughly. A rented tamping machine, or jumping jack, works better than a hand tamper for packing the subbase.

Lay the first course of block, aligning the front edges with the mason's string. (When using flanged block, place the first course upside down and backward.) Check frequently with a level and adjust, if necessary, by adding or removing subbase material below the blocks.

Lay the second course of block according to manufacturer's instructions, checking to make sure the blocks are level. (Lay flanged block with the flanges tight against the underlying course.) Add 3 to 4" of gravel behind the block, and pack it with a hand tamper.

Make half-blocks for the corners and ends of a wall, and use them to stagger vertical joints between courses. Score full blocks with a circular saw and masonry blade, then break the blocks along the scored line with a maul and chisel.

(continued)

8

Add and tamp crushed stone, as needed, to create a slight downward pitch (about ¼" of height per foot of pipe) leading to the drain pipe outlet. Place the drain pipe on the crushed stone, 6" behind the wall, with the perforations face down. Make sure the pipe outlet is unobstructed. Lay courses of block until the wall is about 18" above ground level, staggering the vertical joints.

9

Fill behind the wall with crushed stone, and pack it thoroughly with the hand tamper. Lay the remaining courses of block, except for the cap row, backfilling with crushed stone and packing with the tamper as you go.

10

Before laying the cap block, fold the end of the landscape fabric over the crushed stone backfill. Add a thin layer of topsoil over the fabric, then pack it thoroughly with a hand tamper. Fold any excess landscape fabric back over the tamped soil.

11

Apply construction adhesive to the top course of block, then lay the cap block. Use topsoil to fill in behind the wall and to fill in the base at the front of the wall. Install sod or plants, as desired.

HOW TO ADD A CURVE TO AN INTERLOCKING BLOCK RETAINING WALL

1

Right angle

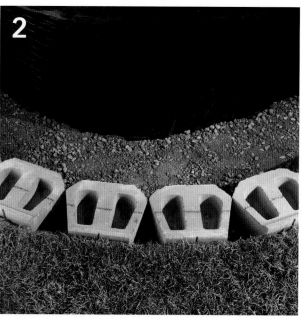

2

Outline the curve by first driving a stake at each end and then driving another stake at the point where lines extended from the first stakes would form a right angle. Tie a mason's string to the right-angle stake, extended to match the distance to the other two stakes, establishing the radius of the curve. Mark the curve by swinging flour or spray paint at the string end, like a compass.

Excavate for the wall section, following the curved layout line. To install the first course of landscape blocks, turn them upside down and backward and align them with the radius curve. Use a 4-ft. level to ensure the blocks sit level and are properly placed.

3

4

Install subsequent courses so the overlapping flange sits flush against the back of the blocks in the course below. As you install each course, the radius will change because of the backwards pitch of the wall, affecting the layout of the courses. Where necessary, trim blocks to size. Install using landscape construction adhesive, taking care to maintain the running bond.

Use half blocks or cut blocks to create finished ends on open ends of the wall.

TIMBER RETAINING WALL

Compactable gravel
Timber (5 × 6 or larger)
12" galvanized spikes
Eye and ear protection
Reciprocating saw
   and long wood blade

Excavation tools
Hand maul
Drill with bits
Landscape fabric
Hand tamper
Work gloves

A low retaining wall built with timbers follows many of the same construction steps as an interlocking block wall (see pages 312 to 314). All steps specific to timber construction are shown here.

When built properly, a timber retaining wall can have a life span of 15 to 20 years. Be sure to use pressure-treated lumber rated for ground contact, and build the wall with 5 × 6 or larger timbers; 4 × 4 and 4 × 6 sizes are not strong enough for retaining walls. Avoid using old, discarded railroad ties that have been soaked in creosote, which can leach into the soil and kill plants.

Cut the timbers with a reciprocating saw and long wood blade (or a chain saw, if you prefer). Before building the retaining wall, prepare the site as directed in steps one to three on page 312.

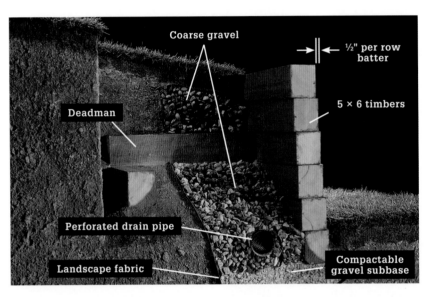

Coarse gravel — **½" per row batter** — **5 × 6 timbers**

Deadman

Perforated drain pipe

Landscape fabric

Compactable gravel subbase

Timber retaining walls must be anchored with "deadmen" that extend from the wall back into the soil. Deadmen prevent the wall from sagging under the weight of the soil. For best results with timber retaining walls, create a backward angle (batter) by setting each row of timbers ½" behind the preceding row. The first row of timbers should be buried.

Tips for Strengthening a Timber Retaining Wall ▸

Timber depth equal to ½ exposed height

Install vertical anchor posts to reinforce the wall. Space the posts 3 ft. apart, and install them so the buried depth of each post is at least half the exposed height of the wall. Anchor posts are essential if it is not practical to install deadmen.

HOW TO BUILD A RETAINING WALL USING TIMBERS

Spread a 6"-layer of compactable gravel subbase into the prepared trench, then tamp the subbase and begin laying timbers, following the same techniques as with interlocking blocks (steps 4 to 11, pages 313 to 314). Each row of timbers should be set with a ½" batter, and end joints should be staggered so they do not align.

Use 12" galvanized spikes or reinforcement bars to anchor the ends of each timber to the underlying timbers. Stagger the ends of the timbers to form strong corner joints. Drive additional spikes along the length of the timbers at 2-ft. intervals. If you have trouble driving the spikes, drill pilot holes.

Install deadmen, spaced 4 ft. apart, midway up the wall. Build the deadmen by joining 3-ft-long lengths of timber with 12" spikes, then insert the ends through holes cut in the landscape fabric. Anchor deadmen to the wall with spikes. Install the remaining rows of timbers, and finish backfilling behind the wall (steps 6 to 11, pages 313 to 314).

Improve drainage by drilling weep holes through the second row of landscape timbers and into the gravel backfill using a spade bit. Space the holes 4 ft. apart, and angle them upward.

STONE RETAINING WALL

Rough-cut wall stones may be dry stacked (without mortar) into retaining walls, garden walls, and other stonescape features. Dry-stack walls move and shift with the frost, and they drain well so they don't require deep footings and drain tiles.

In the project featured here, we use rough-split limestone blocks about eight inches by about four inches thick and in varying lengths. Walls like this may be built up to three feet tall, but keep them shorter if you can, to be safe. Building multiple short walls is often a more effective way to manage a slope than to build one taller wall. Called terracing, this practice requires some planning. Ideally, the flat ground between pairs of walls will be approximately the same size.

A dry-laid natural stone retaining wall is a very organic-looking structure compared to interlocking block retaining walls (pages 312 to 314). One way to exploit the natural look is to plant some of your favorite stone-garden perennials in the joints as you build the wall. Usually one plant or a cluster of three will add interest to a wall without suffocating it in vegetation or compromising its stability. Avoid plants that get very large or develop thick, woody roots or stems that may affect the stability of the wall.

A well-built retaining wall has a slight lean, called a batter, back into the slope. It has a solid base of compacted gravel, and the first course is set below grade for stability.

Tools & Materials ▸

Mason's string	Coarse sand
Line level	Drainage gravel
Stakes	(1½ to 3"
Hand maul	river rock is
Torpedo level	recommended)
Straight 2 × 4	Stone chisel
Hand tamper	4-ft. level
Compactable gravel	Tape measure
Ashlar wall stone	Hammer
Landscape fabric	Scissors
Caulk gun	Work gloves
Block and	Eye and
stone adhesive	ear protection
Excavation tools	

A natural stone retaining wall blends into its surroundings immediately and only looks better with age. Building the wall with ashlar, or cut wall stone, is a much easier project than a wall built with round fieldstones or large boulders.

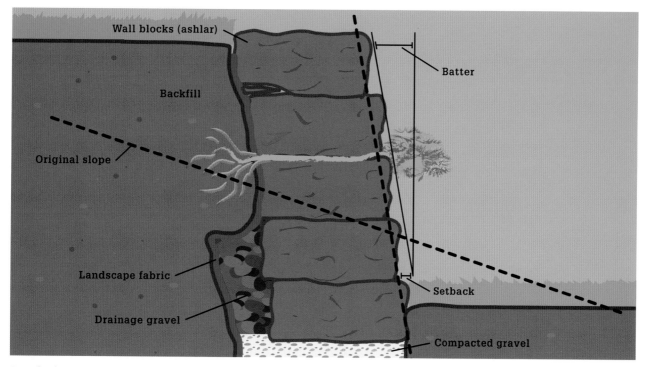

Labels on diagram:
- Wall blocks (ashlar)
- Backfill
- Batter
- Original slope
- Landscape fabric
- Drainage gravel
- Setback
- Compacted gravel

Our single-row retaining wall has a ½" batter, created by setting each course of stone ½" back from the face of the course below. The base of the wall includes a compacted gravel subbase topped with sand to help level the first course of stones. Roots of plants sewn into the wall crevices (an optional decorative embellishment) will eventually reach into the soil behind the wall.

HOW TO BUILD A STONE RETAINING WALL

Begin excavating the wall site. Dig a trench for the base of wall, making it 6" wider than the wall thickness. If necessary, dig into the slope, creating a backward angle that roughly follows the ½" batter the wall will have. If desired, dig returns back into the slope at the end(s) of the wall.

Measure the depth of the trench against a level mason's string running parallel to the trench. The bottom of the trench should be level and 8" below grade (ground level) for the main section of wall and any returns. If the trench becomes too shallow due to natural contours, step it down the height of one stone.

(continued)

Complete the wall base by tamping the soil in the trench, and then adding a 3"-layer of compactable gravel and tamping it flat and level. Cover the gravel with landscape fabric, draping the fabric back over the slope. Add a 1"-layer of sand over the fabric in the trench area. Smooth and level the sand with a short 2 × 4 screed board, checking for level with a torpedo level set on the board.

Set the first course with heavy stones, laying long, square-ended stones at the corners first. *Tip: Organize your stones by size, and plan to set each course with stones of similar thicknesses.* Set up a level mason's string just in front of the top front edge of the course, letting the stones roughly guide the string placement.

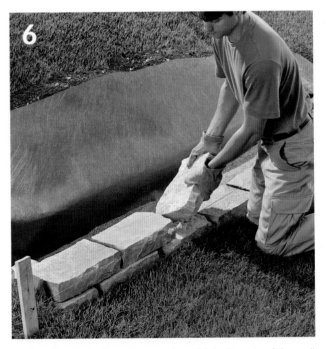

Add or remove sand beneath the stones as needed so they are nearly touching the string. Level the stones front to back with a torpedo level and side to side with a 4-ft. level. If necessary, use a hand maul and stone chisel to chip off irregularities from the edges of stones to improve their fit.

Begin the second course, starting with both ends of the wall face. Reset and level the mason's string at the height of the second course. Place the second-course stones back ½" from the front edges of the first-course stones, overlapping all joints of the first course to create a bond pattern.

Shim beneath stones as needed to level them or add stability, using stone shards and chips. Complete the second course over the main part of the wall.

Complete the returns, as applicable, maintaining the offset joint pattern with the first course. You may need to dig into the slope to create a level base for the return stones. Add a layer of compacted gravel under each return stone before setting it. Complete the remaining courses up to the final (capstone) course.

Backfill behind the base of the wall with drainage rock (not compactable gravel). For a low wall like this, 6 to 10" of gravel is usually sufficient; taller walls may require more gravel and possibly a drainage pipe. Pack the gravel down with a 2 × 4 to help it settle.

Fold the landscape fabric over the gravel, and backfill over the fabric with soil. (The fabric is there to prevent the soil from migrating into the gravel and out through the wall stones.) Trim the fabric just behind the back of the wall, near the top.

Install the final course using long, flat cap stones. Glue the caps in place with block and stone adhesive. After the glue dries, add soil behind the wall to the desired elevation for planting.

YARD & GARDEN STRUCTURES

In this chapter, we turn to the various structures that add to the usefulness of your yard and landscape, either through enhancing the recreational function or by creating places for maintenance or storage or outdoor hobbies, such as recreational gardening. These projects go beyond the hardscaping features demonstrated in the earlier chapters, providing instead a variety of freestanding, self-contained structures that offer either living spaces or practical, hard-working spaces that add functionality to your landscape.

Choosing the correct location for these projects is crucial to their success. While some of these projects are done in conjunction with permanent decks or patios that are already in place, with others you will have a choice of where to locate them; picking the right location spells the difference between a feature that is useful and attractive and one that becomes an obstacle or even an eyesore. Give careful consideration to the overall map of your landscape before committing to a permanent structure that will remain in place for years.

And because these are permanent structures, always consult with your municipal residential construction offices to learn about any code requirements for your project. There might be set-back rules for a shed, for example, specifying location of the project relative to property boundaries. Or your region might have unique foundation or structural requirements that can't be fully addressed by the instructions in this book.

IN THIS CHAPTER:
- Arbor Retreat
- Patio Enclosure
- Patio Arbor/Trellis Enclosure
- Adding a Trellis to an Arbor
- Under-deck Enclosure
- Sun Porch
- DIY Gabled Greenhouse
- Freestanding Kit Greenhouse
- PVC Hoophouse
- Metal & Wood Kit Sheds
- Lean-to Tool Bin

ARBOR RETREAT

The airy, sun-filtered space under an arbor always makes you want to stay awhile—thus, it's a perfect place for built-in seating. The arbor getaway we've chosen (facing page) has plenty of room for lounging or visiting, but it's designed to do much more: Viewed from the front, the arbor retreat becomes an elegant passageway. The bench seating is obscured by latticework, and your eyes are drawn toward the central opening and striking horizontal beams. This makes the structure perfect as a grand garden entrance or a landscape focal point. For added seclusion, tuck this arbor behind some foliage.

Sitting inside the retreat you can enjoy privacy and shade behind the lattice screens. The side roof sections over the seats are lowered to follow a more human scale and create a cozier sense of enclosure. Each bench comfortably fits three people and the two sides face each other at a range that's ideal for conversation.

A classic archway with a keystone motif gives this arbor retreat its timeless appeal.

An arbor with benches makes an ideal resting spot that will become a destination when hiking to remote areas of your property.

A slatted roof and lattice walls are designed to cut sun and wind, creating a comfortable environment inside the arbor retreat.

A few subtle touches turn this cedar arbor into a true standout. The arches at the tops of the sidewall panels give the design visual lift and a touch of Oriental styling.

Materials List

Description (No. finished pieces)	Quantity/Size	Material
Posts		
Inner posts (4)	4 @ field measure	4 × 4
Outer posts (4)	4 @ field measure	4 × 4
Concrete	Field measure	3,000 psi concrete
Gravel	Field measure	Compactable gravel
Roof		
Beams (6 main, 4 cross)	8 @ 8'	4 × 4
Roof slats (10 lower, 11 upper)	21 @ 8'	2 × 2
Seats		
Seat supports, spacers, slats (6 horizontal supports, 6 vertical supports, 4 spacers, 16 slats)	16 @ 8'	2 × 6
Aprons (2)	2 @ 6'	1 × 8
Lattice Screens		
Arches (4)	1 @ 8'	2 × 8
Slats — arched sides (20 horizontal, 8 vertical)	12 @ 8'	2 × 2
Slats — back (8)	8 @ 8'	2 × 2
Hardware & Fasteners		
⅜" × 7" galvanized lag screws	12, with washers	
3" deck screws		
3½" deck screws		
2½" deck screws		
¼" × 3" galvanized lag screws	16, with washers	

Tools

Mason's string
Laser level or 4-ft. level
Hammer or maul
Stakes
Drill
Ladder
Circular saw
Posthole digger
Concrete
Shovel
Tape measure
Pencil
Work gloves
Eye and ear protection
Clamps
Jigsaw or bandsaw
Random orbit sander
Exterior sealant/protectant

Front Elevation

Beam End Detail

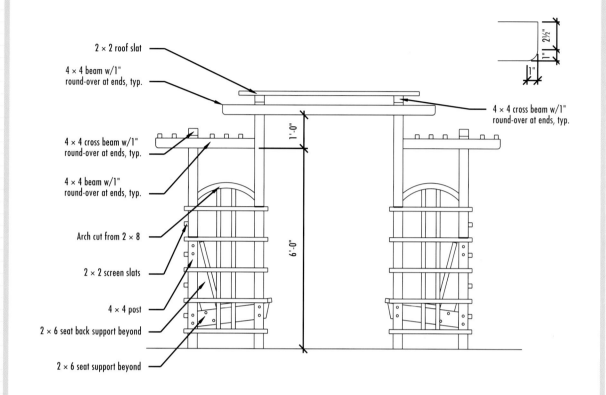

2 × 2 roof slat

4 × 4 beam w/1" round-over at ends, typ.

4 × 4 cross beam w/1" round-over at ends, typ.

4 × 4 cross beam w/1" round-over at ends, typ.

4 × 4 beam w/1" round-over at ends, typ.

Arch cut from 2 × 8

2 × 2 screen slats

4 × 4 post

2 × 6 seat back support beyond

2 × 6 seat support beyond

1'-0"

6'-0"

2½"

1"

1"

Side Elevation

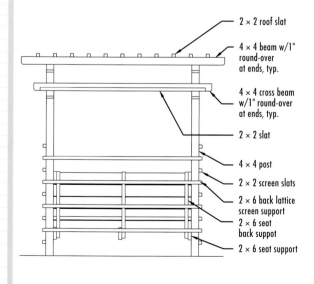

2 × 2 roof slat

4 × 4 beam w/1" round-over at ends, typ.

4 × 4 cross beam w/1" round-over at ends, typ.

2 × 2 slat

4 × 4 post

2 × 2 screen slats

2 × 6 back lattice screen support

2 × 6 seat back suppot

2 × 6 seat support

Post Layout

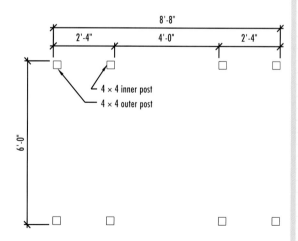

8'-8"

2'-4"

4'-0"

2'-4"

6'-0"

4 × 4 inner post

4 × 4 outer post

HOW TO BUILD THE ARBOR RETREAT

Stake out the project area. Drive a pair of stakes about 2 ft. outside of each corner and string mason's lines from the stakes to create a rectangle that's equal to the total project footprint (6 ft. × 8 ft. 8" as seen here). Mark post locations on the strings, as shown in the Post Layout diagram on page 327, and drive stakes at those points to mark postholes.

Set the eight posts in concrete, making sure that the tops of the four inner posts are at least 84" above the ground, and the four outer posts are 72" above ground. The size and depth of postholes should conform to local building codes. At a minimum, the postholes should be three times the diameter of the post (a 12"-dia. hole) and 24" deep. Use stakes and braces to level and plumb the posts.

Trim post tops. Let the concrete set up overnight and then mark level cutting lines on the posts tops. Use a laser level or a 4 ft. level taped to a straight 2 × 4 to transfer the cutting lines. Make sure to make all four faces of each post. Use a circular saw (a cordless trim saw is best) to trim the post tops.

Cut the lower and upper level beams. The lower level consists of four beams running perpendicular to the seats, and two beams running parallel to the seats. The upper level has two main beams and two cross beams. The 4 × 4 beams have two ends rounded over at the bottom corners with a jig saw. Cut the lower seat level beams to length at 36½". Cut the lower cross beams at 84". Cut upper level main beams to length at 79". Cut upper level cross beams at 96".

Install the lower beams. For each lower level main beam, set the beam on top of an outer post and butt its unshaped end against the corresponding inner post. Hold the beam level, and mark the point where the top face of the beam meets the inner post. Set the beam aside.

Mark a drilling point for a pilot hole on the opposite (inside) face of the inner post. Then, drill a counterbored hole just deep enough to completely recess the washer and head of a ⅜" × 7" lag screw. Reposition each beam so its top face is on the post reference line. Then drill a pilot hole for the lag screw through the inner post and into the end of the beam. Fasten each main beam with a ⅜" lag screw.

(continued)

Drill angled pilot holes through the sides of the cross beams and into the main beams, about ¾" in from the sides of the main beams (to avoid hitting the large screws). Drill two holes on each side of the cross beam at each joint. Fasten cross beams to main beams with 3½" deck screws (eight screws for each cross beam) driven toenail style.

Cut the 10 lower roof slats to length (78"). Mark the roof slat layout onto the tops of the lower main beams, following the plan on page 328. Position slats so they overhang the main beams by 3" at both ends. Drill pilot holes, and fasten the slats to the main beams with 2½" deck screws.

Cut seat supports according to the chart on page 329. Save the cutoffs to make seat slats. Also cut a pair of vertical support spacers from a full 2 × 6. Test-fit the pieces onto the arbor posts and make necessary adjustments. Make 18°-plumb cuts at the fronts of the seat supports.

Position the horizontal seat supports by first measuring up from the ground and marking the inner posts at 16½" and the outer posts at 13". (This marks the top edges of the horizontal supports.) Next, position the seat supports on the marks so their back ends are flush with the outsides of the outer posts. Fasten the supports to the posts with ¼" × 3" lag screws driven through counterbored pilot holes.

Position the vertical seat back support spacers and mark the locations of the support spacer onto the post. Fasten spacers to the post with 3" deck screws driven through pilot holes. Then, fasten the vertical seat back support to the spacer and horizontal seat support with 3½" deck screws; use three or four screws at each end.

Measure and cut 1 × 8 aprons to lengths so they will fit between the outside faces of the side seat supports. Bevel-cut the top edges of the aprons at 7°. Position the aprons against the seat supports. Fasten aprons to the ends of seat supports with 3½" deck screws.

Install seat slats and center supports by first measuring between inner posts for seat slat length; then cutting eight slats for each side. Position a slat on top of the horizontal seat supports so the front edge overhangs the supports by about 1". Fasten the slat to supports with pairs of 3" deck screws. Continue installing slats, leaving a ³⁄₁₆" gap between each.

Assemble the two center seat supports so they match the outer supports, using 2½" deck screws. Install the center supports at the midpoints of the slats by screwing through the slats and into the supports, using 3" deck screws.

(continued)

Build arched lattice screens by first marking the layout of horizontal lattice pieces onto the posts. Mark along one post and use a level to transfer the marks to the other post. Then cut 20 2 × 2 lattice slats to 31". Position them so they overhang the posts by 1½" at both ends and fasten slats to posts with 2½" deck screws driven through pilot holes.

Make the arches using a cardboard template to trace the shape onto a 2 × 8. Cut out the arch with a jigsaw or bandsaw and test-fit the arch between the post pairs. Make necessary adjustments and cut the remaining arches. Sand the cut edges smooth.

Fasten the arches to the posts using 2½" deck screws. First, position arches so they are flush with the outside faces of the posts and, at each end, drill an angled pilot hole upward through the bottom of the arch and into the post.

Cut eight vertical slats to a rough length of 54" (first, mark slats 7" from each post to represent the outside edges of the vertical lattice slats). Mark the top ends of the slats to match the arches by holding each slat on its reference marks. Cut the curved ends and test-fit the slats. Hold each slat in place against the arch (mark bottom for length), then cut them to length.

Install vertical slats with 3" deck screws driven down through tops of the arches and 2½" deck screws driven through the lowest horizontal slats. Make sure all screwheads are countersunk.

Build the back lattice screens by cutting 2 × 2 slats to length at 75", for a 1½" overhang at each end. Position the slats on layout marks, drill pilot holes, and fasten the slats to the posts with 2½" deck screws.

Finish the structure. Sand any rough areas with a random-orbit sander. Wipe down the project, and then apply a coat of exterior wood sealant/protectant.

PATIO ENCLOSURE

If you like the openness and plentiful light of a patio but want more protection from rain and strong winds, this stylish, contemporary patio shelter may be just what you're looking for. Designed as a cross between an open-air arbor or pergola and an enclosed three-season porch, this patio structure has clear glazing panels on its roof and sides, allowing plenty of sunlight through while buffering the elements and even blocking harmful UV rays.

The roof of the patio shelter is framed with closely spaced 2 × 4 rafters to create the same light-filtering effects of a slatted arbor roof. The rafters are supported by a doubled-up 2 × 10 beam and 4 × 6 timber posts. Because the shelter is attached to the house, the posts are set on top of concrete foundation piers, or footings, that extend below the frost line. This prevents any shifting of the structure in areas where the ground freezes in winter.

The patio shelter's side panels cut down on wind while providing a degree of privacy screening. Their simple construction means you can easily alter the dimensions or locations of the panels to suit your own plans. In the project shown, each side has two glazing panels with a 3½-inch space in between, for airflow. If desired, you can use a single sheet of glazing across the entire side section. The glazing is held in place with wood strips and screws so they can be removed for seasonal cleaning.

Slats of white oak sandwich clear polycarbonate panels to create walls that block the wind without blocking light and views.

Building against a solid wall and not in front of a patio door makes the space inside this contemporary shelter much more usable. The corrugated roof panels (see Resources, page 553) made of clear polycarbonate allow light to enter while keeping the elements out.

Patio Enclosure Plans

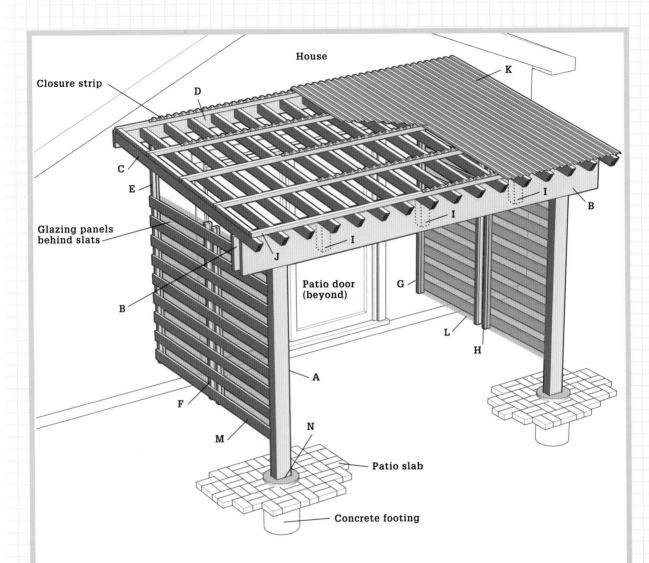

Plan your own patio shelter based on the requirements set by the local building code. Your city's building department or a qualified building professional can help you with the critical structural specifications, such as the size and depth of the concrete post footings, the sizing of beam members, and the overall roof construction. The building department will help make sure your shelter is suitable for the local weather conditions (particularly wind and snow loads).

Cutting List

Key	Part	No.	Size	Material	Key	Part	No.	Size	Material
A	Post	2	3½ × 5½ × 144"	4 × 6 treated pine	H	Slat cleat cap	4	¾ × 1½ × 60"	1 × 2 pine
B	Beam member	2	1½ × 9¼ × 120"*	2 × 10 treated pine	I	Beam blocks	3	3½ × 3½ × 8"	4 × 4 pine
C	Rafter	16	1½ × 3½ × 120"*	2 × 4 pine	J	Purlin	14	1½ × 1½ × 120"	2 × 2 pine
D	Ledger	1	1½ × 5½ × 144"	2 × 6 treated pine	K	Roof panel	6	¼ × 26 × 96"	Corrugated polycarbonate
E	Back post	2	1½ × 1½ × 96"*	2 × 2 pine	L	Side panel	4	¼ × 36 × 58"	Clear polycarbonate
F	Slat cleat	4	1½ × 1½ × 60"	2 × 2 pine	M	Slat	18	¾ × 3½ × 80"*	White oak
G	Back post cap	2	¾ × 1½ × 96"*	1 × 2 pine	N	Post base	2	1½ × 3½ × 3½"	

*Size listed is prior to final trimming

Tools & Materials

Chalk line
4-ft. level
Tape measure
Plumb bob
Mason's string
Digging tools
Concrete mixing tools
Circular saw
Ratchet wrench
Line level
Reciprocating saw or handsaw
Drill with bits
Finish application tools
Gravel
12"-dia. concrete tube forms
Concrete mix
⅝"-dia. J-bolts
⅜ × 4" corrosion resistant lag screws
Flashing
Silicone caulk
Corrosion-resistant metal post bases and hardware

Lumber
Corrosion-resistant 16d and 8d common nails
½"-dia. corrosion-resistant lag bolts and washers
Exterior wood glue or construction adhesive
Corrosion-resistant framing anchors (for rafters)
Deck screws (1½, 3")
Polycarbonate roofing panels
Clear polycarbonate panels
Closure strips
Roofing screws with EPDM washers
Roofing adhesive/sealant
Wood finishing materials
Neoprene weatherstripping
Scrap lumber
Exterior wood stain
Stakes
Eye and ear protection
Hammer
Caulk gun
Table saw, router, or circular saw
Work gloves, plastic gloves

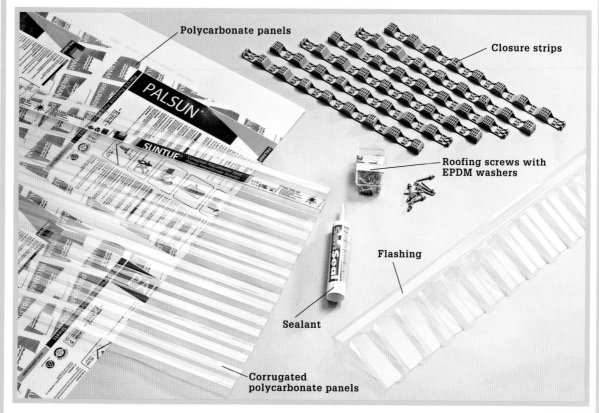

Polycarbonate panels

Closure strips

Roofing screws with EPDM washers

Flashing

Sealant

Corrugated polycarbonate panels

The roofing and side glazing panels of the patio shelter are made with tough polycarbonate materials. The corrugated roofing panels allow up to 90% light transmission while blocking virtually 100% of harmful UV rays. The flat side panels offer the transparency of glass but are lighter and much stronger than glass. Also shown is: wall flashing designed to be tucked under siding; closure strips that fit between the 2 × 2 purlins and the corrugated roof panels; self-sealing screws and polycarbonate caulk.

HOW TO BUILD A PATIO ENCLOSURE

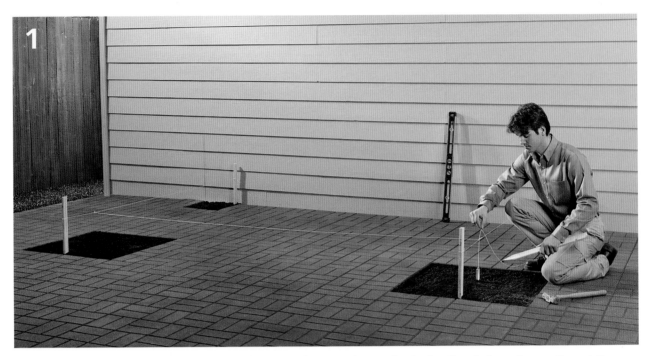

Mark the layout for the ledger board on the house wall. Lay out the post footing locations in the patio area. To mark the cutout for the ledger board, include the width of the ledger board, plus the height of the roofing, plus 1½" for the flashing. The length of the cutout should be 1" longer than the length of the ledger board (12 ft. as shown). Plumb down from the ends of the ledger, then measure in to mark the locations of the post centers. At each of these points, run a perpendicular string line from the house out to about 2 ft. beyond the post locations. Set up a third string line, perpendicular to the first two, to mark the centers of the posts. Plumb down from the string line intersections and mark the post centers on the ground with stakes.

Dig a hole for a concrete tube form at each post location following the local building code for the footing depth. Add 6" of gravel and tamp it down. Position the tube forms so they are plumb and extend at least 2" above the ground. Backfill around them with soil and compact thoroughly.

Fill the tube forms with concrete and screed it level with the tops of the forms. At each post-center location, embed a J-bolt into the wet concrete so it extends the recommended distance above the top of the form. Let the concrete cure.

4

Cut out the house siding for the ledger board using a circular saw. Cut only through the siding, leaving the wall sheathing. *Note: If the sheathing is fiberboard instead of plywood, you may have to remove the fiberboard; consult your local building department.* Replace any damaged building paper covering the sheathing.

5

Stain the wood parts before you begin installing the shelter closure strips and panels. We used a black, semitransparent deck and siding stain.

6

Apply a protective finish to the wood slats as desired. We used a semitransparent deck stain.

(continued)

Install the ledger. First, slip corrugated roof flashing or metal roof flashing behind the siding above the ledger cutout so the vertical flange extends at least 3" above the bottom of the siding. Cut the ledger board to length. Fasten the ledger to the wall using ⅜ × 4" lag screws driven through counterbored pilot holes at each wall-stud location. Seal over the screw heads and counterbores with silicone caulk.

Anchor the post bases to the concrete footing, securing them with the base manufacturer's recommended hardware. Make sure the bases are aligned with each other and are perpendicular to the house wall.

Cut off the bottom ends of the posts so they are perfectly square. Set each post in its base and hold it plumb. Fasten the post to the base using the manufacturer's recommended fasteners. Brace the posts with temporary bracing. *Note: You will cut the posts to length in a later step.*

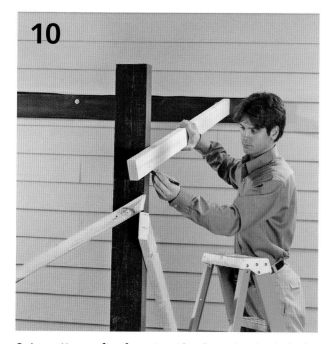

10

Cut a pattern rafter from 2 × 4 lumber using the desired roof slope to find the angle cut for the top end. Angle the bottom end as desired for decorative effect. Set the rafter in position so its top end is even with the top of the ledger and its bottom end passes along the side of a post. Mark along the bottom edge of the rafter onto the post. Repeat to mark the other post. Use a string and line level to make sure the post marks are level with each other.

11

Cut the inner beam member to length from 2 × 10 lumber, then bevel the top edge to follow the roof slope. Position the board so its top edge is on the post markings, and it overhangs the posts equally at both ends (12" of overhang is shown). Tack the board in place with 16d nails.

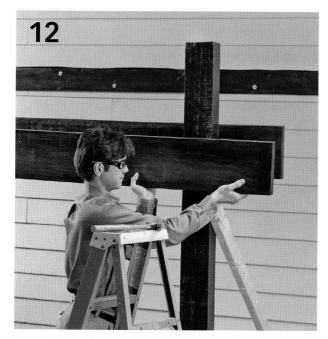

12

Cut the outer beam member to length from 2 × 10 lumber. Bevel the top edge following the roof slope, and remove enough material so that the bottom edges of the two beam members will be level with each other. Tack the member in place with nails.

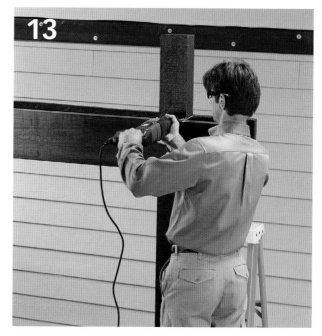

13

Anchor the beam members together and to the posts with pairs of ½"-dia. lag bolts and washers. Cut the posts off flush with the tops of the beam members using a handsaw or reciprocating saw.

(continued)

14

Trim the cutoff post pieces to length and use them as blocking between the beam members. Position the blocks evenly spaced between the posts and fasten them to both beam members with glue and 16d nails. *Note: Diagonal bracing between the posts and beam may be recommended or required in some areas; consult your local building department.*

15

Mark the rafter layout onto the ledger and beam. As shown here, the rafters are spaced 9½" apart on center. The two outer rafters should be flush with the ends of the ledger and beam.

16

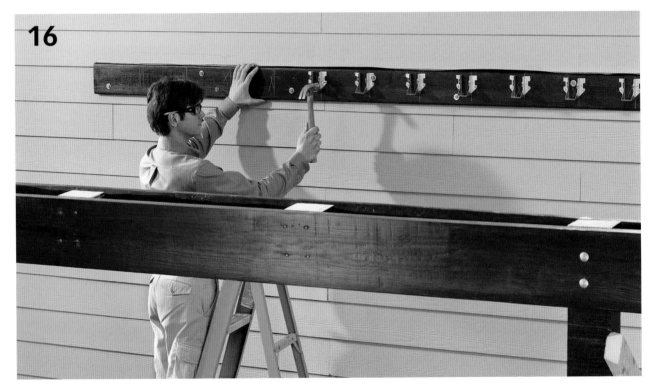

Install metal framing anchors onto the ledger for securing the top rafter ends using the anchor manufacturer's recommended fasteners. Use the pattern rafter or a block to position the anchors so the rafters will be flush with the top of the ledger.

17

Use the pattern rafter to mark the remaining rafters and then cut them. Install the rafters one at a time. Fasten the top ends to the metal anchor using the recommended fasteners. Fasten the bottom ends to both beam members by toenailing one 8d nail through each rafter side and into the beam member.

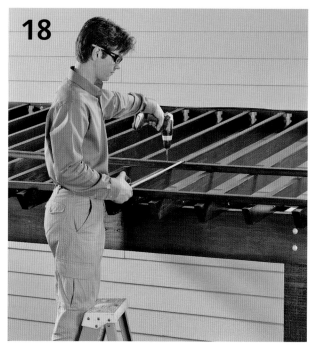

18

Install the 2 × 2 purlins perpendicular to the rafters using 3" deck screws. Position the first purlin a few inches from the bottom ends of the rafters. Space the remaining purlins 24" on center. The ends of the purlins should be flush with the outside faces of the outer rafters.

19

Add 2 × 2 blocking between the purlins along the outer rafters, and fasten them with 3" deck screws. This blocking will support the vertical closure strips for the roof panels.

20

Starting at one side of the roof, install the roof panel closure strips over the purlins using the manufacturer's recommended fasteners. Begin every run of strips from the same side of the roof, so the ridges in the strips will be aligned.

(continued)

21

Add vertical closure strips over the 2 × 2 purlin blocking to fill in between the horizontal strips.

22

Position the first roofing panel along one side edge of the roof. The inside edge of the panel should fall over a rafter. If necessary, trim the panel to length or width following the manufacturer's recommendations.

23

Drill pilot holes, and fasten the first panel to the closure strips with the recommended type of screw and rubber washer. Fasten the panel at the peak (top) of every other corrugation. Drive the screws down carefully, stopping when the washer contacts the panel but is not compressed. This allows for thermal expansion of the panel.

24

Apply a bead of the recommended adhesive/sealant (usually supplied by the panel manufacturer) along the last trough of the roofing panel. Set the second panel into place, overlapping the last troughs on both panels. Fasten the second panel. Install the remaining panels using the same procedure. Caulk the seam between the roof panels and the roof flashing.

25

To create channels for the side glazing panels, mill a rabbet into each of the eight vertical 2 × 2 cleats. Consult the glazing manufacturer for the recommended channel size, making sure to provide space for thermal expansion of the panels. Mill the rabbets using a table saw, router, or circular saw. Stop the rabbets so the bottom edges of the panels will be even with, or slightly above, the bottom edge of the lowest side slat.

Blade guard removed for clarity

If you do not have wall flashing designed to work with the roof profile, place closure strips upside down onto the roof panels and run another bead of adhesive/sealant over the tops of the strips. Work the flashing down and embed it into the sealant. Seal along all exposed edges of the ledger with silicone caulk.

26

Position a cleat on each post at the desired height, with the cleat centered from side to side on the post. The rabbeted corner should face inside the shelter. Fasten the cleats to the posts with 3" deck screws. Fasten two more cleats to the house wall so they are aligned and level with the post cleats.

27

Cut the side slats to length to fit between the posts and the house wall. Mark the slat layouts onto the outside faces of the cleats, and install the slats with 1½" deck screws or exterior trim-head screws. Space the slats 3½" apart or as desired.

(continued)

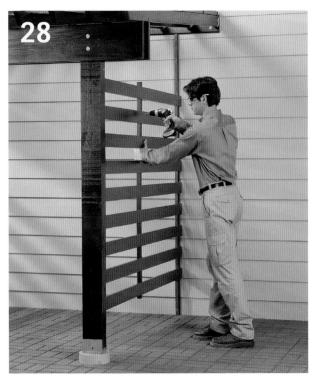

28

Fasten the middle cleats to the slats on each side, leaving about 3½" of space between the cleats (or as desired). The cleats should overhang the top and bottom slats by 1½" (or as desired).

Tip ▶

Used for decorative accent slats on this patio shelter, white oak is a traditional exterior wood that was employed for boatbuilding as well as outdoor furnishings. Although it requires no finishing, we coated the white oak with a dark, penetrating wood stain to bring out the grain.

29

Cut the cap strips for the glazing panels from 1 × 2 material (or rip down strips from the 1 × 4 slat material). Position each cap over a cleat and drill evenly spaced pilot holes through the cap and into the cleat. Make sure the holes go into the solid (non-rabbeted) portion of the cleat. Drill counterbores, too (left). Drive screws to attach the post caps (right).

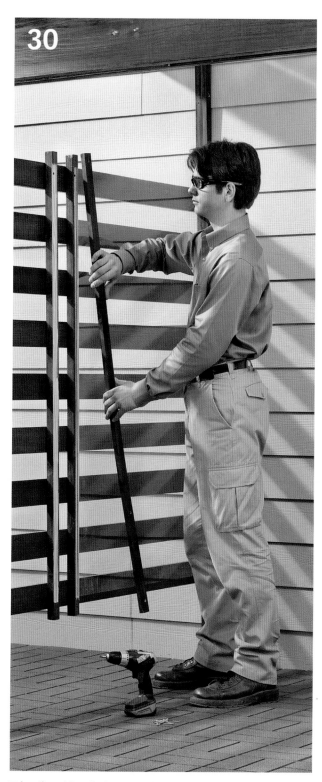

30

Trim the side glazing panels to size following the manufacturer's directions. Apply neoprene or EPDM stripping or packing to the side edges of the panels. Fit each panel into its cleat frame, cover the glazing edges with the 1 × 2 caps, and secure the caps with 1½" deck screws. *Note: If the glazing comes with a protective film, remove the film during this step as appropriate and make sure the panel is oriented for full UV protection.*

Option: Add a 2 × 4 decorative cap on the outside face of each post. Center the cap side-to-side on the post and fasten it with 16d casing nails.

PATIO ARBOR/TRELLIS ENCLOSURE

An arbor is an overhead system of beams, usually supported by posts, that provides shade and is often used to train climbing plants. Arbors can be built as independent yard structures, but they often are combined with a trellis—a lattice wall attached to the side of the arbor (pages 356 to 357). The combined arbor-and-trellis is a traditional, attractive outdoor structure.

Build your arbor structure so it is freestanding—do not attach it directly to your house. A permanent structure that is attached to a house must meet more code requirements than freestanding structures, and there is more risk of structural failure. The arbor featured in this section is made with four-post construction set on sturdy concrete footings. Because it is freestanding, the footings did not need to extend below the frost line. Very small garden arbors can be built with techniques and materials similar to those used for the project shown, but they may not require post footings.

Tools & Materials ▶

Tape measure
Mason's string
Line level
Torpedo level
Carpenter's square
Speed square
Drill
Circular saw
Straight edge
Ratchet-socket set
Ladder
Shovel
Mortar box
Concrete

Isolation boards
Cedar framing lumber
Post anchors
Carriage bolts
Lag screws
Rafter ties
Deck screws or
    6d galvanized nails
J-bolts with nuts
    and washers

YARD & GARDEN STRUCTURES

Arbor structures make a dramatic visual statement when constructed over an ordinary patio. They also help cut down on wind and sun and create a more pleasant outdoor environment.

Freestanding Arbors ▸

An arbor does not need to be attached to your house to function as a patio shelter. In fact, more arbors are built as freestanding units than as attached structures. Because they are so versatile you can locate them so they cast shade only on a portion of a patio, or you can cover the entire area.

The arbor shown here is relatively small. You can easily adapt the design to different sizes, but don't space the posts more than 8 ft. apart. If you want to build a larger arbor, add additional posts between the corner posts. Before you begin construction, check your local building code for footing depth requirements and setback restrictions.

The basics of building a freestanding arbor are as follows. First, lay out the location of the posts using stakes and string. Make sure the layout is square by measuring from corner to corner and adjusting the layout until these diagonal measurements are equal. Dig postholes at the corners to the required depth, using a posthole digger and fill each hole with 6" of gravel.

Next, position the posts in the holes. To brace them in a plumb position, tack support boards to the posts on adjoining faces. Adjust the posts as necessary until they're plumb. Drive a stake into the ground, flush against the base of each 2 × 4. Drive deck screws through the stakes, into the 2 × 4s.

Mix one bag of dry concrete to anchor each post. Immediately check to make sure the posts are plumb, and adjust as necessary until the concrete begins to harden. Let the concrete dry at least 24 hours.

Measure, mark, and cut all the lumber for the arbor. Cut a 3 × 3" notch off the bottom corner of each tie beam, a 2 × 2" notch off the bottom corner of each 2 × 4 rafter, and a 1 × 1" notch off the bottom corner of each cross strip. Position a tie beam against the outside edge of a pair of posts, 7 ft. above the ground. Position the beam to extend about 1 ft. past the post on each side. Level the beam, then clamp it into place with wood screw clamps. Drill pilot holes and attach the tie beam to the posts with 3" lag screws.

Use a line level to mark the opposite pair of posts at the same height as the installed tie beam. Attach the remaining tie beam. Cut off the posts so they're level with the tops of the tie beams.

Next, attach the rafters to the tops of the tie beams, using rafter ties and galvanized nails. Beginning 6" from the ends of the tie beams, space the rafters

2 ft. apart, with the ends extending past each tie beam by 1 ft. Position a cross strip across the top of the rafters, beginning 6" from the ends of the rafters. Center the strip so it extends past the outside rafters by about 6". Drill pilot holes through the cross strip and into the rafters. Attach the cross strip with galvanized screws. Add the remaining cross strips, spacing them 1 ft. apart. Finish your arbor by applying wood sealer/protectant.

This version of a freestanding post-and-slat arbor is a 5 × 5-ft. cedar structure with an extended overhead.

HOW TO BUILD AN ARBOR

Create footings for the arbor posts by digging a hole at least twice the size of the post bottom and at least 12" deep. Fill with concrete, and set a J-bolt in each concrete footing. We positioned the J-bolts so the edges of the posts are flush with the patio.

Allow the footings to harden for at least one day, then attach the post anchor hardware to the J-bolts. Cut and install the arbor posts—for most arbors, 4 × 4 posts are large enough. Cut posts longer than the planned height, and brace them with 2 × 4 braces so they are plumb. Leave the braces in place until the beams and rafters are secured in position.

Use a square to mark the cutting lines for the posts at the desired height: mark the height of the arbor onto the posts at one end, then use a line level to transfer the height mark onto the posts at the other end. With a square, mark cutting lines on all four sides of each post. Trim the posts at the cutting lines using a handsaw. Have a helper steady the post from below while you cut. *Note: You may use a power saw, like a cordless circular saw, to cut off the post tops, but only if your ladder provides enough elevation that you can work from above the cutting line.*

YARD & GARDEN STRUCTURES

Cut beam members from 2 × 8 stock. Because we used two beam members each at the front and back of the project, we cut four beam members. To create a 6" overhang at each side, we cut the beam members 12" longer than the distance between the outside edges of the posts. Mark all beam members with a carpenter's square, then gang-cut them with a circular saw and a straightedge.

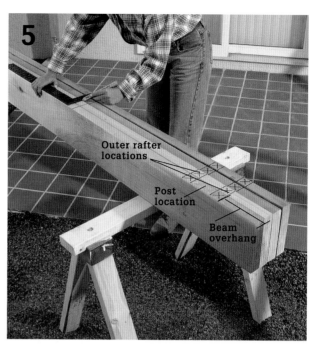

Turn beams on edge, and mark locations for the rafters. Rafters should be no more than 24" apart. Start by marking the outermost rafters—our plan called for a rafter at the inside and outside edge of each post. Don't forget to include the beam overhang in the layout.

Fasten the beam members to the posts at the front and back of the arbor. Screw a guide strip securely to the top of each post, then position the beam members and hold them in place temporarily by driving a screw down through the guide strip and into the top of each beam member. When installing beam pairs, as shown here, use a pair of carriage bolts with washers and nuts at each beam/post joint. Attach a ½" bit with a bit extension to your drill, and drill holes for the carriage bolts through both the beam members and the post.

(continued)

Pound ½"-diameter carriage bolts through the holes. Carriage bolts should be ½" to 1" longer than the combined widths of the outer rafters and the beam. For this project, we used a 7"-long bolt. Slip a washer and nut onto the end of the carriage bolt and tighten with a ratchet. Remove the guide strip.

Measure and mark 2 × 6 rafters to fit on top of the beams, perpendicular to the house. For best appearance, rafters should overhang the beams by at least 6". Cut with a circular saw. For added visual appeal, mark an angled cut of about 30° at the end of one rafter, then cut off with a circular saw. Use the rafter as a template to transfer the angle to the other rafters.

Install the rafters on top of the beams at the rafter layout marks. Position the rafters so the angled ends are at the front of the project, with the shorter side resting on the beam. Use metal rafter ties, mounted to the beams, and deck screws to attach the rafters. *Option: Because the metal rafter ties can be quite visible in the finished product, you may prefer to toenail the rafters in place with 16d galvanized nails.*

Mark the posts and beams for crossbraces. From the inside corner of each post/beam joint, mark an equal distance (about 18") on the beam and the post. For crossbraces that fit between rafters, measure from the post mark to the top of the rafter, following the line created between the post mark and the beam mark. For crossbraces that fit flush with the post and the beam, measure from the post mark to the beam mark for the inside dimension of the crossbrace.

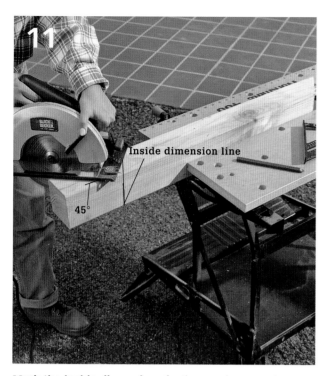

Mark the inside dimensions for the crossbraces onto a piece of lumber of the same type as the posts (here, 4 × 4). Use a square or triangle to draw 45° cutting lines away from each end point of the inside dimension. Cut along these lines with a circular saw to make the crossbraces.

Install the crossbraces. Tack the crossbraces in position, then attach them with ⅜" × 4" lag screws. If the crossbrace is fitted between the rafters, drive the lag screws through the counterbored pilot holes in the rafter and into the cross brace at the top. Attach with lag screws at each joint. Drive lag screws through the counterbored pilot holes that are perpendicular to the post or rafter.

Install the arbor slats on top of the rafters. We used 2 × 2 cedar spaced at 4" intervals. Include an overhang of at least 6". Attach the arbor slats with 2½" deck screws driven down through the slats and into the rafters.

ADDING A TRELLIS TO AN ARBOR

Add a lattice-panel trellis to an arbor structure for a more decorative appearance. Using manufactured lattice panels and lattice molding and hanging the panels with metal fence-panel hangers makes the job inexpensive and quick. Or, you can build your own lattice and frame. Plant climbing-type plants and train them up the trellis to embellish the arbor-and-trellis.

Lattice panels are used to create the trellis portion of an arbor-and-trellis. Most building centers carry cedar, pressure-treated, and vinyl lattice in 2 × 8-ft. and 4 × 8-ft. panels. Standard lattice panels are ¾" thick. For a more customized look, you can build your own lattice panels from exterior-rated lumber.

Tools & Materials ▸

Pencil
Tape measure
Circular saw
Chalk line
Hammer
Clamps
Drill

4 × 8 lattice panels
Lattice molding
Galvanized brads
Fence brackets
Work gloves
Eye and ear protection

HOW TO ADD A TRELLIS TO AN ARBOR

If the planned trellis is wider than 4 ft., you will need additional support posts. Install posts using the same materials and techniques used for the corner posts of the arbor. If possible, install the posts so the lattice panels on either side of each post will be equal in size.

Measure the openings between the posts to determine the sizes for the lattice panels. Generally, panels should be sized so they are installed below the crossbraces between posts. Leave a few inches of open space beneath the panels at ground level. Mark the locations of the panel tops onto the posts using a level to make sure the tops are even.

Subtract 1½" from the frame opening dimensions, and cut the lattice panels to size. To cut lattice panels, sandwich each panel between two boards near the cutting line to prevent the lattice from separating. Clamp the boards and the panel together and cut with a circular saw.

Miter-cut 2 × 2 lattice molding to frame the lattice panels. The finished width of the panel should be ½" narrower than the opening. Nail one vertical and one horizontal frame piece together with galvanized brads. Set the lattice panel into the channels, and attach the other frame pieces. Secure the lattice panels into the molding by driving brads through the molding and into the lattice at 12" intervals.

Attach three fence brackets to the posts, evenly spaced, on each side of the opening using 4d galvanized nails. On the top two brackets, bend the bottom and top flanges flat against the post. Bend all outside flanges flat, away from the post, to allow installation of the lattice panel.

Set the panels in the brackets, and bend the hanger flanges back to their original positions. Drive 1" galvanized nails through the flanges of the fence hangers and into the frames of the lattice panels.

UNDER-DECK ENCLOSURE

Second-story walk-out decks can be a mixed blessing. On top, you have an open, sun-filled perch with a commanding view of the landscape. The space below the deck, however, is all too often a dark and chilly nook that is functionally unprotected from water runoff. As a result, an under-deck area often ends up as wasted space or becomes a holding area for seasonal storage items or the less desirable outdoor furniture.

But there's an easy way to reclaim all that convenient outdoor space—by installing a weatherizing ceiling system that captures runoff water from the deck above, leaving the area below dry enough to convert into a versatile outdoor room. You can even enclose the space to create a screened-in patio room.

The under-deck system featured in this project is designed for do-it-yourself installation. Its components are made to fit almost any standard deck and come in three sizes to accommodate different deck-joist spacing (for 12", 16", and 24" on-center spacing). Once the system is in place, the under-deck area is effectively "dried in", and you can begin adding

amenities like overhead lighting, ceiling fans, and speakers to complete the outdoor room environment.

The system works by capturing water that falls through the decking above and channeling it to the outside edge of the deck. Depending on your plans, you can let the water fall from the ceiling panels along the deck's edge, or you can install a standard rain gutter and downspout to direct the water to a single exit point on the ground.

Tools & Materials ›

4-ft. level	Hacksaw (for optional
Tape measure	rain gutter)
Chalk line	Under-deck ceiling system
Caulking gun	Waterproof acrylic caulk
Drill	1" stainless steel screws
Pencil	Rain gutter system
Aviation snips	(optional)
Work gloves	Eye and ear protection

Made of weather-resistant vinyl, this under-deck system creates an attractive, maintenance-free ceiling that keeps the space below dry throughout the seasons.

DESIGN TIPS

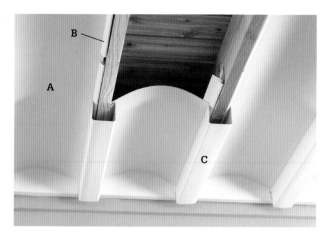

This under-deck system (see Resources, page 553) consists of four main parts: The joist rails mount to the deck joists and help secure the other components. The collector panels (A) span the joist cavity to capture water falling through the deck above. Water flows to the sides of the panels where it falls through gaps in the joist rails (B) and into the joist gutters (C) (for interior joists) and boundary gutters (for outer joists). The gutters carry the water to the outside edge of the deck.

For a finished look, paint the decking lumber that will be exposed after the system is installed. Typically, the lower portion of the ledger board (attached to the house) and the outer rim joist (at the outer edge of the deck) remain exposed.

Consider surrounding architectural elements when you select a system for sealing off the area below your deck. Here, the under-deck system is integrated with the deck and deck stairs both visually and functionally.

HOW TO INSTALL AN UNDER-DECK SYSTEM

Check the undersides of several deck joists to make sure the structure is level. This is important for establishing the proper slope for effective water flow.

How bad is it? If your deck is not level, you must compensate for this when setting the ceiling slope. To determine the amount of correction that's needed, hold one end of the level against a joist and tilt the level until it reads perfectly level. Measure the distance from the joist to the free end of the level. Then, divide this measurement by the length of the level. For example, if the distance is ¼" and the level is 4 ft. long, the deck is out of level by ¹⁄₁₆" per foot.

To establish the slope for the ceiling system, mark the ends of the joists closest to the house: Measure up from the bottom 1" for every 10 ft. of joist length (or approximately ⅛" per ft.) and make a mark. Mark both sides of each intermediate joist and the inside faces of the outer joists.

Create each slope reference line using a chalk line: Hold one end of the chalk line at the mark made in Step 3, and hold the other end at the bottom edge of the joist where it meets the rim joist at the outside edge of the deck. Snap a reference line on all of the joists.

5

Install vinyl flashing along the ledger board in the joist cavities. Attach the flashing with 1" stainless steel screws. Caulk along the top edges of the flashing where it meets the ledger and both joists using quality, waterproof acrylic caulk. Also caulk the underside of the flashing for an extra layer of protection.

6

Begin installing the joist rails, starting 1" away from the ledger. Position each rail with its bottom edge on the chalk line, and fasten it to the joist at both ends with 1" stainless steel screws; then add one or two screws in between. Avoid over-driving the screws and deforming the rail; leaving a little room for movement is best.

7

Install the remaining rails on each joist face, leaving a 1½" (minimum) to 2" (maximum) gap between rails. Install rails along both sides of each interior joist and along the insides of each outside joist. Trim the final rail in each row as needed using aviation snips.

8

Measure the full length of each joist cavity, and cut a collector panel ¼" shorter than the cavity. This allows room for expansion of the panels. For narrower joist cavities, trim the panel to width following the manufacturer's sizing recommendations.

(continued)

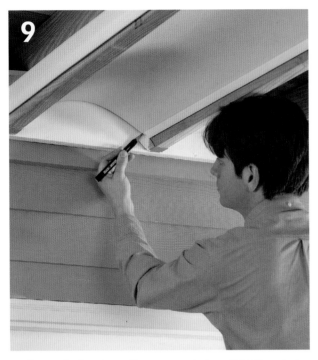

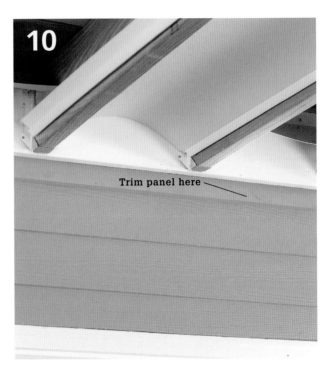

Scribe and trim the collector panels for a tight fit against the ledger board. Hold a carpenter's pencil flat against the ledger, and move the pencil along the board to transfer its contours to the panel. Trim the panel along the scribed line.

Trim the corners of the collector panels as needed to accommodate joist hangers and other hardware. This may be necessary only at the house side of the joist cavity; at the outer end, the ¼" expansion gap should clear any hardware.

Install the collector panels, starting at the house. With the textured side of the panel facing down, insert one side edge into the joist rails, and then push up gently on the opposite side until it fits into the opposing rails. When fully installed, the panels should be tight against the ledger and have a ¼" gap at the rim joist.

Prepare each joist gutter by cutting it ¼" shorter than the joist it will attach to (if the joists rest on a structural beam, see Variation, on page 364). On the house end of each gutter, trim the corners of the flanges at 45°. This helps the gutter fit tightly to the ledger.

13

Cut four or five ⅛" tabs into the bottom surface at the outside ends of the gutters. This helps promote the drainage of water over the edge of the gutter.

14

Caulk here

Attach self-adhesive foam weatherstrip (available from the manufacturer) at the home-end of each joist gutter. Run a bead of caulk along the foam strip to water-seal it to the gutter. The weather strip serves as a water dam.

15

Install each joist gutter by spreading its sides open slightly while pushing the gutter up onto the joist rails until it snaps into place. The gutter should fit snugly against the collector panels. The gutter's home-end should be tight against the ledger, with the ¼" expansion gap at the rim joist.

16

Prepare the boundary gutters following the same steps used for the joist gutters. Install each boundary gutter by slipping its long, outside flange behind the joist rails and pushing up until the gutter snaps into place. Install the boundary gutters working from the house side to the outer edge of the deck.

17

Run a bead of color-matched caulk along the joint where the collector panels meet the ledger board. This is for decorative purposes only and is not required to prevent water intrusion.

18

If collector panels are misshapen because the joist spacing is too tight, free the panel within the problem area, then trim about ⅛" from the side edge of the panel. Reset the panel in the rails. If necessary, trim the panel edge again in slight increments until the panel fits properly.

Working Around Beams ▸

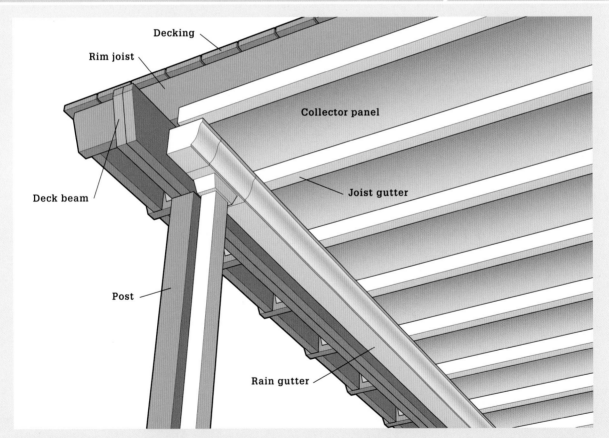

Decking

Rim joist

Deck beam

Post

Collector panel

Joist gutter

Rain gutter

For decks that have joists resting on top of a structural beam, stop the joist gutters and boundary gutters 1½" short of the beam. Install a standard rain gutter along the house-side of the beam to catch the water as it exits the system gutters (see pages 362 to 363). (On the opposite side of the beam, begin new runs of joist gutters that are tight against the beam and stop ¼" short of the rim joist. The joist rails and collector panels should clear the beam and can be installed as usual.) Or, you can simply leave the overhang area alone if you do not need water runoff protection below it.

RUNOFF GUTTERS

A basic gutter system for a square or rectangular deck includes a straight run of gutter channel with a downspout at one end. Prefabricated vinyl or aluminum gutter parts are ideal for this application. Gutter channels are commonly available in 10-ft. and 20-ft. lengths, so you might be able to use a single channel without seams. Otherwise, you can join sections of channel with special connectors. Shop around for the best type of hanger for your situation. If there's limited backing to support the back side of the channel or to fasten into, you may have to use strap-type hangers that can be secured to framing above the gutter.

Tools & Materials ▸

Chalk line
Drill
Hanger clips
Hacksaw
Pain
Work gloves
Eye and ear protection

Runoff gutters are installed at the ends of the under-deck channels to capture runoff water and redirect it away from the enclosed area through downspouts.

HOW TO INSTALL AN UNDER-DECK RUNOFF GUTTER

1

Snap a chalk line onto the beam or other supporting surface to establish the slope of the main gutter run. The line will correspond to the top edge of the gutter channel. The ideal slope is $\frac{1}{16}$" per foot. For example, with a 16-ft.-long gutter, the beginning is 1" higher than the end. The downspout should be located just inside the low end of the gutter channel. Mark the beam at both ends to create the desired slope, then snap a chalk line between the marks. The high end of the gutter should be just below the boundary gutter in the ceiling system.

(continued)

2

Install a downspout outlet near the end of the gutter run so the top of the gutter is flush with the slope line. If you plan to enclose the area under the deck, choose an inconspicuous location for the downspout, away from traffic areas.

3

Install hanger clips (depending on the type of hangers or support clips you use, it is often best to install them before installing the gutter channel). Attach a hanger every 24" so the top of the gutter will hang flush with the slope line.

Tip ▶

Gutters come in several material types, including PVC, enameled steel and copper. In most cases you should try to match the surrounding trim materials, but using a more decorative material for contrast can be effective.

4

Cut sections of gutter channel to size using a hacksaw. Attach an end cap to the beginning of the main run, then fit the channel into the downspout outlet (allowing for expansion, if necessary) and secure the gutter in place.

5

Join sections of channel together, if necessary, for long runs using connectors. Install a short section of channel with an end cap on the opposite side of the downspout outlet. Paint the area where the downspout will be installed if it is unpainted.

6

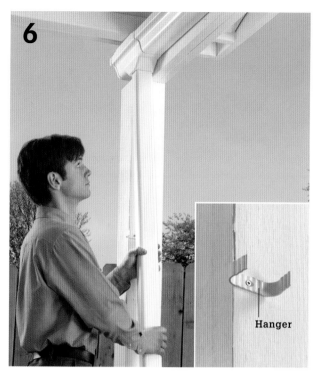

Hanger

Cut the downspout piping to length and fasten an elbow fitting to its bottom end. Attach the downspout to the downspout outlet, then secure the downspout to a post or other vertical support using hangers (inset).

7

Cut a drainpipe to run from the downspout elbow to a convenient drainage point. Position the pipe so it directs water away from the house and any traffic areas. Attach the pipe to the downspout elbow. Add a splash block, if desired.

▶ Routing Drainpipes ▸

You may have to get a little creative when routing the downspout drain in an enclosed porch or patio. Shown here, two elbows allow for a 90° turn of the drainpipe.

SUN PORCH

A sun porch, a sunroom, a three-season porch, a greenhouse, a hothouse, an orangerie, a conservatory . . . these names are not precisely interchangeable but all refer to a similar type of room. The common element all types share is that their walls and usually their roofs are made of clear panel glazing that allows light in and traps it, raising the ambient room temperature to more comfortable levels in cooler times of year. Some of these structures are designed for gardening-related activities; others are meant for enjoyment or entertainment. Some are freestanding, others are attached to a house.

If it is custom-built for you by a professional contractor, a sunroom can be quite expensive. But there is another option: a sunroom in a box. You can have a complete, do-it-yourself sunroom kit delivered to your home in cardboard boxes. A good deal of assembly is required, of course, but with a few basic tools and a helper, most people with basic DIY skills can complete the job in a weekend.

The key features of this sun porch (manufactured by SunPorch Structures Inc., see Resources page 553) are its easy installation and its versatility. First, it's designed to install right on top of an existing concrete patio slab or a wood deck, eliminating the extensive site-prep work required with a custom project. If you don't have a patio or deck in place, you can build an inexpensive foundation with landscape timbers to support the sunroom structure, then create a floor inside using brick pavers, stone, wood decking tiles, or other suitable material. The sunroom manufacturer and your local building department can help you with the planning and construction details.

The sunroom's versatility is apparent in both its design and use. Its modular construction allows you to specify the height, width, and length of the structure to fit your needs and your house. Other modifications can be made at the factory to accommodate special installation requirements, such as installing the room to fit against the roof eave of your house or even slightly above the eave. The standard room design includes two matching end walls and a front wall. If your sunroom will fit into a corner where two house walls meet, simply order the room without one of the end walls. The sizes of end walls also can be adjusted to fit other house configurations.

Operable and removable windows make this sunroom versatile to use. In cooler months, all the windows can be closed against the cold to keep the sun's heat inside. As the weather warms up, you can open either the top or bottom window sash to capture the breezes. And in the summer, you can take the windows out completely to convert the sunroom into a fully screened patio room.

Check In With Your Building Department ▸

It's up to you to gain legal approval for your sunroom project. Contact your city's building department to learn what its rules are. Some municipalities require permits and inspections for DIY sunrooms, while others exclude structures that are installed over existing patios or decks and do not change the home's footprint. In any case, you should also consult with a qualified building professional to make sure your patio, deck, or other foundation can safely support a sunroom.

A DIY sunroom kit comes with all of the parts precut and predrilled for your own custom design. Assembling the kit is a relatively easy task that most couples can accomplish in a weekend.

Commercial-grade, lightweight glazing, and predrilled aluminum frame parts are the key components that make this sunroom kit lightweight and durable enough for shipping and also easy to assemble. Sunrooms can be perfectly acceptable spaces for evening activities, if you equip them with light fixtures (left).

SUN PORCH KIT ACCESSORIES

Skylight shades give you control over light and heat coming through the roof panels. These 2-in-1 shades have a solid reflective panel that blocks most of the sun's light and heat and a translucent panel that blocks only half of the sunlight to reduce glare and heat gain while letting light filter through.

Precisely fitted wall shades are convenient for reducing glare and heat gain right where you need it. They're also great for adding privacy when and where you want it without blocking all of your sunroom views.

Optional roof vents allow hot air to escape and help to flush the interior of the sunroom with fresh air. Adjustable covers let you control the rate of air flow. The opening and closing mechanism is easy to operate from inside the sunporch.

OPTIONS FOR ATTACHING A SUN PORCH TO YOUR HOUSE

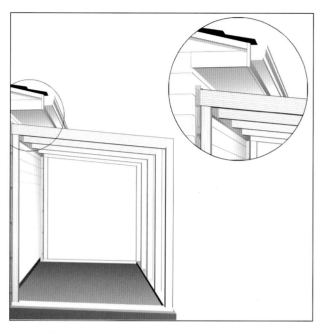

Attach the ledger directly to the wall if there is no eave overhang or if there is at least 6" of clear working space between the top of the ledger and the bottom of the eaves.

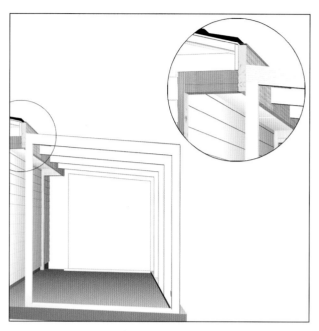

If the maximum height of the sun porch brings it up against or within 6" of the bottom of the eave overhang, extend the fascia on the eave downward and fill in with boards or siding between the cornice and the back post for the sun porch.

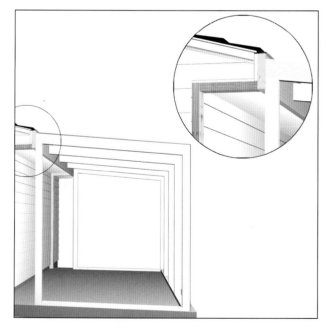

The ledger for the sun porch can be attached directly to the fascia board as long as the highest point of the sun-porch roof remains slightly lower than the roof covering. Be sure to attach the ledger so the lag screws hit into the ends of the rafter tails.

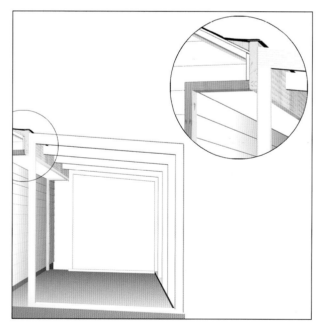

If the sun porch is slightly taller than the roof eaves, you can add a ledger that's taller than the fascia, but it cannot extend more than a couple of inches higher. Fill in the open area beneath the roof covering created at the side using a full-width wood wedge and caulk. The roof covering must retain a slight slope with no swales.

PREPARING THE INSTALLATION SITE

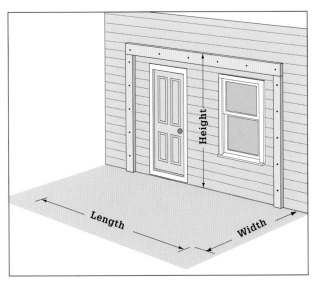

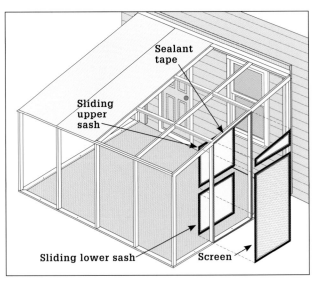

When attaching a sun porch directly to your exterior wall, install 2 × 6 or 2 × 8 edges and hang the roof support beams from it. Also install 2 × 4 vertical nailers beneath the ends of the edges for attaching the walls to the house. Ledgers also may be mounted to rafter ends in the eave area (see previous page).

Sun porch kits with non-glass panels can be mounted on practically any hard surface because they are light enough that they do not require a reinforced floor. You do need to make sure the floor is level, however (see page 375), and that the base channels you lay out create square corners.

THE BENEFITS OF ROOF VENTILATION

Without roof vents, hot air is trapped in the sunroom, making it uncomfortable for users and inhospitable to plants.

A single roof vent creates an escape route for hot air, allowing you to regulate the temperature and keep the room cooler during hot weather. Multiple roof vents increase the ventilation efficiency, but increase the chances for leaks.

OPTIONS FOR ANCHORING A SUN PORCH

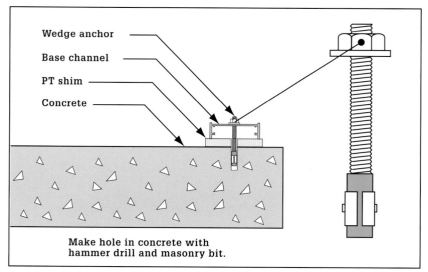

Wedge anchor
Base channel
PT shim
Concrete

Make hole in concrete with
hammer drill and masonry bit.

On concrete patios, attach the base channel to the concrete surface with masonry anchors. There are many styles of anchors you can use. The hardware shown here is a wedge anchor that is driven into a hole drilled through the base channel and into the concrete. If your concrete slab is not level, you'll need to insert shims underneath the base channel in low spots.

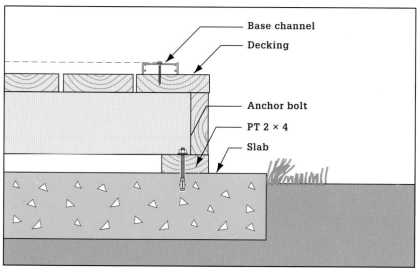

Base channel
Decking
Anchor bolt
PT 2 × 4
Slab

Building a new ground-level deck is a good way to create a stable floor for your sun porch if your concrete patio is in poor condition or if there is no other floor structure in the installation area. Attach pressure-treated 2 × 4 sleepers to the concrete surface to create a raised surface to set the deck on.

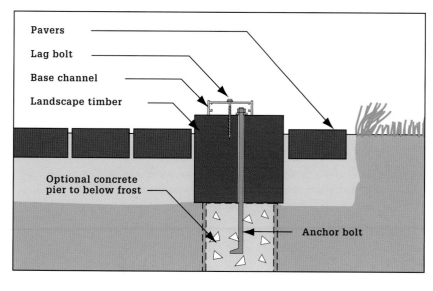

Pavers
Lag bolt
Base channel
Landscape timber
Optional concrete pier to below frost
Anchor bolt

Set treated wood timbers onto a concrete footing for a sturdy wall base that you can attach to directly when installing the base channels. The footings should extend below your frost line to keep the structure from shifting, but you can use a less permanent floor system, such as sand-set pavers, if you wish.

Tools & Materials

4-ft. level	Exterior house paint
Drill and bits	Metal roof flashing
¼" and ⅜" hex nut drivers	100% silicone caulk
#2 square screw (Robertson) bit	¼" × 1½" and ¼" × 2½" corrosion-resistant lag screws
Socket wrench set	and washers
Chalk line	Additional fasteners for securing sunroom to house
Caulking gun	and supporting surface
Rubber mallet	Work gloves
Pressure-treated 2 × 4 and 2 × 6 lumber	Eye and ear protection

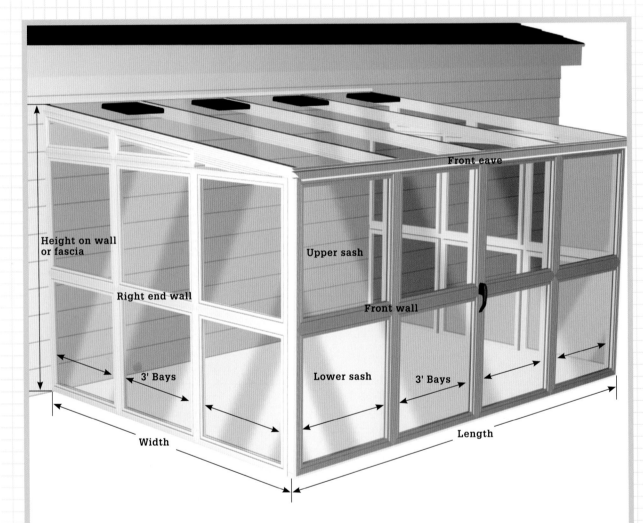

Sun Porch Terms

Mounting surface: May be a level wood deck, concrete slab or patio.

Right and left end walls: Reference point is with your back to the house looking outwards.

Kneewall (not shown): A site built wall used to increase the height of the structure.

Door Information

Door (included with kit) may be mounted in any front or end wall bay.

Door opening is 33" wide and 72" high.

Door swings outward and can be hinged for left-hand or right-hand operation.

HOW TO BUILD A SUN PORCH KIT

1

Install pressure-treated 2 x 4 vertical support cleats and a 2 × 6 horizontal support ledger onto the house wall, following the manufacturer's specifications (See page 371 for options). On non-lap siding, mount the support pieces directly over the siding. For lap siding, cut away the siding and mount the ledger and support cleats over the wall sheathing and building paper. Paint the ledger and cleats before installation, and add roof flashing over the header, leaving it unfastened until the sunroom roof is completely assembled. Make sure the ledger is perfectly level and the vertical cleats are plumb.

Countering Slope ▸

Make sure the wood deck, patio, or other installation base is level before installing the sunroom. If not, you may need to install long wood wedges that fit under the floor plates or take other corrective measures as suggested in your installation manual.

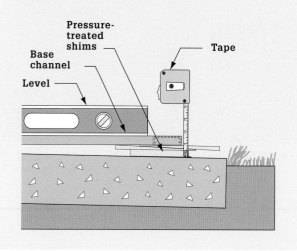

2

Lay out the base channel pieces onto your surface in the installation area. Join the pieces using the provided splice brackets and screws.

(continued)

YARD & GARDEN STRUCTURES

Position the free ends of the base channel against the wall cleats. Use a 4-ft. level to make sure the channel sections are level. If necessary, use tapered shims to level the channel. Then, check the base frame for square by measuring diagonally from corner to corner. Make adjustments as needed until the measurements are equal.

Fasten the base frame to the surface using a recommended fastener at each of the predrilled mounting holes. Apply a bead of silicone caulk where the channel meets the surface on both sides of the channel. Install the base channel vertical brackets to the base channels using the provided screws (inset photo). These brackets will join the vertical end-wall tubes and front-wall columns to the base channel frame.

To begin assembling the wall and roof structures, first join the end-wall headers (the two outside rafters) and the rafters (the interior rafters) to the front-wall columns using the provided mounting brackets and screws. Also install the mounting brackets onto the free ends of the headers and rafters; these are used to mount the headers and rafters to the 2 × 6 support ledger (per step 1 on page 375) on the house wall.

Complete the end-wall assemblies by joining the vertical wall tubes to the end-wall headers using the provided hardware. Finally, install the mullion brackets onto the sides of the rafters and end-wall headers; these will join the horizontal mullions to the rafters and headers to tie the roof frame together (see Step 11).

With a helper, raise one of the end-wall assemblies into position and set the vertical tubes over the base channel brackets. Fasten the tubes to the brackets with screws. Install the other end-wall assembly the same way.

Anchor the end-wall assemblies to the 2 × 4 support cleats and the 2 × 6 support ledger on the house wall. Use a level to position the vertical tubes perfectly plumb, and secure the tubes to the cleats using the recommended fasteners driven through the predrilled holes. Secure the end-wall headers to the 2 × 6 support header using the recommended fasteners.

(continued)

Snap a chalk line across the face of the 2 × 6 support ledger so the line is flush with the tops of the end-wall headers. This line corresponds to the tops of the rafters and the bottom edge of the top mullion pieces.

Working from one end wall to the other, position the first rafter-front column assembly in place, and secure the column to the base channel using the provided screws. Then, install the horizontal mullions between the end-wall header and the first rafter using the provided screws. Repeat this process to install the remaining rafter assemblies and mullions.

Install the top mullion pieces: Apply silicone caulk to the 2 × 6 support ledger to seal the vertical flange of the top mullions to the ledger. Also caulk where the horizontal flanges of the mullions will meet the end-wall headers and rafters. Working from the right end wall to the left, secure the top mullions to the end-wall headers and the rafters using the provided screws.

Anchor the rafters to the 2 × 6 support ledger using the recommended fasteners driven through the mounting brackets you installed on the rafter ends in Step 6.

Install the header caps over the tops of the end-wall headers; these will help secure the roof glazing panels. First apply a bead of caulk down the center of each header, stopping it 3" from the end of the header. Set each cap into the wet caulk and secure it with the provided screws. Install the rafter caps following the same procedure.

Install the eave mullions over the exposed ends of the rafters and end-wall headers. Apply caulk over the center of each frame part and around each predrilled hole. Set the mullions into the wet caulk and secure them with screws. *Note: Complete all additional caulking of the framing as recommended by the manufacturer.*

(continued)

Prepare the roofing panels for installation by taping the ends: Cover the top end of each panel with a strip of aluminum tape, and cover the bottom end with vented tape; both tapes are provided. Follow the manufacturers instructions to install any optional roof vents.

Apply adhesive foam gasket strips (provided) to the roof battens that will secure the glazing panels to the roof framing, following the manufacturer's directions. Be careful not to pull or stretch the gaskets. Also apply gaskets to the roof framing, along the end-wall headers, rafters, top mullions, and eave mullions, as directed.

Remove the protective film from the first roofing panel, making sure the UV-protected side of the panel is facing up. With a helper, place the panel on top of the end-wall header and the adjacent rafter at one end of the roof. The panel should rest against the eave mullion along the front wall.

Secure the outside edge and ends
of the panel with the appropriate battens, using the provided screws. To fasten battens to the eave mullion, first drill pilot holes into the mullion, using the predrilled batten holes as a guide. Carefully caulk the panel and battens at the prescribed locations.

Position the next roofing panel
onto the rafters, and secure it with battens. The long, vertical batten covers both long edges of the first two panels. *Tip: You have to reach across a panel to fasten vertical battens. This is easiest when you have a tall ladder and use a magnetic nut driver on your drill, which allows you to drive the screws with one hand.* Complete the flashing details along the 2 × 6 roof header as directed.

Install the remaining roofing panels,
following the same procedure. Be sure to caulk the roofing carefully at all prescribed locations.

(continued)

21

Begin the wall section installation by adding a triangular aluminum filler piece to the front section of each end wall. Install the fillers with the provided brackets and screws, then caulk along the top and ends of the fillers as directed.

22

Apply sealant tape along the perimeter of the first section on the front wall. Press the strips of tape firmly together to create a seal at each corner. *Tip: Storing the roll of tape in the refrigerator prior to installation makes it easier to work with.*

Tip ▶

The sunroom's door can go into any one of the wall sections. When choosing the location, plan for easy access to both the house and yard. Also consider how the sunroom's layout will be affected by traffic flow into and out of the door. The door itself always opens out, but it can be hinged on either the right or left side.

23

Determine the door location (see Tip, previous page). Install the first screen/window frame: Set the panel onto the base channel, making sure the frame's weep holes are at the bottom. Align the frame within the opening, and press inward firmly to seat it into the sealant tape. Secure the frame with the provided screws. Install the remaining frames using the same techniques.

24

Install the trapezoidal windows under the headers on the end walls: Apply sealant tape as before, position the window, then secure it with the provided screws.

(continued)

25

Complete the window installation by removing the bottom and top sash of each window frame. Peel off the protective film from the glazing, then reinstall each sash, following the manufacturer's directions.

26

Begin the door installation by fastening the door threshold to the base channel, using the provided screws. Then, add the weatherstripping to the hinge bar and latch bar pieces and the header piece. Trim the excess weatherstripping.

27

Decide which side of the door will be hinged. Align the hinge bar (with door attached) to the markings on the vertical wall tube or front column, drill pilot holes, and mount the door to the column with screws.

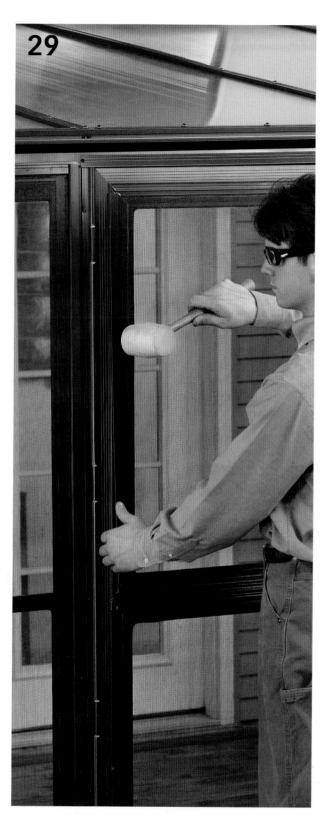

28

Install the latch bar, leaving a ⅛" gap between the bar and the door edge. Install the header piece, also with a ⅛" gap. Complete the door assembly to add the handle, sweep, and closer, following the manufacturer's instructions.

29

Apply sealant tape to the door frame, and install the two glazing panels as directed. Add the decorative cover on each side of the door, seating it with a rubber mallet. If the door is located on one of the end walls, install the trapezoidal window above the door, using the same techniques described in Step 24.

DIY GABLED GREENHOUSE

A greenhouse can be a decorative and functional building that adds beauty to your property. A greenhouse also can be a quick-and-easy, temporary structure that serves a purpose and then disappears. The wood-framed greenhouse seen here fits somewhere between these two types. The sturdy wood construction will hold up for many seasons. The plastic sheeting covering will last one to four or five seasons, depending on the materials you choose, and it is easy to replace when it starts to degrade.

The five-foot-high kneewalls in this design provide ample space for installing and working on a conventional-height potting table. The walls also provide some space for plants to grow. For a door, this plan simply employs a sheet of weighted plastic that can be tied out of the way for entry and exit. If you plan to go in and out of the greenhouse frequently, you can purchase a prefabricated greenhouse door from a greenhouse materials supplier. To allow for ventilation in hot weather, we built a wood-frame vent cover that fits over one rafter bay and can be propped open easily.

You can use hand-driven nails or pneumatic framing nails to assemble the frame if you wish, although deck screws make more sense for a small structure like this.

A wood-frame greenhouse with sheet-plastic cover is an inexpensive, semipermanent gardening structure that can be used as a potting area as well as a protective greenhouse.

Tools, Materials & Cutting List

(1) 20 × 50-ft. roll 4- or 6-mil
   polyethylene sheeting
(12) 24"-long pieces of No. 3 rebar
(8) 8" timber screws
Compactable gravel (or drainage gravel)
Excavation tools
Level
Circular saw
Drill/driver with nut-driver bit
Reciprocating saw
Maul
Hammer
3" deck screws
Speed square
Jigsaw or handsaw
Wire brads
Brad nailer (optional)
Scissors
Utility knife
Tape measure
Work gloves
Eye and ear protection

Key	No.	Part	Dimension	Material
A	2	Base ends	3½" × 3½" × 96"	4 × 4 landscape timber
B	2	Base sides	3½" × 3½" × 113"	4 × 4 landscape timber
C	2	Sole plates end	1½" × 3½" × 89"	2 × 4 pressure-treated
D	2	Sole plates side	1½" × 3½" × 120"	2 × 4 pressure-treated
E	12	Wall studs side	1½" × 3½" × 57"	2 × 4
F	1	Ridge support	1½" × 3½" × 91"	2 × 4
G	2	Back studs	1½" × 3½" × 76" *	2 × 4
H	2	Door frame sides	1½" × 3½" × 81" *	2 × 4
I	1	Cripple stud	1½" × 3½" × 16"	2 × 4
J	1	Door header	1½" × 3½" × 32"	2 × 4
K	2	Kneewall caps	1½" × 3½" × 120"	2 × 4
L	1	Ridge pole	1½" × 3½" × 120"	2 × 4
M	12	Rafters	1½" × 3½" × 60" *	2 × 4

*Approximate dimension; take actual length and angle
measurements on structure before cutting.*

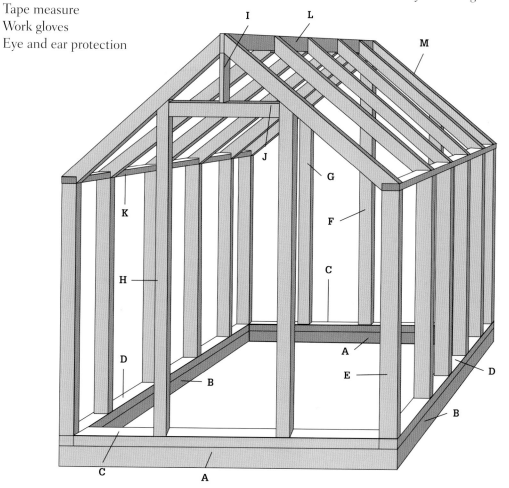

HOW TO BUILD A GABLED GREENHOUSE

Prepare the installation area so it is flat and well drained; then cut the base timbers (4 × 4 landscape timbers) to length. Arrange the timbers so they are flat and level and create a rectangle with square corners. Drive a pair of 8" timber screws at each corner, using a drill/driver with a nut-driver bit.

Cut 12 pieces of #3 rebar to length at 24" (if necessary), using a reciprocating saw or hacksaw. Drill a ⅜"-dia. pilot hole through each timber, near both ends and in the middle. Confirm that the timber frame is square by measuring diagonally between opposing corners (the measurements must be equal). Drive a rebar spike through each hole, using a sledgehammer, until the bar is flush with the timber.

Cut the sole plates, caps, and studs for the two kneewalls. Mark the stud layouts onto the plates and caps, spacing the studs at 24" on center. Assemble each kneewall by driving 3" deck screws through the sole plates and caps and into the ends of the studs.

Install the kneewalls onto the timber base. Set each wall onto a side timber so the sole plate is flush with the ends and side edges of the timber frame. Fasten the sole plate to the timber with 3" deck screws.

5
Temporary post

Begin the end walls by cutting and installing the end sole plates to fit between the side plates, using 3" deck screws. Cut the ridge support posts to length. Install one post at the center of each end sole plate, using screws or nails driven at an angle (toenailed). Check the posts with a level to make sure they're plumb before fastening. *Note: The front post will be cut later to create the door opening.*

6
Ridge pole

Set the ridge pole on top of the support posts and check it for level. Install temporary cross braces between the outer kneewall studs and each support post, making sure the posts are plumb before fastening the braces. Double-check the posts and ridge for plumb and level, respectively.

7

Create a template rafter by cutting a 2 × 4 at about 66" long. Hold the board against the end of the ridge and the top outside corner of a kneewall cap. Trace along the face of the ridge and the cap to mark the cutting lines for the rafter. Cut along the lines, then test-fit the rafter and make any necessary adjustments for a good fit.

8

Mark and cut the remaining rafters, using the template to trace the cutting lines onto each piece of stock. *Tip: A jigsaw or handsaw is handy for making the bottom-end cuts without having to over-cut, as you would with a circular saw.*

(continued)

9

Install the rafters, using the deck screws driven at an angle into the kneewall caps and the ridge. The rafters should be aligned with the studs and perpendicular to the ridge.

10

Mark the two door frame studs by holding them plumb and tracing along the bottom edge of the rafter above. Position the studs on-the-flat, so the inside edge of each is 16" from the center of the support post (for a 32"-wide door, as shown). Install the studs with angled screws. Cut and install two studs on the rear end wall, spacing them evenly between the kneewalls and support post.

11

Complete the door frame: Mark the front support post 78" (or as desired) up from the sole plate. Make a square cut at the mark, using a circular saw or cordless trim saw (inset), then remove the bottom portion of the post. Cut the door header (from the post waste) to fit between the door studs. Fasten the header to the door studs and remaining post piece with screws.

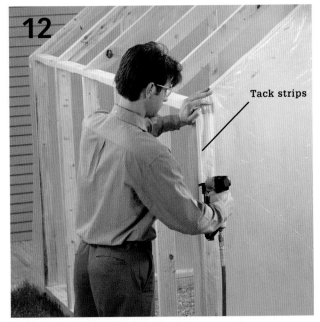

12

Tack strips

Begin covering the greenhouse with the desired cover material (6-mil poly sheeting shown here), starting at the end walls. Cut the sheeting roughly to size and secure it to the framing with wood tack strips fastened with wire brads. Secure the sheeting at the top first, the sides next, and the bottom last. Trim the excess material along the edges of the strips with a utility knife.

YARD & GARDEN STRUCTURES

13

Attach sheeting to the edges of the sole plate on one side of the greenhouse, then roll the sheeting over the top and down the other side. Draw it taut, and cut it a little long with scissors. Secure the sheeting to the other sole plate (using tack strips), then attach it to the outside edges of the corner studs.

14

Door

2 × 4 weight

Create the door, using a piece of sheeting cut a little larger than the door opening (or purchase a door kit; see photo below). Secure the top of the door to the header with a tack strip. Weight the door's bottom end with a 2 × 4 scrap cut to length.

Option: Make a vent window. First, cut a hole in the roof in one rafter bay and tack the cut edges of the plastic to the faces (not the edges) of the rafters, ridge pole and wall cap. Then build a frame from 1 × 2 stock that will span from the ridge to the top of the kneewall and extend a couple of inches past the rafters at the side of the opening. Clad the frame with plastic sheeting and attach it to the ridge pole with butt hinges. Install a screw-eye latch to secure it at the bottom. Make and attach props if you wish.

Greenhouse Doors ▸

Plastic door kits, available from greenhouse suppliers, include self-adhesive zipper strips and are easy to roll up and tie for access or ventilation. You can also create your own roll-up door with zipper strips and plastic sheeting purchased from a building center.

FREESTANDING KIT GREENHOUSE

Building a greenhouse from a prefabricated kit offers many advantages. Kits are usually very easy to assemble because all parts are prefabricated and the lightweight materials are easy to handle. The quality of kit greenhouses varies widely, though, and buying from a reputable manufacturer will help ensure that you get many years of service from your greenhouse.

If you live in a snowy climate, you may need to either provide extra support within the greenhouse or be ready to remove snow whenever there is a significant snowfall because the lightweight aluminum frame members can easily bend under a heavy load. Before buying a kit, make sure to check on how snowfall may affect it.

Kit greenhouses are offered by many different manufacturers, and the exact assembly technique you use will depend on the specifics of your kit. Make sure you read the printed instructions carefully, as they may vary from this project.

The kit we're demonstrating here is made from aluminum frame pieces and transparent polycarbonate panels and is designed to be installed over a subbase of gravel about five inches thick. Other kits may have different subbase requirements.

When you purchase your kit, make sure to uncrate it and examine all the parts before you begin. Make sure all the pieces are there and that there are no damaged panels or bent frame members.

A perfectly flat and level base is crucial to any kit greenhouse, so make sure to work carefully. Try to do the work on a dry day with no wind, as the panels and frame pieces can be hard to manage on a windy day. Never try to build a kit greenhouse by yourself. At least one helper is mandatory, and you'll do even better with two or three.

Construction of a kit greenhouse consists of four basic steps: laying the base, assembling the frame, assembling the windows and doors, and attaching the panels.

Tools & Materials ▸

Cordless drill/driver with nut-driver accessory	Compactible gravel
	Tamper
	Greenhouse kit
Shovels and rakes	Straight 2 × 4
Mason's string	Gravel or other fill material for floor
Stakes	
Commercial-grade landscape fabric	Work gloves
	Eye and ear protection

Kit greenhouses come in a wide range of shapes, sizes, and quality. The best ones have tempered-glass glazing and are rather expensive. The one at left is glazed with corrugated polyethylene and is at the low end of the cost spectrum.

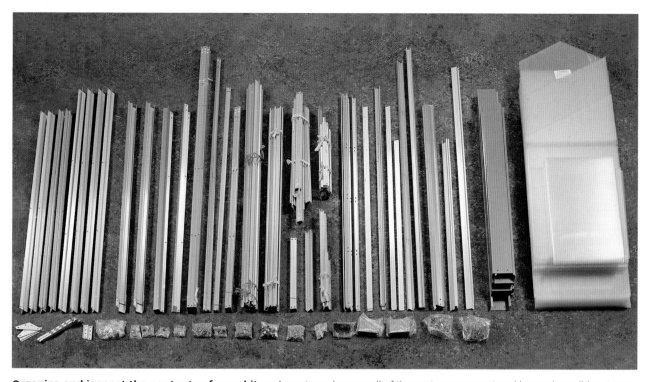

Organize and inspect the contents of your kit cartons to make sure all of the parts are present and in good condition. Most manuals will have a checklist. Staging the parts makes for a more efficient assembly. Just be sure not to leave any small parts loose, and do not store parts in high-traffic areas.

A cordless drill/driver with a nut-driver accessory will trim hours off of your assembly time compared with using only hand tools.

Rent outdoor power equipment if you need to do significant regrading to create a flat, level building base. Be sure to have your local utility company inspect for any buried utility lines first. (You may prefer to hire a landscaping company to do re-grading work for you.)

HOW TO BUILD A FREESTANDING KIT GREENHOUSE

Establish layout lines for the gravel subbase, using stakes or batterboards and mason's string. The excavation area for the subbase should be at least 2" wider and longer than the outside dimensions of the greenhouse kit base. Make sure the layout is perfectly square (the lines are perpendicular to one another) by measuring diagonally between opposing corners: the layout is square when the measurements are equal.

Excavate the site to a depth of 5", using the layout strings as a guide. As you work, use a straight 2 × 4 and a 4-ft. level to check the excavation to make sure it is level and flat. Tamp any loose soil with a plate compactor or hand tamp. Cover the excavation with commercial-grade landscape fabric (do not use plastic; the membrane must be water-permeable). Fill the area with 2 or 3" of compactible gravel, grade and level it, then tamp it thoroughly. Add more gravel, level, and tamp for a final subbase depth of 5".

Assemble the greenhouse base, using the provided corner and end connectors. Set the base onto the subbase and make sure the base is level. Measure the diagonals to check for square, as before. Add a top dressing of gravel or other fill material inside the base, up to about 1" below the base's top lip. Smooth and level the gravel as before.

Attach the bottom wall plates to the base pieces so that the flanged edges face outside the greenhouse. In most systems, the floor plates will interlock with one another, end to end, with built-in brackets.

Fasten the four corner studs to the bottom wall plates, using hold-down connectors and bolts. In this system, each corner stud is secured with two connectors.

Install the ceiling plates: Assemble the pieces for each side ceiling plate. Attach each side plate against the inside of the two corner studs along each side of the greenhouse, making sure the gutter is positioned correctly. Attach the front ceiling plate to the outsides of the corner studs at the front of the building.

(continued)

7

Corner bracket

Stud connectors

Attach the other side ceiling plate
along the other side, flat against the inside of the corner studs. Then attach corner brackets to the rear studs, and construct the back top plate by attaching the rear braces to the corners and joining the braces together with stud connectors.

8

Fasten the left and right rear studs
to the outside of the rear floor plate, making sure the top ends are sloping upward, toward the peak of the greenhouse. Attach the center rear studs to the rear floor plate, fastening them to the stud connectors used to join the rear braces.

Backwards and Forwards ▸

With some kits you need to go backward to go forward. Because the individual parts of your kit depend upon one another for support, you may be required to tack all the parts together with bolts first and then undo and remake individual connections as you go before you can finalize them. For example, in this kit you must undo the track/ brace connections one at a time so you can insert the bolt heads for the stud connectors into the track.

Install the doorway studs at either side of the greenhouse door, on the front end of the building. Install the side studs along both side walls of the greenhouse.

Add diagonal struts, as directed by the manufacturer. The struts help to stiffen and square up the walls. As you work, take diagonal measurements between opposing corners at the tops of the walls, to make sure the structure remains square.

Fasten the gable-end stud extensions to the front and back walls of the greenhouse. The top ends of the studs should angle upward, toward the peak of the greenhouse.

Assemble the roof frame on a flat area near the wall assembly. First assemble the crown-beam pieces; then attach the rafters to the crown, one by one. The end rafters, called the crown beams, have a different configuration, so make sure not to confuse them.

(continued)

With at least one helper, lift the roof into place onto the wall frames. The gable end studs should meet the outside edges of the crown beams, and the ends of the crown beams rest on the outer edge of the corner bracket. Fasten in place with the provided nuts and bolts.

Side braces

Roof window support

Attach the side braces and the roof-window support beams to the underside of the roof rafters, as specified by the manufacturer's instructions.

Build the roof windows by first connecting the two side window frames to the top window frame. Slide the window panel into the frame; then secure it by attaching the bottom window frame. Slide the window into the slot at the top of the roof crown; then gradually lower it in place. Attach the window stop to the window support beam.

Assemble the doors, making sure the top slider/roller bar and the bottom slider bar are correctly positioned. Lift the door panels up into place onto the top and bottom wall plates.

Install the panels one by one, using panel clips. Begin with the large wall panels. Position each panel and secure it by snapping a clip into the frame, at the intervals specified by the manufacturer's instructions.

Add the upper panels. At the gable ends, the upper panels will be supported by panel connectors that allow the top panel to be supported by the bottom panel. The lower panels should be installed already.

Install the roof panels and roof-window panels so that the top edges fit up under the edge of the crown or window support and the bottom edges align over the gutters.

Test the door and window operation, and make any necessary adjustments so they open and close smoothly.

PVC HOOPHOUSE

The hoophouse is a popular garden structure for two main reasons: it is cheap to build and easy to build. In many agricultural areas you will see hoophouses snaking across vast fields of seedlings, protecting the delicate plants at their most vulnerable stages. Because they are portable and easy to disassemble, they can be removed when the plants are established and less vulnerable.

While hoophouses are not intended as inexpensive substitutes for real greenhouses, they do serve an important agricultural purpose. And building your own is a fun project that the whole family can enjoy.

The hoophouse shown here is essentially a Quonset-style frame of bent ¾-inch PVC tubing draped with sheet plastic. Each semicircular frame is actually made from two 10-foot lengths of tubing that fit into a plastic fitting at the apex of the curve. PVC tubes tend to stay together simply by friction-fitting into the fittings, so you don't normally need to solvent glue the connections (this is important to the easy-to-disassemble and store feature). If you experience problems with the frame connections separating, try cutting four- to six-inch-long pieces of ½-inch (outside diameter) PVC tubing and inserting them into the tubes and fittings like splines. This will stiffen the connections.

A hoophouse is a temporary agricultural structure designed to be low-cost and portable. Also called Quonset houses and tunnel houses, hoophouses provide shelter and shade (depending on the film you use) and protection from wind and the elements. They will boost heat during the day, but are less efficient than paneled greenhouses for extending the growing season.

PVC Hoophouse

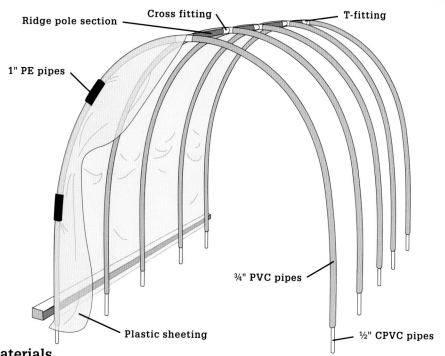

Ridge pole section · Cross fitting · T-fitting

1" PE pipes

¾" PVC pipes

½" CPVC pipes

Plastic sheeting

Tools & Materials

Hand sledge
Plastic tubing cutter or hacksaw
Wood or rubber mallet
Circular saw
Stapler
Drill
Utility knife
Stakes and mason's string
Eye and ear protection
Tape measure

Work gloves
(5) ½" × 10 ft. CPVC pipes
(14) ¾" × 10 ft. PVC pipes
(3) ¾" PVC cross fittings
(2) ¾" PVC T-fittings
16 × 24 ft. clear or translucent plastic sheeting
(4) 16-ft. pressure-treated 2 × 4s
2½" deck screws
(1) 1" × 6 ft. PE tubing (black, flexible)
2 × 4 lumber

Building a Hoophouse ▸

- Space frame hoops about 3 ft. apart.
- Leave ridge members a fraction of an inch (not more than ¼") shorter than the span, which will cause the structure to be slightly shorter on top than at the base. This helps stabilize the structure.
- Orient the structure so the wall faces into the prevailing wind rather than the end openings.
- If you are using long-lasting greenhouse fabric for the cover, protect the investment by spray-painting the frame hoops with primer so there is no plastic-to-plastic contact.

- Because hoophouses are temporary structures that are designed to be disassembled or moved regularly, you do not need to include a base.
- Hoophouses can act a lot like boat sails and will fly away if they're not anchored securely. Be sure to stake each hoop to the ground at both ends (with 30"-long or longer stakes), and carefully weight down the cover with boards (as shown here) or piles of dirt.
- Clip the hoophouse covers to the end frames. Clips fastened at the intermediate hoops will either fly off or tear the plastic cover in windy conditions.

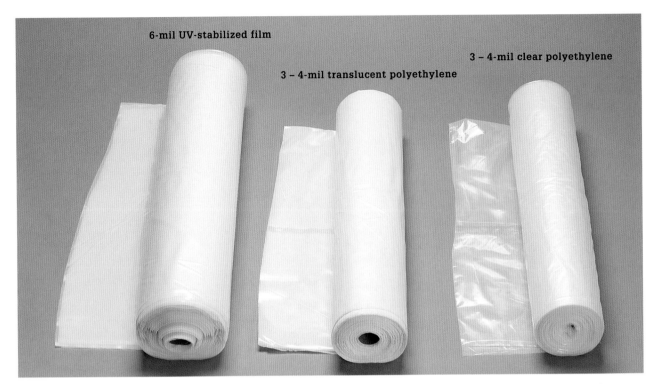

6-mil UV-stabilized film

3 – 4-mil translucent polyethylene

3 – 4-mil clear polyethylene

Sheet plastic is an inexpensive material for creating a greenhouse. Obviously, it is less durable than polycarbonate, fiberglass or glass panels. But UV-stabilized films at least 6-mil thick can be rated to withstand four years or more of exposure. Inexpensive polyethylene sheeting (the kind you find at hardware stores) will hold up for a year or two, but it becomes brittle when exposed to sunlight. Some greenhouse builders prefer to use clear plastic sheeting to maximize the sunlight penetration, but the cloudiness of translucent poly makes it effective for diffusing light and preventing overheating. For the highest quality film coverings, look for film rated for greenhouse and agricultural use.

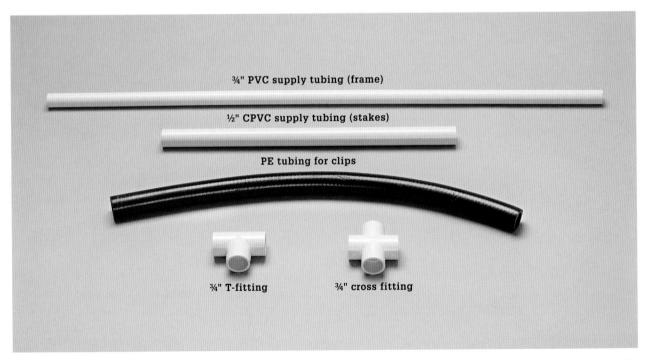

¾" PVC supply tubing (frame)

½" CPVC supply tubing (stakes)

PE tubing for clips

¾" T-fitting

¾" cross fitting

Plastic tubing and fittings used to build this hoophouse include: Light-duty ¾" PVC tubing for the frame (do not use CPVC—it is too rigid and won't bend properly); ½" CPVC supply tubing for the frame stakes (rigidity is good here); polyethylene (PE) tubing for the cover clips; T-fittings and cross fittings to join the frame members.

HOW TO BUILD A PVC HOOPHOUSE

Lay out the installation area, using stakes and mason's string. Stake the four corners to create a rectangle that is 10 ft. wide and 15 ft. long. To make sure the layout is square (the strings are perpendicular), measure diagonally between opposing corner stakes: when the measurements are equal, the layout is square.

Cut a 30"-long stake from ½" CPVC pipe for each leg of each frame hoop. Plastic pipe is easy to cut with a plastic tubing cutter or a hacksaw. Mark the layout strings at 36" intervals, using tape or a marker. Drive a stake at each marked location, using a hand sledge or hammer. Keep the stakes plumb and drive them in 20" deep, so only 10" is above ground.

Join the two legs for each frame hoop with a fitting. Use a T-fitting for the end hoop frames and a cross fitting for the intermediate hoop frames. No priming or solvent gluing is necessary. (The friction-fit should be sufficient, but it helps if you tap on the end of the fitting with a mallet to seat it.)

(continued)

Slip the open end of one hoop-frame leg over a corner stake so the pipe is flush against the ground. Then bend the pipes so you can fit the other leg end over the stake at the opposite corner. If you experience problems with the pipes pulling out of the top fitting, simply tape the joints temporarily until the structure frame is completed.

Continue adding hoop frames until you reach the other end of the structure. Wait until all the hoop frames are in place before you begin installing the ridge poles. Make sure the cross fittings on the intermediate hoop frames are aligned correctly to accept the ridge poles.

Add the ridge pole sections to tie together the hoop frames. The correct length for the ridge poles depends on the socket depth of the fitting you use, so you'll have to measure the fittings and calculate length of the ridge pieces. If necessary, tap the end of each ridge piece with a wood or rubber mallet to seat it fully in the fitting socket.

Cut four 2 × 4s to length (15 ft. as shown). Cut the cover material to length at 16 ft. (or as needed so it is several inches longer than the house at both ends). Staple one edge of the cover to one of the 2 × 4s, keeping the material taut and flat as you work from one end to the other

Lay another 2 × 4 over the first so their ends and edges are flush and the cover material is sandwiched in between. Fasten the two boards together with 2½" deck screws driven every 24" or so. Position the board assembly along the base of the hoops and pull the free end of the material over the tops of the hoops to the other side.

Pull the cover taut on the other side of the house, and repeat the process of stapling it to one board then sandwiching with the other.

Secure the cover at the ends with 6" lengths of 1" PE tubing. Cut the tubing pieces to length, then slit them lengthwise to create simple clips. Use at least six clips at each end of the house. Do not use clips on the intermediate hoops.

Option: Make doors by clipping a piece of cover material to each end. (It's best to do this before attaching the main cover.) Then cut a slit down the center of the end material. You can tie or tape the door material to the sides when you want it open and weigh down the pieces with a board or brick to keep the door shut. This solution is low-tech but effective.

METAL & WOOD KIT SHEDS

The following pages walk you through the steps of building two new sheds from kits. The metal shed measures eight by nine feet and comes with every piece in the main building pre-cut and pre-drilled. All you need is a ladder and a few hand tools for assembly. The wood shed is a cedar building with panelized construction—most of the major elements come in preassembled sections. The walls panels have exterior siding installed, and the roof sections are already shingled. For both sheds, the pieces are lightweight and maneuverable, but it helps to have at least two people for fitting everything together.

As with most kits, these sheds do not include foundations as part of the standard package. The metal shed can be built on top of a patio surface or out in the yard, with or without an optional floor. The wood shed comes with a complete wood floor, but the building needs a standard foundation, such as wooden skid, concrete block, or concrete slab foundation. To help keep either type of shed level and to reduce moisture from ground contact, it's a good idea to build it over a bed of compacted gravel. A four-inch-deep bed that extends about six inches beyond the building footprint makes for a stable foundation and helps keep the interior dry throughout the seasons.

Before you purchase a shed kit, check with your local building department to learn about restrictions that affect your project. It's recommended—and often required—that lightweight metal sheds be anchored to the ground. Shed manufacturers offer different anchoring systems, including cables for tethering the shed into soil, and concrete anchors for tying into a concrete slab.

Kit sheds offer the storage you need, a quick build, and an attractive addition to your backyard. The metal shed kit shown here is constructed on pages 410 to 415.

This all-cedar kit shed is constructed on pages 416 to 423.

BUILDING A METAL OR WOOD KIT SHED

If you need an outbuilding but don't have the time or inclination to build one from scratch, a kit shed is the answer. Today's kit sheds are available in a wide range of materials, sizes, and styles—from snap-together plastic lockers to Norwegian pine cabins with divided-light windows and loads of architectural details. Equally diverse is the range of quality and prices for shed kits. One thing to keep in mind when choosing a shed is that much of what you're paying for is the materials and the ease of installation. Better kits are made with quality, long-lasting materials, and many come largely preassembled. Most of the features discussed below will have an impact on a shed's cost.

The best place to start shopping for shed kits is on the Internet. Large manufacturers and small-shop custom designers alike have websites featuring their products and available options. A quick online search should help you narrow down your choices to sheds that fit your needs and budget. From there, you can visit local dealers or builders to view assembled sheds firsthand. When figuring cost, be sure to factor in all aspects of the project, including the foundation, extra hardware, tools you don't already own, and paint and other finishes not included with your kit.

Tools & Materials ▸

Landscape grading or leveling tools	Eye and ear protection
Landscape fabric	Tape measure
Compactible gravel	Drill
Work gloves	Straight 2 × 4

High-tech plastics like polyethylene and vinyl are often combined with steel and other rigid materials to create tough, weather-resistant—and washable—kit buildings.

If you're looking for something special, higher-end shed kits allow you to break with convention without breaking your budget on a custom-built structure.

Features to Consider ▶

Here are some of the key elements to check out before purchasing a kit shed:

MATERIALS

Shed kits are made of wood, metal, vinyl, various plastic compounds, or any combination thereof. Consider aesthetics, of course, but also durability and appropriateness for your climate. For example, check the snow load rating on the roof if you live in a snowy climate, or inquire about the material's UV resistance if your shed will receive heavy sun exposure. The finish on metal sheds is important for durability. Protective finishes include paint, powder-coating, and vinyl. For wood sheds, consider all of the materials, from the framing to the siding, roofing, and trimwork.

EXTRA FEATURES

Do you want a shed with windows or a skylight? Some kits come with these features, while others offer them as optional add-ons. For a shed workshop, office, or other workspace where you'll be spending a lot of time, consider the livability and practicality of the interior space, and shop accordingly for special features.

WHAT'S INCLUDED?

Many kits do not include foundations or floors, and floors are commonly available as extras. Other elements that may not be included:

- Paint, stain, etc.—Also, some sheds come pre-painted (or pre-primed), but you won't want to pay extra for a nice paint job if you plan to paint the shed to match your house.
- Roofing—Often the plywood roof sheathing is included but not the building paper, drip edge, or shingles.

Most shed kits include hardware (nails, screws) for assembling the building, but always check this to make sure.

ASSEMBLY

Many kit manufacturers have downloadable assembly instructions on their websites, so you can really see what's involved in putting their shed together. Assembly of wood sheds varies considerably among manufacturers—the kit may arrive as a bundle of pre-cut lumber or with screw-together prefabricated panels. Easy-assembly models may have wall siding and roof shingles already installed onto panels.

EXTENDERS

Some kits offer the option of extending the main building with extenders, or expansion kits, making it easy to turn an 8 × 10-ft. shed into a 10 × 12-ft. shed, for example.

FOUNDATION

Check with the manufacturer for recommended foundation types to use under their sheds.

Shed hardware kits make it easy to build a shed from scratch. Using the structural gussets and framing connectors, you avoid tricky rafter cuts and roof assembly. Many hardware kits come with lumber cutting lists so you can build the shed to the desired size without using plans.

HOW TO ASSEMBLE A METAL KIT SHED

Prepare the building site by leveling and grading as needed, and then excavating and adding a 4"-thick layer of compactible gravel. If desired, apply landscape fabric under the gravel to inhibit weed growth. Compact the gravel with a tamper and use a level and a long, straight 2 × 4 to make sure the area is flat and level.

Note: Always wear work gloves when handling shed parts—the metal edges can be very sharp. Begin by assembling the floor kit according to the manufacturer's directions—these will vary quite a bit among models, even within the same manufacturer. Be sure that the floor system parts are arranged so the door is located where you wish it to be. Do not fasten the pieces at this stage.

Once you've laid out the floor system parts, check to make sure they're square before you begin fastening them. Measuring the diagonals to see if they're the same is a quick and easy way to check for square.

Fasten the floor system parts together with kit connectors once you've established that the floor is square. Anchor the floor to the site if your kit suggests. Some kits are designed to be anchored after full assembly is completed.

5

Begin installing the wall panels according to the instructions. Most panels are predrilled for fasteners, so the main trick is to make sure the fastener holes align between panels and with the floor.

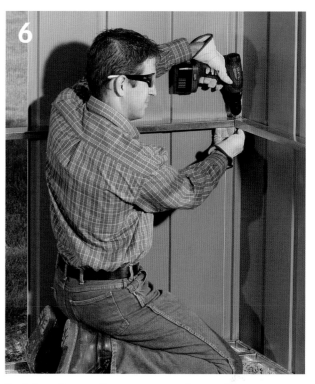

6

Tack together mating corner panels on at least two adjacent corners. If your frame stiffeners require assembly, have them ready to go before you form the corners. With a helper, attach the frame stiffener rails to the corner panels.

7

Install the remaining fasteners at the shed corners once you've established that the corners all are square.

8

Lay out the parts for assembling the roof beams and the upper side frames and confirm that they fit together properly. Then, join the assemblies with the fasteners provided.

(continued)

YARD & GARDEN STRUCTURES

9

Attach the moving and nonmoving parts for the upper door track to the side frames if your shed has sliding doors.

10

Fasten the shed panels to the top frames, making sure that any fasteners holes are aligned and that crimped tabs are snapped together correctly.

11

Fill in the wall panels between the completed corners, attaching them to the frames with the provided fasteners. Take care not to overdrive the fasteners.

12

Fasten the doorframe trim pieces to the frames to finish the door opening. If the fasteners are colored to match the trim, make sure you choose the correct ones.

Insert the shed gable panels into the side frames and the door track and slide them together so the fastener holes are aligned. Attach the panels with the provided fasteners.

Fit the main roof beam into the clips or other fittings on the gable panels. Have a helper hold the free end of the beam. Position the beam and secure it to both gable ends before attaching it.

Drive fasteners to affix the roof beam to the gable ends and install any supplementary support hardware for the beam, such as gussets or angle braces.

(continued)

Begin installing the roof panels at one end, fastening them to the roof beam and to the top flanges of the side frames.

Apply weatherstripping tape to the top ends of the roof panels to seal the joints before you attach the overlapping roof panels. If your kit does not include weatherstripping tape, look for adhesive-backed foam tape in the weatherstripping products section of your local building center.

As the overlapping roof panels are installed and sealed, attach the roof cap sections at the roof ridge to cover the panel overlaps. Seal as directed. *Note: Completing one section at a time allows you to access subsequent sections from below so you don't risk damaging the roof.*

Attach the peak caps to cover the openings at the ends of the roof cap and then install the roof trim pieces at the bottoms of the roof panels, tucking the flanges or tabs into the roof as directed. Install plywood floor, according to manufacturer instructions.

20

Assemble the doors, paying close attention to right/left differences on double doors. Attach hinges for swinging doors and rollers for sliding doors.

21

Install door tracks and door roller hardware on the floor as directed and then install the doors according to the manufacturer's instructions. Test the action of the doors and make adjustments so the doors roll or swing smoothly and are aligned properly.

Tips for Maintaining a Metal Shed ▸

Touch up scratches or any exposed metal as soon as possible to prevent rust. Clean the area with a wire brush, and then apply a paint recommended by the shed's manufacturer.

Inspect your shed once or twice a year and tighten loose screws, bolts, and other hardware. Loose connections lead to premature wear.

Sweep off the roof to remove wet leaves and debris, which can be hard on the finish. Also clear the roof after heavy snowfall to reduce the risk of collapse.

Seal open seams and other potential entry points for water with silicone caulk. Keep the shed's doors closed and latched to prevent damage from wind gusts.

Anchor the Shed ▸

Metal sheds tend to be light in weight and require secure anchoring to the ground, generally with an anchor kit that may be sold separately by your kit manufacturer. There are many ways to accomplish this. The method you choose depends mostly on the type of base you've built on, be it concrete or wood or gravel. On concrete and wood bases, look for corner gusset anchors that are attached directly to the floor frame and then fastened with landscape screws (wood) or masonry anchors driven into concrete. Sheds that have been built on a gravel or dirt base can be anchored with auger-type anchors that are driven into the ground just outside the shed. You'll need to anchor the shed on at least two sides. Once the anchors are driven, cables are strung through the shed so they are connected to the roof beam. The ends of the cables should exit the shed at ground level and then be attached to the anchors with cable clamps.

HOW TO BUILD A WOOD KIT SHED

Tools & Materials ▸

Surface preparation tools
Pressure-treated lumber
Circular saw

Level
Drill
Screws

Tape measure
Square or straight edge

Work gloves
Eye and ear protection

Prepare the base for the shed's wooden skid foundation with a 4" layer of compacted gravel. Make sure the gravel is flat, smooth, and perfectly level. *Note: For a sloping site, a concrete block foundation may be more appropriate (check with your shed's manufacturer).*

Cut three 4 × 4 (or 6 × 6) pressure-treated timbers to match the length of the shed's floor frame. Position two outer skids so they will be flush with the outside edges of the frame, and center one skid in between. Make sure that each skid is perfectly level and the skids are level with one another.

Prepare for the Delivery ▸

Panelized shed kits are shipped on pallets. The delivery truck may have a forklift, and the driver can take off the load by whole pallets. Otherwise, you'll have to unload the pieces one at a time. Make sure to have two helpers on hand to help you unload (often drivers aren't allowed to help due to insurance liability).

Once the load is on the ground, carry the pieces to the building site and stack them on pallets or scrap-wood skids to keep them clean and dry. Look through the manufacturer's instructions and arrange the stacks according to the assembly steps.

Assemble the floor frame pieces with screws. First, join alternating pairs of large and small pieces to create three full-width sections. Fasten the sections together to complete the floor frame.

Attach the floor runners to the bottom of the floor frame, using exterior screws. Locate the side runners flush to the outsides of the frame, and center the middle runner in between. Set the frame on the skids with the runners facing down. Check the frame to make sure it is level. Secure the floor to the skids following the manufacturer's recommendations.

Cover the floor frame with plywood, starting with a large sheet at the left rear corner of the frame. Fasten the plywood with screws. Install the two outer deck boards. Lay out all of the remaining boards in between, then set even gapping for each board. Fasten the remaining deck boards.

Lay out the shed's wall panels in their relative positions around the floor. Make sure you have them right-side-up: the windows are on the top half of the walls; on the windowless panels, the siding tells you which end is up.

(continued)

Position the two rear corner walls upright onto the floor so the wall framing is flush with the floor's edges. Fasten the wall panels together. Raise and join the remaining wall panels one at a time. Do not fasten the wall panels to the shed floor in this step.

Place the door header on top of the narrow front wall panel so it's flush with the wall framing. Fasten the header with screws. Fasten the door jamb to the right-side wall framing to create a ½" overhang at the end of the wall. Fasten the header to the jamb with screws.

Confirm that all wall panels are properly positioned on the floor: The wall framing should be flush with edges of the floor frame; the wall siding overhangs the outsides of the floor. Fasten the wall panels by screwing through the bottom wall plate, through the plywood flooring, and into the floor framing.

Install the wall's top plates starting with the rear wall. Install the side wall plates as directed—these overhang the front of the shed and will become part of the porch framing. Finally, install the front wall top plates.

11

Assemble the porch rail sections using the screws provided for each piece. Attach the top plate extension to the 4 × 4 porch post, and then attach the wall trim/support to the extension. Fasten the corner brackets, centered on the post and extension. Install the handrail section 4" up from the bottom of the post.

12

Install each of the porch rail sections: Fasten through the wall trim/support and into the side wall, locating the screws where they will be least visible. Fasten down through the wall top plate at the post and corner bracket locations to hide the ends of the screws. Anchor the post to the decking and floor frame with screws driven through angled pilot holes.

13

Hang the Dutch door using two hinge pairs. Install the hinges onto the door panels. Use three pairs of shims to position the bottom door panel: ½" shims at the bottom, ⅜" shims on the left side, and ⅛" shims on the right side. Fasten the hinges to the wall trim/support. Hang the top door panel in the same fashion, using ¼" shims between the door panels.

14

Join the two pieces to create the rear wall gable, screwing through the uprights on the back side. On the outer side of the gable, slide in a filler shingle until it's even with the neighboring shingles. Fasten the filler with two finish nails located above the shingle exposure line, two courses up. Attach the top filler shingle with two (exposed) galvanized finish nails.

(continued)

Position the rear gable on top of the rear wall top plates and center it from side to side. Use a square or straightedge to align the angled gable supports with the angled ends of the outer plates. Fasten the gable to the plates and wall framing with screws. Assemble and install the middle gable wall.

Arrange the roof panels on the ground according to their installation. Flip the panels over and attach framing connectors to the rafters at the marked locations, using screws.

With one or two helpers, set the first roof panel at the rear of the shed, then set the opposing roof panel in place. Align the ridge boards of the two panels, and then fasten them together with screws. Do not fasten the panels to the walls at this stage.

18

Position one of the middle roof panels, aligning its outer rafter with that of the adjacent rear roof panel. Fasten the rafters together with screws. Install the opposing middle panel in the same way. Set the porch roof panels into place one at a time—these rest on a ½" ledge at the front of the shed. From inside the shed, fasten the middle and porch panels together along their rafters.

19

Check the fit of all roof panels at the outside corners of the shed. Make any necessary adjustments. Fasten the panels to the shed with screws, starting with the porch roof. Inside the shed, fasten the panels to the gable framing, then anchor the framing connectors to the wall plates.

20

Install the two roof gussets between the middle rafters of the shed roof panels (not the porch panels): First measure between the side walls—this should equal 91" for this kit (see resources). If not, have two helpers push on the walls until the measurement matches your requirement. Hold the gussets level, and fasten them to the rafters with screws.

(continued)

21

Add filler shingles at the roof panel seams. Slide in the bottom shingle and fasten it above the exposure line two courses up, using two screws. Drive the screws into the rafters. Install the remaining filler shingles the same way. Attach the top shingle with two galvanized finish nails.

22

Cover the underside of the rafter tails (except on the porch) with soffit panels, fastening to the rafters with finish nails. Cover the floor framing with skirting boards, starting at the porch sides. Hold the skirting flush with the decking boards on the porch and with the siding on the walls, and fasten it with screws.

23

Add vertical trim boards to cover the wall seams and shed corners. The rear corners get a filler trim piece, followed by a wide trim board on top. Add horizontal trim boards at the front wall and along the top of the door. Fasten all trim with finish nails.

24

At the rear of the shed, fit the two fascia boards over the ends of the roof battens so they meet at the roof peak. Fasten the fascia with screws. Install the side fascia pieces over the rafter tails with finish nails. The rear fascia overlaps the ends of the side fascia. Cover the fascia joints and the horizontal trim joint at the front wall with decorative plates.

25

Place the two roof ridge caps along the roof peak, overlapping the caps' roofing felt in the center. Fasten the caps with screws. Install the decorative gusset gable underneath the porch roof panels using mounting clips. Finish the gable ends with two fascia pieces installed with screws.

26

Complete the porch assembly by fastening each front handrail section to a deck post, using screws. Fasten the handrail to the corner porch post. The handrail should start 4" above the bottoms of the posts, as with the side handrail sections. Anchor each deck post to the decking and floor frame with screws (see below).

Drilling Counterbored Pilot Holes ▸

Use a combination piloting/counterbore bit to pre-drill holes for installing posts. Angle the pilot holes at about 60°, and drive the screws into the framing below whenever possible. The counterbore created by the piloting bit helps hide the screw head.

LEAN-TO TOOL BIN

The lean-to is a classic outbuilding intended as a supplementary structure for a larger building. Its simple shed-style roof helps it blend with the neighboring structure and directs water away and keeps leaves and debris from getting trapped between the two buildings. When built to a small shed scale, the lean-to (sometimes called a closet shed) is most useful as an easy-access storage locker that saves you extra trips into the garage for often-used lawn and garden tools and supplies.

This lean-to tool bin is not actually attached to the house, though it appears to be. It is designed as a freestanding building with a wooden skid foundation that makes it easy to move. With all four sides finished, the bin can be placed anywhere, but it works best when set next to a house or garage wall or a tall fence. If you locate the bin out in the open—where it won't be protected against wind and extreme weather—be sure to anchor it securely to the ground to prevent it from blowing over.

As shown here, the bin is finished with asphalt shingle roofing, T1-11 plywood siding, and 1× cedar trim, but you can substitute any type of finish to match or complement a neighboring structure. Its 65-inch-tall double doors provide easy access to its 18 square feet of floor space. The 8-foot-tall rear wall can accommodate a set of shelves while leaving enough room below for long-handled tools.

Because the tool bin sits on the ground, in cold climates it will be subject to shifting with seasonal freeze-thaw cycles. Therefore, do not attach the tool bin to your house or any other building set on a frost-proof foundation.

Tools & Materials ▸

Site prepartation tools and materials
Square
Hammer
Circular saw
Tape measure
Pencil
Plumb bob
Screws
Insect mesh
Shingles
Roof sheathing
Work gloves
Eye and ear protection

Keep your tools safe and dry in the lean-to tool bin located next to a house, garage, fence, or wall.

Cutting List

DESCRIPTION	QTY./SIZE	MATERIAL
Foundation		
Drainage material	0.5 cu. yd.	Compactible gravel
Skids	2 @ 6'	4 × 4 treated timbers
Floor Framing		
Rim joists	2 @ 6'	2 × 6 pressure-treated
Joists	3 @ 8'	2 × 6 pressure-treated
Floor sheathing	1 sheet @ 4 × 8	¾" tongue-&-groove ext.-grade plywood
Joist clip angles	4	3 × 3 × 3" × 16-gauge galvanized
Wall Framing		
Bottom plates	1 @ 8', 2 @ 6'	2 × 4
Top plates	1 @ 8', 3 @ 6'	2 × 4
Studs	14 @ 8', 8 @ 6'	2 × 4
Header	2 @ 6'	2 × 6
Header spacer	1 piece @ 6'	½" plywood — 5" wide
Roof Framing		
Rafters	6 @ 6'	2 × 6
Ledger*	1 @ 6'	2 × 6
Roofing		
Roof sheathing	2 sheets @ 4 × 8'	½" ext.-grade plywood
Shingles	30 sq. ft.	250# per square min.
Roofing starter strip	7 linear ft.	
15# building paper	30 sq. ft.	
Metal drip edge	24 linear ft.	Galvanized metal
Roofing cement	1 tube	
Exterior Finishes		
Plywood siding	4 sheets @ 4 × 8'	⅝" Texture 1-11 plywood siding, grooves 8" O.C.

DESCRIPTION	QTY./SIZE	MATERIAL
Door trim	2 @ 8'	1 × 10 S4S cedar
	2 @ 6'	1 × 8 S4S cedar
Corner trim	6 @ 8'	1 × 4 S4S cedar
Fascia	3 @ 6'	1 × 8 S4S cedar
	1 @ 6'	1 × 4 S4S cedar
Bug screen	8" × 6'	Fiberglass
Doors		
Frame	3 @ 6'	¾" × 3½" (actual) cedar
Stops	3 @ 6'	1 × 2 S4S cedar
Panel material	12 @ 6'	1 × 6 T&G V-joint S4S cedar
Z-braces	2 @ 10'	1 × 6 S4S cedar
Construction adhesive	1 tube	
Interior trim (optional)	3 @ 6'	1 × 3 S4S cedar
Strap hinges	6, with screws	
Fasteners		
16d galvanized common nails	3½ lbs.	
16d common nails	3½ lbs.	
10d common nails	12 nails	
10d galvanized casing nails	20 nails	
8d galvanized box nails	½ lb.	
8d galvanized finish nails	2 lbs.	
8d common nails	24 nails	
8d box nails	½ lb.	
1½" joist hanger nails	16 nails	
⅞" galvanized roofing nails	¼ lb.	
2½" deck screws	6 screws	
1¼" wood screws	60 screws	

Note: 6-foot material is often unavailable at local lumber stores, so buy half as much of 12-foot material.

Floor Framing Plan

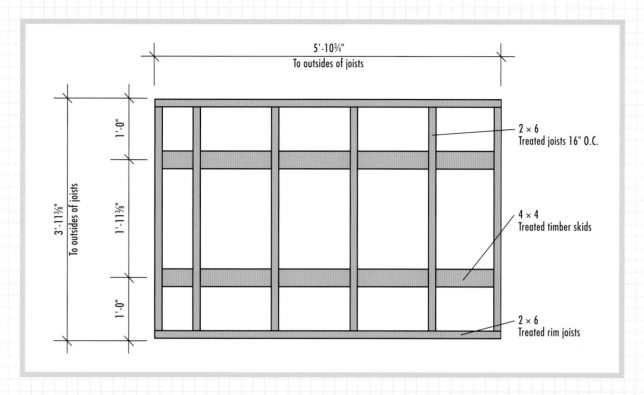

5'-10¾"
To outsides of joists

3'-11⅜" To outsides of joists

1'-0"

1'-11⅜"

1'-0"

2 × 6
Treated joists 16" O.C.

4 × 4
Treated timber skids

2 × 6
Treated rim joists

Roof Framing Plan

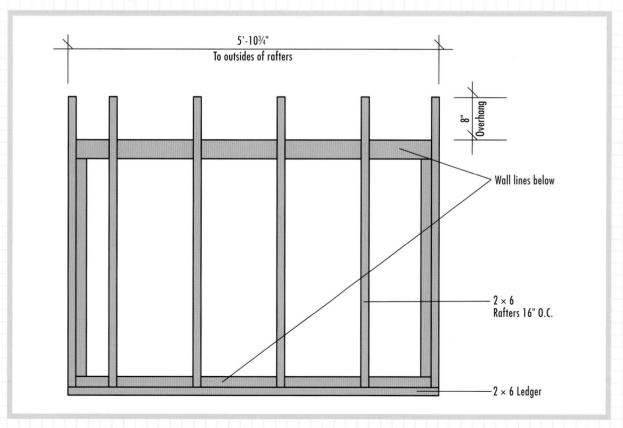

5'-10¾"
To outsides of rafters

8" Overhang

Wall lines below

2 × 6
Rafters 16" O.C.

2 × 6 Ledger

Front Framing Elevation

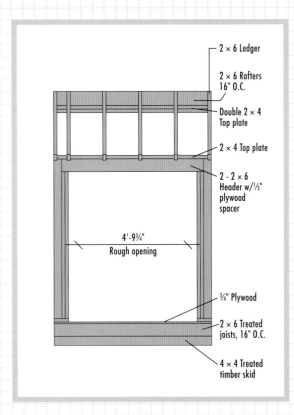

2 × 6 Ledger

2 × 6 Rafters 16" O.C.

Double 2 × 4 Top plate

2 × 4 Top plate

2 - 2 × 6 Header w/½" plywood spacer

4'-9¾" Rough opening

¾" Plywood

2 × 6 Treated joists, 16" O.C.

4 × 4 Treated timber skid

Left Framing Elevation

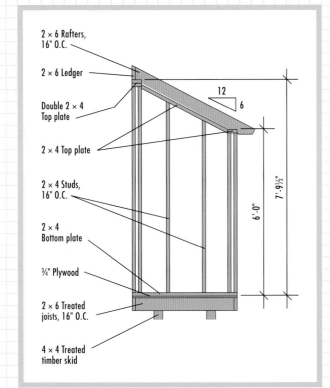

2 × 6 Rafters, 16" O.C.

2 × 6 Ledger

Double 2 × 4 Top plate

2 × 4 Top plate

2 × 4 Studs, 16" O.C.

2 × 4 Bottom plate

¾" Plywood

2 × 6 Treated joists, 16" O.C.

4 × 4 Treated timber skid

12

6

7'-9½"

6'-0"

Rear Side Framing Elevation

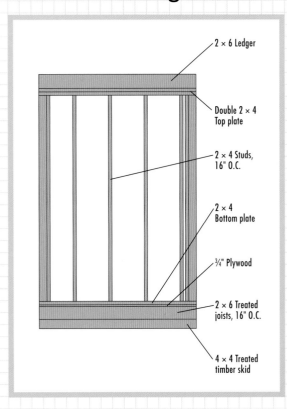

2 × 6 Ledger

Double 2 × 4 Top plate

2 × 4 Studs, 16" O.C.

2 × 4 Bottom plate

¾" Plywood

2 × 6 Treated joists, 16" O.C.

4 × 4 Treated timber skid

Right Side Framing Elevation

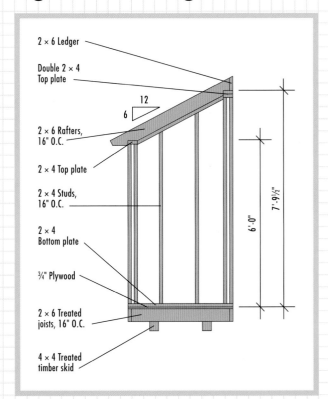

2 × 6 Ledger

Double 2 × 4 Top plate

2 × 6 Rafters, 16" O.C.

2 × 4 Top plate

2 × 4 Studs, 16" O.C.

2 × 4 Bottom plate

¾" Plywood

2 × 6 Treated joists, 16" O.C.

4 × 4 Treated timber skid

12

6

7'-9½"

6'-0"

Building Section

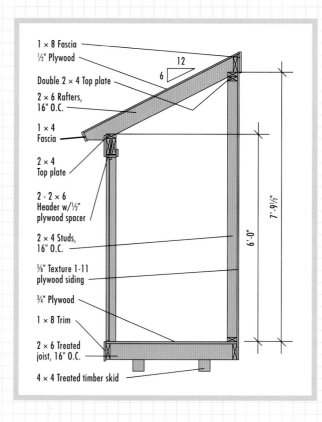

1 × 8 Fascia
½" Plywood
Double 2 × 4 Top plate
2 × 6 Rafters, 16" O.C.
1 × 4 Fascia
2 × 4 Top plate
2 - 2 × 6 Header w/½" plywood spacer
2 × 4 Studs, 16" O.C.
⅝" Texture 1-11 plywood siding
¾" Plywood
1 × 8 Trim
2 × 6 Treated joist, 16" O.C.
4 × 4 Treated timber skid

12
6

7'-9½"
6'-0"

Side Elevation

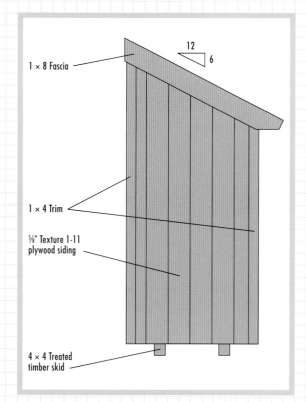

1 × 8 Fascia
12
6
1 × 4 Trim
⅝" Texture 1-11 plywood siding
4 × 4 Treated timber skid

Front Elevation

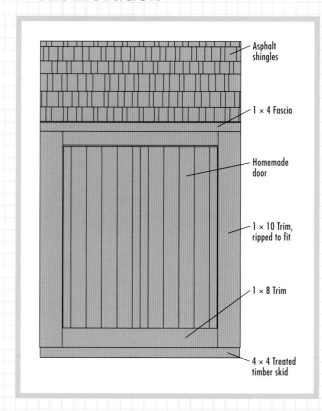

Asphalt shingles
1 × 4 Fascia
Homemade door
1 × 10 Trim, ripped to fit
1 × 8 Trim
4 × 4 Treated timber skid

Rear Elevation

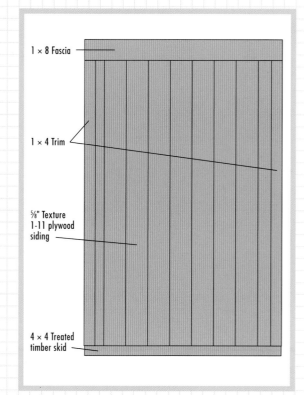

1 × 8 Fascia
1 × 4 Trim
⅝" Texture 1-11 plywood siding
4 × 4 Treated timber skid

Wall Plan

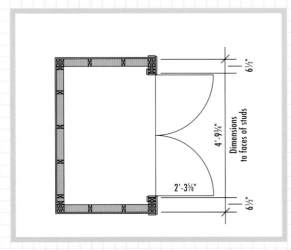

6½"

4'-9¾"

Dimensions to faces of studs

2'-3⅝"

6½"

Rafter Template

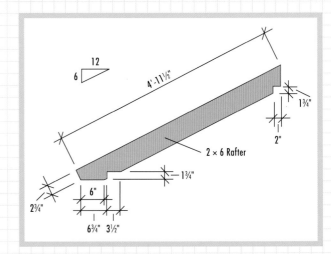

12
6

4'-11½"

1¾"

2"

2 × 6 Rafter

1¾"

2¾"

6"

6¾" 3½"

Side Roof Edge Detail

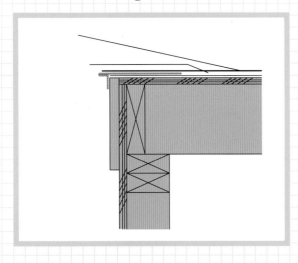

Overhang Detail

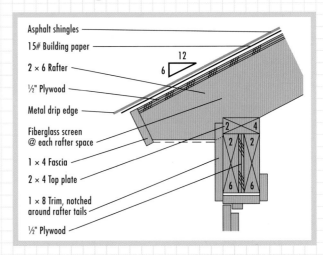

Asphalt shingles

15# Building paper

2 × 6 Rafter

½" Plywood

Metal drip edge

Fiberglass screen @ each rafter space

1 × 4 Fascia

2 × 4 Top plate

1 × 8 Trim, notched around rafter tails

½" Plywood

12
6

2 4

2 2

6 6

Door Jamb Detail

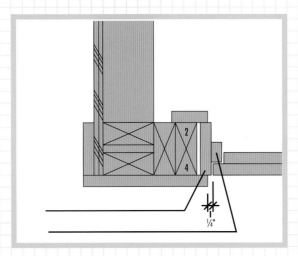

2

4

¼"

Door Elevation

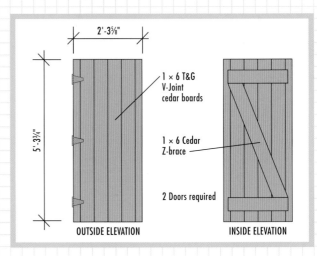

2'-3⅝"

5'-3¾"

1 × 6 T&G V-Joint cedar boards

1 × 6 Cedar Z-brace

2 Doors required

OUTSIDE ELEVATION

INSIDE ELEVATION

HOW TO BUILD THE LEAN-TO TOOL BIN

Prepare the site with a 4" layer of compacted gravel. Cut the two 4 × 4 skids at 70¾". Set and level the skids following Floor Framing Plan (page 427). Cut two 2 × 6 rim joists at 70¾" and six joists at 44⅜". Assemble the floor and set it on the skids as shown in the Floor Framing Plan. Check for square, and then anchor the frame to the skids with four joist clip angles (inset photo). Sheath the floor frame with ¾" plywood.

Cut plates and studs for the walls: Side walls—two bottom plates at 47⅜", four studs at 89", and four studs at 69"; Front wall—one bottom plate at 63¾", one top plate at 70¾", and four jacks studs at 63½". Rear wall—one bottom plate at 63¾", two top plates at 70¾", and six studs at 89". Mark the stud layouts onto the plates.

Fasten the four end studs of each side wall to the bottom plate. Install these assemblies. Construct the built-up 2 × 6 door header at 63¾". Frame and install the front and rear walls, leaving the top plates off at this time. Nail together the corner studs, making sure they are plumb. Install the rear top plates flush to the outsides of the side wall studs. Install the front top plate in the same fashion.

Cut the six 2 × 6 rafters following the Rafter Template (page 430). Cut the 2 × 6 ledger at 70¾" and bevel the top edge at 26.5° so the overall width is 4⁵⁄₁₆". Mark the rafter layout onto the wall plates and ledger, as shown in the Roof Framing Plan (page 427), then install the ledger flush with the back side of the rear wall. Install the rafters.

(continued)

YARD & GARDEN STRUCTURES

5

Complete the side wall framing: Cut a top plate for each side to fit between the front and rear walls, mitering the ends at 26.5°. Install the plates flush with the outsides of the end rafters. Mark the stud layouts onto the side wall bottom plates, then use a plumb bob to transfer the marks to the top plate. Cut the two studs in each wall to fit, mitering the top ends at 26.5°. Install the studs.

6

Sheath the side walls and rear walls with plywood siding, keeping the bottom edges ½" below the floor frame and the top edges flush with the tops of the rafters. Overlap the siding at the rear corners, and stop it flush with the face of the front wall.

7

Add the 1 × 4 fascia over the bottom rafter ends as shown in the Overhang Detail (page 430). Install 1 × 8 fascia over the top rafter ends. Overhang the front and rear fascia to cover the ends of the side fascia, or plan to miter all fascia joints. Cut the 1 × 8 side fascia to length, and then clip the bottom front corners to meet the front fascia. Install the side fascia.

8

Install the ½" roof sheathing, starting with a full-width sheet at the bottom edge of the roof. Fasten metal drip edge along the front edge of the roof. Cover the roof with building paper, then add the drip edge along the sides and top of the roof. Shingle the roof, and finish the top edge with cut shingles or a solid starter strip.

Cut and remove the bottom plate inside the door opening. Cut the 1 × 4 head jamb for the door frame at 57⅛" and cut the side jambs at 64". Fasten the head jamb over the sides with 2½" deck screws. Install 1 × 2 door stops ¾" from the front edges of jambs, as shown in the Door Jamb Detail (page 430). Install the frame in the door opening, using shims and 10d casing nails.

For each door, cut six 1 × 6 tongue-and-groove boards at 63¾". Fit them together, then mark and trim the two end boards so the total width is 27⅝". Cut the 1 × 6 Z-brace boards following the Door Elevation (page 430). The ends of the horizontal braces should be 1" from the door edges. Attach the braces with construction adhesive and 1¼" screws. Install each door with three hinges.

Staple fiberglass insect mesh along the underside of the roof from each side 2 × 6 rafter. Cut and install the 1 × 8 trim above the door, overlapping the side door jambs about ¼" on each side (see the Overhang Detail, page 430).

Rip vertical and horizontal trim boards to width, then notch them to fit around the rafters, as shown in the Door Jamb Detail (page 430). Notch the top ends of the 1 × 10s to fit between the rafters and install them. Add 1 × 8 trim horizontally between the 1 × 10s below the door. Install the 1 × 4 corner trim, overlapping the pieces at the rear corners.

TREEHOUSES & PLAY STRUCTURES

This chapter offers a chance for the kids to get even after all the time you've spent building yourself that deck or patio or some other major landscape feature using the project instructions from other chapters in the book. Or maybe you're choosing to be proactive, building the youngsters a play structure from this chapter at the very beginning, in order to give them something to do while you build that deck or patio or shed for yourself.

This chapter offers something for every kid's interest, with plans ranging from a simple tree swing to an impressive treehouse with enclosed walls, windows, and a weatherproof roof. You'll find complete building plans, clear step-by-step directions, and helpful tips along the way.

When building projects for children, safety is always of utmost concern. Always consult with local government to learn about any applicable permit and inspection requirements, and never scrimp on materials when it comes to investing in the safety of projects your kids will use.

IN THIS CHAPTER:
- Open-air Treehouse
- Enclosed Treehouse
- Playground Safety
- Precut Playground Kit
- DIY Playset
- DIY Swingset
- Classic Tree Swing
- Skateboard Ramp
- Bocce Court

OPEN-AIR TREEHOUSE

This house design could just as easily be called the All-ages Treehouse. Adults will like it because they can move around in the house without having to see their chiropractor the next day and because the broad deck surface and ample headroom make it a great venue for outdoor entertaining and everyday cocktails at sundown. Kids will love it because, well, because it's a treehouse, but also because it's large enough to fit loads of them. The open sides are ideal for backyard games, and the deck makes the perfect stage for picnics and campouts. Best of all, everyone can use the treehouse at once, although this may require a willingness to dodge water balloons or act as a captive on a pirate ship.

The house shown in this project has an 8 × 12-foot floor plan and measures about 9 feet from the deck to the roof peak. It's supported along the front side by two posts and along the rear side by two trees (see page 438), using special anchors designed specifically for treehouses. The treehouse deck stands about eight feet off the ground.

The instructions here provide a detailed overview of building the house as shown, for this particular site. They can serve as a general guide to help you design and build a similar house of your own. However, all of the construction specifications for your project must be geared for your specific house design, the intended use of the house, the tree(s), and the building site, as well as any applicable local building codes and zoning restrictions.

Water-resistant cushions are ideal for the open-air treehouse, perfect for extra seat padding or just throwing on the ground—it's a treehouse, after all.

The open-air treehouse combines the versatility of an elevated deck with the shelter of a covered porch, but of course it's far better than both because it's found in the trees.

Open-air Treehouse

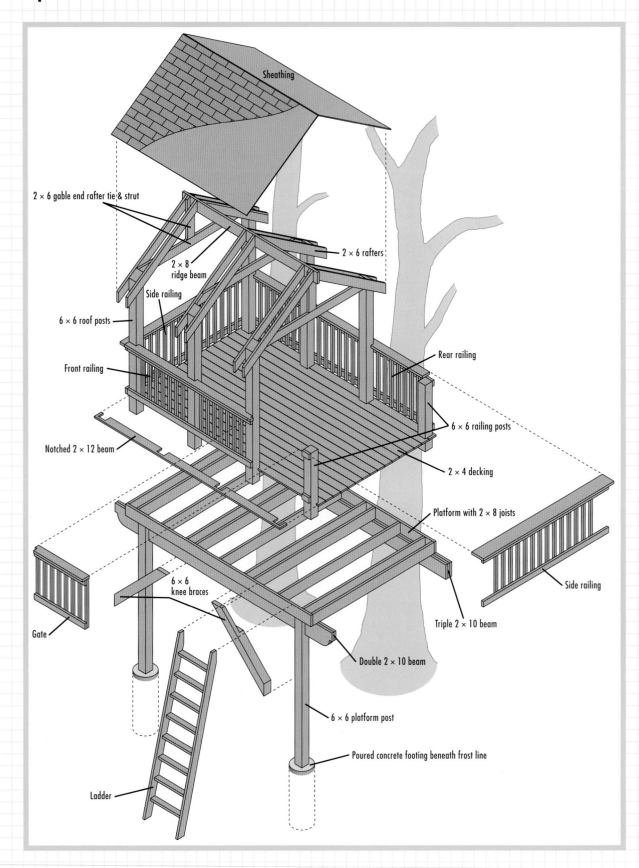

Sheathing

2 × 6 gable end rafter tie & strut

2 × 6 rafters

2 × 8 ridge beam

Side railing

6 × 6 roof posts

Front railing

Rear railing

Notched 2 × 12 beam

6 × 6 railing posts

2 × 4 decking

Platform with 2 × 8 joists

Side railing

6 × 6 knee braces

Gate

Triple 2 × 10 beam

Double 2 × 10 beam

Ladder

6 × 6 platform post

Poured concrete footing beneath frost line

PLAN VIEW: PLATFORM FRAMING

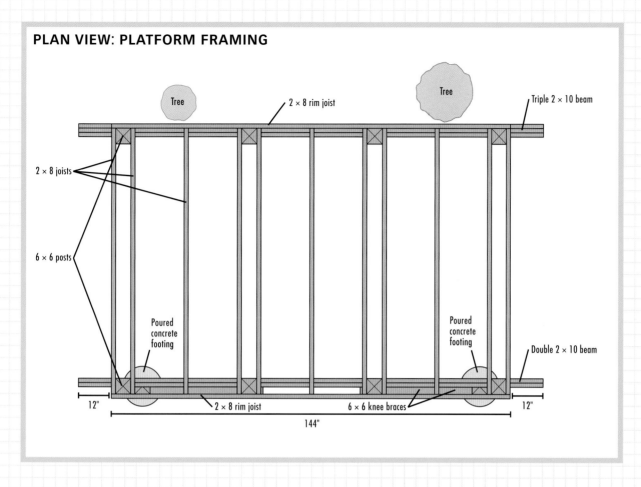

Tree

Tree

2 × 8 rim joist

Triple 2 × 10 beam

2 × 8 joists

6 × 6 posts

Poured concrete footing

Poured concrete footing

Double 2 × 10 beam

12"

2 × 8 rim joist

6 × 6 knee braces

12"

144"

FRONT ELEVATION

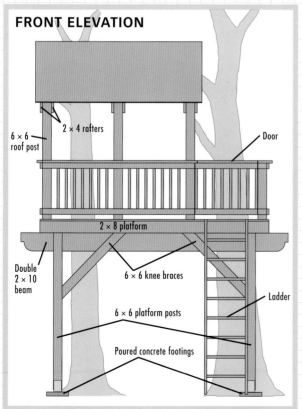

6 × 6 roof post

2 × 4 rafters

Door

Double 2 × 10 beam

6 × 6 knee braces

2 × 8 platform

6 × 6 platform posts

Ladder

Poured concrete footings

SIDE ELEVATION

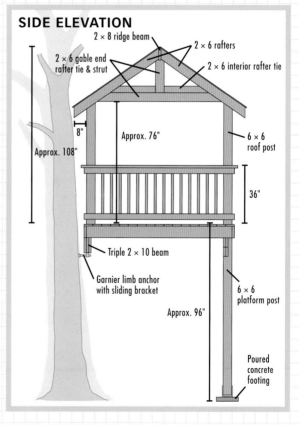

2 × 8 ridge beam

2 × 6 rafters

2 × 6 gable end rafter tie & strut

2 × 6 interior rafter tie

8"

Approx. 76"

6 × 6 roof post

Approx. 108"

36"

Triple 2 × 10 beam

Garnier limb anchor with sliding bracket

6 × 6 platform post

Approx. 96"

Poured concrete footing

DETAIL: LADDER

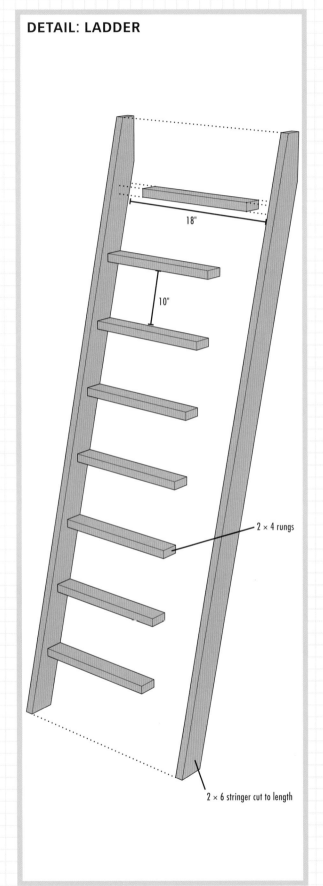

18"

10"

2 × 4 rungs

2 × 6 stringer cut to length

DETAIL: ROOF FRAMING

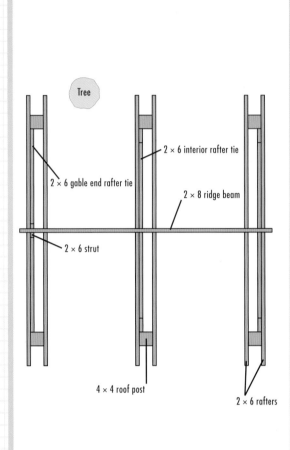

Tree

2 × 6 interior rafter tie

2 × 6 gable end rafter tie

2 × 8 ridge beam

2 × 6 strut

4 × 4 roof post

2 × 6 rafters

DETAIL: CEILING

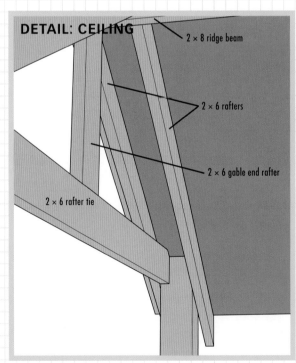

2 × 8 ridge beam

2 × 6 rafters

2 × 6 gable end rafter

2 × 6 rafter tie

HOW TO BUILD AN OPEN-AIR TREEHOUSE

1

Use a level board as a visual reference to determine the best height and location for your tree anchors.

2

Drill the pilot hole with a heavy-duty ½" drill (available at any rental center). Brace yourself and pay attention to avoid injury with this powerful tool.

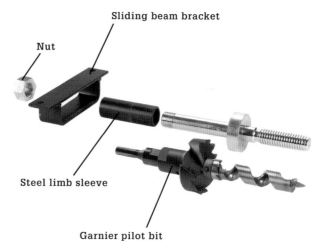

Nut

Sliding beam bracket

Steel limb sleeve

Garnier pilot bit

The GL anchor and its specially designed piloting bit. The middle collar section on the anchor compresses into the tree to help prevent rot and disease.

3

Level the anchor carefully as it begins to bite into the tree. A big pipe wrench (and maybe a cheater bar) is the key to getting the anchor tight (below).

(continued)

TREEHOUSES & PLAY STRUCTURES

Nail three 2 × 10s together to create the built-up rear beam. Stagger the nails between the upper and lower portions of the beam.

With the beam in position, add a nut to the end of each anchor (using a washer, if applicable) to trap the bracket on the anchor.

Embed an anchor bolt into the wet concrete of each footing. The bolt should be centered on the footing.

Build the front beam with two 2 × 12 boards, staggering 10d nails with 16" spacing. Shape the ends with decorative cuts, if desired.

TREEHOUSES & PLAY STRUCTURES

8

Level across from the top of the rear beam to mark the top cutoff lines on the posts.

9

Use a square to extend the cutting lines across the post faces for the top end cutoff and notches.

10

Fasten the posts to their bases. Make sure the base is tightened down to the anchor bolt with the provided nut.

11

Beam side

Fasten the front beam to the posts with pairs of carriage bolts inserted through the posts and secured on the beam side with washers and nuts. (continued)

Trace along the front beam to mark the top cuts and notches for the knee braces. When installed, the faces of the posts and braces are aligned.

Anchor the knee braces to the posts with lag screws driven straight through the inside faces of the braces, roughly centered on the joint.

Use a scrap of 6 × 6 post as a spacer when marking the joist layout and installing the joists. The roof posts should fit snugly between the joist pairs.

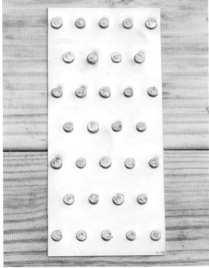

Metal framing connectors create a strong connection between the treehouse platform and the beams and are important for resisting wind uplift.

16

Follow chalk lines to set the initial rows of decking (since you can't start at the edge of the platform). A few extra chalk lines can help you stay on track during the installation.

17

Anchor the bottom ends of the roof posts with carriage bolts, sandwiching the posts between the joists at either side.

18

Use a string line to ensure the posts are on the same plane across each side of the treehouse.

19

Cut the ends of the pattern rafters at 33.7° and test-fit them on a pair of roof posts, using a piece of 2 × 8 scrap to serve as the ridge beam.

20

Mark the ridge beam for rafters, using the roof posts. Make an "X" to the outside of each post marking to show where the rafter goes.

(continued)

21

Interior rafter ties span across the rafters on the interior roof posts. Their ends are cut to match the roof slope.

22

The gable-end rafter ties are combined with a strut to create a truss detail. The strut is notched to fit around the ridge beam (below).

23

24

Tongue-and-groove roof decking is required for the relatively wide spans of the rafters. Follow the manufacturer's specifications for gapping between panels.

A decorative layer of cedar plywood conceals roofing nails and creates a finished ceiling. Notch the panels as needed to fit around the roof framing.

25

Composition shingles make for an inexpensive, long-lasting roof. Consider the shingle color carefully, as you'll probably be looking at it most of the year.

26

Install the rails with their top edges on the chalk lines. The 3" gap below the bottom rail makes it easy to sweep off the treehouse deck.

27

Use a baluster and level to mark the sides of each baluster location, and use a 2 × 4 block cut to length at 3⅞" to set the gaps between balusters.

28

Notch the caps to fit around the posts (inset), leaving about a 1½" overhang on the outside of the railing and a 1" overhang on the inside. (continued)

29

Self-closing hinges keep the gate closed when it's not in use—a handy safety feature for anyone using the treehouse.

30

Swing direction →

Mating notches in the caps and rails of the gate and treehouse railing create safety stops that also prevent undue wear and tear on the gate.

31

Access to this treehouse happens to be at the front, but it could also be at either end or even the back, if you'd prefer a cleaner look at the front.

32

Strategically placed accessories, such as swings and climbing ropes, turn the treehouse into the best kind of backyard play structure.

ENCLOSED TREEHOUSE

A treehouse that feels like a home. Solid walls, sturdy windows and doors, and some simple decorative touches add up to a cozy retreat where kids can really let their imaginations run wild.

This nicely proportioned house is a great example of what you can do with one good, stout tree. And the design is simpler than it looks. It starts with a square platform that's framed around the trunk and supported by knee braces at the corners. Apart from the cutout for the door and entry deck, the house is just a box with a gable roof, much like the houses you find in kids' drawings. This classic look is no coincidence—with its traditional lines and fully enclosed interior, the treehouse has an especially homey feel, a theme that's enhanced by the Dutch door and playhouse-size entry deck. The interior layout also lends itself to built-in accessories, like shelves and tables.

A single-tree house of this size requires a large, mature tree. The specimen must be healthy, of course, and should measure at least five feet in circumference at its base. Because the tree alone will bear the burden of the house and its occupants, it's a good idea to have it inspected by an arborist before making any serious construction plans. Think about where you'd like to place the house, so you can give special attention to the installation areas.

Note: The instructions here provide a detailed overview of building the house as shown, for this particular site. They can serve as a general guide to help you design and build a similar house of your own. However, all of the construction specifications for your project must be geared for your specific house design, the intended use of the house, the tree, and the building site, as well as any applicable local building codes and zoning restrictions.

Tools & Materials ›

Lag screws	Anchor brackets	Drill	Work gloves
Level	Compass	Hammer	Eye and ear protection
Nails or screws	Circular saw	Tape measure	

Self-closing hinges keep the gate shut when it's not in use—a handy safety feature for anyone using the treehouse.

Gable House with Entry Deck

GABLE HOUSE EXPLODED VIEW

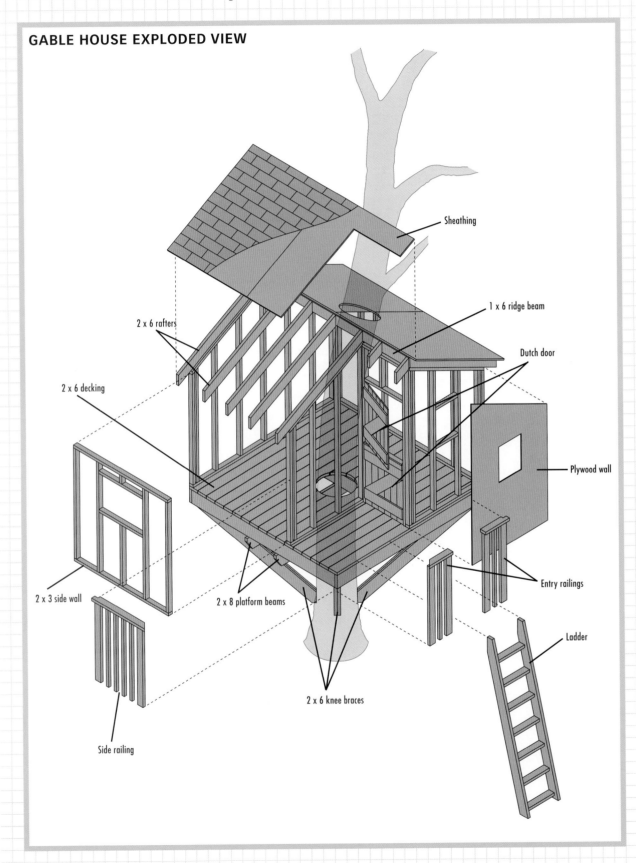

Sheathing

1 x 6 ridge beam

Dutch door

2 x 6 rafters

Plywood wall

2 x 6 decking

2 x 3 side wall

2 x 8 platform beams

Entry railings

Ladder

2 x 6 knee braces

Side railing

PLATFORM FRAMING

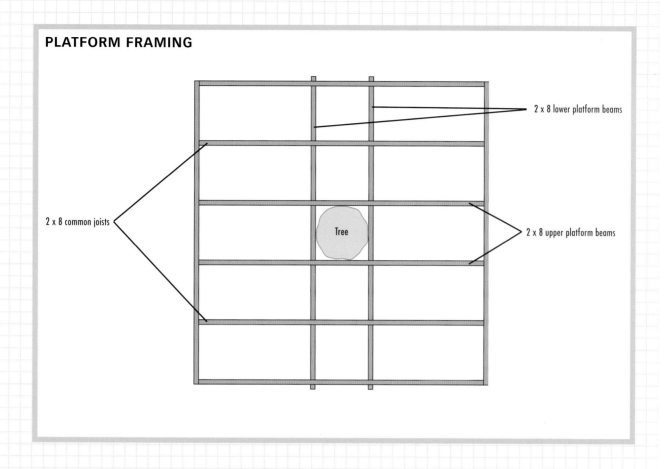

2 x 8 lower platform beams

2 x 8 common joists

2 x 8 upper platform beams

Tree

FRONT ELEVATION

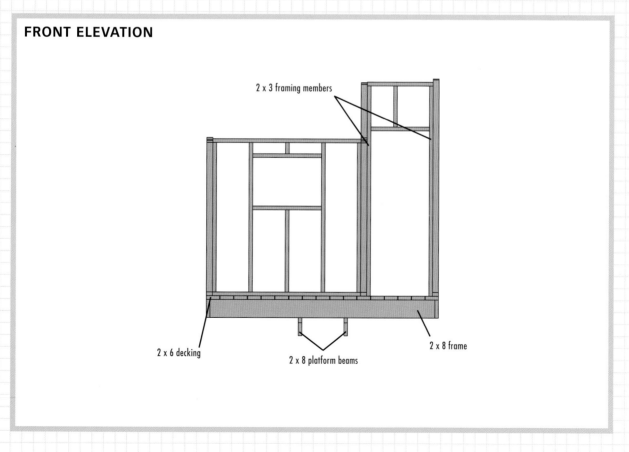

2 x 3 framing members

2 x 6 decking

2 x 8 platform beams

2 x 8 frame

SIDE ELEVATION LEFT

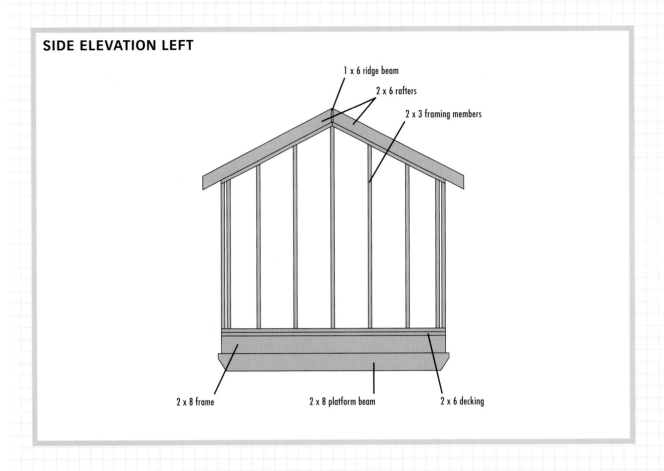

1 x 6 ridge beam

2 x 6 rafters

2 x 3 framing members

2 x 8 frame

2 x 8 platform beam

2 x 6 decking

FLOOR PLAN

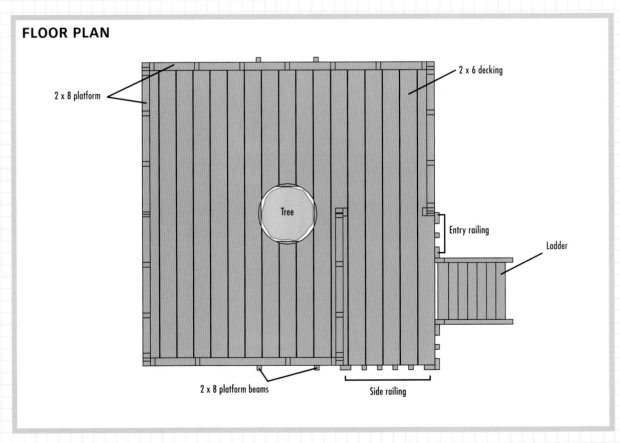

2 x 8 platform

2 x 6 decking

Tree

Entry railing

Ladder

2 x 8 platform beams

Side railing

BACK ELEVATION

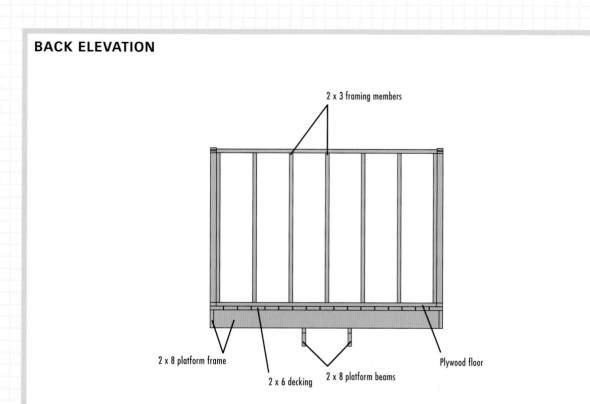

2 x 3 framing members

2 x 8 platform frame

2 x 6 decking

2 x 8 platform beams

Plywood floor

SIDE ELEVATION RIGHT

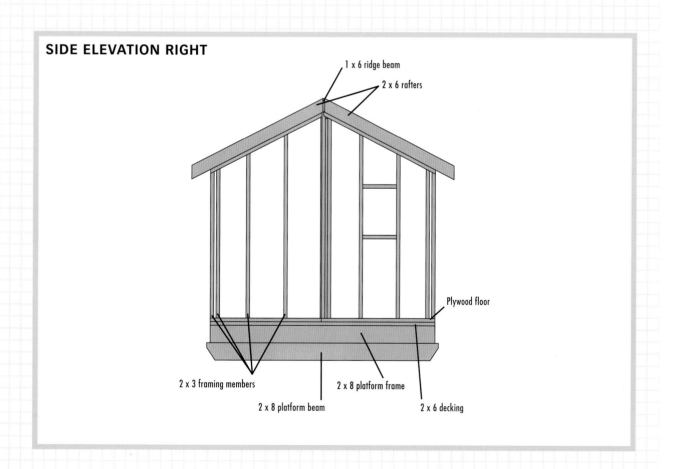

1 x 6 ridge beam

2 x 6 rafters

Plywood floor

2 x 3 framing members

2 x 8 platform beam

2 x 8 platform frame

2 x 6 decking

HOW TO BUILD AN ENCLOSED TREEHOUSE

Anchor the lower beams to the center of the tree. Remember that the lag screws should be just below center (top-to-bottom) on the beams.

Install the upper beams, checking all of the beams for level as you go. If necessary, use wood shims to make a beam stand plumb against the tree (detail below).

3

Fasten the rim joists to the common joists with nails or screws. Here, the interior common joists are centered between the outer commons and the upper beams.

4

Secure the knee braces to the tree with anchor brackets (detail below) and to the platform frame with toenailed screws or nails and framing connectors.

(continued)

457

5

2" gap

Custom fit the decking boards around the tree by butting each piece up to the tree and using a compass set at 2" to transfer the tree's contours to the board.

The left gable wall spans the width of the house and is centered on the roof peak. The extra stud at each end is for installing interior finishes.

Use ropes and a pulley, a block and tackle, or any other mechanical aids to hoist the walls up to the platform.

Fasten the walls together at the corners with deck screws, following the same plan you used for the dry assembly on the ground.

(continued)

7

Installing the ridge beam first makes it easy to mark and test-fit the pattern rafters.

8

The rafters overhang the front and rear walls by about 8" (measured horizontally) to create the traditional eaves.

The custom gable rafters are installed so their outside faces are flush with the outside of the wall siding.

Salvaged windows with exterior trim are a breeze to install. Others might call for some creative carpentry, but they're well worth the effort.

(continued)

Preassembling a homemade window can save you some trips to and from the treehouse, but it requires careful measuring of the window opening.

This sample Dutch door shows the simple construction of tongue-and-groove siding boards joined with 1 × 6 Z-bracing.

This simple railing is made with 2 × 4s and 2 × 2s anchored to the platform framing and the house walls.

PLAYGROUND SAFETY

Safety is paramount to enjoying your backyard playground. And safety starts in the basic planning stage. For example, if you plan to build multiple play structures, keep at least nine feet of space between them. Securely mount the structures or anchor them to the ground and always follow manufacturer instructions.

In addition to planning your playground project wisely, you can make your play area safer by observing some basic rules when building it.

- Drive nailheads and set screwheads completely into the wood so the heads are flush with the surfaces. Nails or screws that stick out of the wood can pose a serious risk to children. When you've finished building your project, examine it for fasteners that are popping out. Also check for nails or screws that have gone completely through boards and are sticking out the other side. If that happens, clip the end off or grind it down flush with the board.
- Countersink or counterbore holes for anchor bolts so the heads and nuts are recessed.
- Crimp hooks with pliers so sharp edges are not exposed.
- Conduct regular inspections of the structures and look for unusual wear and tear, loose boards or connections, and loose rails. Replace hardware if needed, only with identical hardware.

Playground Safety ▸

For more in-depth information on playground safety, visit the following websites:

- National Program for Playground Safety: uni.edu/playground
- US Consumer Product Safety Commission: cpsc.gov

Attention to safety details along with a thick cushion of soft mulch around the entire play area ensures that all the landings will be happy ones.

Are Post Footings Necessary? ▸

Pouring concrete footings to anchor structural components results in a rock-solid playground, but the process adds hard work and expense. Poured footings are not always necessary, especially if you're building a wide or low structure or using angled supports (like those used for swingsets). Here's a breakdown of the advantages and disadvantages of pouring concrete post footings:

ADVANTAGES
- Creates a stable, permanent base that won't tip or move or sag
- Anchors swingsets and other play equipment solidly
- Makes building on uneven ground easier
- Allows you to make tall, narrow structures and cantilevers without danger of tipping or movement
- Structure can eventually be converted to a storage or garden shed

DISADVANTAGES
- Adds time and expense to the project, especially if you are building in rocky or hard clay soil
- Structures that can't be moved or disassembled easily may interfere with future landscaping

SECURING PLAYGROUND EQUIPMENT

Add a wide, stable base to playground structure supports. Stabilize the base as much as possible by angling the supporting posts and adding crosspieces. Add additional stability by driving and fastening anchor stakes next to the base.

Screw-in anchors help keep playground structures from rocking or tipping, though they can be difficult to install in hard clay or rocky soil. Make sure anchors don't create a tripping hazard.

Spread the Playground Mulch ▸

According to the Consumer Product Safety Commission, about 40,000 children a year visit hospital emergency rooms due to falls from playground equipment. A safe playground will have a cushioning surface, such as mulch or wood chips. Most home playgrounds, however, are located directly on grassy lawns because that is an easy, cost-free surface. However, any grass lawn will become compacted and hard eventually, making falls dangerous. And, of course, you should never build a playground on hard surfaces like concrete or asphalt.

The supports for playground structures need to be anchored on solid, undisturbed ground, so the mulch layer is usually added after the playground is constructed. Once all of the structural elements are anchored, remove some dirt from around the play area—slightly slope the grade away from the supports for the tower and swings. The mulch should extend at least six feet out from all structures and 16 feet beyond the support

beam of a swing. The cushion layer should be installed over landscape fabric to a depth of at least 12 inches. You can reach that depth either by excavating or by adding landscape timbers around the edges to contain the mulch.

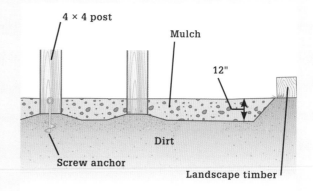

465

PRECUT PLAYGROUND KIT

If you want to design and build a backyard playground that meets your needs, but you don't want to start from scratch, a good option is to buy a precut playground kit. Most home centers and a number of Internet suppliers sell do-it-yourself playground packages containing parts and hardware to make a complete play area. Some of the kits include all of the wood, while others include a list of lumber that you must buy with the set. Dozens of different designs are available, from a basic swingset and slide to elaborate, multilevel play areas with numerous extra features. Most manufacturers design their systems so that optional features can be easily added on.

Most playground systems are designed to be installed with poured concrete footings, but in some cases you may be able to get by with simply anchoring the posts (see page 465). If you choose not to pour footings, it's even more important for the ground underneath the tower and swingset to be very level. To level and smooth the playground area and to stop grass and weeds from growing through it, cut out the sod in the play area, or at least in the area where the structures go, before you begin building.

Some playground kits include all the necessary drill bits and drivers. If your kit doesn't, you'll need a standard selection of spade bits and drill bits, as well as countersink bits for #6 and #8 screws. You'll also need a magnetized Phillips head driver for your drill.

Note: The instructions in the following project are intended as a general guide for installing a playground kit that includes precut lumber. The type of playground you purchase may use different materials and techniques than shown here.

Precut playground packages contain everything you need except tools. A homeowner with basic skills can put together a play area like this in one or two weekends.

Playground Kit

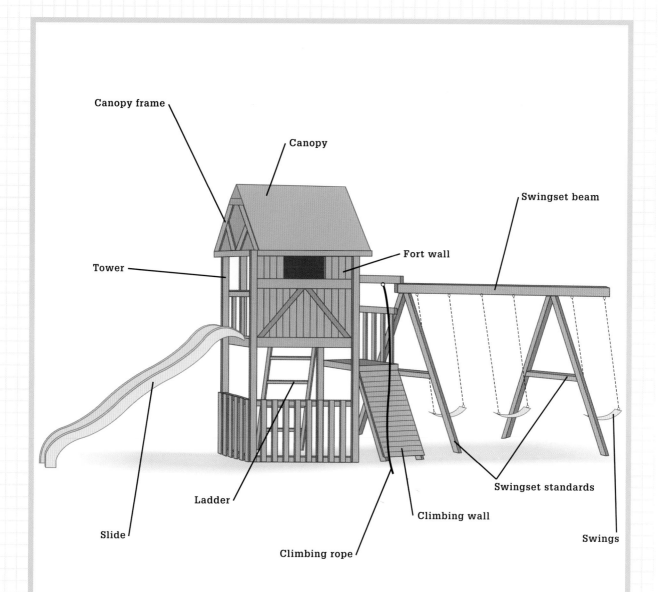

Canopy frame

Canopy

Swingset beam

Tower

Fort wall

Ladder

Climbing wall

Slide

Swingset standards

Swings

Climbing rope

Tools & Materials

Framing square
Carpenter's level
Socket wrench
Adjustable wrench
Drill/driver
Sawhorses
Shovels
Posthole digger
   (if screw-in anchors don't
   work with your soil)
Stakes

Mason's string
Line level
Power saw
Clamps
Ladder
Spacers
Screwdriver
Lag screws
Anchor screws
Playset kit
Eye and ear protection

Work gloves
2×6 or 2×8
Brackets
Bolts
$1\frac{1}{2}$", $2\frac{1}{2}$" deck screws
Tape measure
Swing hangers
$1\frac{1}{2}$" panhead screws
Landscape fabric
Mulch
Screw-in anchors

HOW TO INSTALL A PLAYGROUND KIT

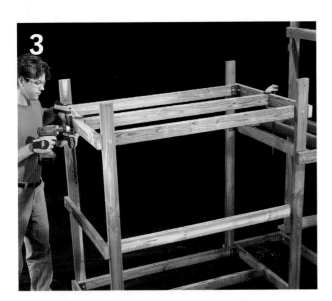

Before you begin, properly prepare the installation area (see pages 464-465). Begin assembling a tower. Towers are the principal structural elements in any playground kit. They support slides and other accessories. Generally, they are comprised of fairly simple frames and beams. For the kit shown here, assemble the framework of the tower one side at a time, and then join the sides together on top of flat pieces of 2 × 6 or 2 × 8. Use the drilling template included in the kit as a guide for driving countersunk screws. Locate screws carefully—metal brackets that cover the screwheads are often added later, so the screws have to be positioned carefully. Raise the tower.

Screw the brackets to the tower frame corners, making sure that the bolt hole on the long side of the bracket lines up with the centers of the 2 × 4s behind it. Using the large holes in the brackets as guides, drill holes for the bolts. To avoid splintering the back sides, stop drilling as soon as the bit starts to poke through the back, then finish drilling from the other side. Check to make sure everything is still square, and then install and tighten the bolts.

Install the center joists that connect the platform frames, fastening them with countersunk 2½" deck screws. Make certain all screwheads are fully seated beneath the wood surface.

Install the deckboards with 1½" deck screws driven into countersunk pilot holes, starting with the two outside pieces. Try to make sure the ends of the deck boards are aligned during installation—clamping a stop block or spacer block to the deck-board support will help align your workpieces. The drainage gaps between the deck boards must be less than ¼".

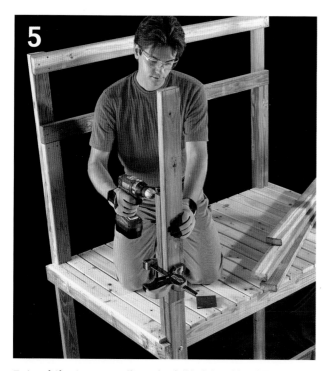

Extend the tower walls to the full height with additional 2 × 4 pieces. Use the drill guide or template (if provided with your kit) to ensure regular alignment of all screws.

Install the outer framework of 2 × 4s to support the roof of the playground structure, using corner brackets provided by the kit manufacturer.

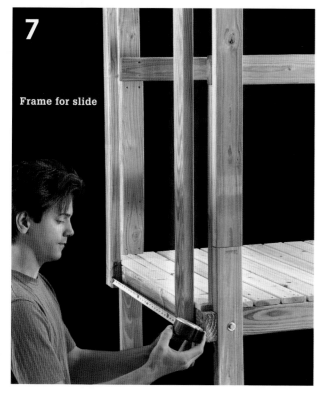

Frame for slide

Spacer

Add additional framing to strengthen the sides of the tower. The framing on the right will help support the swingset and the climbing bar and climbing wall; the 2 × 4s on the left are used to support the slide.

Install the bottom railings and the top back and side railings for the tower structure. Clamp a straight piece of wood on top of (or underneath) the railing at the 1" point to create the setback and to make installation easier. Cut spacers to make the gap even, but check the gap before screwing in the last few boards, just in case, and adjust if necessary.

(continued)

9

Attach railings, siding, and trim. Install the front railing first, using a ³⁄₁₆" spacer. Then, add the trim pieces. This step is easier if you tilt the structure backwards to the ground—but don't try this without a helper.

10

Install the rest of the roof frame. Use clamps to hold pieces in position before attaching them. Check the center vertical pieces with a carpenter's level to make sure they are plumb.

11

Begin building the swingset. The swing structure shown here is supported by a pair of angled posts in an A-frame configuration on the end farther from the tower, and a single angled leg on the tower end. Fasten the three legs of the swingset together (they are made with doubled 2 × 4s), and then bolt on the triangular bracket for each leg. Construct the assembly by bolting the triangular brackets together and then screwing on the crosspiece. Add the small brackets to the inside of the crosspiece, with the short legs against the crosspiece (inset). Trim the leg bottoms so they will lie flat on the ground.

12

Join the beams and legs. Screw the 2 × 6 beam pieces to the brackets, making sure the legs are exactly parallel and square to the beam. Drill the ³⁄₈" holes for the bolts using the brackets as a guide. Then screw the second layer of 2 × 6s to the first with 2½" screws.

13

Swing hanger

Attach the swing hardware. First, turn the swing assembly over and place it on sawhorses. Drill guide holes and fasten the sides together with bolts. Drill guide holes for the swing hangers and lag screws and install them so that the moving hanger swings perpendicular to the beam.

14

Add the swingset to the tower. Lift the swingset into place and fasten it to the tower with a bolt through the swing beam and a 2 × 4 crosspiece near the base fastened with metal angles and bolts.

15

Installing the climbing wall. Attach the climbing wall supports to the tower frame with the provided brackets. The ends of the supports are angle-cut at the top and the bottom. Attach the top and bottom crossboards to the outer supports and then center the middle support board and attach it by driving deck screws through the crossboards and into the support.

16

Add the remaining crossboards in the climbing wall, working down from the top and making sure the boards are fitted tightly together.

(continued)

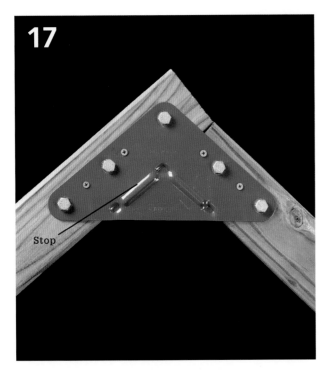

17

Stop

Start building the climbing bar assembly. The climbing bars function as a ladder that is mounted to the tower on the side opposite from the climbing wall. Assemble the climbing bar standards with four triangular metal brackets included with the kit. The stops on the sides of the brackets that contact the standard will set the correct angle for the standards if the boards are tight against the stops.

18

Attach the climbing bars to the standards, making sure the standards are parallel and oriented correctly. Use 1¼" panhead screws to attach the bars at 12" intervals on the bottom leg and at 10¾" intervals along the top (or as directed by the instructions for your kit).

19

Connect the climbing bar to the tower. First, dig holes into the play surface at the correct locations for the legs of the climbing bar standards. Set the legs into the 2"-deep holes (inset), and then fasten the top ends of the standards to the tower with brackets and lag screws.

20

Anchor all sides of the swingset, along with the climbing bar and climbing wall, using screw-in anchors (see page 465). If the anchors don't work properly in your soil type, dig a 2-ft.-deep posthole, fill it with concrete, and set the anchor in that. Bolt the anchor to the structure with ⅜ × 1½" lag screws.

21

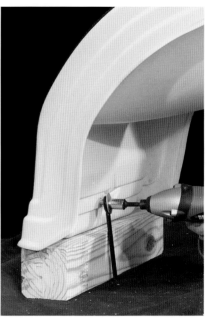

Attach the slide. First, position the slide (left photo) and then attach it to the tower at the top with fasteners as provided (or recommended) by the manufacturer. Then, bolt the slide at the base to a screw-in anchor. *Tip: Attach the bottom of the slide to a 4 × 4 spacer and then attach the spacer to a screw-in anchor (right photo). This provides a solid footing for the slide while raising it so the bottom is not completely covered by groundcover or mulch.*

22

Add other accessories, including swings, the roof, and the climbing rope. You'll need to drill access holes for the climbing rope in the climbing wall. Add approved groundcover (see page 465).

DIY PLAYSET

If you want a playset, designing and building your own from scratch is not as easy or fast as buying a precut system, but if you have the tools and know-how you can save money and create a more unique and imaginative playset by doing it yourself.

The simplest way to get started is to design and build the playground in separate parts, beginning with a simple, rectangular platform. You can then add slides, a swingset, a climbing rope, and other features as your time and budget allow. Before you start, mark the area where the play structure will go in your yard, then add additional area for playground mulch (at least six feet out in all directions). Cut away the sod in this area and level the ground—preferably by digging out soil instead of filling in, since fill will continue to compress even after it is compacted.

Playset Hardware ▸

Although it's a little more work initially, the best way to make sure your playground will be solid and stable is to pour concrete footings and anchor the platform posts to the footings. Ideally, the footings should extend below the frostline (check with your local building department if you do not know your frostline depth). If you pour concrete footings, make sure that the concrete is covered by several inches of dirt or playground mulch to prevent injuries.

When building your playset, you can set the posts into postholes, add a few inches of gravel, and then fill the hole with concrete, or you can set the posts into exterior-rated metal post bases that are anchored to the concrete.

Note: Metal post bases are designed to work in groups and are not a good choice for single posts or even post pairs. They do not provide sufficient side-to-side rigidity.

If your structure is very wide or low to the ground, you can forego footings and instead bolt the posts to a framework of 2 × 6s (or larger), which will spread the weight over a large area and keep the platform stable. If you attach a swing or cantilevered beam to the platform, use one of these methods to hold the structure in place: fasten long screw anchors at the corners; attach structure to concrete footings; or weigh structure down with an attached sandbox.

Hardware and equipment specially designed for playgrounds can be purchased in kits or as needed. In addition to saving time, using engineered hardware is a safe method for designing critical joinery. For example, if you are wondering how many lag bolts you need to make a post/beam connection on a swingset, you'll find the easiest answer is zero if you purchase an engineered A-frame bracket instead. A-frame bracket (A), screw-in anchors (B), swing hardware (C), swing chain and seat (D), galvanized joist hangers and brackets (E), hot-dipped galvanized fasteners (F), hot-dipped glavanized eye bolt (G).

Save money by designing and building your own play structure using standard building materials and your own ingenuity.

Playset

Materials

(4) 4 × 4" post bases
(4) 8"-dia. × 2-ft. tube forms
Concrete
Landscape fabric
(1) 1 × 3" × 8 ft.
(1 lb.) 2" deck screws
(2 lb.) 2½" deck screws
(44) ⅜ × 5" carriage bolts, washers, nuts
Joist hanger brackets and nails
(8) 2¾" metal corners
(2) 1¼ × 8⅝ × 3⁹⁄₁₆" u-shaped metal straps
(6) ⅜ × 6" carriage bolts, washers, nuts
(1) ⅜ × 5" eyebolt with washer, lock washer, nut
18 ft. ¾" thick rope
Metal thimble for rope

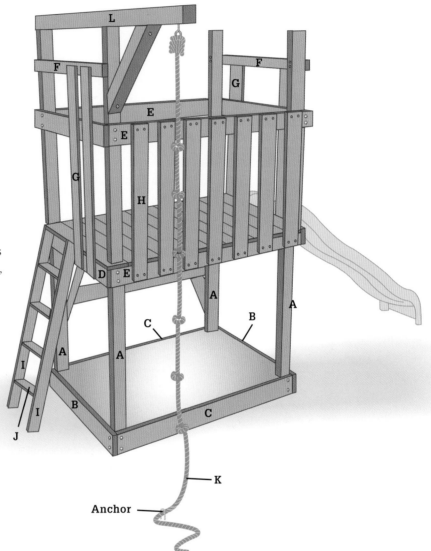

Cutting List

Key	No.	Dimension	Material
Base & Platform			
A	4	3½ × 3½ × 10'	Pine (PT)
B	2	1½ × 7¼ × 51"	"
C	2	1½ × 7¼ × 69"	"
D	2	1½ × 5½ × 51"	"
E	4	1½ × 5½ × 58"	"
F	2	1½ × 3½ × 48"	"
G	4	5/4 × 5½ × 58"	Decking (PT)

Key	No.	Dimension	Material
H	14	5/4 × 5½ × 42"	Decking (PT)
Ladder			
I	2	1½ × 3½ × 61½"	Pine (PT)
J	4	1½ × 3½ × 17"	"
Climbing Rope			
K	1	3½ × 3½ × 7'	Pine (PT)
L	1	3½ × 3½ × 30"	"

HOW TO BUILD A DIY PLAYSET

1

Lay out the project area, including the required excavation of surface materials for the buffer zone around the playset. Use batterboards and mason's string to outline the area, making sure the corners are square. Tie a second set of strings to the squared layout strings so they intersect directly over the centers of the post locations.

2

Mark digging points on the ground directly below post locations. Untie the mason's strings. *Note: Contact your local utilities company to have them mark buried gas, plumbing, or electrical lines before you start digging.*

3

Dig holes for concrete footings using a posthole digger or a power auger. Where feasible, dig at least a few inches past the frostline for your area.

4

Fill the forms with concrete, tie the mason's string back onto the batterboards and level them, and then set J-bolts into the concrete directly beneath the centers of the planned post locations.

(continued)

Set the metal post bases and washers over the bolts and hand-tighten the nuts (a standoff base is designed to elevate the post bottom to eliminate ground contact while still holding the post securely). Leave one side of the post base open so you have access with an open-end wrench to tighten each nut after trimming and aligning the post tops.

Fasten the bottoms of the posts to the standoff hardware with 10d galvanized nails, joist hanger nails or other fasteners as specified by the post base manufacturer. All predrilled guide holes in the hardware should be filled with a fastener. Plumb and brace the posts. *Note: The tops of the 4 × 4 posts should be high enough that they can all be trimmed back to final height later.*

Temporary brace

Attach 2 × 6 pressure-treated frame boards to the posts so the bottoms are level with one another and slightly above grade. Cut the 2 × 6s so they form a complete frame around the posts once installed. Use clamps and deck screws to tack the members in place until they are leveled and located exactly where you want them. After drilling the bolt guide holes, use a 1¼" spade bit to counterbore ½"-deep holes. Wrap masking tape around the spade bit to mark the ½" depth.

Install landscape fabric. To prevent weeds and grass from growing through the sand, spread landscape fabric over the ground inside the structure area and staple it to the inside surfaces of the 2 × 6 frame. Hold the top of the fabric back about 3" from the tops of the frame boards. For extra holding power, use thin wood strips as retainers for stapling or nailing the fabric.

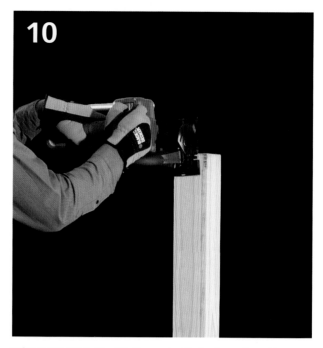

Attach the platform side boards so the tops are approximately 59" above grade. First, tack the side boards to the 4 × 4 posts with a 2½" deck screw at each end. Make sure the sides and all other members are level and plumb and then drill two bolt holes at each end for ⅜ × 5" carriage bolts. The end of each hole that will receive the nut and washer should have a 1¼"-dia. × ½" deep counterbore. Do not counterbore for carriage bolt heads. Tighten nuts onto the carriage bolts with a socket wrench or impact driver.

Trim post tops. Identify the post with the lowest post base and measure up on that post to the finished post height for the project. Mark the height and then use a laser level (or a straight board with a carpenter's level attached to it) to transfer the post top height to the other posts. After the frame and platform are installed, trim the posts along the lines. A cordless circular saw is a good tool for trimming post tops.

Add the platform support joists, using joist hanger hardware to support the 2 × 6 joist material between the side boards. Space the joists equally. The tops of the joists should be flush with the tops of the side boards.

(continued)

12

Cut pieces of 5/4 decking (actual thickness is 1") for the platform and install them with deck screws driven into the support joists. Arrange the boards on the joist supports first and adjust them so the gaps between boards are equal, consistent, and do not exceed ¼". Drive screws in a regular pattern, as the screwheads will be visible.

13

Fasten 2 × 6 railings to the posts on the sides of the structure, using ⅜ × 5" carriage bolts. The tops of the railings should be 8 ft. above ground. Counterbore the posts so the nuts and washers are recessed. Also install 2 × 4 railings on the other two sides (narrow sides) at 111" high. Paint or stain the playset with exterior-grade paint if desired.

Safety Tip ▸

For safety, add wide balusters made from deck boards to the sides. The gaps between boards should not exceed 3". Leave openings for ladders, slides, and any other accessories you wish to attach.

14

Fill the framed base enclosure with sand to create a sandbox (or use mulch or pea gravel, if you prefer).

TREEHOUSES & PLAY STRUCTURES

HOW TO BUILD A LADDER

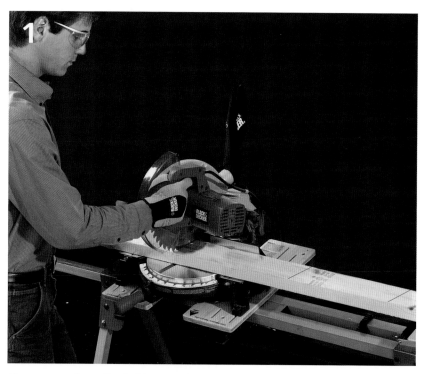

A wooden ladder provides easy, safe access up into the fort portion of your project. This ladder is sturdy and simple to build. You'll need: (2) 2 × 4 × 61½", (4) 2 × 4 × 17", (1) 2 × 4 × 24", and (8) 2¾" metal corners.

Measure and cut the ladder standards from a pressure-treated 2 × 4. Look for tight-grained lumber with no visible defects. The steps are set at a 15° angle so they'll be level when the angled standards are set on flat ground. The back edges of the standards at the top are cut at a 75° angle.

Attach the steps. Nail one plate of each metal corner brace to the ladder sides at the correct spacing (the steps generally are 12" apart on-center) and then nail the bracket to the underside of the step using joist hanger nails.

Attach a ladder base to the bottom of the ladder to function as a spreader. Screw the 24"-long base to the bottoms of the ladder sides with deck screws, then set the ladder in place on a bed of gravel. Secure the ladder to the playset deck through the back with two deck screws per side driven into the frame.

HOW TO ATTACH A SLIDE

A slide is perhaps the most necessary accessory for any playset. Although it is possible to build your own from scratch, the likelihood of obtaining satisfactory results is low. Any building center that carries playset parts will also sell plastic slides in many styles, colors, and sizes. You'll need a slide, three #14 × 1¼" panhead screws, a screw-in ground anchor, and a ⅜ × 1" hex bolt with washers and nuts.

Mark the slide anchor location onto the ground using a cap nail. When using a thick bed of playground mulch, raise the bottom of the slide by attaching it to a 4 × 4. This 60" slide is secured to the playset tower so the top edge is 60" above ground. To attach the slide temporarily, drive #14 × 1¼" panhead screws through the screw holes in the slide lip.

Drive an anchor for the slide base into the ground, after removing the slide, at the post marked in Step 1. The eye hook at the top should be aligned with the bolt hole in the slide.

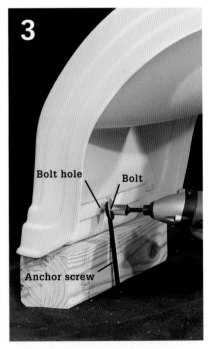

Bolt hole
Bolt
Anchor screw

Reinstall the slide, driving the fasteners through the top lip and into the playset structure. Use an exterior bolt (⅜ × 1" is used here) to attach the base of the slide to the anchor you've driven for it. The base should be resting on solid ground (not on mulch or other loose materials) or a spacer, as shown.

HOW TO ADD A CLIMBING ROPE

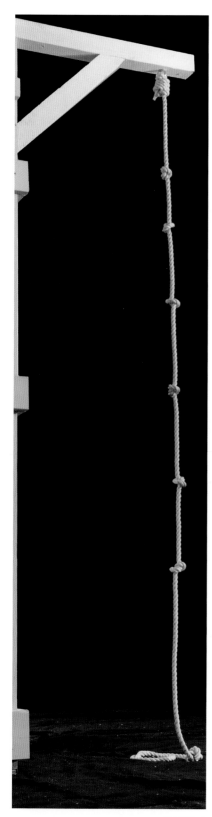

A climbing rope can be attached to a cantilevered support beam that is securely affixed to the top of your play structure.

Attach a 7-ft.-long 4 × 4 to the top of the playset structure to support a climbing rope. Use joist hanger nails and U-shaped metal straps or long metal straps to fasten the cantilevered 4 × 4 to the post tops.

Add a 4 × 4 brace with a 45° angle cut at each end. The brace is attached with a ⅜ × 6" bolt at each end and reinforced with the same U-shaped strap hardware used to attach the beam.

Hang the climbing rope. A ⅜ × 5" eyebolt can be attached to the cantilevered end of the beam, about 6" in, for an easy tie-off point. You can purchase fancier hardware, such as a swivel hook. Tie knots every foot or so in the rope for better gripping while climbing.

Anchor the bottom of the rope to a screw-in anchor or a board that's bolted to the base of the fort. The rope should not hang loose for safety reasons. If you are tying the rope to a screw-in anchor, use a large enough knot to cover the top of the anchor screw eye.

DIY SWINGSET

Swingsets are fairly simple projects to build, and can be anchored to a larger playset for more stability, as is the case with the model seen here. If your swingset will be freestanding, anchor all four legs with screw-in anchors. Swings can be higher or longer, as long as the A-frame supports are widely spaced and securely bolted together.

Swing seats, chains, and hardware usually come as a package. Generally, the plastic-encased chain is easier to work with and has a greater chance of success than rope, which is difficult to adjust and may stretch or loosen over time.

Swings are virtually a requirement in any playset. This swingset is bolted to a DIY playset, but it can easily be modified into a freestanding swinging structure.

Swingset

65°

B

A

A

A

A

C

C

25°

Tools & Materials

Pencil
Circular saw
Protractor
Power miter saw
Drill/driver
Sawhorses
Clamps
Stepladder
Eye and ear protection
Work gloves
(8) ⅜ × 5" carriage bolts, nuts, washers
(2) ⅜ × 6" carriage bolts, nuts, washers
(2) Swingworks A-frame brackets
    (see Resources, page 553)
Swing seats, chains, and hardware

Cutting List

Key	No.	Dimension	Material
A	4	3½ × 3½ × 104"	Pine (PT)
B	1	3½ × 5½ × 8'	"
C	2	1½ × 5½ × 6'	"

HOW TO BUILD A SWINGSET

Mark the posts for cutting. If you are using A-frame brackets (strongly recommended), purchase the hardware beforehand and mark the posts using the A-frame bracket as a guide. If you are not using brackets, use a protractor or a speed square as a gauge to mark the tops of the posts at around 65° so they will meet to form a stable A-shaped structure with sufficient leg spread.

Cut the long angles on each post with a circular saw, then square off the top edge with a power miter saw or circular saw.

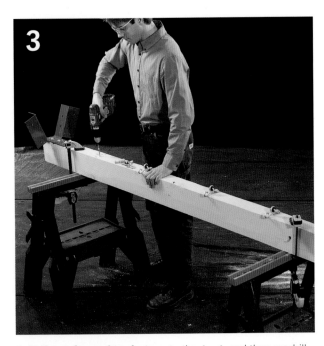

Bolt the A-frame brackets onto the 4 × 6, and then predrill the holes for the eye bolts that hold the swing. Use a long spade bit for the holes.

Assemble the legs. Lay the 4 × 4 legs for one side on a flat area, set the 4 × 6 on top of them, and then bolt the legs to the brackets. Use the fasteners recommended by the hardware manufacturer. You'll need a helper to hold the 4 × 6 steady.

Attach the second leg. Use a stepladder or helpers to hold the 4 × 4s steady and in place as you finish bolting into the brackets.

Clamp the 2 × 6 ties in position. Drill the bolt holes, and then counterbore the holes on the inside. Bolt the 2 × 6 on with 5" carriage bolts.

Anchor the swingset. Tack the swingset structure in place against the platform of the adjoining playset. Using a long drill bit, drill through each 4 × 4 leg and bolt the swing to the platform.

Hang the swings using the mounting hardware and chains or rope supplied with or recommended by the manufacturer. Test to make sure the ground clearance is adequate and adjust as necessary.

CLASSIC TREE SWING

A rope hung from a large tree may be a simple swinging apparatus, but kids and even adults will find it completely irresistible. The rope may be hung with just a knot at the bottom for gripping or it may support a swing seat or an old tire.

All that is really required to build a rope swing is a healthy tree, a length of heavy rope, and the ability to tie a good knot. Use one-half-inch diameter or larger rope (larger is better) made of nylon or hemp. Tie a few knots in the bottom of the rope as grips and to prevent unraveling, even if you plan to add a swing seat. Watch the rope for signs of wear, and test it often. Make sure smaller children understand how to use it safely, and that they should never make loops in it.

When siting your swing, look for a tree that has a sturdy limb at least eight inches in diameter and nearly horizontal. The limb should be at least 10 feet above ground and the swinging area should be free and clear of all obstacles, including the tree trunk, which should be at least six feet from the point where the swing is tied (farther if the rope is longer than 10 feet). Landing and access areas should be clear of hazards and have shock-absorbing mulch or ground cover. Do not allow small children to use the swing without adult supervision.

Tools & Materials ▸

½"-dia. rope or larger (nylon or hemp)
⅝"-dia. hot-dipped galvanized eyebolt
    with washer and nut
Metal thimble (to match rope)
Old tire (optional) or swing
Drill and spade bit for eye bolt
Stepladder
Eye and ear protection
Work gloves

A tree swing can be installed practically anywhere that you have a tree, clear swinging area, and safe spots for landing and access.

HOW TO HANG A TREE SWING

Attach a ⅝" galvanized eyebolt through the center of a branch that's at least 8" in diameter. Insert a thimble through the eye bolt; then tie the rope onto the eyebolt, threading it through the thimble to make the top curve. This is a tree-friendly approach to hanging a swing

Option: Tie the rope to the tree. If the branch is too high to easily reach with a ladder, throw a small cord with a weight over the branch, then use it to pull the rope up. Tie a loop in the end of the rope and pull it tight. Test the knot to make sure it is secure and does not slip. *Note: Wrapping a rope or chain around a tree limb is okay as a short-term swinging solution, but it can actually cause more long-term harm to the tree than an eyebolt. Prolonged friction from a tight rope can eventually start to strangle the limb by cutting through the bark.*

Rope Selection ▸

Use ½"-dia. or larger nylon or hemp rope for a rope swing. Hemp is a traditional rope for swings, but will eventually start to rot if left out year round. Nylon is almost indestructible, but will stretch slightly and is more expensive than hemp. Nylon is available in fun colors. A 12" galvanized steel eyebolt with thimble inserted into the eye offers a safe, tree-friendly hanging method.

Hang the tire or swing seat. Swings are an excellent use for an old tire, but avoid steel-belted types with exposed steel strands, and clean the tire thoroughly before using it. Drill large holes in the tread of the tire to drain water away (inset). Do not use hard objects or objects with sharp corners (such as wood planks) as tree swings—they can cause damage or injury.

SKATEBOARD RAMP

Because good places to practice can be few and far between, every skateboarder dreams of having a skateboard ramp of his or her own. Sidewalks may get dull, city streets are dangerous, and most public areas are rarely skateboarder-friendly; but your own ramp in your own yard is always ready and available.

This skateboard ramp (knowledgeable boarders would describe it as a mini half-pipe ramp) is a fun, challenging, and safe place to learn new skills—and it offers a softer landing than a hard concrete sidewalk. It's also fun to build and can be constructed in two to four days using only standard hand and power tools.

This 4-foot-high ramp measures 24 feet long by 8 feet wide. It is built in three sections: a pair of curved ramps on each end and a flat stretch in between. To keep the plywood that forms the curves from wicking up moisture and rotting, build it on top of concrete footings or pads. If you build it on a flat driveway or patio, set the corners and center transitions on concrete pads to keep the wood dry.

Skateboarding is a dangerous activity on ramps or anywhere else. Always wear a helmet, kneepads, and other protective clothing and equipment when skateboarding. *Note: This ramp is based on a free plan designed by Rick Dahlen and available for downloading.*

Tools & Materials ▸

Jigsaw	2 × 4 lumber (no. 2 or
Power miter saw	better)
Circular saw	Deck screws (1⅝, 2, 2½")
Trammel	Lag screws (⅜ × 3") with
Sander	washers
Paint or wood	Carriage bolts (⅜ × 4")
preservative	with washers and nuts
¾" exterior plywood	#6 panhead screws (1½")
⅜" exterior plywood	Schedule 40 PVC tubing
(sanded)	(2" dia.)
2 × 4 lumber	Work gloves
(pressure-treated)	Eye and ear protection

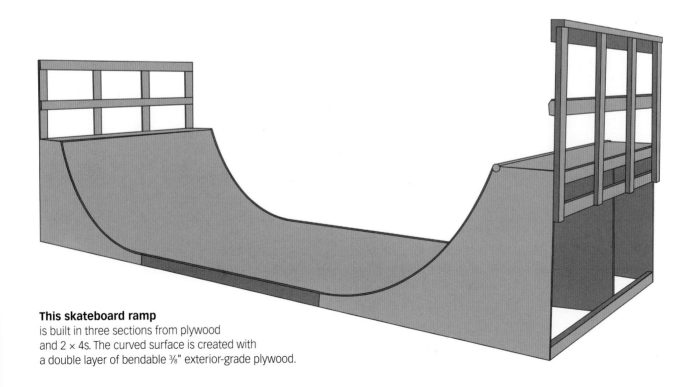

This skateboard ramp
is built in three sections from plywood
and 2 × 4s. The curved surface is created with
a double layer of bendable ⅜" exterior-grade plywood.

HOW TO BUILD A SKATEBOARD RAMP

1

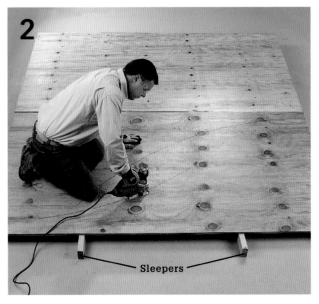

2

Sleepers

Mark the curves for the ramp sides using a modified trammel. First, lay two sheets of ¾"-thick exterior plywood next to each other on a flat surface. The long edges should be touching, with the ends flush. Cut a thin strip of wood to 8 ft. long and tack one end 3½" up from one of the back ends. Measure 7 ft.-6" from the point where the trammel strip is tacked and drill a ⅜"-dia. guide hole for a pencil. Insert a pencil into the guide hole and trace a curve on the plywood. Mark four pieces of plywood this way.

Cut out the curves using a jigsaw equipped with a fast wood-cutting blade. Watch the lines carefully as you cut to avoid drifting away from the curve, and make sure both the workpiece and the waste are well supported. Setting the plywood on 2 × 4 sleepers creates access space for the jigsaw blade.

3

4

Cut notches for the coping pipe at the top of each curved plywood upright, using a jigsaw. The notches allow the PVC coping pipe that is used to overhang the ramp slightly.

Build the ramp side assemblies. Cut the 2 × 4 spreaders to length using a power miter saw equipped with a stop block for uniform lengths. Install the spreaders between pairs of ramp sides at intervals of approximately 8". Drive several 2½" deck screws through the plywood and into the ends of the spreaders at each joint.

TREEHOUSES & PLAY STRUCTURES

Bevel the top spreaders. Two spreaders are butted together at the top of each ramp to create a cradle for the coping tube (here, a piece of 2" PVC pipe). Butt a spreader up against the face of the top spreader in each ramp and mark a bevel cut on the edge so you can trim the spreader to be flush with the plywood base. Rip the bevel cut on a table saw or clamp the workpiece securely to a support board and cut the bevel with a straightedge guide and a circular saw. Set the saw blade angle to match the bevel angle.

Construct the 2 × 4 platform for the flat middle area in two sections and then fasten the sections together with deck screws. Alternate driving directions between frames to create a stronger joint.

Join all the curved and flat sections with deck screws, aligning the edges carefully. By this time, you should have moved the parts to the installation area and confirmed that the area is flat. Ideally, the ramp should be installed on a concrete slab or concrete footings that minimize ground contact.

Coping tube
shown cutaway for clarity

Add the coping tube to the tops of the ramps—we used 2"-dia. Schedule 40 PVC tubing, but you can use rigid conduit or water pipe if you prefer metal. Drill eight evenly spaced $\frac{3}{16}$" holes through the coping, then enlarge the entry holes to $\frac{1}{2}$". Fasten the coping to the beveled top spreaders with $1\frac{1}{2}$", #6 panhead screws.

(continued)

9

Install a layer of ¾" plywood to the flat areas of the ramp using 2" deck screws driven every 8" into the platform frames. Choose exterior-rated plywood with a sanded face facing upward to create a smooth skateboarding surface. Make sure joints between panels fall over 2 × 4 supports and make sure all screw heads are recessed slightly below the wood surface.

10

Attach a double layer of ⅜" plywood to the curved parts of the ramp. Standard ¾" plywood is too thick to bend along the ramp curves, so we used two layers of ⅜" plywood, which is limber enough to manage the gradual curves of the ramp. Make sure the seams for both layers are offset by at least 18" and that all joints fall over 2 × 4s. Leave ⅛" gaps between sheets for expansion and drainage. Attach with 1⅝" deck screws driven every 8". *Tip: To help the plywood bend more easily, dampen the reverse side.*

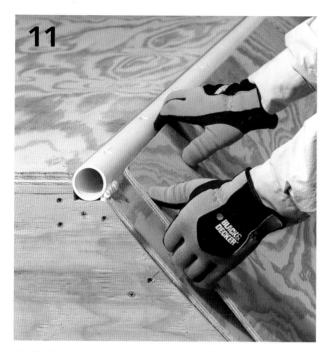

At the joint between the coping and the deck, spread a bead of caulk along the top edge of the first layer to keep water from wicking in between the sheets and rotting the wood. Caulk the gap between the coping tube and the first course before you butt the second course of plywood up to the coping. Fasten the plywood with 2" deck screws. *Tip: For a better joint, bevel-rip the top edge of the second course slightly.*

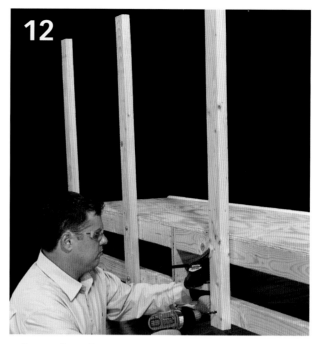

Bolt 2 × 4" × 4-ft. posts to the back of each platform using ⅜ × 4" carriage bolts. Attach an additional 2 × 4" × 4-ft. corner post at each side to create L-shaped corners. Draw the corner post boards together with 2½" deck screws, closing the joint.

Install horizontal rails between the posts and then top-off each end rail system with a 2 × 4 cap plate attached with 2½" deck screws.

Sand the plywood to eliminate roughness and splinters, and set any protruding screws beneath the surface of the plywood. Vacuum the dust off, then coat all wood with paint or wood preservative. For best protection and ease of cleaning, coat the entire ramp with two or three thin coats of gloss exterior paint.

BOCCE COURT

Like many sports and games, bocce can be played casually on any reasonably level lawn with a minimum of rules, depending on how flexible you and your playing companions are. But if you are serious about playing bocce as a pastime and you have the space in your yard, consider building a regulation bocce court with a smooth, flat surface and a permanent border.

Developed in Italy as a variation of an ancient Roman game and then spread around the world, bocce is played at clubs, public courts, and backyards all over the world. Although not an Olympic sport, various bocce federations and clubs organize tournaments for enthusiastic amateurs, and competition can be fierce.

Official bocce courts for tournament play are 13 feet wide by 91 feet long, but recreational courts can be anywhere from 8 to 14 feet wide and 60 to 91 feet long. If you're trying to squeeze a court into your backyard, you can adjust those measurements as needed. Often the game is played without a court at all, or with an irregular-shaped court that accommodates the dimensions and shape of your yard. Standard courts are made from gravel topped with a fine clay or shell mixture and surrounded by a low wood wall, with the depth and composition of gravel and the construction of the wood wall determined by local climate and soil conditions.

Borders should be made of wood, and can be constructed of 4 × 4s, 4 × 6s, 2 × 10s, or other combinations of sizes. No matter which size you use, the border should be protected from frost heave and moisture, either by anchoring it to 4 × 6 posts set in concrete below the frost line or by building it on a thick bed of gravel.

Large, pressure-treated timbers like 6 × 6s and 6 × 8s make an excellent border, but these can be difficult to work with unless you're using a bobcat. You can substitute built-up layers of 2× lumber and 4 × 4s instead, overlapping seams and nailing and bolting them together. Bolt or screw them together from the outside, so that there are no visible fasteners on the inside of the court.

Bocce is a popular backyard game that has been around for centuries. It can be played free-form in any backyard, but for the truly authentic bocce experience you'll want a hard-surface bocce court.

Tools & Materials ▸

4 × 6 pressure-treated timbers	Maul
2 × 10 pressure-treated timbers	Circular saw
	Concrete mix
1½ to 2"-dia. drainage rock	Drill and spade bits
	Laser level
Compactable gravel	Stakes
Tennis court clay, crushed oyster shells, or similar blend	Mason's string
	Flat nose spade
	Shovel
Lag bolts, washers, and nuts	Rake
	Trowel
2½" deck screws	Power tamper
Construction adhesive	Construction adhesive
Posthole digger	Eye and ear protection
Gravel compactor	Work gloves

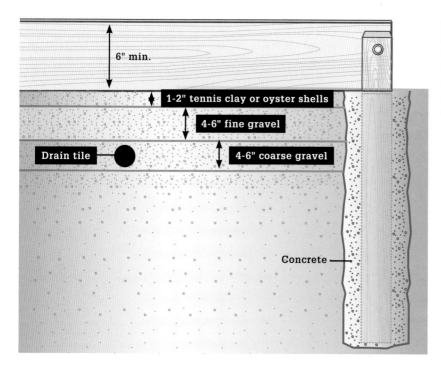

Frame the court with wood planks or timbers supported by frost footings or a thick gravel pad. Build the court surface from coarse gravel topped with finer, crushed limestone or similar stone, topped with crushed oyster shells, tennis clay or other similar material.

6" min.

1-2" tennis clay or oyster shells

4-6" fine gravel

Drain tile

4-6" coarse gravel

Concrete

How to Play Bocce ▸

Bocce is played between two players or two teams of up to four players each. Eight large balls and one small ball called a "pallino" are used. The pallino is thrown out first. The object of the game is to get one of the large balls as close as possible to the pallino. Knocking the other team's balls away from the pallino is acceptable. For a much more in-depth version of the rules, along with playing strategies and penalties, visit www.boccestandardsassociation.org and the United States Bocce Federation at www.bocce.com.

Bocce is played with a set of eight bocce balls and one target ball. Introductory sets made from composites can be purchased for less than $50. A traditional set of bocce balls made from clay and imported from Italy costs considerably more, but is a near-necessity if you develop a serious attachment to the game.

HOW TO BUILD A BOCCE COURT

1

Find or create a level area in your yard and stake out the corners of the bocce court. See previous page for discussion of court dimensions. Strip back the sod from the court area with a sod cutter or a flat nose spade.

2

Excavate the topsoil in the court area. A regulation bocce court should be dug out a minimum of 10" so the proper subbase material can be put in. If your plans are more casual, you can cheat this step a little as long as the ground in your yard is not soft enough that the court will sink.

3

Dig postholes. To support the walls (and prevent them from moving) set pressure-treated 4 × 6 landscape timbers every 4 ft. around the perimeter of the court. Ideally, the timbers (installed vertically) should extend past the frostline for your area. The tops will be trimmed to about 6" above grade after they're set.

4

Set the 4 × 6 timbers into the post holes, with a 4 to 6" layer of drainage gravel at the bottom. Fill around the timbers with concrete, sloping the tops to shed water. After all of the posts are set and the concrete is dry, use a laser level to mark level cutting lines on all the post tops and then trim them to height with a circular saw or reciprocating saw.

Option: After cutting the posts to height, use a circular saw set at 45°, a planer, or a trim router with a chamfer bit to cut chamfer profiles into the tops of the posts. Cut the outer edge and side edges of each post. Do not cut a chamfer on the side that will butt against the court walls.

Spread a 4 to 6" layer of drainage rock, such as 1½" river rock, onto the court. Cover this with a 4 to 6" layer of compactable gravel and tamp the gravel thoroughly with a power tamper. Add more gravel and tamp until you have attained a very firm base that is at or slightly below ground level.

Build the walls. Lay pressure-treated 2 × 10 lumber around the perimeter inside the posts. This first layer of the wall should be laid on edge, with the end seams falling at post locations. Fasten the boards to the posts with counterbored lag bolts, washers, and nuts. Then, attach a second layer of 2 × 10 inside the first layer. Use heavy duty construction adhesive and 2½" deck screws driven through the outer layer and into the inner layer.

Add a 1 to 2"-thick top layer of court clay, crushed oyster shells or other suitable medium. Here, crushed stone is being raked in preparation for compaction. Some top-dress layers do not require tamping, as the material will settle naturally. If the surface remains loose, however, you can use a power compactor to harden the surface so the bocce balls will roll more easily.

OUTDOOR FURNISHINGS & ACCESSORIES

The earlier chapters in *The Complete Outdoor Builder* mostly involved the hardscape for your yard—the permanent structural elements that turn your landscape into space where meaningful family living is possible. But just as your home is not very livable if it consists only of rooms with walls and floors, your outdoor landscape needs furnishings and accessories to become truly functional.

This final chapter gives you complete plans and instructions for building a dozen of the most useful and basic landscape accessories—the projects that will put the finishing touches on your yard. Some are self-contained yard elements that serve recreational or functional purposes, such as the Backyard Firepit or the Mailbox Stand. Others are useful for landscape gardeners of any skill level, such as Raised Planting Beds, the Compost Bin, or two different plans for Cold Frames. Other projects, though, are offered as completing touches for other major projects from earlier in the book. Your newly constructed deck, for example, will become uniquely yours with the addition of Deck Planters or a Deck Swing. Or a Privacy Screen might be just the touch for finishing your patio.

There are, of course, hundreds of outdoor furnishings and landscape accessories you can build yourself. These 12 are just an introduction to teach you the necessary skills and to show you what's possible.

IN THIS CHAPTER:

- Deck Planters
- Privacy Screen
- Deck Benches
- Porch Swing
- Versailles Planter
- Mailbox Stand
- Simple Potting Bench
- Compost Bin
- Backyard Firepit
- Classic Garden Bridge
- Raised Planting Bed
- Cold Frame Box
- Jumbo Cold Frame

DECK PLANTERS

What better way to truly integrate a deck with your landscaping than to introduce plants right on top of the surface? Supplement your deck design with one or more planters and you have the opportunity to grow just about any vegetation that catches your fancy.

The easiest planters to build are simple squares or rectangles like the one featured here. However, you shouldn't feel confined to those basic shapes; most planter plans can easily be adapted to just about any shape. That adaptability can come in handy when you need to tuck the planter into the odd corner of an unusual deck design.

Regardless of what shape you choose, it's always helpful to have some idea of what you want to plant in the planter. Different plants can require radically different types of soil and space for roots. A tree will require a much different planter than a small display of blooming annuals. In any case, it's wise to attach the planter to the deck to prevent it from falling over due to high winds or rambunctious party guests.

Tools & Materials ▸

Circular saw	3" galvanized deck screws
Miter saw	2½" galvanized deck screws
Power drill & bits	¾" exterior grade plywood
Tape measure	Nail set
4 × 4 lumber	Pond liner or 6-mil poly
1 × 3 lumber	Stapler
1 × 1 nailing strips	Work gloves
1 × 4 lumber	Eye and ear protection

A planter like this is relatively easy to construct and adds immeasurably to the look of the deck, not only with its design, but also by hosting attractive plant life.

HOW TO BUILD A DECK PLANTER

Use a miter saw or circular saw to cut all the framing members. Mark and cut four 4 × 4 legs and 20 1 × 4 side panels, all 18" long. Cut four 1 × 2 rails 21" long, and four 14" long. Cut eight 1 × 1 nailing strips 14" long.

Assemble the end panels by laying four 1 × 4s side by side, aligning them perfectly. Lay a short 1 × 2 rail across one end, running it perpendicular to the boards. Drill pilot holes, and screw the rail to each of the panel boards.

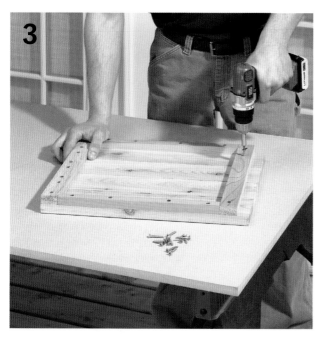

Position the nailing strips along the outside edges of the panel and drill pilot holes. Screw the nailing strips in place, and then screw the bottom rail in place as you did with the top rail. Butt it up against the bottom of the nailing strips (there should be a gap between the bottom edge of the rail and the bottom edges of the panel boards). Repeat the process using six 1 × 4s to construct the side panels.

Set a leg on the worktable and align a panel with the leg. Drill pilot holes through the nailing strip on the back of the panel, into the leg, and screw the panel to the leg using a screw every 2". Continue attaching the legs in the same manner until the box of the planter is complete.

(continued)

5

Cut a rectangle of exterior-grade ¾" plywood, 26½" × 19½". Notch the corners by cutting in 2¾" from each edge.

6

Turn the planter box upside down and screw the plywood bottom into place, drilling pilot holes at the edges into the bottom rails, and then screwing the bottom to the rails. Use a ¼" bit to drill holes in the center of the plywood to allow for drainage.

7

Cut the 1 × 4s for the plinth and top frame. Cut four 28" long, and four 21" long. Miter the ends of all pieces 45°.

8

Attach the planter box to the deck by measuring and setting it into position. Drive 2½" decking screws down through the plywood bottom and into the deck. Use one screw at each corner, located as close to the outer panel as possible.

Screw the plinth pieces in place around the base of the planter by driving 2" deck screws from the inside of the box, through the bottom rail and into the plinth piece. Use three screws per side.

Staple the planter box liner all around, attaching it over the top rail, but not so that it overlaps onto the outside of the side panels. Cut some holes in the bottom for drainage.

Drill pilot holes through the outside edges of the top frame pieces through the miters. Position the frame in place on the planter and drill pilot holes down through the frame and into the legs. Nail the frame in place with galvanized finish nails, and use a nailset to sink the nails.

Sand and finish the box if desired. Add a few inches of gravel at the bottom, then soil and plants. Water thoroughly.

PRIVACY SCREEN

Today's deck has the potential to be much, much more than just a simple step-out platform. You can design your deck to be an outdoor dining room with a secluded nook for quiet, intimate meals, a discrete sunbathing platform, or a sanctuary to read the paper in peace and get away from it all. But for all of these, privacy is key. A romantic brunch is no fun when it's in direct view of a neighbor's yard or kitchen window. And that's where a privacy screen can come in mighty handy.

Deck-mounted privacy screens have to conform to the same codes—or in some cases, more stringent versions—that the deck railings do. You have to be very careful that the placement of a screen does not impede on an egress opening, and that the clearance around windows and vents is adequately maintained. If you live in an area subject to strong winds, code issues will be even more of a concern and the screen may require special reinforcement so that it can withstand added wind load. Ultimately, you may also have to install blocking between the joists running

to where the screen is mounted, to help combat the stress from the wind load.

As important as code issues are, don't lose sight of the fact that a privacy screen is a substantial deck feature. Take the time to make sure the design adds to the look, as well as the function, of your deck.

Tools & Materials ›

Power drill and bits
Jigsaw or circular saw
1⅜" spade bit
5 × ½" lag screws and washers
3" deck screws
2½" deck screws
1½" 4d galvanized finish nails
Exterior grade ¾" lattice
Pyramid or other post finial
Eye and ear protection

4 × 4 lumber
1 × 2 lumber
2 × 4 lumber
Tape measure
Miter saw
Level
Speed square
Clamps
Work gloves

A lattice privacy screen allows for airflow and some light to filter through, and offers privacy from other yards.

HOW TO BUILD A PRIVACY SCREEN

Measure and cut the 4 × 4 posts for the screen. Each post should be 6'5" long. Miter the bottom ends of the posts to a 22½° angle. Seal the cut ends with a sealant/preservative, even if you're using pressure treated wood.

Measure and mark 2" up from the bottom of the backside of the posts, and 2" above that mark. Drill ½" deep holes at these marks, using a 1⅜" spade bit. Drill ⅜" pilot holes in the center of the larger holes, all the way through the post.

Mark the locations of the top and bottom plates on the inside faces of the posts. Mark the post positions on the side of the deck and double check your measurements (the posts should be exactly 46" apart on center). Hold the posts in position and mark through the pilot holes for the joist holes.

Attach the privacy screen posts to the edge of the deck with the aid of a helper. Hold each post in place, checking plumb with a level, and use 5 × ½" lag screws and washers to connect the post to the deck.

(continued)

5

6

Position the bottom plate between the two posts, using spacers to hold the plate in place. Screw the plate to the posts from the top, in toenail fashion, using two 3" deck screws on both sides.

Cut the screen frame pieces from 1 × 2 stock: 2 side pieces 5 ft. long, and top and bottom pieces 43" long. Miter the ends of the framing pieces to 45°. Mark a 4 × 8 sheet of lattice and use a jigsaw or circular saw to cut the sheet down to 4 × 5.

7

8

Drill countersunk pilot holes in the edges of all the screen framing pieces for the 3" deck screws that will secure the frame to the posts and plates. Space the holes about 10" apart.

Assemble the front frame by clamping pieces at the mitered joints, drilling pilot holes for 2" deck screws. Measure diagonally after the frame is finished to ensure square. Assemble the rest of the frame in the same way, and repeat to construct the back frame.

Add the outside frame. Drill pilot holes into the post and attach with 3" deck screws.

Place the lattice in position and install the inner frame. Predrill and nail the inner to the outer frame through a lattice strip every 8" with 4d galvanized nails.

Screw the top plate into place, and screw the top frame pieces to the top plate and to each other. Finish the screen by covering the post tops with finials. The finials used here are glued to the post top with construction adhesive.

Add additional segments by repeating these steps and adding a 2 × 6 cap mitered at 22½° at the mated ends. This plate will replace the finials.

MAILBOX STAND

This weekend project combines building skills and a love for flowering perennial plants. In addition to the building materials, visit a salvage yard to find an interesting rectangular planter to suspend below the mailbox. We used a brass planter with an antique patina.

Or, build your own planter from material of your choosing. This mailbox stand is made from a 4 × 4 cedar post that supports a pair of cross arm rails on which you set the mailbox. It is designed for a typical rural mailbox that's sized from 6 to 7 inches wide and 19 to 20 inches long. The planter is mounted by hanging it from ropes attached to Shaker pegs in the cross arm rails. Of course, you may prefer to leave the planter off entirely.

It is recommended that you set your mailbox stand post into concrete. It doesn't need to extend all the way down past the frost line unless you're really worried about your mailbox height changing by a fraction of an inch as the ground freezes and thaws. A depth of around 20 inches is more than adequate for relatively stable soil. A post cap at the top of the post keeps moisture out of the post's end grain and gives your project a neat, finished appearance.

This appealing mailbox stand creates a welcome entry marker for your driveway, especially if you hang the optional planter from it and fill it with bedding plants.

Materials ▸

1 4 × 4" × 8 ft. cedar post	16 #6 × 1½" brass wood screws
2 2 × 4" × 8 ft. cedar	Exterior wood glue
1 1 × 6" × 8 ft. cedar	Mailbox
1 2 × 8" × 8 ft. cedar	Rectangular planter box
1 1 × 2" × 8 ft. cedar	
1 decorative post cap	Nylon rope (or cord or chain)
6 ¼ × 5½" stainless steel bolts with nuts and washers	Potting soil
	12 wood caps
6 #8 × 2" brass wood screws	8 Shaker pegs

MAILBOX STAND

MAKE THE PARTS

Cut the side rails as indicated on the cutting list. On one end of each side rail, make a mark at 14" and another mark at 17½". Set the depth on a circular saw to ¼"; starting at the first mark and working to the second, make a series of cuts ¼" apart. Using a mallet and chisel, remove the waste material between the cuts (photo 1). Sand the face of the mortise as necessary. On each end of each side rail, use a jigsaw to cut a 3½"-radius arc.

Cut two braces as indicated on the cutting list. Use a jigsaw to cut an arc 5½" in radius in each end of each brace (photo 2).

ASSEMBLE THE POST & RAILS

Cut the spacers. Lay out one side rail, and set the post into the mortise. Position the spacers and the braces and add the second side rail. Square and clamp the assembly. Use a 1" spade bit to drill six counterbored holes that are ½" deep and centered at each bolt location. Turn the assembly over and drill holes on the other side.

Use a ⁵⁄₁₆" spade bit to through-drill the six bolt holes. Fasten the assembly with bolts, washers, and nuts (photo 3). Set the nuts finger tight, plus a half-turn. Use exterior wood glue and a wooden cap to plug each bolt hole (photo 4). Tap each cap into place, using a rubber mallet wrapped with a soft cloth.

1

Cut a mortise into each side rail by making a series of ¼"-deep kerf cuts and then removing the waste wood with a mallet and chisel.

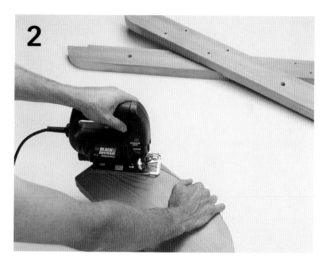

2

Cut and shape two braces. Draw an arc with a 5½" radius on the braces and cut with a jigsaw.

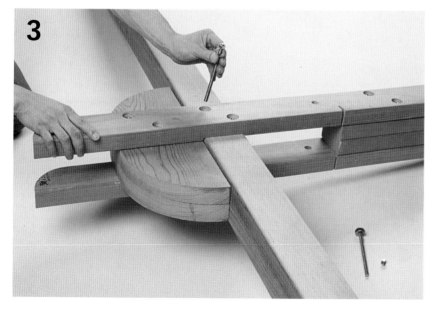

3

Fasten the post, rails, and braces with lag bolts. Drill counterbores for the bolt heads and the nuts.

(continued)

Drill four receiving holes for the four Shaker pegs that will support the planter. Use exterior wood glue to fasten the pegs into the side rails (photo 5). The heads of the pegs should extend 1" from the side rails. Trim off the excess peg shank so the ends are flush with the inside faces of the rails. Attach the decorative cap onto the top of the post.

ATTACH THE SHELF & MAILBOX

Cut the box shelf as indicated on the cutting list. Position the shelf on top of the side rails, 2½" from the front. Drill pilot holes and attach the mailbox shelf to the side rails using six #8 wood screws (photo 6). Fasten the mailbox to the mailbox shelf with eight #6 wood screws driven through the side flanges

(photo 7). Adjust the box position to allow the door to open freely.

MAKE THE PLANTER HANGING FRAME

Cut two long frame pieces and two short frame pieces. Drill pilot holes for four Shaker pegs. Position the short frame pieces between the long frame pieces. Drill pilot holes and fasten the frame with two #6 wood screws at each corner (photo 8). Glue the pegs into their guide holes and trim the ends. Allow the assembly to dry overnight.

Fill the planter box with potting soil and plants. Water thoroughly. Insert the planter box into the support frame and suspend it from the cabinet pulls with nylon rope, cord, or chain.

Glue a wood cap into both counterbores for each bolt.

Insert a Shaker peg into each guide hole so the cap extends 1" out from the rail. Glue in place and trim the end flush.

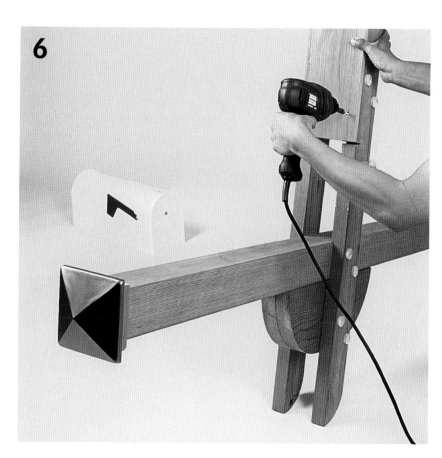

6

Attach the shelf for the mailbox to the side rails.

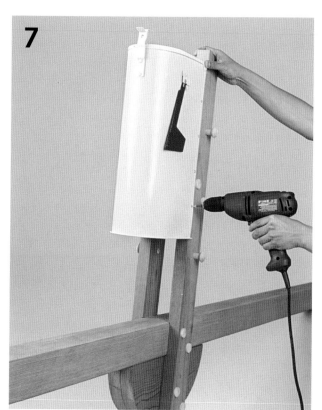

7

Attach the mailbox to the box shelf by driving screws through the side flanges of the mailbox.

8

Fasten the planter hanging frame with a pair of #6 wood screws driven in pilot holes at each corner.

PORCH SWING

A beautiful evening outdoors gets a little better when you're sitting and enjoying it from a porch swing. The gentle, rhythmic motion of the swing is a relaxing coda to any stressful day.

Essentially, a porch swing is a garden bench with chains instead of legs. Like garden benches, swings can be built to suit just about any style. Also like garden benches, too often the style of a porch swing comes at the expense of comfort. In fact, if you were to test each of the thousands of porch swing designs in existence, you might be amazed to discover how many are simply not comfortable. This porch swing was designed with both style and comfort in mind. It sits a bit deeper than many other versions and the back is pitched at just the right angle. Another key to its comfort is that the back rails don't extend all the way down to the seat slats, creating open space that is ergonomically important.

Despite the custom appearance of this porch swing, it is actually built from common ⅞" cedar boards, ⁵⁄₄" cedar deck boards, and cedar 2× lumber.

This porch swing can be hung from eyehooks in a porch ceiling that features sufficient structural framing, including joists that are no smaller than 2 × 8. Or, you can hang it in a variety of locations from a freestanding porch swing stand. The swing stand shown on pages 522 to 527 is designed to complement this swing.

Materials ▶

2 1 × 6" × 8 ft. cedar boards	4⅜"-dia. locknuts
1 ⁵⁄₄" × 12 ft. cedar deck board	Jigsaw
4 2 × 4" × 8 ft. cedar	Tape measure
Deck screws (2½", 3")	Clamps
Eyebolts (exterior):	Compass
2 @ ⅜ × 3½"	Speed square
2 @ ⅜ × 6½"	Drill and bits
8 ⅜"-dia. washers	Exterior glue
Eye and ear protection	Sander
Finishing materials	Work gloves

This cedar swing is roomy enough for two but compact enough to hang from either a stand or a front porch ceiling. Made of cedar, it is lightweight yet durable and moisture-resistant.

Porch Swing

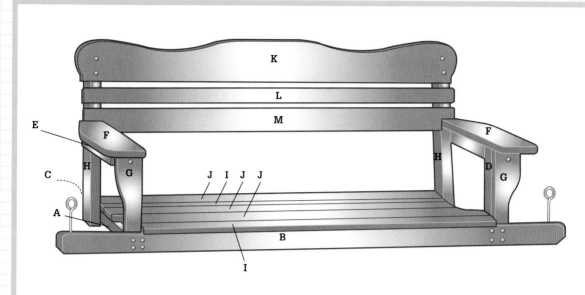

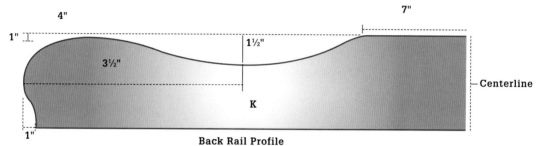

Back Rail Profile

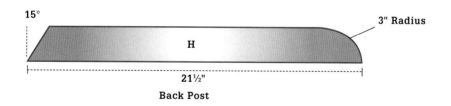

Back Post

Cutting List

Key	Part	Dimension	Pcs.	Material
A	Seat supports	$1\frac{1}{2} \times 3\frac{1}{4} \times 17\frac{1}{2}$"	3	Cedar
B	Front rail	$1\frac{1}{2} \times 3 \times 68$"	1	Cedar
C	Back rail	$1\frac{1}{2} \times 2\frac{1}{2} \times 48$"	1	Cedar
D	Front posts	$1\frac{1}{2} \times 2\frac{1}{2} \times 11\frac{3}{4}$"	2	Cedar
E	Arm support	$1\frac{1}{4} \times 2 \times 22$"	2	Cedar
F	Armrest	$1\frac{1}{4} \times 5\frac{1}{2} \times 24\frac{1}{4}$"	2	Cedar
G	Arm front	$1\frac{1}{4} \times 3\frac{1}{4} \times 9\frac{1}{4}$"	2	Cedar

Key	Part	Dimension	Pcs.	Material
H	Back posts	$1\frac{1}{2} \times 3 \times 21\frac{1}{2}$"	2	Cedar
I	Seat slats	$\frac{7}{8} \times 2\frac{3}{8} \times 48$"	2	Cedar
J	Seat slats	$\frac{7}{8} \times 5 \times 48$"	3	Cedar
K	Top back rail	$\frac{7}{8} \times 5\frac{1}{2} \times 54$"	1	Cedar
L	Middle back rail	$\frac{7}{8} \times 2 \times 52$"	1	Cedar
M	Bottom back rail	$\frac{7}{8} \times 3 \times 52$"	1	Cedar

PORCH SWING

BUILD THE SEAT FRAME

Make the workpieces for the seat supports by cutting three 17½" lengths of 2 × 4. Cedar is shown here; you can also use treated pine if you want a natural wood finish or untreated SPF (spruce, pine, or fir) if you plan to paint the swing. Lay out the seat support profile on one of the seat support pieces (photo 1) using the diagram on page 515 as a reference. The seat support is scooped on the top edge so the seat slats follow a comfortable flow. At the low point in the middle of

each support, the thickness of the part drops to 1¾". At the back end the part should be 2½" from top to bottom and at the front end it should peak at 3¼" and then drop down slightly over the last inch. Plot the profile so the tops of the part follow straight lines that conform to the width of the slats that will rest on them. The back edge of the part should be mitered at 15° to follow the backrest angle. Cut along the layout line with a jigsaw and then use the first seat support as a template to trace the profile onto the remaining

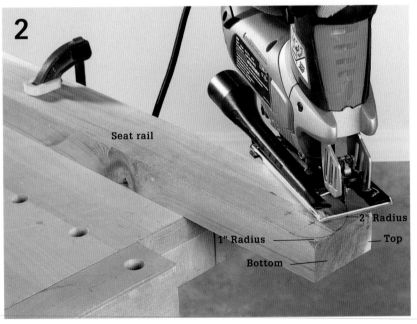

Lay out the parts. Plot the seat support profile onto one of the seat support workpieces using the dimensions given on page 515 as a reference.

Cut the end profiles. Use a compass to draw the front rail end radius and cut along these lines with a jigsaw. Sand the cuts smooth.

Seat rail

2" Radius
1" Radius
Top
Bottom

two seat supports. Also use the jigsaw to cut out the second and third seat supports. Gang the seat supports together with clamps and sand the profiles all at the same time so they are exactly the same.

Make the seat front rail by cutting a 2 × 4 to 68" long and rip-cutting ¼" off each edge to remove the rounded edges, leaving a workpiece that's 3" wide. On the front face of the front rail first mark a 2" radius on the bottom corners and then draw a 1" radius on the top corners. Cut along the corner radius lines with a jigsaw (photo 2). Make the seat back rail by cutting a 2 × 4 to 48" in length and then rip-cutting it down to 2½" wide. Attach the seat supports to the seat front and back rails with 3" deck screws (photo 3).

ATTACH THE BACK & ARM SUPPORTS

Cut a pair of 11¾" lengths of cedar 2 × 4 and rip-cut these pieces to 2½" wide to make the front posts. Drill counterbored pilot holes and attach the front posts to the front rail and outside seat supports with 2½" deck screws (photo 4). *Note: Counterbore pilot holes for all structural joints.* If you're looking to save a bit of time, consider attaching the seat slats with screws driven through pilot holes that are countersunk only.

Join rails and seat supports. Drive two 3" deck screws through the front rail and into the front ends of the seat supports. Also drive one 3" screw through the back rail and into the back end of each seat support. Apply exterior glue to the mating parts first to reinforce the joints.

Attach the front posts. Drive two 2½" deck screws through the side of the front post and into the outside seat supports. Drive two 2½" deck screws through the front rail and into the front posts.

(continued)

Next, cut two 21½" lengths of 2 × 4 and rip them to 3" wide, and then miter-cut the bottom ends to 15° to make the back posts. Next, draw a 3" radius on the back top corners of each back post and cut along the radius line with a jigsaw. Attach the back posts to the outside seat supports with 2½" screws (**photo 5**).

Cut one 22" length from a ¾ deck board (actual thickness is 1" to 1¼") and rip-cut that piece into two 2"-wide pieces to make the two arm supports. Attach the arm supports to the front and back posts with 2½" screws (photo 6). Cut two 9¼" pieces of the ¾ deck board to

make the arm fronts. Lay out the arm front profile on each piece and cut the profiles with a jigsaw. Attach the arm fronts to the front posts with 2½" deck screws.

ATTACH THE BACK RAILS & SEAT SLATS

Cut two 24¼" pieces of ¾ deck boards to make the armrests. Lay out the armrest profile on each deck board and cut the boards using a jigsaw. The backside edge should have a curved taper of 1" starting 7" from the end. The armrests should be rounded at a 1" radius on both front corners. Cut four 48" long pieces of ⅞ × 5½"

Attach the back posts. Drive two 2½" deck screws through each back post and into the outside seat supports.

Attach the arm supports. Drive two 2½" deck screws through each end of the arm supports and into the front and back posts. Then attach the arm front with two 2½" deck screws.

(nominal 1 × 6) boards to make the seat slats. Rip-cut three of the boards to 5" wide and then rip-cut the fourth deck board into two 2⅝" wide pieces.

Cut a 54" piece of ⅝ deck board to make the top back rail. Make a template of one-half of the top back rail on a piece of cardboard according to the profile drawing on page 33. Cut the template out with scissors or an X-acto knife. Trace the template onto each half of the top back rail (photo 7). Then, cut along the layout line with a jigsaw. Sand smooth. Cut a 52" piece of ⅝ deck board to make the middle

and bottom rails. Rip-cut this piece into one 2" wide board and one 3" wide board. Use a router and ¼" roundover bit to ease the edges of the armrests, seat slats, and back rails (photo 8). Attach the armrests, seat slats, and back rails with 2½" deck screws (photo 9).

FINISH THE SWING

Although you may choose to leave the swing unfinished if it is made of a good exterior wood, such as cedar or redwood, most people prefer to apply a top coat or even

7

Lay out the back rail profile. Use the information on page 33 to make a cardboard template of half of the top back rail. Use this template to lay out the first half of the top back rail profile and then flip the template to lay out the second half.

(continued)

an exterior wood stain and a top coat. Protecting the wood not only allows the wood tone to retain its color, it also minimizes the raised wood grain effect that occurs when water soaks into unprotected wood. The raised grain is not uncomfortable in and of itself, but it can lead to splintering.

Before applying your finish of choice, sand all of the wood surfaces up to 150 grit using a pad sander. Do not use an aggressive sander, such as a belt sander. Cut or buy wood plugs from the same species as the swing wood. Glue the plugs into the counterbored holes at screw locations. Once the glue has set, trim the plugs flush with the wood surface using a flush-cutting saw, or simply sand the tops down so they are even with the surrounding wood surface. Then, wipe down the entire project with a rag dipped in mineral spirits or rubbing alcohol, wait for the wood to dry, and then apply your finish. If you have access to an HVLP sprayer, it is an excellent choice for applying the finish smoothly and quickly. Two or three light coats will yield much better results than one or two heavier coats.

8

Ease the edges. Round over all edges of the armrests, back rails, and the top edges (smooth face) of the seat slats. Use a router with a ¼" radius roundover bit to make these profile cuts.

9

Finish the assembly. Attach the armrests, seat slats, and back rails with 2½" deck screws.

HANGING THE SWING

Install the four ⅜"-dia. eyebolts that will be fastened to the hanging chains or ropes (photo 10). Of these two options, chains take a bit longer to install but they won't need adjusting once they're set, and you don't have to tie and retie knots. Porch swing chains can be purchased as kits from hardware stores and from online sellers. Each kit contains a pair of chain assemblies with two swing chains, which consist of a Y-fitting that connects to an S-hook at the end of a single chain dropping from the ceiling or stand. Make sure the chain you buy is of sufficient strength and rated for outdoor usage. If you are using rope, choose rope that won't shrink or stretch (such as ⅝"-dia. nylon rope).

Two bolts are attached through the front rail and two bolts are attached through the back edges of the armrests and back posts. Hang the porch swing from chains or ropes so that the front edge is approximately 16" off the ground. The back edge of the swing should be level with the front edge or slightly lower. Adjust the hanging height to suit the primary users.

10

Prepare for hangers. Drill ⁷⁄₁₆"-dia. guide holes for each ⅜" eyebolt. Fasten the eyebolts with washers and locknuts.

Porch Swing Stand

CUT THE PARTS

Cut each 76"-long 4 × 4 leg with parallel 14° miters at the ends (photo 1). You need a 10" or 12" power miter saw for enough capacity to cut the legs in a single pass. Be sure to provide ample support for the workpiece, including the cutoff portion. If you don't have a miter saw, mark the angled cutting lines with a protractor or speed square, and cut them with a circular saw or handsaw. Cut the two 44" long cross braces from a piece of 2 × 8. Miter-cut each end to 14°.

The bottom edge of the cross brace features a decorative arc profile. Draw this arc using a flexible strip of wood (such as 1"-wide strip of ¼" lauan plywood) as a gauge. Mark points on the workpiece that are 4" from the outside edges of the long side of the cross brace. At each mark, tap two small nails into the face of the cross brace near the edge. Tap a third rail centered across the length of the brace and 2" up from the bottom to mark the apex of the arc. Flex a thin scrap of wood against the nails to create a smooth

Cut the stand legs to length. If you have a 10" or 12" power miter saw, you should be able to make the 14° end cuts in one pass. Be sure the end of the workpiece is supported.

Trace the cross-brace arcs. Flex a thin piece of wood or metal against two nails to act as a template for laying out the arc profile on the leg cross braces.

arc profile. Trace the arc with a pencil (photo 2) and then remove the nails and cut along the line with a jigsaw.

Miter-cut the 14° ends of the two 21"-long 2 × 6 inside beam supports to length. Miter-cut the 14° of the two 21¾"-long 2 × 8 outside beam supports. Use the same method that you used to create the arc on the cross braces to create an arc along the bottom edge of the outside beam supports.

Cut the beam gussets 14¾" long. Make two marks 3½" in from each end along the top edge of each gusset, and draw a 45° line from each mark to the outside end of the gusset. Then, draw a second 45° line from the outside edge down to the bottom edge of the gusset (photo 3). Cut off the corners of each gusset on these marked cutting lines.

The top beam is an 8-foot long 4 × 6 timber. Miter-cut the top corners of the beam to 45°, starting 3½" in from each end of the beam.

ASSEMBLE THE STAND

To attach the gussets to the inside beam supports, first mark the center of each beam support and then measure out 1¾" from the center to designate the

3

Make the gussets. Draw 45° cutting lines at ends of the beam gussets using a try square as a guide. Trim along the cutting lines.

4

Attach the gussets. Bore counterbore holes and guide holes for bolts, washers, and nuts through the beam supports, cross braces and legs. Drive ⅜" × 6½" lag screws with washers to secure the gussets.

(continued)

positions of the inside edges of the gussets. Draw alignment lines on these marks, perpendicular to the top and bottom edges of the beam supports. Position your drill ¾" to the outside of these lines and bore ³⁄₁₆"-dia. guide holes through the beam supports. Hold the gussets in position and drill ⅛" pilot holes in the ends of the gussets using the beam pilot holes as a guide. Attach the gussets to the beam supports with 3" deck screws.

Lay the legs on a flat surface. Position the outside beam support and cross brace under the legs. Then, position the inside beam support and gusset assembly on top of the legs. Clamp the legs between the beam supports and clamp the cross brace to the legs. Drill two 1⅛"-dia. × ½" deep counterbore holes and ⁷⁄₁₆"-dia. guide holes through each joint and attach the parts with ⅜"-dia. × 5" and ⅜"-dia. × 6½" bolts (photo 4).

Raise the leg assembly. Position the beam on the beam supports so it fits in between the gussets. Clamp the beam in place and then drill counterbores and guide holes through the joints, just as you did for the leg assembly. Fasten the beam with ⅜"-dia. × 6½" bolts secured by washers and locknuts (photo 5).

The chain or rope that supports the swing will be fastened to an eyebolt that runs down through the beam. Drill two ⁹⁄₁₆"-dia. vertical pilot holes through the center of the beam, spaced the same measured distance as there is between your swing's hanging chains or ropes. To avoid creating a place for water to pool, a counterbore hole is not drilled for the nuts that fasten the eyebolts. Fasten two ½"-dia. × 6" eyebolts with lock washers and nuts to the beam (photo 6).

INSTALL THE STAND & HANG THE SWING

The swing stand should be placed on level ground. A porch swing is not intended to swing fast or in a long arc, like a play swing does, so there is no need under normal use to anchor the stand to the ground. Hang the porch swing so the top front edge of the seat is approximately 16" off the ground (photo 7). The back edge of the swing should be level with the front edge or slightly lower. Adjust the hanging height to suit the primary users.

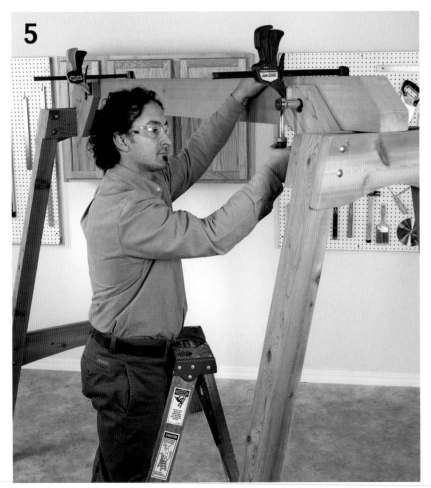

Attach the beam. Drill counterbores for washers on both gussets and drill guide holes for ⅜"-dia. x 6½"-long lag bolts. Insert the bolts and secure with lock washers and nuts.

Install eyebolts on the beam. Fasten ½"-dia. eyebolts to the beam with washers and locknuts.

Hang the swing. Use chains (preferred) or rope to hang the porch swing from the eyebolts in the swing stand beam. The front edge of the swing seat should be roughly 16" off the ground, and the swing should be level or tilted slightly backwards when at rest.

SIMPLE POTTING BENCH

A multi-functional workstation offers great versatility that makes it useful for a host of different gardening projects. But sometimes, all you really want from your work area is a big, broad surface with plenty of room to spread out and get busy. This workhorse of a bench is modeled after the most-used workspace in any home: the kitchen countertop. At 36 inches tall, the bench is the same height as most kitchen counters, and at 28 inches wide, it's slightly deeper than standard countertops—but not so deep that you can't easily reach across to the other side. The symmetrical configuration allows you to push any part of the bench against a wall or leave it out in the open for easy access to all sides.

There's also no need to worry about leaving the bench out in the rain. The understructure is made with moisture-resistant, pressure-treated lumber, and the top is made up of composite decking boards that won't split, rot, or splinter and require no protective finish.

Of course, if you've always wished your kitchen counters were a bit higher or lower, you can simply add or subtract a few inches from the given dimension for the bench legs. You can also change the length of the bench to fit a tight space, if necessary. Shortening the whole thing by two feet allows you to build it with standard 8-foot lumber and decking instead of 12-foot and 10-foot pieces.

This potting bench has a 28 × 71" top and is built with four 2 × 4s and three standard-size decking boards. The handy pot shelf below the bench top is made with a cutoff from one of the deck boards.

Simple Potting Bench

¾" overhang all sides

Tools & Materials

Tape measure
Circular saw
Drill
Piloting-countersink bit
Framing square
Clamps
(3) 12-ft. pressure-treated 2 × 4
3½" and 2½" deck screws
(1) 10-ft. pressure-treated 2 × 4
(3) 12-ft. 1 × 6 composite decking boards
Sandpaper
Eye and ear protection
Work gloves

Cutting List

KEY	Part	Dimension	Pieces	Material
A	Top frame side	1½ × 3½ × 69½"	2	2 × 4
B	Top frame end	1½ × 3½ × 23½"	2	2 × 4
C	Top supports	1½ × 3½ × 23½"	4	2 × 4
D	Leg	1½ × 3½ × 35"	4	2 × 4
E	Leg support	1½ × 3½ × 16½" (field measure)	2	2 × 4
F	Stretcher	1½ × 3½ × 63½" (field measure)	1	2 × 4
G	Top decking	1 × 5½ × 71"	5	1 × 6 decking
H	Pot shelf	1 × 5½ × 68"	1	1 × 6 decking

HOW TO BUILD THE SIMPLE POTTING BENCH

Cut the two top frame sides from one 12-ft. 2 × 4, using a circular saw or power miter saw. Cut the two top frame ends and the four top supports from another 12-ft. 2 × 4. Fit the side pieces over the ends of the end pieces so all top edges are flush. Drill countersunk pilot holes and fasten the pieces together with two 3½" deck screws at each joint.

Mark the layout for the top supports: Measuring from one end of the top frame, mark both frame sides every 13⅝". Check the top frame for square, using a framing square. Install the top supports between the frame sides with 3½" deck screws driven through the frame sides and into the supports. Make sure the supports and frame sides are flush across the top.

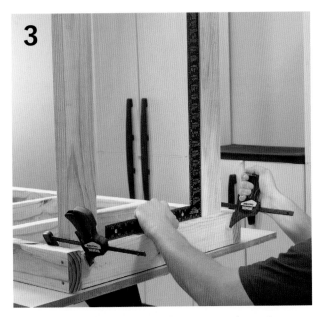

Cut the four legs from one 12-ft. 2 × 4. Round-over the edges on the bottom end of each leg, using sandpaper, a file, or a router and roundover bit; this prevents splintering if the table is slid around. Install the legs at the inside corners of the top frame, driving 2½" deck screws through the legs and into the top frame ends. Also screw through the top frame sides and into the legs. Make sure the legs are square to the frame before fastening.

Mark the inside edge of each leg, 10" up from its bottom end. Measure the distance between each leg pair and cut a leg support to fit snugly between the legs, using the 10-ft. 2 × 4. Install the leg supports with their bottom edges on the marks; drive 3½" screws toenail style through the top and bottom edges of the supports and into the legs.

5

Cut the 2 × 4 stretcher to fit snugly between the leg supports, using the remainder of the 10-ft. 2 × 4. Install the stretcher so it's centered side-to-side on each support, with the top edges flush. Drive 3½" screws through the outsides of the leg supports and into the stretcher ends.

6

Cut the top decking boards to length. Clamp the first board in place so it overhangs the front and ends of the top frame by ¾". If the deck boards are crowned (slightly curved across the face), make sure the convex side faces up. Drill two pilot holes at the center of each top frame end and top support location, countersinking the holes slightly. Fasten the board with 2½" deck screws.

7

Install the remaining deck boards so all of their ends are perfectly aligned and each board is gapped ⅛" from the next (without gaps, the joints would trap dirt). Use pieces of ⅛"-thick hardboard or two ⅛"-dia. drill bits to set the gaps. The last board should overhang the rear frame side by ¾".

8

Complete the pot shelf by cutting the remaining half piece of deck board to length. Position the board so it is centered side-to-side over the stretcher and overhangs both leg supports by ¾". Fasten the board to the stretcher and leg supports with 2½" deck screws driven through pilot holes.

COMPOST BIN

The byproducts of routine yard maintenance can pile up. Consider the waste generated by your landscaping during a single year: grass clippings, deadheaded blossoms, leaves, branches, and weeds. All this can be recycled into compost and incorporated back into plant beds as a nutrient-rich soil amendment.

Compost is nature's own mulch, and it effectively increases soil porosity, improves fertility, and stimulates healthy root development. Besides, making your own mulch or soil amendment through composting is much less expensive than buying commercial materials. Kitchen waste and yard refuse are all the ingredients you need.

So how does garbage turn into plant food? The process works like this: Organisms such as bacteria, fungi, worms, and insects convert compost materials into humus, a loamy, nutrient-rich soil. Humus is the end goal of composting, and it can take as long as a couple of years or as short as a month to produce.

With the right conditions, you can speed up Mother Nature's course and yield several helpings of fresh compost for your yard each season. This is called managed composting, as opposed to passive composting, when you allow a pile of plant debris and such to decompose on its own. The conditions must be just right to manage compost and speed the process. You'll need a balance of carbon and nitrogen, the right temperature, good air circulation, and the right amount of water. By mixing, chopping materials, and monitoring conditions in your compost pile, you'll increase your yield each season.

Tools & Materials ▸

(8) Cedar 2 × 4	U-nails (or narrow crown staples)	Caulk	Hammer
(10) Cedar 1 × 2		Circular saw	Pneumatic stapler (optional)
(3 × 12 ft.) Galvanized hardware cloth (½")	(2) 2 × 2" galvanized butt hinges	Table saw (optional)	
		Power miter saw	Caulk gun
Deck screws (3")	Exterior wood glue	Clamps	Work gloves
18-gauge brads (galvanized)	Galvanized finish nails	Tape measure	
Eye and ear protection	Exterior wood sealant	Drill/driver	

Browns and Greens ▸

A fast-burning compost pile requires a healthy balance of "browns" and "greens." Browns are high in carbon, which is food energy microorganisms depend on to decompose the pile. Greens are high in nitrogen, which is a protein source for the multiplying microbes. A ratio of 3-to-1 brown-to-green materials is the best balance.

- Browns: Dry brown plant material, straw, dried brown weeds, wood chips, saw dust (used with caution)
- Greens: Grass clippings, kitchen fruit and vegetable scraps, green leaves, and manure (no pet droppings)

Note: If you use chemical lawn care products on your lawn, do not include grass clippings in your compost pile.

Compost Bin

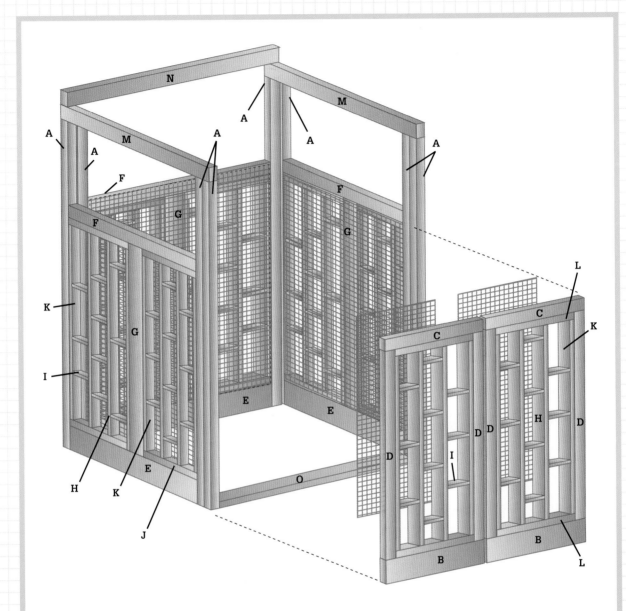

Cutting List

Key	Part	No.	Dim.	Material
A	Post	8	1½ × 1¾ × 48"	Cedar
B	Door rail	2	1½ × 3½ × 16"	Cedar
C	Door rail	2	1½ × 1¾ × 16"	Cedar
D	Door stile	4	1½ × 1¾ × 30½"	Cedar
E	Panel rail	3	1½ × 3½ × 32½"	Cedar
F	Panel rail	3	1½ × 1¾ × 32½"	Cedar
G	Panel stile	3	1½ × 3½ × 30½"	Cedar
H	Infill	16	¾ × 1½ × 30½"	Cedar

Key	Part	No.	Dim.	Material
I	Filler	80	¾ × 1½ × 4"	Cedar
J	Panel grid frame-h	12	¾ × 1½" × Cut to fit	Cedar
K	Grid frame-v	16	¾ × 1½" × Cut to fit	Cedar
L	Door frame-h	4	¾ × 1½" × Cut to fit	Cedar
M	Top rail-side	2	1½ × 1¾ × 39"	Cedar
N	Top rail-back	1	1½ × 1¾ × 32½"	Cedar
O	Front spreader	1	1½ × 3½ × 32½"	Cedar

HOW TO BUILD A COMPOST BIN

Prepare the wood stock. At most building centers and lumber yards you can buy cedar sanded on all four sides, or with one face left rough. The dimensions in this project are sanded on all four sides. Prepare the wood by ripping some of the stock into 1¾" wide strips (do this by ripping 2 × 4s down the middle on a tablesaw or with a circular saw and cutting guide).

Cut the parts to length with a power miter saw or a circular saw. For uniform results, set up a stop block and cut all similar parts at once.

Assemble the door frames. Apply exterior-rated wood glue to the mating parts and clamp them together with pipe or bar clamps. Reinforce the joints with 3" countersunk deck screws (two per joint). Reinforce the bottom joints by drilling a pair of ¾"-dia. × 1" deep clearance holes up through the bottom edges of the bottom rails and driving 3" deck screws through pilot holes up into the stiles.

Assemble the side and back panels. Clamp and glue the posts and rails for each frame, making sure the joints are square. Then, reinforce the joints with countersunk 3" deck screws—at least two per joint.

(continued)

OUTDOOR FURNISHINGS & ACCESSORIES

Hang the door frames. With the posts cut to length and oriented correctly, attach a door frame to each post with a pair of galvanized butt hinges. The bottoms of the door frames should be flush with or slightly higher than the bottoms of the posts. Temporarily tack a 1 × 4 brace across both door bottom rails to keep the doors from swinging during construction.

Join the panels and the door assembly by gluing and clamping the parts together and then driving 3" countersunk deck screws to reinforce the joints. To stabilize the assembly, fasten the 2 × 4 front spreader between the front, bottom edges of the side panels. Make sure the spreader will not interfere with door operation.

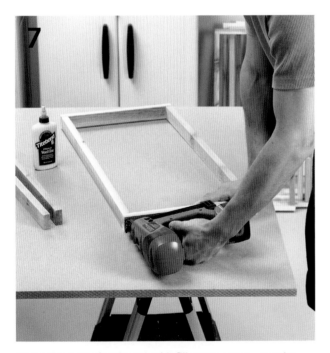

Make the grids for the panel infill areas. Use 1 × 2 cedar to make all parts (you may have to rip-cut cedar 2 × 4s for this, depending on availability in your area. Use exterior glue and 18-gauge brads (galvanized) to connect the horizontal filler strips to the vertical infill pieces. Vary the heights and spacing of the filler for visual interest and to make the ends accessible for nailing.

Frame the grids with 1 × 2 strips cut to the correct length so each frame fits neatly inside a panel or door opening. Install the grid frames in the openings, making sure all front edges are flush.

9

Attach the top rails that conceal the post tops and help tie the panels together. Attach the sides first using exterior glue and galvanized finish nails. Then, install the back rail on top of the side rails. Leave the front of the project open on top so you can load, unload, and turn over compost more easily.

10

Line the interior surfaces of the compost bin with ½" galvanized hardware cloth. Cut the hardware cloth to fit and fasten it with fence staple or galvanized U-nails driven every 6" or so. Make sure you don't leave any sharp edges protruding. Grind them down with a rotary tool or a file.

11

Set up the bin in your location.
Apply a coat of exterior wood sealant to all wood surfaces—use a product that contains a UV inhibitor. *Tip: Before setting up your compost bin, dig a 12"-deep hole just inside the area where the bin will be placed. This will expand your bin's capacity.*

BACKYARD FIREPIT

A firepit is a backyard focal point and gathering spot. The one featured here is constructed around a metal liner, which will keep the firepit walls from overheating and cracking if cooled suddenly by rain or a bucket of water. The liner here is a section of 36-inch-diameter corrugated culvert pipe. Check local codes for stipulations on pit area size. Many codes require a 20-foot-diameter pit area.

Ashlar wall stones add character to the firepit walls, but you can use any type of stone, including cast concrete retaining wall blocks. You'll want to prep the base for the seating area as you dig the firepit to be sure both rest on the same level plane.

Tools & Materials ▸

Wheelbarrow
Landscape paint
String and stakes
Spades
Metal pipe
Landscape edging
Level
Garden rake
Plate vibrator

Metal firepit liner
Compactable gravel
Top-dressing rock
   (trap rock)
Wall stones
Eye protection
   and work gloves

Some pointers to consider when using your firepit include: 1) Make sure there are no bans or restrictions in effect; 2) Evaluate wind conditions and avoid building a fire if winds are heavy and/or blowing toward your home; 3) Keep shovels, sand, water, and a fire extinguisher nearby; 4) Extinguish fire with water and never leave the fire pit unattended.

CROSS SECTION: FIREPIT

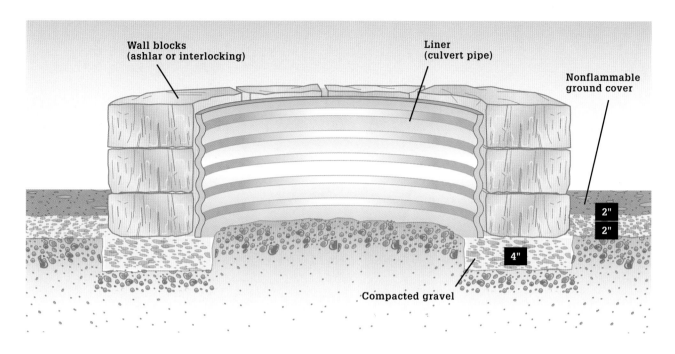

Wall blocks
(ashlar or interlocking)

Liner
(culvert pipe)

Nonflammable
ground cover

2"

2"

4"

Compacted gravel

PLAN VIEW: FIREPIT

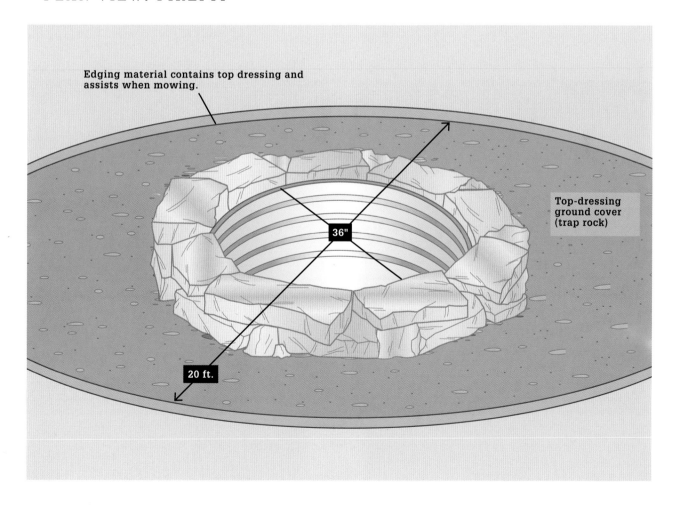

Edging material contains top dressing and
assists when mowing.

Top-dressing
ground cover
(trap rock)

36"

20 ft.

HOW TO BUILD A FIREPIT

Outline the location for your firepit and the firepit safety area by drawing concentric circles with landscape paint using a string and pole for guidance.

Remove a 4"-deep layer of sod and dirt in the firepit and safety areas (the depth of the excavation depends on what materials you're installing in the safety zone).

Dig a 4"-deep trench for the perimeter stones that will ring the pit liner.

Fill the trench for the perimeter stones with compactable gravel and tamp thoroughly. Then scatter gravel to within 2½" of the paver edging top throughout the project area. It is not necessary to tamp this layer at this time.

Place your metal fire ring so it is level on the gravel layer and centered around the center pipe.

Arrange the first course of wall blocks around the fire ring. Keep gaps even and check with a level, adding or removing gravel as needed.

Install the second course of retaining wall block, taking care to evenly stagger the vertical joints on the first and second courses. Add the remaining courses.

Compact the compactable gravel in the seating/safety area using a rental plate vibrator.

Place and compact a layer of top-dressing rock in the seating/safety area to complete the firepit.

CLASSIC GARDEN BRIDGE

An elegant garden bridge invites you into a landscape by suggesting you stop and spend some time there. Cross a peaceful pond, traverse an arroyo of striking natural stone, or move from one garden space to the next and explore. While a bridge is practical and functions as a way to get from point A to point B, it does so much more. It adds dimension, a sense of romanticism, and the feeling of escaping to somewhere special.

The bridge you see here can be supported with handrails and trellis panels, but left simple as pictured, its Zen appeal complements projects such as an arroyo, a garden pond, or a rain garden. We think the sleek, modern design blends well in the landscape, providing a focal point without overwhelming a space.

Tools & Materials ▸

4 × 4" × 8' cedar (4)
2 × 10" × 8' cedar (2)
2 × 4" × 8' cedar (10)
1 × 8" × 8' cedar (2)
1 × 3" × 8' cedar (2)
1 × 2" × 8' cedar (8)
½" × 2" × 8' cedar
   lattice (2)
Lag screws (⅜ × 4")
Deck screws (2", 3")

Finishing materials
Jigsaw
Circular saw
Drill
Hammer
Sander
Work gloves
Eye and ear protection

Unlike many landscape and garden bridges that are large, ornate, and designed to be the center of attention, this low cedar bridge has a certain refined elegance that is a direct result of its simple design.

Cutting List

Key	Part	Dim.	PCS.	Material
A	Stringer	1½ × 9¼ × 96"	2	Cedar
B	Stretcher	1½ × 3½ × 27"	4	"
C	Tread	1½ × 3½ × 30"	26	"

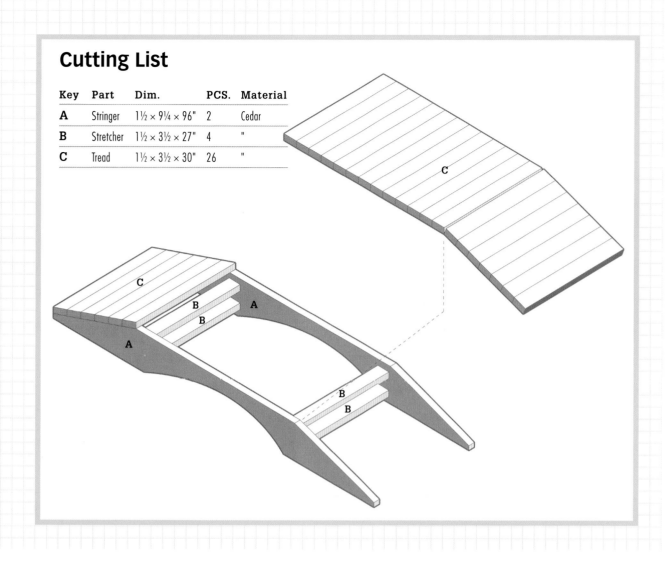

PREPARING BRIDGE PIECES

Study the cutting list carefully and take care when measuring for cuts. The building blocks of this bridge are: stringers, a base, and treads. Read these preliminary instructions carefully, then study the steps before you begin.

Stringers: This first step involves cutting the main structural pieces of the bridge. The stringers have arcs cut into their bottom edges, and the ends of stringers are cut at a slant to create a gradual tread incline. Before you cut stringers, carefully draw guidelines on the wood pieces:

- A centerline across the width of each stringer
- Two lines across the width of each stringer 24" to the left and right of the centerline
- Lines at the ends of each stringer, 1" up from one long edge

- Diagonal lines from these points to the top of each line to the left and right of the center

Base: Four straight boards called stretchers form the base that support the bridge. Before cutting these pieces, mark stretcher locations on the insides of the stringers, 1½" from the top and bottom of the stringers. The outside edges of the stretchers should be 24" from the centers of the stringers so the inside edges are flush with the bottoms of the arcs. When working with the stretchers, the footboard may get quite heavy, so you will want to move the project to its final resting place and finish constructing the project there.

Treads: Cut the treads to size according to the cutting list. Once laid on the stringers, treads will be separated with ¼" gaps. Before you install the treads, test-fit them to be sure they are the proper size.

HOW TO BUILD A GARDEN BRIDGE

Use a circular saw to cut the ends of stringers along the diagonal lines, according to the markings described on the previous page.

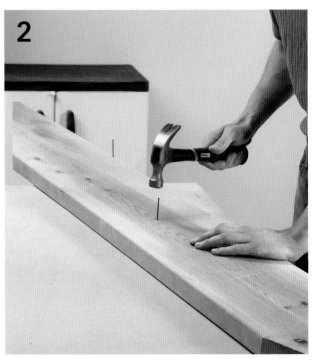

Tack a nail on the centerline, 5¼" up from the same long edge. Also tack nails along the bottom edge, 20½" to the left and right of the centerline.

Make a marking guide from a thin, flexible strip of scrap wood or plastic, hook it over the center nail, and slide the ends under the outside nails to form a smooth curve. Trace along the guide with a pencil to make the arc cutting line.

Use a jigsaw to make arched cut-outs in the bottoms of the 2 × 10 stringers after removing the nails and marking guide.

Assemble the base by preparing stringers as described on facing page and positioning the stretchers between them. Stand the stringers upright (curve at the bottom) and support bottom stretchers with 1½"-thick spacer blocks for correct spacing. Fasten stretchers between stringers with countersunk 3" deck screws, driven through the stringers and into the ends of the stretchers.

Turn the stringer assembly upside down and attach the top stretchers.

Attach treads after test-fitting them. Leave a ¼" gap between treads. Secure them with 3"-long countersunk deck screws.

Sand all surfaces to smooth out any rough spots, and apply an exterior wood stain to protect the wood, if desired. You can leave the cedar untreated and it will turn gray, possibly blending with other landscape features.

COLD FRAME BOX

An inexpensive foray into greenhouse gardening, a cold frame is practical for starting plants six to eight weeks earlier in the growing season and for hardening off seedlings. Basically, a cold frame is a box set on the ground and topped with glass or plastic. Although mechanized models with thermostatically controlled atmospheres and sashes that automatically open and close are available, you can easily build a basic cold frame yourself from materials you probably already have around the house.

The back of the frame should be about twice as tall as the front so the lid slopes to a favorable angle for capturing sunrays. Build the frame tall enough to accommodate the maximum height of the plants before they are removed. The frame can be made of brick, block, plastic, wood, or just about any material you have on hand. It should be built to keep drafts out and soil in.

If the frame is permanently sited, position it facing south to receive maximum light during winter and spring and to offer protection from wind. Partially burying it takes advantage of the insulation from the earth, but it also can cause water to collect, and the direct soil contact will shorten the lifespan of the wood frame parts. Locating your frame near a wall, rock, or building adds additional insulation and protection from the elements. Keep an inexpensive thermometer in a shaded spot inside the frame for quick reference. A bright spring day can heat a cold frame to as warm as 100°, so prop up or remove the cover as necessary to prevent overheating. And remember, the more you vent, the more you should water. On cold nights, especially when frost is predicted, cover the box with burlap, old quilts, or leaves to keep it warm inside.

A cold frame is positioned over tender plants early in the growing season to trap heat and moisture so they get a good, strong start. This cold frame doesn't rely on finding old windows for the top, so anyone can build it.

Cold Frame Box

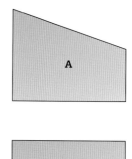

A

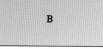

B

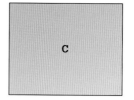

C

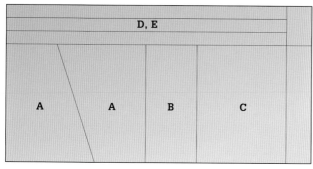

D, E

A   A   B   C

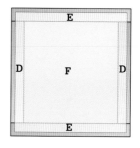

E

D   F   D

E

Tools & Materials

Tape measure
Carpenter square
(2) 3 × 3" butt hinges (ext.)
Exterior paint
(2) 4" utility handles
2" or 2½" deck screws
(4) Corner L-brackets (¾ × 2½")
#8 × ¾" wood screws
(1) ¾" × 4 × 8 ft. plywood (ext.)
Circular saw
⅛ × 37 × 38" clear Plexiglas
Drill/driver
Exterior caulk/adhesive
Caulk gun
Pipe clamps
Exterior wood glue

Straightedge cutting guide
Dark exterior paint
Eye and ear protection
Work gloves

Cutting List

Key	Part	No.	Size	Material
A	Side	2	¾ × 16/28 × 36"	Ext. Plywood
B	Front	1	¾ × 16 × 36"	Ext. Plywood
C	Back	1	¾ × 28 × 36"	Ext. Plywood
D	Lid frame	2	¾ × 4 × 31"	Ext. Plywood
E	Lid frame	2	¾ × 4 × 38"	Ext. Plywood
F	Cover	1	⅛ × 37 × 38"	Plexiglas

HOW TO BUILD A COLD-FRAME BOX

Cut the parts. This project, as dimensioned, is designed to be made entirely from a single 4 × 8 sheet of plywood. Start by cutting the plywood lengthwise to make a 36"-wide piece. *Tip: Remove material in 4" wide strips and use the strips to make the lid frame parts and any other trim you may want to add.*

Cut the parts to size with a circular saw or jigsaw and cutting guide. Mark the cutting lines first (See Diagram, previous page).

Assemble the front, back and side panels into a square box. Glue the joints and clamp them together with pipe or bar clamps. Adjust until the corners are square.

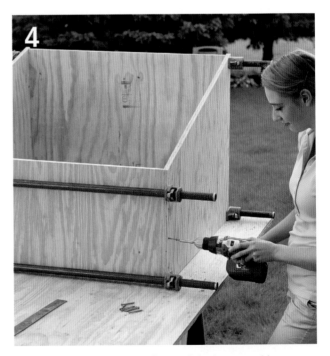

Reinforce the joints with 2" or 2½" deck screws driven through countersunk pilot holes. Drive screws every 4 to 6" along each joint.

Make the lid frame. Cut the 4"-wide strips of ¾" plywood reserved from step 1 into frame parts (2 @ 31" and 2 @ 38"). Assemble the frame parts into a square 38 × 39" frame. There are many ways to join the parts so they create a flat frame. Because the Plexiglas cover will give the lid some rigidity, simply gluing the joints and reinforcing with an L-bracket at each inside corner should be more than adequate structurally.

Paint the box and the frame with exterior paint, preferably in an enamel finish. A darker color will hold more solar heat.

Lay thick beds of exterior adhesive/caulk onto the tops of the frame and then seat the Plexiglas cover into the adhesive. Clean up squeeze-out right away. Once the adhesive has set, attach the lid with butt hinges and attach the handles to the sides.

Move the cold frame to the site. Clear and level the ground where it will set if possible. Some gardeners like to excavate the site slightly.

JUMBO COLD FRAME

A cold frame of any size works on the same principle as a greenhouse, capturing sunlight and heat while protecting plants from cold winds and frost. But when your planting needs outgrow a basic backyard cold frame with a window-sash roof, it makes sense to look to the greenhouse for more comprehensive design inspiration. This jumbo version offers over 17 square feet of planting area and combines the convenience of a cold frame with the full sun exposure of a greenhouse. Plus, there's ample height under the cold frame's canopy for growing taller plants.

The canopy pivots on hinges and can be propped all the way up or partially opened to several different positions for ventilating the interior to control temperature. The hinges can be separated just like door hinges (in fact, they are door hinges), so you can remove the canopy for the off season, if desired. Clear polycarbonate roofing panels make the canopy lightweight yet durable, while admitting up to 90 percent of the sun's UV rays (depending on the panels you choose).

The base of the cold frame is a simple rectangle made with 2 × 6 lumber. You can pick it up and set it over an existing bed of plantings, or give it a permanent home, perhaps including a foundation of bricks or patio pavers to protect the wood from ground moisture. For additional frost protection and richer soil for your seedlings, dig down a foot or so inside the cold frame and work in a thick layer of mulch. Because all sides of the canopy have clear glazing, you don't have to worry about orienting the cold frame toward the sun; as virtually all of the interior space is equally exposed to light.

Tools & Materials ▶

Circular saw
 or miter saw
Cordless drill and bits
Hacksaw
Deck screws 2", 2½", 3"
(5) ½" × 10-ft. thin
 wall PVC pipes (the
 flexible type used for
 lawn irrigation, not
 schedule 40 type)
(2) 25 × 96" corrugated
 polycarbonate
 roofing panels
30 × 24" clear
 acrylic panel
16" treated stakes

Roofing screws with
 EPDM washers
(2) 3½" exterior-
 grade butt hinges
 with screws
(2) ¼ × 4" eyebolts
3½ × ⁵⁄₁₆" stainless steel
 machine bolts
 (2 bolts with
 8 washers and 2 nuts)
(2) Heavy-duty hook-
 and-eye latches
Outdoor thermometer
 with remote sensor
Work gloves
Eye and ear protection

A cold frame can extend the growing season in your garden to almost—or truly—year round. Use an oversized cold frame like the one in this project and there may be no need to put up vegetables in the fall, because you'll have all the fresh produce you can handle.

Building a Jumbo Cold Frame

Cutting List

Key	No.	Part	Dimension	Material
A	2	Frame side	1½ x 2½ x 94"	2 x 3
B	2	Frame end	1½ x 2½ x 30"	2 x 3
C	2	Base side	1½ x 5½ x 94"	2 x 6
D	2	Base end	1½ x 5½ x 30"	2 x 6
E	4	Frame brace	1½ x 2½ x 8"	2 x 3
F	2	Prop stick	¾ x 1½ x 30"	1 x 2
G	4	Rib	½ x ½ x 37"	½ PVC tubing

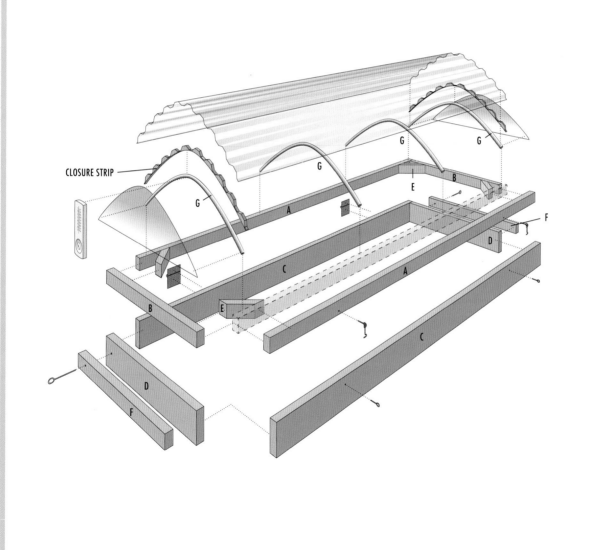

CLOSURE STRIP

HOW TO BUILD A JUMBO COLD FRAME

Drill pilot holes and fasten the frame end pieces between the frame side pieces with 3" deck screws to create the rectangular frame. Do the same with the base pieces to create the base. Use two screws for each joint.

Stabilize the corners of the canopy frame with braces cut to 45° angles at both ends. Install the braces on-the-flat, so their top faces are flush with the tops of the canopy frame. Drill pilot holes and fasten through the braces and into the frame with one 2½" screw at each end. Then, drive one more screw through the outside of the frame and into each end of the brace. Check the frame for square as you work.

Assemble the canopy glazing framework using ½" PVC pipe. Cut all the ribs 37" long. You can cut these easily with a miter saw, hacksaw, or jigsaw.

Use 2" deck screws as receptors for the PVC pipes. Drive the screws in 1" from edge and ¾" from the ends, angling the screws at about 35 to 45° toward the center. Leave about ¾" of the screw exposed. Drive two additional screws in at 32¼" from each end.

Install the PVC ribs by putting one end over the 2" screw, then curving the PVC until the other end fits over the opposite screw. Take your time with this, and use a helper if you need. *Note: Hopefully you've remembered to buy the flexible PVC, not the Schedule 40 type used for indoor plumbing.*

6

Hold up and mark a smooth piece of clear acrylic for the end panels. The clear acrylic should cover the 2 × 3 and follow the curving top of the PVC. Cut the clear acrylic with a plastic-cutting jigsaw blade.

7

Drill ¼" holes along the bottom of both panels about ⅝" up from the edge of the panel. Space the holes 2½" from ends, then every 16". Also mark and drill rib locations on the roof panels about 6" up from bottom, spacing the holes at 1⅝" and 33¼" from each end. Install the panels 1½" up from the bottom of the 2 × 3 with the roofing screws. The ends of the panels should extend 1" beyond the 2 × 3s.

8

Adjust the PVC ribs until the predrilled holes in the roof panels are centered on them, then predrill the PVC with a ⅛" bit. Fasten the panels to the two center ribs.

(continued)

Lap the second sheet over the first, leaving roughly the same amount of panel hanging over the 2 × 3. Fasten the second sheet the same way as the first. Insert filler strips at each end under the polycarbonate, then drill through those into the PVC ribs. Now add additional screws about every ⅛". You can just predrill the holes with the ⅛" bit (the polycarbonate panels are soft enough that the screws will drive through them without cracking).

Set the clear acrylic end panels in place, butting them against the filler at the top. Mark screw locations. Place the panel on a piece of plywood and predrill with a ¼" diameter bit to avoid cracking the clear acrylic, which isn't as soft or flexible as the polycarbonate. Screw the panels in place with roofing screws, hand-tightening with a screwdriver to avoid cracking the clear acrylic. Don't overtighten.

Mount the canopy to the cold frame base with two exterior hinges. The canopy frame should fit flush over the base on all sides. Screw in two hook-and-eye latches in front.

Attach a prop stick to each side with a stainless steel bolt and nut. Insert three washers (or more) between the prop stick and the 2 × 6 base so the prop stick clears the clear acrylic side panel. Drill a few additional 5/16" holes in the stick and the frame for the eyebolts, so that you can prop the canopy open at different heights. Now, prepare the ground and place the cold frame in the desired location. Anchor the base to the ground using 16" treated stakes or heavy-duty metal angles driven into the ground and secured to the frame.

RESOURCES

ACG Greenhouses
888 888 9050
www.littlegreenhouse.com

American Institute of Architects
800 364 9364
www.aiaonline.com

American Society of Landscape Architects
202 898 2444
www.asla.org

Asphalt Roofing Manufacturers Association
202 207 0917
www.asphaltroofing.com

The Betty Mills Company
www.bettymills.com

The Big eZee
Metal Kit Sheds
101 N. Fourth St.
Breese, IL 62230
800 851 1085

Black & Decker (US), Inc.
800 544 6986
www.blackanddecker.com
www.bdk.com

Brick Institute of America
703 620 0010
www.brickinfo.org

California Redwood Association
888 225 7339
www.calredwood.org

Cedar Shake & Shingle Bureau
604 820 7700
www.cedarbureau.org

Certified Wood Products Council
503 224 2205
www.certifiedwood.org

Construction Materials Recycling Association
630 548 4510
www.cdrecycling.com

Finley Products, Inc.
888 626 5301
www.2×4basics.com

Greenhouses.com
800 681 3302
www.greenhouses.com

GreenhouseKit.com
877 718 2865
www.greenhousekit.com

HDA Inc.
www.houseplansandmore.com

Juliana Greenhouses
www.julianagreenhouses.com

Masonry Society
303 939 9700
www.masonrysociety.com

National Concrete Masonry Association
703 713 1900
www.ncma.org

Paint Quality Institute
www.paintquality.com

Portland Cement Association
847 966 6200
www.portcement.com

Simpson Strong-Tie Co.
800 999 5099
www.strongtie.com

Southern Pine Council
www.southernpine.com

Sturdy-built Greenhouses
Redwood greenhouse kits
800 344 4115
www.sturdi-built.com

Summerwood Products
866 519 4634
www.summerwood.com

PHOTO CREDITS

METRIC CONVERSIONS

Metric Equivalent

Inches (in.)	1/64	1/32	1/25	1/16	1/8	1/4	3/8	2/5	1/2	5/8	3/4	7/8	1	2	3	4	5	6	7	8	9	10	11	12	36	39.4
Feet (ft.)																								1	3	3 1/12
Yards (yd.)																									1	1 1/12
Millimeters (mm)	0.40	0.79	1	1.59	3.18	6.35	9.53	10	12.7	15.9	19.1	22.2	25.4	50.8	76.2	101.6	127	152	178	203	229	254	279	305	914	1,000
Centimeters (cm)							0.95	1	1.27	1.59	1.91	2.22	2.54	5.08	7.62	10.16	12.7	15.2	17.8	20.3	22.9	25.4	27.9	30.5	91.4	100
Meters (m)																								.30	.91	1.00

Converting Measurements

To Convert:	To:	Multiply by:
Inches	Millimeters	25.4
Inches	Centimeters	2.54
Feet	Meters	0.305
Yards	Meters	0.914
Miles	Kilometers	1.609
Square inches	Square centimeters	6.45
Square feet	Square meters	0.093
Square yards	Square meters	0.836
Cubic inches	Cubic centimeters	16.4
Cubic feet	Cubic meters	0.0283
Cubic yards	Cubic meters	0.765
Pints (U.S.)	Liters	0.473 (Imp. 0.568)
Quarts (U.S.)	Liters	0.946 (Imp. 1.136)
Gallons (U.S.)	Liters	3.785 (Imp. 4.546)
Ounces	Grams	28.4
Pounds	Kilograms	0.454
Tons	Metric tons	0.907

To Convert:	To:	Multiply by:
Millimeters	Inches	0.039
Centimeters	Inches	0.394
Meters	Feet	3.28
Meters	Yards	1.09
Kilometers	Miles	0.621
Square centimeters	Square inches	0.155
Square meters	Square feet	10.8
Square meters	Square yards	1.2
Cubic centimeters	Cubic inches	0.061
Cubic meters	Cubic feet	35.3
Cubic meters	Cubic yards	1.31
Liters	Pints (U.S.)	2.114 (Imp. 1.76)
Liters	Quarts (U.S.)	1.057 (Imp. 0.88)
Liters	Gallons (U.S.)	0.264 (Imp. 0.22)
Grams	Ounces	0.035
Kilograms	Pounds	2.2
Metric tons	Tons	1.1

Converting Temperatures

Convert degrees Fahrenheit (F) to degrees Celsius (C) by following this simple formula: Subtract 32 from the Fahrenheit temperature reading. Then mulitply that number by 5/9. For example, 77°F - 32 = 45. 45 × 5/9 = 25°C.

To convert degrees Celsius to degrees Fahrenheit, multiply the Celsius temperature reading by 9/5, then add 32. For example, 25°C × 9/5 = 45. 45 + 32 = 77°F.

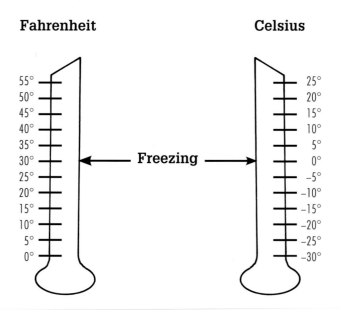

Fahrenheit   **Celsius**

← **Freezing** →

INDEX